문풀집

독한독해 3.0

문제 뽀개기

| 저자 전경식 |

▲ 네이버 카페 '맨발의 청춘 영어'
http://cafe.naver.com/rudyenglish

▶ 동영상 강의
www.withstars.co.kr | www.eduwill.net

PREFACE

독한독해 3.0 문제뽀개기를 펴내며

정확하고 꼼꼼한 해석과 의미덩어리를 강조하는 꼬장꼬장한 독독 1.0 문장뽀개기.
문장분석에서 한 걸음 더 나아가 전반적인 지문의 구성을 파악하는 독독 2.0 지문뽀개기

이제는....
그렇다 실전이다!
가장 실전적인 독해법을 지향해서 집필한 것이 독독 3.0 유형별 뽀개기이다.

루디가 생각하는 가장 실전적인 독해전략은 무엇인가?
실전이라는 것은 언제나 우리가 목표로 하는 시험과의 연직선에서 생각해 볼 수밖에 없다.
그리고 모든 시험에는 제한된 시간에 자신의 모든 실력을 발휘해야 한다는 공통점이 있다.

따라서 '가장 실전적 독해법'이란 제한된 시간을 어떻게 가장 효과적으로 활용할 수 있느냐의 문제이다.

그러기 위해서는 독해 유형별로 해결 전략을 수립하고, 그 전략을 지속 반복적으로 적용하는 훈련이 가장 효과적인 해결방안이라고 생각한다.

1. 3.0에서는 너무나 중요하지만 많은 수업서들이 간과하고 있는 객관식 문제의 특징과 한계를 명확하게 규정, 정리했다. 주관식 문제와 객관식 문제는 유형에 따른 해결전략의 차이점이 분명히 존재하지만, 많은 학습자들이 이 근본적인 차이점을 인식하지 못하고 있다. '지피지기면 백전백승'이란 고사성어처럼 우리가 대비하는 객관식 문제의 특성을 명확히 이해하는 것이 모든 전략의 첫 걸음이다.

2. 주제에서 시작해서 '순삽탈'에 이르기까지 모든 유형에 가장 실전적인 해결방안을 다양한 'CASE STUDY'를 통해서 제시했다. 다만 너무나 다양한 풀이전략은 개별적인 문제에는 적용될 수 있지만, 실전의 적용에 한계를 지닐 수 있기에, 최대한 엄선해서 활용성이 높은 전략들만을 제시했다.

3. 3.0의 '풀이전략'은 철저하게 '2.0'과의 연계성에 존재한다. 독독시리즈들이 개별적인 특성을 지니면서도 동시에 다음 과정에 철저하게 연계성을 지니게 집필했다. '2.0'에서 강조했던 'GS, 플러스&마이너스, RESTATEMENT'의 모든 핵심이론을 3.0의 풀이 전략에 고스란히 녹이려고 노력했다.

4. 결국 실전은 제한된 시간안에 문제를 해결하는 시험 방식에 익숙해지는 것이다. 이때 초중급자에게 가장 중요한 것은 눈높이에 맞는 유형별 문제들을 직접 제한된 시간 안에 해결해 보는 것이다. 이를 위해서 '10분 모의고사' 30회를 정말 정성스럽게 준비했다. 반복적인 유형들을 제한된 시간 안에 해결하면서 단기간에 걸쳐 성적 향상에 든든한 디딤돌이 될 것이라 확신한다.

재즈의 거장 Miles Davis은 이렇게 말했다.
'우선 찬사를 보내라. 내 연주를 들으면 그렇게 할 테니까'

이런 삶의 관록과 여유를 독한독해 시리즈를 통해서 나 스스로에게 부여하고 싶었다.
그런 찬사는 독자들의 몫이지만, 독한독해 시리즈들을 집필하면서 진정성 어린 시간을 보낸 나 자신에게, 작지만 흐뭇한 미소를 보내고 싶다.

"For a long time it had seemed to me that life was about to begin. But there was always some obstacle in the way, something to be gotten through first, some unfinished business, time still to be served, a debt to be paid. Then life would begin. At last it dawned on me that these obstacles were my life."

"오랫동안 나에게 삶이란 이제 시작되려는 것처럼 보였다. 하지만 항상 장애물이 있었고, 먼저 극복해야 할 것이 있었고, 끝내지 못한 일들이, 그래서 쏟아야 하는 시간과 정리해야 할 빚이 있었다. 그런 다음에야 삶이 시작되는 것처럼 보였다. 하지만 마침내 나는 알았다. 이런 장애물들 자체가 내 삶이었다는 것을"
― Alfred D. Souza ―

전경식 드림

INTRO

INTRO. Skimming
(skimming은 독한독해 2.0 참고)

Skimming은 Keyword를 중심으로 핵심적인 부분만을 속독으로 이해하는 것이다. 이런 속독 전략은 전반적인 글의 논지를 묻는 주제와 빈칸추론, 순서배열 문제 등에 매우 효과적인 풀이 전략이 될 수 있다.

스키밍에 능숙하기 위해서는 언제나 개별 문장에 몰입하지 말고, 지문 전체를 전반적으로 파악하는 시야를 가져야 한다. 이를 위해서는 독독2.0에서 학습한 'GS, Restatement, 플러스&마이너스'의 문장들의 관계를 파악하는 관점과 'GS, MT, ST'로 지문을 분석하는 능력이 기반이 되어야 한다.

What to think about for skimming
G&S 진술을 구분해 본다.
전후 문장들의 관계를 플러스&마이너스 구조로 분석해 본다.
글의 구조를 'GS&MT&ST' 분류해 본다.

ℝ GS (General Specific) - 서론에 주제문이 등장하고, 이후에 구체적인 재진술이 등장하는 구조의 영문
　MT (Myth Truth) - 통념을 비판하고, 기존의 잘못된 상식을 비판하는 구조의 영문
　ST (Story Telling) - 이야기 구조로 예시와 열거의 재진술로 구성된 영문

How to do skimming
지문의 서론과 마지막 문장을 살펴보며 G/S 진술을 살펴본다. 이때 서론과 결론에 동일한 표현이 등장하는지에 특히 유의한다.
각 문장들의 연결어들을 '플러스&마이너스'를 중심으로 살펴본다.
S 포인트에 해당하는 '연도, 통계치, 인명, 사건의 개요, 실험 과정' 등은 빠르게 넘어가고 해당 진술 전후에 G진술이 등장하는가를 살펴본다.

ℝ (general statement 일반, 포괄적 진술) & S (specific statement 구체, 예시적 진술)

[CASE STUDY 1]

It's long been part of folk wisdom that birth order strongly affects personality, intelligence and achievement. However, most of the research claiming that firstborns are radically different from other children has been discredited, and it now seems that any effects of birth order on intelligence or personality will likely be washed out by all the other influences in a person's life. In fact, the belief in the permanent impact of birth order, according to Toni Falbo, a social psychologist at the University of Texas at Austin, comes from the psychological theory that your personality is incorrect. The better, later and larger studies are less likely to find birth order a useful predictor of anything. When two Swiss social scientists, Cecile Ernst and Jules Angst, reviewed 1,500 studies a few years ago, they concluded that "birth order differences in personality are nonexistent in our sample. In particular, there is no evidence for a firstborn personality."

VOCA folk wisdom n. 상식, 민간의 지혜 firstborn n. 장남, 장녀 radically av. 급진적으로 discredit v. 불신하다 wash out v. 제거하다 birth order n. 출생순서 predictor n. 예언자

출생 순서가 성격, 지능 그리고 성취에 상당한 영향을 끼친다는 것이 오랫동안 일반 사람들이 갖는 생각이었다. 그러나 대부분의 연구가 첫 자녀가 다른 자녀들과 근본적으로 다르다는 주장이 의심을 받게 되었고 이제는 출생 순서가 지능이나 성격에 미치는 어떤 영향도 한 사람의 인생에서 모든 다른 영향력 있는 요소에 의해서 약화되는 것처럼 보인다. 사실 오스틴 텍사스 대학의 사회 심리학자인 토니 팔도에 따르면 출생 순서의 영구적 영향에 대한 믿음은 성격이 부정확하다는 심리적 이론에서 유래한다. 더 나은, 더 향후의 그리고 더 광범위한 연구가 출생 순서가 어떤 것도 유용하게 예측할 수 있게 해주는 가능성이 낮다는 것을 알아낼 것이다. 두 명의 사회학자 Cecile Ernst 그리고 Jules Angst가 몇 년 전 1,500건의 연구를 검토해 본 결과, 이들은 "성격의 출생 순서 차이가 우리의 샘플에서는 존재하지 않았으며 특히 첫 아이의 성격이라는 것에 대한 증거는 없다."는 결론을 내렸다.

INTRO

[CASE STUDY 2]

The concept of incarcerating individuals as a punishment for crimes did not exist in Wales before or during the medieval period. The early castles of the Welsh rulers did possess dungeons, but the purpose of these facilities was for the confinement of hostages and political prisoners, people who may have committed no crime. Up to the 17th century the most common punishments for criminal offences were fines, corporal punishment and executions. From the 18th century the institutions that would begin to have the function of modern prisons began to appear. Existing buildings were used to house criminals for a set period of time after being sentenced by a court. Early prisons in Wales were rudimentary and had few amenities for the imprisoned. In 1878 the prison system in Wales was nationalized and came under centralized government control. This led to better conditions and fewer, larger prisons. The smaller prisons and jails across the country were closed and the location of the prisons centralized.

VOCA incarcerate v. 투옥시키다   dungeon n. 지하 감옥   confinement n. 감금, 억류   hostage n. 인질   commit v. (범죄를) 저지르다   fine n. 벌금형   corporal punishment n. 태형   execution n. 사형   institution n. 제도, 기관   house v. 수용하다   criminal n. 범죄자   sentence v. (형을) 선고하다   rudimentary a. 기본적인   amenity n. 편의시설   nationalize v. 국유화하다   condition n. 여건, 조건   centralize v. 중앙 집권하다

범죄에 대한 처벌로써 개인을 투옥시키는 개념은 중세 이전과 중세 동안의 웨일즈에는 존재하지 않았다. 웨일즈 통치자들의 초기 성들은 지하 감옥을 가지고 있었지만, 이러한 시설들의 목적은 인질과 정치범 즉, 범죄를 저지르지 않았을 사람들을 감금하는 것이었다. 17세기까지 가장 보편적인 범죄의 처벌은 벌금형, 체형, 그리고 사형이었다. 18세기부터, 현재 감옥 기능을 갖기 시작하는 제도들이 나타나기 시작하였다. 기존의 건물들은 법원에서 형선고를 받은 이후 정해진 기간 동안 범죄자들을 수용하는 데에 사용되었다. 웨일즈의 초기 감옥들은 원시적이었고 수감자들을 위한 편의 시설이 거의 없었다. 1878년에 웨일즈의 감옥 제도는 국유화 되었고, 중앙 정부의 통제 하에 놓이게 되었다. 그 결과 감옥의 상태는 나아졌고, 수는 적어졌으며, 규모는 커졌다. 전국에 있던 작은 감옥과 구치소들은 문을 닫았고, 감옥의 위치는 집중화되었다.

[CASE STUDY 3]

Children usually feel sick in the stomach when traveling in a car, airplane, or train. This is motion sickness. While traveling, different body parts send different signals to the brain. Eyes see things around and they send signals about the direction of movement. The joint sensory receptors and muscles send signals about the movement of the muscles and the position in which the body is. The skin receptors send signals about the parts of the body which are in contact with the ground. The inner ears have a fluid in the semicircular canals. This fluid senses motion and the direction of motion like forward, backward, up or down. When the brain gets timely reports from the various body parts, it finds a relation between the signals and sketches a picture about the body's movement and position at a particular instant. But when the brain isn't able to find a link and isn't able to draw a picture out of the signals, it makes you feel sick.

VOCA motion sickness n. 멀미 signal n. 신호 joint sensory receptor n. 관절 감각 기관 semicircular a. 반원의 canal n. 수로, (신체)관

아이들은 대개 자동차, 비행기 혹은 기차를 타고 여행할 때 메스꺼워한다. 이것이 멀미이다. 여행하는 동안, 신체의 다른 기관들은 두뇌로 다른 신호들을 보낸다. 눈은 주변의 사물들을 보고 움직임의 방향에 대한 신호들을 보낸다. 관절 감각기관들과 근육들은 근육의 움직임과 신체가 취하고 있는 자세에 대한 신호들을 보낸다. 피부 수용기는 땅과 접촉하고 있는 신체의 부분에 대한 신호들을 보낸다. 내이(內耳)는 반고리관 안에 액체를 가지고 있다. 이 액체는 움직임과 앞뒤 혹은 위아래와 같은 방향을 감지한다. 뇌가 다양한 신체의 기관으로부터 적절한 신호들을 받을 때, 뇌는 신호들 사이의 관계를 찾아서 신체의 움직임과 어떤 특정한 순간에 신체의 자세에 대한 그림을 그린다. 그러나 뇌가 신호들로부터 연결점을 찾지 못하고 그림을 그릴 수 없을 때, 그것은 당신을 메스껍게 만든다.

CONTENTS

CONTENTS

이 책의 목차

Chapter 01 파트별 전략 / 13

- UNIT 01 문제 분석 ·· 14
- UNIT 02 PARAPHRASE ·· 32
- UNIT 03 TOPIC ·· 38
- UNIT 04 내용일치 ·· 44
- UNIT 05 빈칸 추론(Blank) ·· 50
- UNIT 06 순삽탈(순서배열 문장삽입 논지일탈) ·· 56

Chapter 02 10분 모의고사 / 73

직관적으로는 사실처럼 들리지만, 냉정히 분석해 보면 사실이 아닌 이야기들이 많다. '영어 실력과 영어 점수는 정비례한다' 라는 주장이 그러하다. 학창 시절에 평상시 실력은 매우 좋은데, 시험 점수는 그렇지 못한 경우를, 실력이 그렇게 좋은 것은 아닌데 시험만 보면 점수는 잘 나오는 경우가 그런 예이다.

특정 목표를 이루기 위해서는 내가 그 목표에 도달하는 가장 효과적인 방법이 무엇인지에 대해서 냉철하게 고민해 봐야 한다. 그냥 열심히 하면 되겠지 라는 막연한 자세와 전략은 막연한 결과만을 가져올 뿐이다.

지금 이 순간, 이 자리에서 우리가 간절히 원하는 것은 시험 점수의 상승이다! 그렇다면 시험의 특징은 무엇일까?

1. 기출 문제 분석을 통해서 문제들의 유형과 난이도를 알 수 있다.
2. 반드시 정해진 시간 안에 문제를 해결해야 한다.

따라서 시험에 대비하는 우리의 해결책은 다음과 같다.
1. 문제 유형별 분석을 통해서 가장 효과적인 풀이 전략(Reading Skill)을 학습하고, 이를 지속적으로 반복해서 체득해야 한다.
2. 연습을 실전같이! 평상시에 시간을 정해서 문제를 해결하는 연습을 해야한다.

CH1에서 우리는 독해 유형별 풀이 전략을 학습할 것이다. 여기서 핵심적인 것은 유형별로 분류할 때의 기준은 독해지문이 아니라, 문제들이다. 따라서 문제를 분석하고, 보기문항들을 분석하는 전략이 제일 중요하다.

CH2에서는 시간을 정해서 문제를 해결하는 연습에 집중할 것이다. 시간 안에 문제를 해결하는 연습이 연계되지 않으면, CH1에서 학습한 풀이 전략을 효과적으로 활용할 수 없다.

CHAPTER 1
파트별 전략

CHAPTER ❶ UNIT 01

문제 분석

수업 때 자주 묻는 질문 중 하나!
만약 두 문제 중에 하나만 선택해야 한다면 어느 것을 선택할 것인가?

1) 지문은 처음 보는 아랍어. 문제는 한글.
2) 지문은 한글. 문제는 처음 보는 아랍어.

대부분 큰 어려움 없이 1번을 선택한다. 2번처럼 지문을 완벽하게 이해해도 문제에 대한 이해를 전혀 할 수 없다면 문제를 풀 수 없기 때문이다. 하지만 1번은 지문에 대한 이해는 전혀 없지만, 문제와 보기 문항을 이해할 수 있기에, 적어도 이런 저런 궁리 끝에 답을 선택해 볼 수는 있기 때문이다.

그러나... 너무나 많은 수험생들이 지문에 대한 난이도에는 민감하지만, 문제의 중요성을 간과하고 있다. 기억하자! 언제나 정답은 문제와 문항 속에 있다는 것을!

시험문제의 정답률은 지문의 난이도 보다는 문제의 난이도가 절대적으로 결정한다.
따라서 언제나 문제와 보기 문항을 분석하는 것이 제일 중요한 문제풀이 전략의 핵심이다!

 모든 해답은 언제나 문제와 문항에 있다

1 텍스트 의존성

모든 객관식 문제들은 **'텍스트 의존성'**을 기준으로 2가지로 나눌 수 있다.
텍스트 의존성이란 문제가 얼마나 텍스트(지문)에 의존하고 있는지를 의미한다. 실전에서 텍스트 의존성이 중요한 것은 텍스트 의존성이 높은 문제일수록, 본문에 대한 내용을 전달 하기에 문제를 해결하는데 도움이 되기 때문이다.

1) 텍스트 의존성이 낮은 문제들

의존성이 낮은 문제들은 지문에 대한 어떤 사전 정보도 제공해 주지 않는다. 실전에서 이런 문제들은 단순히 유형 파악으로만 충분하다.

Which of the following is true according to the passage?
What is the most plausible title of the presentation?

Which of the following is most appropriate for the blank?
What is the main idea of the passage?
Which of the following does the passage mainly discuss?
Which of the following is the author most likely to admit?

2) 텍스트 의존성이 높은 문제들

의존성이 높은 문제들은 대체로 문제가 길다. 평소에 텍스트 의존성에 대한 학습이 되어 있지 않다면, 직관적으로 어렵다고 느낄 여지가 다분하다. 여기서 독독1.0 학습의 가치가 빛을 드러낸다. 문제가 길다는 것은 그만큼 지문에 대한 정보를 주는 것이기 때문에, 이것을 적극적으로 이용할 수 있다면 정답률을 비약적으로 높일 수 있다.

텍스트 의존성이 있는 문제들은 언제나 지문에 관한 내용을 알려주는 keyword를 등장하기에 이를 적극적으로 활용하자.

---

1 According to the passage, creditors seldom talk about money when sending bills because mentioning money _____.

채권자들은 돈을 보낼 때 돈 이야기를 거의 하지 않는다. 돈을 언급하는 것은 _____ 때문이다.

① is conventional
② is a taboo
③ is inhibited by law
④ is not professional

이 문제는 지문에 대한 아무런 정보가 없어도, 빈칸에는 부정적인 표현이 적절하다는 것을 문제 분석을 통해서 알 수 있다.

---

2 If the coin is a "fair coin," what is the expected number of ducats that Paul will receive from Peter?

만약 동전이 정확하다면, 폴이 피터에게서 받을 수 있는 더컷은 얼마인가?

이 문제를 통해서, 지문은 동전과 폴이 피터에게서 돈을 받는다는 내용임을 알 수 있다.

2. 텍스트 의존성 Practice

Q 텍스트 의존성 높은 keyword를 선별해 보자.

01 The above passage suggests that in order to fully understand the literary excellence of the English Bible, we should first _____.

02 How have we been able to learn about the mummification process?

03 Which of the following is true about the ceremonies at Gettysburg during the Civil War?

04 When did Lincoln's Gettysburg Address begin to receive public acclaim?

05 What is the main reason city officials created official spots for the locks?

06 According to the advisory, what is one possible consequence of misuse of the equipment?

07 According to the passage, what can make cycling in traffic less perilous?

08 What prompted Briggs to alter its asthma medication?

09 What is a requirement of the reception desk agent job?

10 Which of the following is a social science discipline that the author mentions as being possibly over-utilized?

11 According to the passage, which one is not correct as a possible cause of the end of the Earth?

12 According to the passage, which of the following transformed the men from a mob of individual fighters into an army?

13 Why did some critics doubt the antiquity of the inscriptions?

14 What does the writer think of the heedlessness of children?

15 Why were X-rays given to older women more than younger women?

16 What will probably be the first stage of change as the Sun becomes a red giant?

17 It can be inferred from the passage that the author believes which of the following about the current state of public awareness concerning nuclear power?

18 According to the passage, short stories are popular in the United States today primarily because they _____.

19 Mathematical laws explaining the movement of the planets according to the Copernican theory were made by _____.

20 Why did the people of Macondo decide not to return to the movies?

21 Which design principle does this passage focus on as most important for dashboard visualizations?

22 Rosa Parks usually didn't take the bus home from work, because _____.

23 According to the passage, blue monkeys of different groups can live together as long as _____.

24 According to the passage, why did the Census Bureau revise the definition of urban in 1950?

25 According to the passage, what kind of difficulty would the astronauts have?

26 According to the passage, what is the most comprehensive explanation for the success of Asian immigrants in the US?

27 According to the passage, which of the following is not a reason for travel becoming increasingly unnecessary?

28 Which of the following best describes the relation between physical exercise and brain exercise?

29 According to the passage, why are architects taking into account of the environment in designing buildings?

30 For a company registering a business in Delaware what is not necessary?

3 보기 문항 Keyword

Topic이나 내용일치 문제 유형에서 빈번하게 발생하는 어려움은 두 개의 보기 문항 중에 하나를 선택해야 하는 일이다. 복수의 보기 문항 중에서 2개까지는 골랐는데, 그 두 개 중 하나를 선택해야 하는 시점에서 실제적인 지침이 될 수 있는 것이 보기 문항에서 대표적인 keyword를 선별하는 것이다. 2개 중 하나를 선별 해야하는 시점에서 일반적으로 수험생들은 다시 본문을 읽고, 보기 문항을 보고, 또다시 본문을 읽고 보기 문항을 보고… 이런 과정을 반복한 뒤에 확신 없이 답을 선택하는 경우가 대부분이다. 하지만 보기 문항에서 keyword를 선별하는 훈련이 되면, 본문을 읽을 때 특정 표현이나 내용에 초점을 맞추고 독해할 수 있기에 좀 더 수월하게 정답에 접근할 수 있다.

1) 모든 문항에 중복되는 표현들이 있는 경우

상대적으로 수월한 경우로 보기문항들에서 중복되는 표현이 있는 경우로, 중복되는 표현들을 소거하고 보기문항들의 차별성을 보여주는 표현을 keyword로 선택하면 된다.

(1) Handling Everyday ~~Worries~~ (다루는 방법?)
(2) Negative Effect of ~~Worries~~ (부정적인 영향?)
(3) How I Conquered My ~~Fears~~ (정복하는 방법?)
(4) ~~Worries~~ : Its Cause and Cure (원인과 치료법?)

Worries가 중복되기에 반복되는 표현을 빼고 남은 표현들을 중심으로 본문의 내용을 파악해 보면 수월하게 주제를 찾을 수 있다.

(1) The Reasons Why ~~Women~~ Have Jobs (일을 하는 이유?)
(2) ~~Women~~'s Power in the Nuclear Family (능력, 영향력?)
(3) ~~Women~~'s Economic Dependence on Men (경제적 의존?)
(4) Working ~~Women~~'s Difficulties in Marriage Life (결혼생활에서의 어려움?)

2) 복수의 보기문항에 중복되는 표현들이 등장하는 경우

가장 많은 경우에 해당하는 유형들로 2개~3개의 보기문항들에 중복되는 보기문항들이 등장하는 유형이다.

아래 보기 문항들은 두 개의 표현들이 중복되는데,

첫째 Asia을 중심으로 파악하면

(1) Importance of the ~~Asiaen Market~~ (중요성?)
(2) How to Master English Quickly (영어를 빠르게 배우는 방법?)
(3) Rapid Growth of ~~Asian Economy~~ (빠른 성장?)
(4) Popularity of English in ~~Asia~~ (영어의 인기?)

Or English 중심으로 파악하면

(1) Importance of the Asiaen Market (아시아 시장의 중요성?)
(2) How to Master ~~English~~ Quickly (배우는 방법?)
(3) Rapid Growth of Asian Economy (아시아 시장의 빠른 성장?)
(4) Popularity of ~~English~~ in Asia (아시아에서 인기?)

이 때, 아시아 또는 English 중 둘 중 하나를 소거해서 생각할지, 아님 둘 다 모두 소거해서 생각할지는 지문의 내용에 따라서 선택적으로 적용하면 된다.

아래 보기 문항에서는 3개의 보기문항에 conflict가 중복되는데, (3)번에서 aggressive acts (공격적인 행동)을 conflict와 유의어로 보는 것이 요점이 될 수 있다. 지문에 따라서는 전혀 다른 의미가 될 수 있지만, 일반적으로 conflict가 발생하는 경우에 aggressive act가 일어날 가능성이 많기 때문에 유의어로 보고 다른 표현들을 중심으로 보기문항들을 비교해 보는 것이 실전적이다.

(1) Why Individual ~~Conflicts~~ Happen (왜 개인에게 발생?)
(2) Patterns of Reacting to ~~Conflict~~ (반응의 패턴?)
(3) Results of ~~Aggressive Acts~~ (결과들?)
(4) Changing Other's Behavior (타인의 행동을 변화시키기?)

아래 보기문항들에서는 서로 다른 두 개의 문항들에서 반복되는 표현들이 등장한다. 이런 경우에는 본문을 토대로 2개 정도의 보기 문항을 선별한 후에 2개를 비교해 보는 것이 실전적이다.

(1) Hard Work of Town Officials (도시 공무원들의 노고)
(2) How to Find <u>Number Patterns</u> (숫자 패턴들을 찾는 방법)
(3) Importance of Community's Services (지역사회 서비스의 중요성)
(4) Using <u>Number Patterns</u> in Town Planning (도시계획에서 수치패턴들을 활용하는 것)

만약 예상 정답으로 (1)&(3)으로 두 개를 선택했다면 양자 사이에서는 반복되는 표현들이 없다. 이런 경우에는 본문의 내용을 토대로

(1) Hard Work of Town Officials (도시 공무원들의 노고)
(3) Importance of Community's Services (지역사회 서비스의 중요성)

양자의 보기 문항을 비교해서 어떤 특정 표현이나 내용이 더 빈번하게 등장하는지를 고려해서 정답을 유추해야 한다.

하지만 만약 (2)&(4)를 예상 정답으로 선택했다면

(2) How to Find ~~Number Patterns~~ (찾는 방법?)
(4) Using ~~Number Patterns~~ in Town Planning (활용하는 것?)

반복되는 표현을 소거해서 나머지 내용을 토대로 정답을 유추할 수 있다.

3) 개별적인 문항들이 있는 경우

반복되는 표현들이 없는 경우에는 상대적으로 특정 keyword를 선별하기가 애매하다. 특정 표현으로 볼 것인지, 보기 문항을 전체적으로 조망할지에 대한 선택에 직면하는데... 결론적으로 이런 경우에는 지문의 내용을 토대로 keyword를 선택할 수밖에 없다. 하지만 이런 경우에도 보기문항들만의 비교를 통해서 대략적인 keyword를 선별할 수 있다.

아래의 보기문항들에서는 중복되는 표현은 없지만, 모두 '명사+ 장소의 전치사구'들이 나열되어 있다. 이런 경우에는 장소를 제외한 나머지 특정 어구들을 keyword로 파악하면 효율적인 경우가 많다.

(1) Religious Freedom in North America (종교의 자유?)
(2) The Founding Idea of Dutch West India Company (건국이념?)
(3) The Quakers in the New World (퀘이커 교도?)
(4) The Puritan Orthodoxy in the New Colony (청교도 윤리?)

아래의 보기문항들은 대체로 '명사 + 부사구'의 구조들이다. 이런 경우 또한 해당 명사들을 keyword로 선택해도 큰 무리는 없다.

(1) The relationship between environmental change and women's lives (관계?)
(2) The development plan of the rural areas in India (발전 계획?)
(3) The reason to support the women of the underdeveloped countries (이유?)
(4) The global issue of deforestation in the underdeveloped countries (산림 파괴?)

아래의 보기 문항들에서는 반복되는 표현들이 보이지 않는다. 하지만, 우리는 '건강', '질병'이라는 **포괄적 개념을 유추**해 볼 수 있다. 이처럼 보기문항들을 통해서 본문의 내용을 미루어 짐작해 볼 수 있는 것 또한 보기문항들을 활용하는데 있어서 매우 유익한 실전스킬이다.

(1) Benefits of Jogging (조깅의 이점들)
(2) Sources of High Fats (고지방의 원천)
(3) Importance of Checkup (건강검진의 중요성)
(4) Causes of Heart Attack (심장마비의 원인들)

4 문항 Practice

Q 보기 문항들에서 Keyword를 파악하자.

01 ① How to Protect the Wild Life
    ② The Life of the Passenger Pigeon
    ③ Hunting in Nineteenth-Century America
    ④ How Passenger Pigeon Became Extinct

02 ① Climate Changes in Recent Years
    ② Why Americans Move to the South
    ③ What caused Stress of Modern People
    ④ The Increase of Living Cost in America

03 ① Sharing of Our Problems
    ② The Importance of Job
    ③ Types of Family Business
    ④ How to Cope with Crisis

04 ① How Can We Make Snow?
    ② Two Sides of Artificial Snow
    ③ The Importance of 'Safety First'
    ④ The Increasing Number of Skiers

05 ① Harmful Effects of Computer
   ② Increasing Needs for Computer
   ③ Computer: A Useful Tool of Art
   ④ Various History of Computer Graphics

06 ① Effects of the Sun's Heat
   ② Causes of Weather Changes
   ③ Mysteries of the Solar System
   ④ Results of the Earth's Movement

07 ① Advantage of Small Family
   ② Importance of Family Bond
   ③ Nuclear and Extended Family
   ④ Element of Family Organization

08 ① Greatness of Barack Obama
   ② Barack Obama : the 44th US President
   ③ Possible Threat to the Inauguration
   ④ Public safety plan for Obama Inauguration

09 ① To Get a Job, Be a Pleasant Person
   ② More Qualifications Bring Better Chances
   ③ It Is Ability That Counts, Not Personality
   ④ Show Yourself As You Are at an Interview

10 ① The restaurant presents a culinary performance.
   ② The restaurant is highly praised in Beijing.
   ③ The restaurant features a special champagne bar.
   ④ The restaurant only serves dishes from the Beijing region.

11 ① Time your feedback well.
   ② Customize negative feedback.
   ③ Tailor feedback to the person.
   ④ Avoid goal-oriented feedback.

12 ① the development of legal names
   ② the concept of attractive names
   ③ the benefit of simple names
   ④ the roots of foreign names

13 ① In the past, the study of history required disenchantment from science
   ② Recently, science has given us lots of clever tricks and meanings
   ③ Today, we teach and learn about our world in fragments
   ④ Lately, history has been divided into several categories

14 ① The increase in the number of working women boosted the expansion of food service programs.
　② The US government began to feed poor children during the Great Depression despite the food shortage.
　③ The US school food service system presently helps to feed children of poor families.
　④ The function of providing lunch has been shifted from the family to schools.

15 ① What effects does worry have on life?
　② Where does worry originate from?
　③ When should we worry?
　④ How do we cope with worrying?

16 ① Insomnia can be classified according to its duration.
　② Transient insomnia occurs solely due to an inadequate sleep environment.
　③ Acute insomnia is generally known to be related to stress.
　④ Chronic insomnia patients may suffer from hallucinations.

17 ① to improve the quality of teacher training facilities
　② to bridge the gap through virtual classrooms
　③ to get students familiarized with digital technology
　④ to locate qualified instructors across the nation

18 ① Governments must control the flow of trade to revive the economy.
   ② Globalization can be beneficial regardless of one's economic status.
   ③ The global economy grows at the expense of the poor.
   ④ Globalization deepens conflicts between rich and poor.

19 ① There was an increase in the knowledge of the Earth and heavens in the early 17th century.
   ② Dependence on the philosophy of Aristotle was on the decline in universities in the 17th century.
   ③ Natural philosophy proposed four elements to explain the movements of bodies.
   ④ In natural philosophy, numbers were routinely put to use for measurable external quantities.

20 ① Your grandfather's stress when he was an adolescent might make you more anxious.
   ② Early stressful experiences alleviate anxiety later in life.
   ③ Constant moving from one place to another can benefit offspring.
   ④ Chronic social stress cannot be caused by relocation.

21 ① Sponsorship is necessary for a successful career.
   ② Building a good network starts from your accomplishments.
   ③ A powerful network is a prerequisite for your achievement.
   ④ Your insights and outputs grow as you become an expert at networking.

22 ① Some writers struggle for teaching positions to teach creative writing courses.
   ② As a doctor, William Carlos Williams tried to find the time to write.
   ③ Teaching is a common way for writers to make a living today.
   ④ Salman Rushdie worked briefly in advertising with great triumph.

23 ① Public adoption agencies are better than private ones.
   ② Parents pay huge fees to adopt a child from a foster home.
   ③ Children in need cannot be adopted through public agencies.
   ④ Private agencies can be contacted for international adoption.

24 ① the better world that is still within our reach
   ② the accumulation of wealth in fewer pockets
   ③ an effective response to climate change
   ④ a burning desire for a more viable future

25 ① children's identification with teachers at school
   ② low intelligence of primary school children
   ③ influence of poor working memory on primary school children
   ④ teachers' efforts to solve children's working-memory problem

26 ① The Brookfield Zoo ran a program that supports free admission for low-income families.
② The Brookfield Zoo assisted African-American kids in tracing their family history.
③ The Newberry Library and the Brookfield Zoo won a $10,000 award respectively.
④ The Newberry Library was awarded the medal for an extensive number of maps.

27 ① Science is very helpful in modern society.
② Science and technology are developing quickly.
③ The absolute belief in science is weakening.
④ Scientific research is getting more funds from private sectors.

28 ① Movie and concert schedules will be notified twice a month.
② During the weekdays, the cafeteria and the library will open at noon.
③ Campus buses will run every hour and make all of the regular stops.
④ A valid identification card is required to use the athletic and entertainment facilities during the summer session.

29 ① In the nineteenth century, opening windows was irrelevant to the density of miasma.
　② In the nineteenth century, it was believed that gentlemen did not live in places with bad air.
　③ Vaccines were invented after people realized that microbes and bacteria were the real cause of diseases.
　④ Cleaning cuts and scrapes could help people to stay healthy.

30 ① People tend to explain behavior in terms of individual personality.
　② Individual behaviors in a given situation are determined by the objective conditions.
　③ The social environment shapes the thoughts, feelings, and behaviors of the individual.
　④ People often distort reality in order to view themselves favorably.

CHAPTER ❶ UNIT 02

PARAPHRASE

'Paraphrase'는 본문 내용을 다르게 표현해서 동일한 내용을 전달하는 방식이다.
'대부분 밥을 먹는다 = 주식으로 쌀을 소비한다'

패러프레이즈가 중요한 이유는 다음과 같다.
1. 주제&요지 문항들은 본문의 핵심 내용을 패러해서 등장하는 것이 대부분이다.
2. 내용일치&불일치 문제들은 본문의 진술을 패러해서 보기 문항에 등장한다.
3. 패러 보기문항들을 '플러스&마이너스'로 분류했을 때, 정답문항을 좁힐 수 있다.
4. 보기문항 분석을 통해서 선택한 Keyword를 본문에서 패러한 표현을 찾아서 정답을 선출할 수 있다.

Case Study 1

중복되는 표현들이 있는 문항을 선별하고, 패러표현(동의어)들을 선택하자!

> He couldn't care less that his neighbors were moving.

(A) He was very disappointed that his neighbors were going away.
(B) He had mixed feelings about his neighbors' leaving.
(C) He secretly wished that his neighbors would stay.
(D) He was indifferent to his neighbors' moving.

Case Study 2

상관접속사에 주목하자.

> We have to deal not so much with actual facts as with various questions concerning the origins.

(A) We have to deal with more questions about actual facts than about the origins.
(B) Actual facts are more urgent issues to be addressed than questions concerning the origins.
(C) We are as much concerned with actual facts as with diverse issues surrounding the origins.
(D) Our discussion should be more focused on questions about the origins than on actual facts.

Case Study 3

비교급에 주목하자.

> The enduring values of freedom of thought outweigh any particular advantages that demand its violation.

(A) The long-held merits of freedom of thought are greater than benefits gained from restricting it.
(B) Freedom of thought endured long persecution and it gives advantages even when it is partially violated.
(C) Advantages coming from the breach of freedom of thought are often greater than those from upholding it.
(D) The values of freedom of thought are so great that its violation must be tolerated only when warranted.

Case Study 4

가진목적어 구문에 주목하자.

> Most people consider it discourteous to arrive at an appointment later than the time agreed upon.

(A) As a general rule, one needs to obtain advance permission to arrive late.
(B) Being tardy for an appointment is generally regarded as unmannerly.
(C) Arriving after the prearranged time is not considered rude.
(D) Most people do not take timely arrival for an appointment too seriously.

Case Study 5

강조용법에 주목하자.

> It was the man's flamboyant self-indulgence that allowed himself to become an election issue at the expense of his own achievements.

(A) The man attempted to mask his personal behavior in the election through emphasizing his achievements.
(B) The man's self-centeredness caused attention to be focused on his achievements and not on himself.
(C) In the election, the man's achievements received less attention than his character because he was generous.
(D) Because of the man's conceitedness, he himself became an election issue rather than his achievements.

Case Study 6

가정법 의미에 주목하자.

> If your teammates had shown the same level of devotion and diligence as you have shown, the project could not have been concluded so satisfactorily.

(A) Your teammates should have followed your example in completing the project successfully.
(B) The team project was successful despite your lack of effort and care.
(C) Despite your diligence and devotion, the project could not be completed satisfactorily.
(D) Without your input, the team could not have successfully completed the project.

CHAPTER ❶

UNIT 03

TOPIC

가장 대표적인 문제 형식인 주제 관련 문제들은 전형적인 Macro 문제 유형들이다. 매크로 문제의 특징은 세부적인 내용 파악이 안 된다 해도, 전반적인 논지를 파악해서 충분히 정답을 도출할 수 있다는 것이다.

TOPIC 문제에서는 가장 논쟁거리가 되는 것은 4개의 선지 중에서 2개까지 좁힌 후에, 그 2개 중에서 하나를 선택해야 하는 경우에 발생한다. 이런 경우에는 언제나 보기문항 Keyword를 분석과 대조를 통해서 정답을 선별할 수 있다.

1. 보기문항 Keyword를 분석한다.
2. 스키밍한다.
3. GS & MT & ST 구조로 분류해 본다.

Case Study 1

반복적인 단어는 KEYWORD !

> Some people become blind because a part of the eye called the cornea doesn't let in enough light. The cornea becomes clouded over. These people can be made to see again, however, if they are able to get clear corneas to let in the light. The blind must get the corneas from people with healthy eyes - people who agree to let blind people use their eyes after they die.

주제로 적절한 것은?

(A) Why corneas get clouded over.
(B) Why healthy eyes need more light.
(C) How people can see better.
(D) How clear corneas can help the blind.

VOCA cornea n. 각막　let in v. 통과시키다　clouded a. 구름 낀, 흐린

Case Study 2

대립문항들에 주목하자!

> There are those who say: "War is part of human nature, and human nature cannot be changed. If war means the end of man, we must sigh and submit." But they forget that what is called "human nature" is, in the main, the result of custom and tradition and education, and in civilized men, only a very tiny fraction is due to primitive instinct. If the world could live for a few generations without war, war would come to seem as absurd as dueling has come to seem to us.

Which of the following best expresses the idea of the writer?

(A) War means the end of man.
(B) Man is selfish by nature.
(C) War is part of human nature.
(D) Man can avoid war.

VOCA nature n. 본성, 본질, 자연 end n. 목적, 종말 sigh v. 한숨 쉬다 submit v. 굴복하다, 제출하다 custom n. 관습 civilized a. 문명화된 tiny a. 매우 적은 fraction n. 부분, 일부 primitive a. 원시의 instinct n. 본능 absurd a. 어리석은 dueling n. 결투 by nature ad. 타고난

Case Study 3

'difference'를 통해서 대조 구조를 파악해 보자.

> There is an enormous difference in the ways various public officials respond to public pressures, and in the means and methods they employ to deal with them. The best possess understanding of the forces that must be taken into account, determination not to be swerved from the path of public interest, a willingness to make enemies along with a gift for avoiding them, and faith that public support will be forthcoming for the correct course. The poorest are over-hesitant, evasive and preoccupied with their relationships with their colleagues, superiors, the press or the political support on which they lean. They will make no move unless the gallery is packed. They confront all embarrassment with a stale general formula.

What is the most plausible title of the presentation?

(A) Political Pressure Groups
(B) Mistakes for Public Officials to Avoid
(C) Characteristics of Public Officials
(D) Gaining Political Support

VOCA enormous a. 거대한, 막대한 gallery n. 관람석, 관객 swerve v. 빗나가다 embarrassment n. 당황 forthcoming a. 다가오는 stale a. 진부한(=trite) evasive a. 파악하기 어려운(=elusive) over-hesitant a. 우유부단한

Case Study 4

'sound change'를 중심으로 문항들의 차이점에 주목하자.

> All living languages are characterized by sound changes that have occurred and will continue to occur in the course of their history. Some linguists choose to consider the sound change as something that operates with the regularity of physical laws. "Sound law" is a term devised by linguist August Leskien to describe the supposed absolute regularity of this kind of structural change in language. The term "Sound law" means that, in a given area and at a given period of a sound change, the change will be universal and will gave no exceptions. This rule loses some of its inflexibility by amendments to the effect that, if apparent exceptions are found, they are due to some extraneous factor, such as foreign or dialectal borrowing.

What is the main topic of the passage?

(A) The history of languages
(B) A theory of sound change
(C) Some exceptions to the rule of sound change
(D) Some reasons for sound change

VOCA characterize v. 특성을 나타내다 inflexibility n. 불가변성 term n. 용어 amendment n. 개정, 수정(안) devise v. 고안하다 apparent a. 명백한, 분명한 universal a. 보편적인 due to prep. 기인하는 extraneous a. 외래의, 이질적인 dialectal a. 방언의 exception n. 예외 analogy n. 유사, 유추 influence n. 영향

Case Study 5

처음과 마지막에 등장한 동의어 표현에 주목하자.

> An essay which appeals chiefly to the intellect is France Bacon's 'Of Studies.' His careful tripartite division of studies expressed succinctly in aphoristic prose demands the complete attention of the mind of the reader. He considers studies as they should be: for pleasure, for self-improvement, for business. He considers the evils of excess study; laziness, affectation, and precocity. Bacon divides books into three categories; those to be read in part, those to be read cursorily, and those to be read with care. Studies should include reading, which gives depth; and writing, which trains in preciseness. The author ascribes certain virtues to individual fields of study: wisdom to history, wit to poetry, subtlety to mathematics, and depth to natural philosophy. Bacon's four-hundred-word essay, studded with Latin phrases and highly compressed in thought, has intellectual appeal indeed.

Which of the following is the most appropriate title for the passage?

(A) Francis Bacon
(B) 'Of Studies': A Tripartite Division
(C) An Intellectual Exercise: Francis Bacon's 'Of Studies'
(D) The Categorization of Books According to Bacon

VOCA tripartite a. 3부로 이루어진 succinctly ad. 간단명료하게 aphoristic a. 경구적인, 금언의 prose a. 산문의 n. 산문 precocity n. 조숙 precise a. 정확한 subtlety n. 섬세함, 미묘함 studded with a. 많이 들어있는 stud n. 장식 못(단추) v. ~에 장식 못을 박다 cursorily ad. 피상적으로, 대충

Case Study 6

'One of 최상급'에 keyword가 등장한다.

> Many of the scientific achievements that we take for granted today have reached far beyond the dreams of scientists and science fiction writers of just seventy-five years ago. One of the most spectacular of these scientific accomplishments was the splitting of the atom. Life has never been the same since that event. From microwave ovens to electrical power and nuclear medicine, to ships that can sail the seas for as long as twelve years without refueling, the atom provides a better life for many of the inhabitants of the earth. Yet, this same power that is used today to detect genetic disorders in unborn children or to destroy a malignant cancer cell was the destructive, for that killed over one hundred thousand people in Hiroshima and Nagasaki at the end of World War II. The splitting of the atom, the unleashing of its terrific power, poses the greatest single threat known to humanity. We now have the power to destroy in a matter of minutes a civilization that has taken centuries to develop. Never before has the power for such potential good or such total destruction existed.

이글은 다음 중 무엇에 대한 글인가?

(A) examples of scientific achievements
(B) examples of destructive power
(C) powers resulting from splitting of the atom
(D) potentially good and destructive powers

VOCA science fiction n. 과학소설　spectacular a. 장관의, 구경거리가 될 만한　the splitting of the atom n. 원자 분열　microwave oven n. 전자레인지　refuel v. 연료를 다시 채우다　detect v. 찾아내다　genetic disorder n. 유전적인 질병　malignant a. 악성의　unleash v. 해방하다　potential a. 잠재력이 있는 n. 가능(성) 잠재력　philosophical a. 철학적인　laudatory a. 칭찬하는　sarcastic a. 냉소적인　factual a. 사실적인

CHAPTER ❶   UNIT 04

내용일치

내용일치 문제는 독해 문제에서 가장 정석적인 유형이다. 즉, 주제나 빈칸 문제들이 부분적인 읽기나 글의 구성을 통해서 정답을 도출할 수 있는 반면에, 내용일치 문제들은 지문의 세부 정보를 파악해야 해결할 수 있다. 이것은 더 많은 시간과 더 많은 집중력을 우리에게 요구한다. 텍스트 의존성과 보기문항 S 포인트를 중심으로 본문을 스키밍하는 방법이 최선의 전략이다.

1. 텍스트 의존성 문제라면 본문 내용의 Keyword를 파악한다.
2. 상호 모순적인 문항들은 둘 중 하나가 정답일 가능성이 크다.
3. 문항에 글의 주제가 등장한다면 정답이다.
4. 보기문항에서 S 포인트 파악하고 본문을 스키밍한다.

Case Study 1

'negative event'를 중심으로 본문을 스키밍하자.

> The self-serving bias is the tendency for us to attribute positive events to ourselves and negative ones to external factors. For example, a star athlete interviewed after winning a big game attributes his success to his hard work. The same athlete interviewed a few weeks later after losing a game explains, "Today just wasn't my day." Psychologists say it is human nature to think this way in order to protect our self-esteem and reputation. The advantages of the self-serving bias are: it prevents us from getting depressed in the face of failure, and it allows us to remain confident about the future. However, blaming negative outcomes on external sources robs us of opportunities to learn from our mistakes and become better people. If we continue to avoid looking honestly at how we contributed to a negative outcome, we will remain stagnant.

According to the passage, what do we usually do after experiencing a negative event?

(A) Think of ourselves as responsible
(B) Listen to critique from other people
(C) Try to learn from our mistakes
(D) Blame things other than ourselves

VOCA self-serving n. 확증 편향   tendency n. 성향   attribute v. ~탓으로 돌리다   stagnant a. 침체된   critique n. 비평   blame v. 비난하다

Case Study 2

보기 문항을 Globalization 중심으로 이분법하자.

> How on earth will it help the poor if governments try to strangle globalization by stemming the flow of trade, information, and capital — the three components of the global economy? That disparities between rich and poor are still too great is undeniable. But it is just not true that economic growth benefits only the rich and leaves out the poor, as the opponents of globalization and the market economy would have us believe. A recent World Bank study entitled "Growth Is Good for the Poor" reveals a one-for-one relationship between income of the bottom fifth of the population and per capita GDP. In other words, incomes of all sectors grow proportionately at the same rate. The study notes that openness to foreign trade benefits the poor to the same extent that it benefits the whole economy.

본문의 내용과 일치하는 것은?

(A) Governments must control the flow of trade to revive the economy.
(B) Globalization can be beneficial regardless of one's economic status.
(C) The global economy grows at the expense of the poor.
(D) Globalization deepens conflicts between rich and poor.

VOCA strangle v. 억압하다   stem v. 막다   component n. 요소, 성분   disparity n. 격차   undeniable a. 부정할 수 없는   entitled a. 제목이 붙은   proportionately ad. 비례해서

Case Study 3

보기문항을 Speedking vs Sesta로 이분법해서 본문을 스키밍하자.

> Electric cars were always environmentally friendly, quiet, clean—but definitely not sexy. The Speedking has changed all that. A battery-powered sports car that sells for $120,000 and has a top speed of 125m.p.h., the Speedking has excited the clean-tech crowd since it was first announced. Some Hollywood celebrities also joined a long waiting list for the Speedking; magazines like Wired drooled over it. After years of setbacks and shake-ups, the first Sesta Speedkings were delivered to customers this year. Reviews have been ecstatic, but Sesta Motors has been hit hard by the financial crisis. Plans to develop an affordable electric sedan have been put on hold, and Sesta is laying off employees. But even if the Speedking turns out to be a one-hit wonder, it's been an exciting electric ride.

글의 내용과 일치하는 것은?

(A) Speedking is a new electric sedan.
(B) Speedking has received negative feedback.
(C) Sesta is hiring more employees.
(D) Sesta has suspended a new car project.

VOCA clean-tech a. 친환경 기술의   drool over v. 군침을 흘리다   setback n. 방해, 역경   shake-ups n. 대개편   ecstatic a. 황홀한   put on hold v. 지연하다   lay off v. 정리해고 하다   one-hit wonder n. 하나뿐인 히트상품

Case Study 4

문항이 한글인 경우에 반복적인 표현을 통해서 본문의 내용을 예측하자.

> Langston Hughes was born in Joplin, Missouri, and graduated from Lincoln University, in which many African-American students have pursued their academic disciplines. At the age of eighteen, Hughes published one of his most well-known poems, "Negro Speaks of Rivers." Creative and experimental, Hughes incorporated authentic dialect in his work, adapted traditional poetic forms to embrace the cadences and moods of blues and jazz, and created characters and themes that reflected elements of lower-class black culture. With his ability to fuse serious content with humorous style, Hughes attacked racial prejudice in a way that was natural and witty.

다음 글의 내용과 일치하지 않는 것은?

(A) Hughes는 많은 미국 흑인들이 다녔던 대학교를 졸업하였다.
(B) Hughes는 실제 사투리를 그의 작품에 반영하였다.
(C) Hughes는 하층 계급 흑인들의 문화적 요소를 반영한 인물을 만들었다.
(D) Hughes는 인종편견을 엄숙한 문체로 공격하였다.

VOCA academic disciplines n. 전공, 학업   incorporate v. 통합하다   authentic a. 진짜의, 진정한   dialect n. 사투리   embrace v. 수용하다   cadences n. 억양   racial prejudice n. 인종적 편견

Case Study 5

보기에 S 포인트(숫자, 인명, 지명)를 중심으로 본문을 스캔하자.

In the U.S., 80% of people ages 65 and older are now living in metropolitan areas, and according to the World Health Organization, by 2030, an estimated 60% of all people will live in cities - many of them over age 60. Cities increasingly rank high on both doctors' and seniors' lists of the best places to age gracefully.

Every year, the Milken Institute Center for the Future of Aging (CFA) ranks the best metropolitan places for successful aging, and most years, major cities sweep the top 10 spots. No wonder: cities tend to have strong health systems, opportunities for continued learning, widespread public transportation, and an abundance of arts and culture. That's not to say that people can't feel isolated or lonely in cities, but you can get lonely in a country cottage too. In cities, the cure can be just outside your door.

"We all long to bump into each other," says Paul Irving, the chairman of the Milken Institute CFA. "The ranges of places where this can happen in cities tend to create more options and opportunities." They tend to be alone especially as we age and families disperse. But there are answers: a 2017 study in the journal Personal Relationships found that it can be friends, not family, who matter most. The study looked at 270,000 people in nearly 100 countries and found that while both family and friends are associated with happiness and better health, as people aged, the health link remained only for people with strong friendship.

"While in a lot of ways, relationships with friends had a similar effect as those with family," says William Chopik, assistant professor of psychology at Michigan State University and the author of the study, "in others, they surpassed them."

Which of the following is NOT true?

(A) Four fifths of Americans at 65 and over are now living in metropolitan areas.
(B) Cities are increasingly favored by doctors as the best places to live gracefully in old age.
(C) The finding of the 2017 study in Personal Relationships was based on the subjects from around 100 countries.
(D) Paul Irving is the author of the 2017 study published in Personal Relationships.

VOCA metropolitan a. 대도시의   long v. 열망하다   bump into v. 우연히 마주치다   surpass v. 능가하다, 추월하다

Case Study 6

보기문항과 관련 없는 내용은 skip 하자.

> When the gong sounds, almost every diner at Beijing restaurant Duck de Chine turns around. That's because one of the city's greatest culinary shows is about to begin — the slicing of a Peking duck. Often voted by local guides in China as the best Peking duck in the city, the skin on Duck de Chine's birds is crispy and caramelized, its meat tender and juicy. "Our roasted duck is a little different than elsewhere," says An Ding, manager of Duck de Chine. "We use jujube wood, which is over 60 years old, and has a strong fruit scent, giving the duck especially crispy skin and a delicious flavor." The sweet hoisin sauce, drizzled over sliced spring onions and cucumbers and encased with the duck skin in a thin pancake, is another highlight. "The goal of our service is to focus on the details," says Ding. "It includes both how we present the roasted duck, and the custom sauces made for our guests." Even the plates and the chopsticks holders are duck-shaped. Duck de chine also boasts China's first Bollinger Champagne Bar. Though Peking duck is the star, there are plenty of other worthy dishes on the menu. The restaurant serves both Cantonese and Beijing cuisine with a touch of French influence.

다음 글의 내용과 일치하지 않는 것은?

(A) The restaurant presents a culinary performance.
(B) The restaurant is highly praised in Beijing.
(C) The restaurant features a special champagne bar.
(D) The restaurant only serves dishes from the Beijing region.

VOCA gong n. (악기)징   turn around v. 몸을 돌리다   culinary a. 요리의   slicing n. 얇게 자름   crispy a. 고소한   caramelized a. 설탕을 입힌   jujube wood n. 대추나무   hoisin sauce n. 해선장(단맛 나는 중국 소스)   drizzle v. 뿌리다   encased a. 덮힌   touch n. 풍미, 분위기   cantonese n. 광둥어

CHAPTER ❶

빈칸 추론 (Blank)

빈칸 넣기는 특히 '부분적인 읽기를 통해서 정답을 유추'해야 하는 파트이다. 내용일치가 글의 전반적인 내용을 스키밍하는 것이 중요한 스킬인데 비해, 빈칸은 철저하게 빈칸을 중심으로 전후의 문맥을 파악하는 것이 핵심이다. 전후의 문맥은 2.0에서 학습한 '플러스 마이너스' 구조의 이분법을 통해서 양분할 수 있다. 이 때 특히, '플러스 재진술'의 문맥을 파악하는 것이 아주 중요하다. 마이너스 연결어들은 언제나 눈에 띄지만, 재진술 구조는 유의하지 않으면 파악하기가 쉽지 않기 때문이다.

1. 빈칸이 처음/마지막이라면 전후에 재진술이 반드시 등장한다.
2. 빈칸이 중간이라면 전후 문맥 (플러스 마이너스)을 살피자.
3. 빈칸 전후에 '동일어구 연결어'에서 단서를 찾자.

Case Study 1

빈칸 뒤에 대명사를 통해서 재진술 구조임을 파악하자.

> Many prophets of information technology (IT) believe that the next big movement in their field will be the "_____." This, they hope, will connect objects hitherto beyond the reach of IT's tendrils so that, for example, your sofa can buzz your phone to tell you that you have left your wallet behind, or your refrigerator can order your groceries without you having to make a shopping list. That, though, will mean putting chips in your sofa, your wallet and your fridge to enable them to talk to the rest of the world.

(A) artificial intelligence (B) internet of things
(C) driverless vehicle   (D) big data

VOCA prophet n. 예언자 information technology n. 정보기술(IT) hitherto ad. 지금까지 tendril n. 덩굴손 buzz v. 소리를 내다 grocery n. 식료품 및 잡화 internet of things n. 사물인터넷 artificial intelligence n. 인공지능

Case Study 2

첫 문장의 빈칸은 주제문이기에 후속 재진술 내용에 유의하자.

> The attitude toward _____ is seen in many aspects of American life. One is invited to dinner at a home that is not only comfortably but even luxuriously furnished. Yet the hostess probably will cook the dinner herself, will serve it herself, and will wash the dishes afterward. Furthermore, the dinner will not consist merely of something quickly and easily assembled from the contents of various cans and a cake or pie bought at the nearby bakery. On the contrary, the hostess usually takes pride in her own careful preparation of special dishes.

(A) family tie
(B) manual labor
(C) social activity
(D) public relations

VOCA manual a. 육체노동의 serve v. 접대하다 consist of v. 구성되다 take pride in v. 자랑스러워하다 dish n. 음식

Case Study 3

마지막 문장의 빈칸은 주제문으로 본문의 재진술 내용을 종합하자.

> Researchers placed "lost" applications to graduate school at an airport and studied how frequently people who found the application helped by putting it in the mail. Results showed that people were more likely to send in the application if the person in the photo, whether male or female, was attractive. On overage, 52 percent of the applications of good-looking people were returned, compared to 35 percent of the applications of less attractive people. In this anonymous situation, willingness to help was affected by _____.

(A) environmental conditions
(B) physical appearance
(C) the number of witnesses
(D) social responsibility

VOCA applications n. 지원서 send in v. 발송하다 anonymous a. 익명의

Case Study 4

빈칸 전후 문장들만을 보고 문맥을 파악해 보자.

"Let's Uber." Few companies offer something so popular that their name becomes a verb. But that is one of the many achievements of Uber, a company founded in 2009 which is now the world's most valuable startup, worth around $70 billion. But Uber's ambitions extend much further: using self-driving vehicles, it wants to make ride-hailing so cheap and convenient that people forgo car ownership altogether. Not satisfied with shaking up the $100-billion-a-year taxi business, it has its eye on the far bigger market for personal transport, worth as much as $10 trillion a year globally. _____. Companies big and small have recognized the transformative potential of electric, self-driving cars, summoned on demand. Technology firms including Apple, Google and Tesla are investing heavily in autonomous vehicles.

(A) Uber is getting bigger and bigger.
(B) That was a mistake.
(C) Uber is not alone in this ambition.
(D) That's not the way it goes.

VOCA verb n. 동사 achievement n. 성취, 달성 startup n. 신규 업체(특히 인터넷 기업) ride-hailing n. 전화나 스마트폰 어플 등을 이용해서 택시를 부르는 교통수단 forgo v. 포기하다 shake up v. 흔들어 섞다, 개편하다 transformative a. 변화[변형]시키는 summon v. 소환하다, 호출하다 on demand ad. 요구만 있으면 autonomous a. 자율적인

Case Study 5

빈칸 뒤의 '문장부호'는 재진술 신호이다.

> Like most patriotic Americans, my father was forever buying gizmos that proved to be disastrous - clothes steamers that failed to take the wrinkles out of suits but had wallpaper falling off the walls in whole sheets, an electric pencil sharpener that could consume an entire pencil in less than a second, a water pick that was so lively it required two people to hold and left the bathroom looking like the inside of a car wash, and much else. But all of this was nothing compared with the situation today. We are now surrounded with items that do things for us to an almost absurd degree - automatic cat food dispensers, electric juicers and can openers, refrigerators that make their own ice cubes, automatic car windows, disposable toothbrushes that come with the toothpaste already loaded. People are so addicted to convenience that they have become trapped in _____: The more labor-saving appliances they acquire, the harder they need to work; the harder they work, the more labor-saving appliances they feel they need to acquire.

The best expression for the blank would be _____.

(A) a vicious circle (B) a dilemma
(C) a balloon effect (D) a domino effect

VOCA patriotic a. 애국적인 gizmo n. 간단한 장치, 기계 wrinkle n. 주름 wallpaper n. 벽지 pencil sharpener n. 연필깎이 to a degree ad. 어느 정도로, 대단히 dispenser n. 디스펜서 load v. (재료를) 넣다 addicted a. 중독된 trap v. (어떤 상태로) 빠뜨리다, 잡다, 덫을 놓다 labor-saving a. 노동력 절약형의 appliance n. 가전제품, 기기

Case Study 6

빈칸 뒤 구체적인 재진술 문장이 등장한다.

> The Nobel Prize in Literature may be the world's most important literary award, but not everyone who wins can make it to the ceremony. Among the reasons given by past laureates for failing to travel to Stockholm to accept the award: being gravely ill and in a wheelchair (Harold Pinter, 2005); and being a Soviet dissident terrified to leave the country because you might not be allowed back in (Aleksandr Solzhenitsyn, 1970). Over the years, some literature prize winners seem to have delighted in making things difficult for the academy by reacting to news of their win with _____. In 1964, Jean-Paul Sartre turned the award down. As for V. S. Naipaul, when the academy telephoned him at home to let him know that he'd won the 2001 prize, he refused to come to the phone.

(A) welcoming gestures
(B) less than complete enthusiasm
(C) fear of public recognition
(D) expressions of excitement

VOCA award n. 상, 수상 ceremony n. 의식 laureate n. 수상자 gravely ad. 중대하게 agoraphobic a. 광장공포증을 가진 suited a. 적절한, 어울리는 dissident n. 반체제 인사 terrify v. 놀라게 하다 react v. 반응하다, 반작용하다 refuse v. 거절하다 grumble v. 불평하다, 투덜대다 complete a. 완벽한, 최대의

CHAPTER ❶

순삽탈 (순서배열 문장삽입 논지일탈)

순서배열, 문장삽입, 논지일탈 3가지 문제 유형은 결국 같은 논리적 사고를 묻는 문제들이다.
문제의 형식은 다르지만, 위 문제들에서 평가하고자 하는 논리성들은 다음과 같다.
G ≫ S (일반적 진술이 구체적 진술보다 앞에 온다)
접속사와 대명사는 첫 문장으로 적절하지 않다.
동일 어구(동의어, 유의어)는 이어진다.
명사와 그것을 지칭하는 대명사는 이어진다. (재진술)

 동일 어구 접대 일구!! + 보기문항 소거법

Case Study 1

G는 S보다 선행한다.

> [I] Music has long been appreciated for its calming effects, but new research shows it also may have the power to restore and keep us healthy.
>
> [II] Soothing sounds, from Tibetan chants to Beethoven symphonies, are being given scientific credit for preventing colds, easing labor pain and even boosting anti-aging hormones. One recent study found that surgery patients who listened to comforting music recovered more quickly and felt less pain than those who did not.
>
> [III] Sound therapy goes beyond recorded music: The International Journal of Arts Medicine reports that infants in intensive care unit go home three days sooner, eat better and gain more weight if the staff talks and sings to them.

(A) I - II - III   (B) II - I - III
(C) III - II - I   (D) III - I - II

VOCA appreciate v. 감상하다 calming a. 안정시키는 restore v. 회복시키다 soothing a. 달래는, 누그러뜨리는 chant n. 구호, 성가 cold n. 감기 ease v. 완화시키다 labor pain n. 분만통 anti-aging a. 노화를 예방하는 surgery n. 수술, 진료 recover v. 회복하다 therapy n. 치료법 go beyond v. 초월하다 infant n. 신생아 intensive care unit n. 중환자실

Case Study 2

시간표시는 일반적으로 서론에 등장한다.

> (a) For the past two years, I have been studying cancer survivors at the university, trying to find out why it is that some people respond much better to their treatment than do others.
> (b) Some patients fared much better in their therapies than others.
> (c) The patients I am talking about here received upon diagnosis whatever therapy - medication, radiation, surgery - their individual cases demanded.
> (d) On closer scrutiny, however, I discovered that severity of the illness was only one of a number of factors that accounted for the difference between those who get well and those who don't.
> (e) Yet the response to such treatments was hardly uniform.
> (f) At first I thought that some patients did well because their illnesses were not as severe as the illnesses of others.

(A) (c)-(b)-(a)-(f)-(d)-(e)   (B) (a)-(f)-(d)-(c)-(e)-(b)
(C) (d)-(c)-(b)-(e)-(f)-(a)   (D) (c)-(b)-(a)-(d)-(f)-(e)

VOCA survivor n. 생존자 treatment n. 치료 therapy n. 치료 diagnosis n. 진단 medication n. 약물 scrutiny n. 정밀조사 severity n. 심함, 혹독함 uniform a. 불변의 fare v. 살아가다, 지내다

Case Study 3

A는 THE 보다 선행한다.

[I] The exact reason is unclear, but it may be related to the effect of carotenoid levels in the blood.

[II] A study conducted by the University of Queensland's School of Pharmacy involving more than 12,000 Australians revealed that the benefits of a fresh produce-rich diet extend beyond physical health.

[III] With every added daily portion of fruits or vegetables (up to eight), the subjects' happiness levels rose slightly.

[IV] The researchers calculated that if someone were to switch from a diet free of fruit and vegetables to eight servings per day, he or she would theoretically gain as much life satisfaction as someone who transitioned from unemployment to a job.

(A) [I] - [III] - [II] - [IV]   (B) [II] - [III] - [IV] - [I]
(C) [III] - [II] - [I] - [IV]   (D) [IV] - [II] - [III] - [I]

VOCA pharmacy n. 약학, 약국   benefit n. 이익   produce-rich a. 농산물이 풍부한   extend v. 퍼지다, 연장되다   portion n. 일부, 부분   calculate v. 계산하다   theoretically ad. 이론적으로   transition v. 이행하다, 변천하다   carotenoid n. 카로티노이드(적황 색소)

Case Study 4

동일어구는 이어진다.

> Thunderstorms are extremely common in many parts of the world, for example, throughout most of North America. Updrafts of warm air set off these storms.

[A] This more buoyant air then rises and carries water vapor to higher altitudes. The air cools as it rises, and the water vapor condenses and starts to drop as rain. As the rain falls, it pulls air along with it and turns part of the draft downward.

[B] An updraft may start over ground that is more intensely heated by the sun than the land surrounding the area. Bare, rocky, or paved areas, for example, usually have updrafts above them. The air in contact with the ground heats up and thus becomes lighter, more buoyant, than the air surrounding it.

[C] The draft may turn upward again and send the rain churning around in the cloud. Some of it may freeze to hail. Sooner or later, the water droplets grow heavy enough to resist the updrafts and fall to the ground, pulling air in the form of downdrafts with them.

(A) [A] - [C] - [B] (B) [B] - [A] - [C]
(C) [B] - [C] - [A] (D) [C] - [A] - [B]

VOCA updraft n. 상승기류 buoyant a. 부력이 있는 altitude n. 고도 condense v. 응결되다, 응축되다 bare a. 벌거벗은, 노출된 pave v. (길을) 포장하다 churn v. 휘젓다 hail n. 우박

Case Study 5

'그러나', 대명사는 처음에 등장할 수 없다.

ⓐ Today, however, trees are being cut down far more rapidly. Each year, about 2 million acres of forests are cut down. That is more than equal to the area of the whole of Great Britain.

ⓑ There is not enough wood in these countries to satisfy the demand. Wood companies, therefore, have begun taking wood from the forests of Asia, Africa, South America, and even Siberia.

ⓒ While there are important reasons for cutting down trees, there are also dangerous consequences for life on earth. A major cause of the present destruction is the worldwide demand for wood. In industrialized countries, people are using more and more wood for paper.

ⓓ There is nothing new about people cutting down trees. In ancient times, Greece, Italy, and Great Britain were covered with forests. Over the centuries those forests were gradually cut back. Until now almost nothing is left.

(A) ⓐ - ⓑ - ⓒ - ⓓ (B) ⓓ - ⓐ - ⓑ - ⓒ
(C) ⓑ - ⓐ - ⓒ - ⓓ (D) ⓓ - ⓐ - ⓒ - ⓑ

VOCA rapidly ad. 급격하게 cut down v. 벌목하다 consequence n. 결과 industrialized a. 산업화된 be covered with v. 덮혀있다 cut back v. 삭감하다, 축소하다

Case Study 6

'also'는 키워드이다.

> Celebrities also sacrifice their private lives.

(A) Many people dream of being celebrities, but they might change their minds if they considered all the disadvantages there are to being famous. (B) For one thing, celebrities have to look perfect all the time. (C) There's always a photographer ready to take an unflattering picture of a famous person looking dumpy in old clothes. (D) Their personal struggles, divorces, or family tragedies all end up as front-page news. Most frighteningly, celebrities are in constant danger of the wrong kind of attention. Threatening letters and even physical attacks from crazy fans are things the celebrity must contend with.

VOCA celebrity n. 유명인 take a picture v. 사진을 찍다 unflattering a. 이상한 dumpy a. 땅딸막한 front-page n. 기사의 앞면 contend with v. (어려운 문제와) 씨름하다

Case Study 7

YES/NO 대답은 의문문 뒤에 위치한다.

> No, these are what two middle-school boys have subjected a classmate to for the past nine months.

> Frequent beatings, Water torture, Being dragged around by the neck and forced to eat crumbs off the floor. Sound like the abuses committed by some soldiers on suspected terrorists in a certain country? (A) The victim leapt to his death lately, leaving a note of painful recollections of his ordeals. (B) The word shock hardly suffices to describe the huge impact this incident has had on society. (C) Even more astounding, however, is most experts agree these kinds of grim episodes can happen anytime, anywhere in the present educational and social environment of Korea. (D) This shows why the nation must waste no more time to drive out bullying in and outside of campus, immediately and fundamentally.

VOCA beating n. 매질 torture n. 고문 drag v. 끌다 crumb n. 부스러기 suffice v. 충분하다 grim a. 암울한 drive out v. 추방하다 subject v. 당하게 하다, 복종시키다 ordeal n. 시련

Case Study 8

However를 중심으로 동일어구를 파악하자.

However, psychologists have developed criteria to determine whether a behavior reveals an intent to communicate.

At around 8 months of age, infants begin to use gestures such as pointing and showing in a communicative manner. (A) It is not easy to determine whether a behavior is meant to communicate something or is simply a behavior that an infant enjoys. (B) The major criteria are waiting, persistence, and development of alternative plans. (C) For example, suppose an infant pulls his or her parent's leg, waits for the parent to look down, and then points at a toy. (D) The fact that the infant waited for the adult to pay attention suggests that the infant was operating on the assumption that we first have to get an adult's attention and then we point out what we want.

VOCA criteria n. 기준   communicate v. (의사) 전달하다   point out v. 지시하다   persistence n. 인내, 지속   intent n. 의도

Case Study 9

삽입문의 대명사는 선행사를 찾는 문제이다.

> "Talking is not an important part of friendship for most of them."

Different ways of speaking are part of gender. As adults, men and women sometimes face difficulties in their communication with each other. [I] Studies of communication show that if a woman tells her husband about a problem, she will expect him to listen and offer sympathy. She may be annoyed when he simply tells her how to solve the problem. [II] Similarly, a husband may be annoyed when his wife wants to stop and ask a stranger for directions to a park or restaurant. Unlike his wife, he would rather use a map and find his way by himself. Language is also part of the different ways that men and women think about friendship. [III] Most American men believe that friendship means doing things together such as camping or playing tennis. [IV] American women, on the other hand, usually identify their best friend as someone with whom they talk frequently.

(A) [I]   (B) [II]   (C) [III]   (D) [IV]

VOCA gender n. 성별   sympathy n. 공감   on the other hand ad. 반면에

Case Study 10

S진술은 G진술 뒤에 온다.

> For example, some cultural groups were often portrayed as gangsters, while others were usually shown as the 'good guys' who arrested them.

One of the challenges we face in the world today is that a lot of the information we get about other people and places comes from the advertising and entertainment we see in the media. (A) You can't always trust these types of information. (B) To the people who make television programs and advertisements, true facts and honest opinions aren't as important as keeping you interested long enough to sell you something! (C) In the past, the messages we received from television programs, advertisements, and movies were full of stereotypes. (D) Even places were presented as stereotypes : European cities, such as Paris and Venice, were usually shown as beautiful and romantic, but cities in Africa and Asia, such as Cairo and Calcutta, were often shown as poor and overcrowded.

VOCA portray v. 묘사하다 arrest v. 체포하다 face n. 얼굴 v. 직면하다 advertising n. 광고 entertainment n. 접대, 오락, 즐거움 stereotype n. 고정관념 v. 정형화하다 overcrowded a. 인구과잉의

Case Study 11

첫 문장의 '우울증은 흔한 질병'이라는 flow을 따라가자.

내용의 흐름상 적절하지 못한 문장은?

> Depression is one of the most common mental illnesses. (A) At least 8% of adults in the United States experience serious depression at some point during their lives, and estimates range as high as 17%. (B) The illness affects all people, regardless of sex, race, ethnicity, or socioeconomic standing. (C) People commonly view depression as a sign of personal weakness, but psychiatrists and psychologists view it as a real illness. (D) However, women are two to three times more likely than men to suffer from depression.

VOCA depression n. 우울증   estimate v. 추정하다   ethnicity n. 민족성   socioeconomic a. 사회 경제적인   standing n. 입장, 지위   psychiatrist n. 정신과 의사

Case Study 12

'과학에서 이론은 유용하다'는 첫 문장의 flow를 따라가자.

내용의 흐름상 적절하지 못한 문장은?

In any science, a good general theory is the handiest tool possible. (A) Not only does it link many seemingly random facts into one coherent framework, but it also acts as a powerful aid to prediction. (B) Making predictions has become one of the leading growth industries of the twentieth century. (C) For instance, if you wanted to find out whether there is a planet beyond the known series, you could ask several hundred astronomers to keep their eyes open at night. (D) However, it would be more fruitful to turn to gravitational theory, which predicts that if there was a further planet out there it would cause detectable movements in the orbit of some other known planets. Indeed that is exactly how Leverrier predicted in 1846 that a planet would be discovered: Uranus.

VOCA irrelevant a. 일관성이 없는 random a. 무작위의 coherent a. 일관된 fruitful a. 생산적인 detectable a. 탐지할 수 있는 Uranus n. 천왕성

Case Study 13

첫 문장 '제품 생산'의 flow를 따라가자.

내용의 흐름상 적절하지 못한 문장은?

Before the Industrial Revolution, most goods were produced by hand in rural homes or urban workshops. (A) Merchants, known as entrepreneurs, distributed the raw materials to workers, collected the finished products, paid for the work, then sold them. (B) Growing demand for consumer products, together with a shortage of labour, placed pressure on entrepreneurs to find new, more efficient methods of production. (C) The great era of European exploration that began in the 15th century arose primarily out of a desire to seek out new trade routes and partners. (D) With the development of power-driven machines, it made economic sense to bring workers, materials and machines together in one place, giving rise to the first factories. For added efficiency, the production process was broken down into basic individual tasks that a worker could specialize in, a system known as the division of labour.

VOCA Industrial Revolution n. 산업혁명 goods n. 물건, 상품 rural a. 시골의, 지방의 workshop n. 일터, 작업장 merchant n. 상인 entrepreneur n. 실업가, 기업가 distribute v. 분배하다, 배급하다 raw material n. 원료 finished product n. 완제품 consumer product n. 소비재 efficient a. 능률적인, 효과적인 era n. 시대, 시기 exploration n. 탐험 specialize in v. 전공하다 division of labor n. 분업

Case Study 14

각 문장의 주어를 비교하자.

내용의 흐름상 적절하지 못한 문장은?

> The earth is a planet full of life. One of the reasons for this is that our sun is the kind of star that can support life on a planet. All the time the sun continues to send out a steady supply of heat and light. For our sun is a stable star. (A) <u>This means that it stays the same size.</u> And its output of energy (heat and light) does not change much. (B) <u>Some stars are not stable.</u> They grow bigger and hotter and then smaller and cooler. (C) <u>The heat and light they send out vary greatly.</u> If our sun behaved like that, the earth would boil and freeze repeatedly. (D) <u>Life could exist under these great changes.</u> We are here because a steady amount of energy pours forth from our sun.

VOCA planet n. 행성, 혹성 support v. 지원하다, 부양하다 continue v. 지속하다 send out v. 발산하다, 파견하다 steady = stable a. 안정적인 boil v. 끓다 freeze v. 얼다, 얼리다 pour v. 퍼붓다 n. 주입, 유출 forth av. 앞으로

Case Study 15

밑줄 문장들만을 연결해 보자.

글의 흐름상 가장 어색한 문장은?

Children's book awards have proliferated in recent years; today, there are well over 100 different awards and prizes by a variety of organizations. (A) <u>The awards may be given for books of a specific genre or simply for the best of all children's books published within a given time period</u>. An award may honor a particular book or an author for a lifetime contribution to the world of children's literature. (B) <u>Most children's book awards are chosen by adults, but now a growing number of children's choice book awards exist</u>. The larger national awards given in most countries are the most influential and have helped considerably to raise public awareness about the fine books being published for young readers. (C) <u>An award ceremony for outstanding services to the publishing industry is put on hold</u>. (D) <u>Of course, readers are wise not to put too much faith in award-winning books</u>. An award doesn't necessarily mean a good reading experience, but it does provide a starting place when choosing books.

VOCA proliferate v. 증가하다 genre n. 유형, 형식 ceremony n. 의식, 행사 outstanding a. 뛰어난 be put on hold v. 연기되다

CHAPTER 2
10분 모의고사

10분 모의고사 01

1 제시된 영문과 가장 가까운 문장을 선택하세요.

> American uniformity is an axiom for the European beyond any experience.

(A) Europeans do not believe in American uniformity until they come to America.
(B) Europeans are more convinced of American uniformity after they have been to America.
(C) Europeans have never believed in American uniformity due to their experience in America.
(D) Europeans believe so strongly in American uniformity that no experience can alter their belief.

2 빈칸에 가장 적절한 표현은?

> Sometimes things change without appearing to have changed at all. Let's take a pebble lying on a beach as an example. During the day the pebble is heated by the sun's rays. At night it cools down. To anyone who did not touch the pebble at both times it would not seem to have changed. However, to an insect walking across the pebble during the day and again at night, the pebble would seem to have changed a great deal. So to some extent, change is _____.

(A) difficult   (B) unusual
(C) relative   (D) unpredictable

---

1 **uniformity** n. 동질성 **axiom** n. 자명한 이치, 원리 **convince** v. 납득시키다, 확신하다
2 **pebble** n. 조약돌 **lying** a. 놓여있는 **cool down** v. 차가워지다 **to some extent** ad. 어느 정도는

3 글의 제목으로 가장 알맞은 것을 고르시오.

If we want to describe our society in terms of age, we may come up with four age groups — childhood, adolescence, maturity, and old age. We take it for granted that people of different ages behave differently. For example, we feel that a man in his thirties should act his age and not behave like an adolescent or an old man. Equally, we expect that, as they go through life, people of the same age will in some ways understand each other better than people of different ages. All this is part of expected ways of behaving in our social life, but it is not something that we can apply to formal institutions governed by hard-and-fast rules.

(A) Age Groups : Their Expected Behavior
(B) Secrets of Aging : Myth and Truth
(C) Formal Institutions : Their Social Rules
(D) Teens' Behavior : Respected or Neglected?

4 주어진 글 다음에 이어질 글의 순서로 가장 적절한 것은?

Footwear has a history which goes back thousands of years, and it has long been an article of necessity.

[A] The earliest footwear was undoubtedly born of the necessity to provide some protection when moving over rough ground in varying weather conditions. In ancient times, as today, the basic type of shoes worn depended on the climate.

[B] Shoes have not always served such a purely functional purpose, however, and the requirements of fashion have dictated some curious designs, not all of which made walking easy.

[C] For instance, in warmer areas the sandal was, and still is, the most popular form of footwear, whereas the modern moccasin derives from the original shoes adopted in cold climates by races such as Eskimos and Siberians.

(A) [A] — [B] — [C] (B) [A] — [C] — [B]
(C) [B] — [C] — [A] (D) [C] — [A] — [B]

---

4 footwear n. 신발 go back v. 거슬러 올라가다 necessity n. 필수품 undoubtedly ad. 확실히 varying a. 다양한 climate n. 기후 functional a. 기능의, 실용적인 requirement n. 필요한 것, 필요조건 derive v. ~에서 파생되다 adopt v. 채용[채택]하다

5 글의 흐름으로 보아 주어진 문장이 들어가기에 가장 적절한 곳은?

'I also learned that her name was Dorothy'

Our nursing professor gave us a quiz. I had easily answered all the questions until I read the last one: "What is the name of the woman who cleans the school?" (A) I knew she was tall, short-haired, and in her fifties, but how would I know her name? I handed in my paper, leaving the question blank. (B) Collecting the papers, the professor said the last question would count. Then she added, "In your careers you will meet many people. All are significant. (C) They deserve your attention and care, even if all you do is smile and say hello." I've never forgotten that lesson. (D)

5 hand in v. 제출하다 significant a. 중대한, 함축성 있는 deserve v. ~할 만하다 attention n. 관심, 주의 count v. 중요하다

6 본문의 내용을 토대로 빈칸에 적절한 것은?

According to a new paper by Paola Acevedo of Tilburg University and Steven Ongena of the University of Zurich, the trauma affects how bankers subsequently do business. The authors look at bank lending after heists in Colombia, a country where 835 bank robberies took place between 2003 and 2011. They find that loan officers treat would-be borrowers differently in the aftermath of an armed robbery. Loan volumes did not change, but the duration of loans issued in the first 90 days after a stickup was 70% longer. The average Colombian loan matures in 5.4 months, but a newly burgled branch typically lends for 8.7 months. The traumatized loan officers also demand more collateral, but offer slightly lower interest rates than normal. All of these changes reduce the need to deal with new customers in person. Lending for longer periods pushes repayment meetings further into the future. Taking more collateral reduces the need to vet customers thoroughly. And the lower interest rates suggest that loan officers spend less time haggling. This behaviour is a classic symptom of post-traumatic stress disorder.

After armed robberies, bankers _____.

(A) give out loans on better terms
(B) tend to reduce the duration of loans
(C) would not give out loans to new customers
(D) do not require any collateral

6 **heist** n. 은행 강도, 절도 **stickup** n. 권총 강도 **mature** v. 어음 등이 만기가 되다 **burgle** v. 강도질하다 **collateral** n. 담보물 **vet** v. 조사하다, 심사하다 **haggle** v. 말다툼하다 **post-traumatic stress disorder** n. 외상 후 스트레스 장애 (큰 정신적 충격 때문에 겪게 되는 의학적 증상)

10분 모의고사 02 문제편

1 제시된 영문과 가장 가까운 문장을 선택하세요.

> It is unlikely that the city subway system will be able to continue its present level of service without a price increase.

(A) In order to increase the level of service, the city subway system will have to raise the subway fare.
(B) The level of service will probably not increase because of the present subway fares.
(C) The city subway system will probably have to raise subway fares in order to continue similar service.
(D) The city subway system will probably face a financial crisis.

2 빈칸에 가장 적절한 표현은?

> As children enter the educational system, traditional expectations for boys and girls continue. In the past, much research focused on how teachers were shortchanging girls in the classroom. Teachers would focus on boys, calling on them more and challenging them. Because boys were believed to be more _____, teachers assumed they would excel in math and science. Teachers encouraged them to go into careers, such as computer science or engineering.

(A) modest (B) arrogant
(C) analytical (D) effeminate

---

1 **present** a. 현재의 **fare** n. 요금 **face** v. 직면하다 **financial crisis** n. 재정위기
2 **shortchange** v. 부당하게 대우하다 **call on** v. 요구하다, 방문하다 **analytical** a. 분석적인 **effeminate** a. 여자 같은 **modest** a. 겸손한, 적당한 **arrogant** a. 건방진

3-4 다음 물음에 답하시오.

> The poor talker sometimes surprises us by being a good writer. Such a one is usually of the Cerebral type. He likes to think out every phase of a thing and put it into just the right words before giving it to the world. So, many a Cerebral does little talking outside; his intimate circle does a good deal of surreptitious writing. It may be only the keeping of a diary, jotting down memoranda or writing long letters to his friends, but he will write something. Some of the world's greatest ideas have come to light first in the forgotten manuscripts of people of this type who died without showing their writings to anyone. Evidently they did not consider them as sufficient importance or did not care as much about publishing them as about putting them down.

3. Which of the following best represents the main idea of the passage?

(A) Actions speak louder than words.
(B) There are people who write better than they talk.
(C) Some of the greatest ideas remain in the dark because of public ignorance.
(D) Speaking does a thousand things while writing does not get you anywhere.

4. According to the passage, which one is true of a Cerebral?

(A) He knows how to make bad ideas sound plausible.
(B) He's reluctant to share his ideas with others.
(C) He's not so interested in delivering his ideas to the public.
(D) His thoughts are more creative than those of ordinary people.

3-4 **cerebral** a. 뇌의, 지적인 **phase** n. 측면 **put into words** v. 말로 표현하다 **intimate** a. 친밀한 **circle** n. 동아리, 단체, 영역 **a good deal of** a. 많은 **surreptitious** a. 내밀한, 은밀한 **keep a diary** v. 일기를 쓰다 **jot down** v. 적다 **memoranda** n. 비망록 **manuscript** n. 원고 **get(go) anywhere** v. 성공하다 **plausible** a. 그럴듯한

5 글의 흐름으로 보아 주어진 문장이 들어가기에 가장 적절한 곳은?

Therefore, they have fewer enemies than most people, and they are probably the most loved of people.

Most people like to talk, but few people like to listen, yet listening well is a rare talent that everyone should treasure. (A) Because they hear more, good listeners tend to know more and to be more sensitive to what is going on around them than most people. (B) In addition, good listeners are inclined to accept or tolerate rather than to judge and criticize. (C) However, there are exceptions to that generality. (D) For example, John Steinbeck is said to have been an excellent listener, yet he was hated by some people. No doubt his ability to listen contributed to his capacity to write, but the results of his listening did not make him popular.

5 rare a. 드문, 진귀한 treasure v. 소중히 하다 be inclined to v. ~하는 경향이 있다 tolerate v. 참다, 견디다 contribute to v. 기여하다

6 아래 영문들의 가장 논리적인 순서는?

[A] These new technologies have another benefit for biologists by allowing them to gain access to the unknown world of communication between animals. For centuries, biologists believed giraffes were the silent giants of Africa. In recent years, however, biologists have been able to listen more carefully by means of these technologies and have realized that giraffes may talk, though not in a way that we can hear.

[B] Communication through infrasound is not limited to giraffes. Over the last few decades, biologists have found that whales, elephants, and some other animals also use this extremely low-pitched sound to communicate. This infrasound, as a means of communication, has special merit: It can travel a greater distance than higher-pitched noise. Such long-distance communication is a must for animals such as giraffes or elephants that roam over wide areas.

[C] Infrasound is a low-pitched sound, whose frequency is far below the range of human ears. Scientists, however, have been able to discover the existence of infrasound by using special technologies. These new technologies have revealed that many things can produce infrasound, from earthquakes and thunderstorms to trains and underground explosions, thus making possible the warning of earthquakes and the monitoring of underground nuclear-explosion tests.

(A) [C] - [B] - [A]   (B) [A] - [C] - [B]
(C) [B] - [A] - [C]   (D) [C] - [A] - [B]

10분 모의고사 03

1 제시된 영문과 가장 가까운 문장을 선택하세요.

> The future, as we stand on the threshold of 2012, looks bleaker than it did during the past few years.

(A) The future only seems bleaker; however, in reality that is because the past few years were great.
(B) As we enter 2012, we are more pessimistic than we have been over the past few years.
(C) From the vantage point of 2012, the situation has no hope of improvement.
(D) Although the future from 2012 looks bleak, it is because we only have the past for perspective.

---

1 **threshold** n. 문지방, 경계 **bleak** a. 암울한 **pessimistic** a. 비관적인 **perspective** n. 관점 **vantage point** n. 관점, 견해

2 글의 흐름으로 보아 주어진 문장이 들어가기에 가장 적절한 곳은?

You read the owner's manual, ask friends for help and call the manufacturer for assistance.

It's important to remember that you must take pride in the work you do. (A) It's like learning how to use a computer. (B) The first time, the computer is intimidating and not very user-friendly: Files are deleted, screens freeze, and software doesn't install. (C) But you don't give up. (D) After a few weeks, you begin to master the intricacies of using a computer and begin to wonder how you ever lived without one. If you didn't take pride in learning how to use a computer, it would probably end up gathering dust instead of making your life more efficient and productive.

2 manual n. 소책자, 입문서 intimidate v. 위협하다, 으르다 user-friendly a. (컴퓨터를) 사용하기 쉬운 intricacy n. 복잡한 일 productive a. 생산적인, 이익을 낳는

3 제시된 영문들의 가장 논리적인 순서는?

[A] Imagine that it's Saturday and you are to meet your friends at the mall at 12:00. You've been busy all morning, and suddenly you notice it is 11:45. You hurry to get ready and then jump in the car. What route is probably the fastest? You know where the mall is, and you choose the best route based on what you know about the distance, the number of stop lights, and the amount of traffic. In short, you make observations and make your best guesses based on what you know and have observed.

[B] True problem solving, however, goes beyond feelings. To solve a problem, you must look beyond how you feel and combine information that you already know with new observations. Then, on the basis of your knowledge of the situation, you can evaluate the problem and come up with the best way to solve it. An example will make this point clear.

[C] Everyone makes decisions every day. What clothes should you wear? Should you go out tonight or stay home and study? Most of the decisions people make are based on what they feel will be the best solution. Feelings and judgments of how others feel toward you play a major role in how you choose to solve your day-to-day problems.

(A) [A] - [B] - [C]   (B) [C] - [B] - [A]
(C) [C] - [A] - [B]   (D) [B] - [C] - [A]

3 mall n. 쇼핑센터 evaluate v. 평가하다 come up with v. 생각해 내다

4 빈칸에 가장 적절한 표현은?

> A wealthy individual, whose basic survival needs are met many times over, buys his pets gourmet, organic food that costs more per week than the weekly earnings of a minimum-wage worker. He is proud that he is able to take such good care of his animals and insists that it's the right thing to do if one really loves one's pets. After all, his vet was the one who recommended that he buy that brand. A minimum-wage worker who loads that food into the rich person's car might feel anger when he realizes how much money this individual spends on his pets. The minimum-wage worker might fume that this man's pets eat better than he does. He might wonder whether this rich man has any concept of _____.

(A) authenticity
(B) validity
(C) anarchy
(D) reality

5 According to the passage, which one is NOT true?

"Heaven helps those who help themselves" is a well-tried maxim, embodying in a small compass the results of vast human experience. The spirit of self-help is the root of all genuine growth in the individual, and as exhibited in the lives of many, it constitutes the true source of national vigor and strength. Help from without is often enfeebling in its effects, but help from within invariably invigorates. Whatever is done for men or classes to a certain extent takes away the stimulus and necessity of doing for themselves. And where men are subjected to overgovernment, the inevitable tendency is to render them comparatively helpless.

(A) Too much intervention goes against the spirit of self-help.
(B) "Heaven helps those who help themselves" is now an obsolete aphorism.
(C) Self-help is an essential requirement to achieve a real progress in the individual.
(D) Selfish motives are generally more stimulating than altruistic ones.

5 **well-tried** a. 충분한 시험을 거친 **embody** v. 구현하다, 포함하다 **in a small compass** ad. 간결하게, 아담하게 **exhaust** v. 다 써버리다, 소진시키다 **daunt** v. 위협하다, 기죽게 하다 **vigor** n. 활기 **bona fide** a. 진실한 **debilitate** v. 약화시키다 **from without** ad. 외부로부터 **from within** ad. 내부로부터 **enfeeble** v. 약화시키다 **invigorate** v. 활기를 북돋우다 **aphorism** n. 경구, 금언 **constitute** v. 구성하다 **obsolete** a. 구식의 **altruistic** a. 이타적인 **take away** v. 빼앗다 **overgovernment** n. 지나친 통제

6 What is the most suitable title for the passage?

In its effort at social engineering to build the perfect society, Singapore has, among other things, banned chewing gum, run campaigns encouraging people to smile, and passed edicts to stop children from climbing trees. Since 1984 the Social Development Unit, a government agency, has even attempted to create smarter Singaporeans. The forum was launched to redress a vexing imbalance: too few bright Singaporean men and women seemed interested in marrying each other, preferring either to wed intellectual inferiors or not to marry at all. Fearing the trend pointed in the direction of dullardism, the government decided to play Cupid by organizing dances for eligible college graduates. The SDU, though, quickly earned a reputation among critics as the port of last resort for the "Single, Desperate and Ugly." But the government's efforts have become effective: more than half of Singapore's graduate men now marry graduate women – an increase of nearly 25% since 1984.

(A) Civilized Wedding
(B) State Matchmaking
(C) Social Welfare Policy
(D) Common Law Marriage

6 engineering n. 토목, 조종 edict n. 포고, 명령 chewing n. 씹기 forum n. 포럼, 토론회 vexing a. 성가신, 애태우는 inexorably ad. 멈춤 없이 dullardism n. 우둔함, 멍청함 (dullard에 ism이 결합한 형태) play Cupid v. 중매자 역할을 하다 matchmaking n. 중매 common law 관습법 effective a. 효과적인, 유효한 redress v. 교정하다

10분 모의고사 04

1 다음 주어진 문장에 이어질 글의 순서로 가장 적절한 것은?

A number of studies showed the relationship between population density and the rates of disease, crime, and mental illness.

[A] But it has lower rates of hospitalization for mental illness and criminal violence than American cities.
[B] Hong Kong, for instance, has a population density 4 times as great as even the most crowded American cities.
[C] The results of these studies were confusing, because they sometimes didn't support the idea of the existence of the relationship.

(A) [A] - [B] - [C]   (B) [A] - [C] - [B]
(C) [C] - [B] - [A]   (D) [C] - [A] - [B]

---

1 density n. (인구의) 밀도 hospitalization n. 입원 criminal violence n. 강력 범죄 crowded a. 혼잡한, 복잡한 confusing a. 혼란스러운

2 제시문과 가장 가까운 의미의 영문은?

> Among their possible uses, smartphones can be used to mobilize individuals for political as well as social purposes.

(A) Smartphones make it easy for individuals to track changes in politics and society.
(B) Smartphones enable people to unite to achieve political goals in addition to enabling social achievement.
(C) Smartphones enable the integration of political and social agendas through a common technology.
(D) Smartphones are blurring lines between diverse political and social trends by causing individuals to merge into one group.

2 **mobilize** v. 동원하다, 모으다 **track** v. 추적하다 **unite** v. 통합하다 **interaction** n. 교류, 상호작용 **integration** n. 통합 **agenda** n. 의제, 안건 **blur** v. 허물다 **merge** v. 합병하다

3 글의 제목으로 가장 알맞은 것을 고르시오.

The average human pulse rate is around seventy beats per minute. This is also the average tempo of most Western music. In fact, it's said that the slow parts of Baroque music induce mental and emotional integration. Concentrating on the rhythm of music affects the rate of breathing, making it more regular, and faster or slower depending on the piece. There are interesting developments involving music. People are making "bioelectric" music, recording the sounds made by the electric impulses that result from brain activity or muscle movement. The sounds are processed through a computerized gadget for the use of composers, musicians, and even handicapped people who can be taught this means of self-expression. It's possible that by studying the "music" made by cells, microscopic creatures, and plants, we will understand biology much better.

(A) New Developments in Music
(B) Relation of Music to Biology
(C) Use of Biology to Music
(D) Ways to Understand Biology

---

3 **pulse** n. 맥박; 진동 **induce** v. 야기하다 **integration** n. 통합 **bioelectric** a. 생체 전기의 **gadget** n. 간단한 장치 **cell** n. 세포, 전지 **microscopic** a. 현미경의, 극미의

4 빈칸에 가장 적절한 표현은?

> The migrant question is a more serious threat to Europe's future than anything in recent memory, because it can't be resolved by a promise from a central bank or an infusion of someone else's cash. This is a question of Europe's identity – whether it means as much to European voters as it did a generation ago. _____, the refugees will keep coming, and it will become harder for governments to make sacrifices to welcome them.

(A) All the while
(B) On the one hand
(C) In conclusion
(D) On the other hand

5 글의 흐름으로 보아 주어진 문장이 들어가기에 가장 적절한 곳은?

> He threw the coin into the air and all watched intently it landed.

> During a momentous battle, a Chinese general decided to attack even though his army was greatly inferior in numbers. (A) He was confident they would win, but his men were filled with doubt. (B) On the way to the battle, they stopped at a religious shrine. After praying with the men, the general took out a coin and said, "I shall now toss this coin. (C) If it is heads, we shall win. If it is tails we shall lose." (D) It was heads. The soldiers were so overjoyed and filled with confidence that they vigorously attacked the enemy and were victorious. After the battle, a lieutenant remarked to the general, "No one can change destiny." "Quite right," the general replied as he showed the lieutenant the coin, which had heads on both sides.

---

4 **migrant** n. 이민자 **resolve** v. 해결하다 **infusion** n. 투입 **identity** n. 정체성 **refugee** n. 난민 **all the while** ad. 그러는 와중에 **on the other hand** ad. 반면에 **on the one hand** ad. 한편으로는

5 **momentous** a. 아주 중요한 **be inferior in numbers** v. 수적으로 열세이다 **shrine** n. 사당, 성지 **intently** ad. 열심히 **overjoyed** a. 미칠 듯이 기뻐하는 **confidence** n. 확신, 자신 **vigorously** ad. 활기 넘치게 **lieutenant** n. 부관 **heads** n. 동전의 앞면 **tails** n. 동전의 면

6 Which of the following statements is probably true?

> An abbreviation is a shortened form of a word or phrase that is used to save space in written form. Certain types of abbreviations, such as some acronyms, may also facilitate memory and are spoken, if easily pronounced, as well as written. The use of abbreviations dates back to ancient times, but the proliferation of abbreviations has been most acute in the 20th century. This is directly related to the vast increase in information, especially in science and technology, and to the ever-burgeoning number of agencies and organizations, both private and governmental.

(A) most acronyms are fairly easy to pronounce and remember
(B) the use of abbreviations has been steady throughout history
(C) abbreviations did not appear in ancient times
(D) proliferation of acronyms may not cease

---

6 **abbreviation** n. 약어, 축약형 **acronym** n. 두문자어 (ex. NATO – North Atlantic Treaty Organization) **facilitate** v. 촉진하다 **date back** v. 거슬러 올라가다 **proliferation** n. 확산, 만연 **acute** a. 날카로운, 급성의 **ever-burgeoning** a. 계속해서 급증하는

10분 모의고사 05

1 제시문과 가장 가까운 의미의 영문은?

> Nowadays religion gets less credit for its staple function of patching up the moral fabric of society.

(A) Religion's heavy task of revising the moral criteria of society is becoming less trustworthy.
(B) Religion is believed to perform an insignificant task in supporting moral standards of society.
(C) Religion's principal role in sustaining moral cohesion of society is not acknowledged as much.
(D) Religion does not recognize its traditional role in creating moral principles of society.

---

1 **get credit** v. 신뢰를 받다 **staple** a. 안정적인 **patch up** v. 연결하다, 종합하다 **revise** v. 개정하다 **criteria** n. 기준 **insignificant** a. 사소한 **cohesion** n. 통합, 응집

2 본문의 내용을 토대로 빈칸에 적절한 것은?

Since the Hawaiian Islands have never been connected to other land masses, the great variety of plants in Hawaii must be a result of the long-distance dispersal of seeds, a process that requires both a method of transport and equivalence between the ecology of the source area and that of the recipient area. There is some of dispute about the method of transport involved. Some biologists argue that ocean and air currents are responsible for the transport of plant seeds to Hawaii. Yet the results of flotation experiments and the low temperatures of air currents cast doubt on these hypotheses. More probable is bird transport, rather externally, by accidental attachment of the seeds to feathers, or internally, by the swallowing of fruit and subsequent excretion of the seeds. While it is likely that fewer varieties of plant seeds have reached Hawaii externally than internally, more varieties are known to be adapted to external than to internal transport.

The author mentions the results of flotation experiments on plants seeds in order to _____.

(A) support the claim that the distribution of plants in Hawaii is the result of the long-distance dispersal of seeds
(B) lend credibility to the thesis that air currents provide a method of transport for plant seeds to Hawaii
(C) suggest that the long-distance dispersal seeds is a process that requires long periods of time
(D) challenge the claim that ocean currents are responsible for the transport of plant seeds to Hawaii

2 land mass n. 육지 dispersal n. 분산, 살포 equivalence n. 동등, 등가 recipient n. 수령자 current n. 흐름, 전류 ocean and air currents n. 해류와 대류 flotation n. 부양 cast doubt v. 의문을 제기하다, 의심하다 swallow v. 삼키다 subsequent a. 뒤이은 excretion n. 배설, 분비물 variety n. 종류, 변화

3 제시된 내용들을 가장 논리적으로 나열한 것은?

(a) In March 1979 Wertheimer and physicist Ed Beeper, Ph. D. published this ominous finding in the American Journal of Epidemiology, one of the foremost epidemiological journals in the world.

(b) In addition, appliances tend to be used sporadically and therefore do not constitute sources of chronic, or continuous, magnetic-field exposure.

(c) They pointed out, however, that unlike the magnetic fields given off by power lines, the fields from most household appliances fall off sharply with distance from the appliance.

(d) Their article noted that certain household appliances - hair dryers, toasters, and electric drills — can also produce strong magnetic fields.

(e) They wrote that power lines "are taken for granted and generally assumed to be harmless," but that assumption had "never been adequately tested."

(A) (a)-(e)-(d)-(c)-(b)
(B) (e)-(d)-(c)-(b)-(a)
(C) (c)-(a)-(d)-(b)-(e)
(D) (a)-(c)-(b)-(e)-(d)

4 글의 흐름으로 보아 주어진 문장이 들어가기에 가장 적절한 곳은?

Then he would hear them when they come to eat the bananas and he could chase them away.

The intelligence of the elephant is widely known. We say, "the elephant never forgets," in honor of its excellent memory. (A) An Indian farmer who kept elephants discovered this fact. (B) He had noticed that his elephants were eating his bananas at night. (C) No fence could keep out the elephants, of course, so he decided to tie bells on them. (D) A few mornings later, however, the bananas were all gone, though he had heard nothing at night. When he checked the elephants he found that they had played a trick on him. They had filled the bells with mud so that they would not make any noise!

4 chase away v. 쫓아 버리다 in honor of ad. 기념해서 keep out v. 막다, 내쫓다 play a trick on v. 속이다 mud n. 진흙

[5-6]

While computer scientists would prefer that our passwords be a hard-to-crack jumble, precisely what makes passwords so flawed is also what computer scientist Joseph Bonneau finds uplifting. "People take a nonnatural requirement imposed on them, like memorizing a password," he said, "and make it _____." Here is a good example. In 1993, when she was 22, Maria T. Allen used for her password a combination of the name of her summer crush, J. D. and the name of a mythological female deity to whom he had compared her when they'd first met. The fling ended, and they went their separate ways. But the password endured. Eleven years later, out of the blue, Maria received a message through "classmates.com" from J. D. himself. They dated a few years, then decided to marry. Before the wedding, J. D. asked Maria if she had ever thought of him during that interim decade. "About every time I logged in to my Yahoo! account," she replied, before recounting to him her secret. He had the password inscribed on the inside of his wedding ring.

5 Choose the most suitable one for the blank.

(A) a true story
(B) a code of conduct
(C) a meaningful human experience
(D) a means of encoding a password

6 Which of the following statements is not true?

(A) Maria's Yahoo! account password had an emotional edge.
(B) J. D. once praised Maria's beauty by likening it to that of a goddess.
(C) It was in 2004 that Maria received a message again from J. D. after the breakup.
(D) Maria stopped using all passwords associated with J. D. right after the breakup.

5-6 **hard-to-crack** a. 깨기 어려운 **jumble** n. 뒤죽박죽 뒤섞인 것 **flawed** a. 흠이 있는 **uplifting** a. 희망을 주는 **crush** v. 부수다 n. 압착, 홀딱 반함 **fling** v. 던지다 n. 내던지기, 방종 **out of the blue** ad. 갑자기, 난데없이 **interim** a. 임시의, 과도기적인 **breakup** n. 이별, 헤어짐 **deity** n. 신, 여신 **log in** v. 로그인하다 **account** n. 계정 **recount** v. 자세히 말하다 **encode** v. 암호화하다 **liken** v. 비유하다

10분 모의고사 06 문제편

1 제시문과 가장 가까운 의미의 영문은?

> It would have been an ideal location for a waste incineration facility except for the opposition of the people in a nearby town.

(A) The people interfered with the construction of a waste incineration facility.
(B) A waste incineration facility was built in spite of the opposition of the people.
(C) The opposition of the people did not prevent the construction of a waste incineration facility.
(D) People have always raised objections to a waste incineration facility even in ideal locations.

---

1 **incineration** n. 소각장 **facility** n. 시설 **interfere with** v. 반대하다 **objection** n. 반대

2 다음 문장들을 논리적인 글이 되도록 배열하라.

(a) So, climate is a long view of weather.
(b) On the other hand, climate refers to the typical weather patterns of an area over many years.
(c) Weather refers to the temperature and amount of rain, wind, sun, and snow during a specific time.
(d) Although weather and climate are closely related, climate is different from weather.
(e) Most people probably spend more time thinking about weather than about climate.

(A) (d)-(c)-(b)-(e)-(a) (B) (e)-(d)-(c)-(b)-(a)
(C) (b)-(c)-(a)-(e)-(d) (D) (c)-(d)-(e)-(a)-(b)

2 view n. 관점, 견해 refer to v. 의미하다 typical a. 전형적인

3 제시된 문장이 들어가기에 적절한 자리는?

> But science alone is not enough: scientific knowledge must be translated into useful products and processes.

The advance of technology is a key force behind economic growth. What drives technology? (A) Scientific advances make new technologies possible. To take the most spectacular example in today's world, the semiconductor chip - which is the basis for all modern information technology - could not have been developed without the theory of quantum mechanics in physics. (B) And that often requires devoting a lot of resources to research and development, or R&D, spending to create new technologies and prepare them for practical use. (C) Although some research and development is conducted by governments, much R&D is paid for by the private sector. (D) The United States became the world's leading economy in large part because American businesses were among the first to make systematic research and development a part of their operations.

3 be translated into v. 전환되다 key force n. 원동력 spectacular a. 눈에 띄는 quantum mechanics n. 양자역학

4 What could be the main idea of this passage?

> Scientists with the National Oceanic and Atmospheric Administration say that with the sun now moving toward solar maximum, power outages, computer problems, and communication failures are likely to increase during 2018 and 2019. Solar max refers to the sun reaching the most active stage of its 11-year cycle where the number and intensity of solar events increase. During solar max, the surface of the sun spews electrically charged particles into space. Depending on the movement of the particles, they could head towards Earth. Since the last solar max in 1999, most nations have increased their dependency on wireless and satellite services, making them even more vulnerable.

(A) Solar max increases our dependency on science.
(B) We can prevent solar max from activating sooner or later.
(C) The sun moves toward solar max.
(D) Scientists anticipate solar max problems.

---

4 **solar maximum** n. 솔라맥스 (태양 활동이 가장 활발한 시기) **outage** n. 정전 **spew** v. 토하다, 쏟아내다 **vulnerable** a. 취약한, 공격당하기 쉬운 **sooner or later** ad. 조만간

[5-6]

How do you feel about sending women into combat? I'm a woman who will be going through Army basic training in a few months. I think it would be foolish of me to say that I want to go into battle, but I think it's totally unfair to exclude women from combat duty when they can handle it as well as men. Women should be expected to do the same work as men in the military and in wartime. When are the people going to realize that women are a viable source of our national defense? Canadian law has been revised, and now women are allowed to serve in all military positions – except on submarines – in the Canadian armed forces. There are plenty of men out there who would gladly give up their combat positions to women, and plenty of women who would _____ in a battle.

5 According to the passage, the writer believes _____.

(A) all women are eager to go into combat
(B) it is fair to exclude women from combat duty
(C) men are unwilling to yield their positions to women
(D) women can play an important role in national defense

6 Which best fits in the blank?

(A) jump at the chance to prove themselves
(B) be likely to be missing in action
(C) be afraid to substantially participate
(D) fight fiercely against women's rights

5-6 combat duty n. 전투 go through v. 경험하다 viable a. 실행 가능한 revise v. 개정하다 submarine n. 잠수함 fiercely ad. 사납게 yield v. 생산하다, 양보하다 substantially ad. 실질적으로 jump at v. 기꺼이 응하다

10분 모의고사 07

1 제시문과 의미가 가장 가까운 문장을 고르시오.

> Your persistence in being chronically late is only matched by your inability to recognize the inconvenience it causes to those it affects.

(A) Your lateness is causing you to become stubborn towards people you know.
(B) Your chronic lateness makes you unable to recognize its inconvenience.
(C) You do not realize the problems your constant lateness causes.
(D) You are aware of your lateness though you criticize others for being inconsiderate.

1 persistence n. 고집, 지속 chronically ad. 만성적, 습관적으로 inconvenience n. 불편함 stubborn a. 고집스러운 inconsiderate a. 사려깊지 못한

2 제시된 문장이 들어가기에 적절한 자리는?

"Unfortunately, the guarantee is often also a lie."

How can you recognize a quack? Sometimes it's easy because he or she offers something we know is impossible. A drink to keep you young is an example of this. But many times, these people lie, saying that their product was made because of a recent scientific discovery. (A) This makes it more difficult to know if the person is real or a fraud. Another way to recognize quackery is that many quacks will say their product is good for many different illnesses, not just for one thing. (B) They usually like to offer money-back guarantees if their treatment doesn't work. (C) Finally, the fraudulent clinic will often be in another country. (D) Laws in the United States will not allow a quack to have a clinic in the United States because the quack doesn't have the proper medical training.

2 recognize v. 알아보다 quack n. 돌팔이 의사, 사기꾼 guarantee n. 보증, 담보 treatment n. 치료 fraudulent a. 사기의 discovery n. 발견 money-back a. 환불해 주는

3 주어진 글에 이어질 문장의 순서로 가장 알맞은 것은?

> For decades, doctors have been intrigued by the apparent health benefits of the so-called Mediterranean diet, which is not really a diet the way most people think of one. It's more of a dietary pattern or rather, several complementary dietary patterns that have existed around the Mediterranean basin for centuries.

[A] But most people tend to focus on one component of these diets — olive oil — as if it were a magical potion that you could drizzle over any meal to make it healthy.

[B] Typical Mediterranean diets emphasize lots of fruits, cooked vegetables and legumes, grains and, in moderation, wine, nuts, fish and dairy products, particularly yogurt and cheese.

[C] According to the most rigorously controlled study of a Mediterranean diet, people with the most Mediterranean-like eating habits seem to have a reduced risk of dying from heart disease. But the study was unable to link the health benefits to any one ingredient, not even olive oil.

(A) [A] — [B] — [C] (B) [A] — [C] — [B]
(C) [B] — [A] — [C] (D) [C] — [A] — [B]

---

3 intrigue v. 흥미를 끌다 dietary a. 식이요법의 complementary a. 보충의 basin n. (강)유역 component n. 구성요소 drizzle v. 뿌리다 legume n. 콩과 식물

4 빈칸에 적절한 연결어들은?

The best poetry seems to be fully appreciated only by the few and to be beyond the comprehension of the many. The best advertising, _____, is thought about, laughed over, and acted upon by multitudes. Poetry is, in the general apprehension, something special to be studied in schools, to be enjoyed by cultivated people who have time for that sort of thing and to be read on solemn or momentous occasions. _____, advertising is part of everyday life.

(A) for example - However
(B) however - By contrast
(C) however - In short
(D) therefore - Otherwise

[5-6]

The idea that liars are easy to spot is still with us. Just last month, Charles Bond, a psychologist at Texas Christian University, reported that among 2,520 adults surveyed in 63 countries, more than 70 percent believe that liars avert their gazes. The majority believe that liars squirm, stutter, touch or scratch themselves or tell longer stories than usual. The liar stereotype exists in just about every culture, Bond wrote, and its persistence "would be less puzzling if we had more reason to imagine that it was true." What is true, instead, is that there are as many ways to lie as there are liars; there's no such thing as a dead giveaway.

Most people think ①_____, but studies show otherwise. A very small minority of people, probably fewer than 5 percent, seem to have some innate ability to sniff out deception with accuracy. But, in general, even professional lie-catchers, like judges and customs officials, perform, when tested, at a level not much better than chance. In other words, even the experts would have been right as if they had just flipped a coin. Most of mechanical devices now available, like the polygraph, detect not the lie but anxiety about the lie. So it can miss the most dangerous liars: the ones who don't care that they are lying or have been trained to lie. It can also miss liars ②_____, the true believers willing to die for the cause.

5 빈칸에 적절한 표현들은?

(A) ① they are good at spotting liars
    ② with nothing to lose if they are detected
(B) ① liars cannot but be detected
    ② who believe the machine can detect the lie
(C) ① experts are not reliable in spotting liars
    ② who believe they are innocent
(D) ① beliefs about lying are plentiful and contradictory
    ② with unusual sensitivity to conscientiousness

6 글에 따르면 적절한 것은?

(A) Most people can spot deception by paying sufficient attention to liars' physical signals.
(B) Learning to detect serious lies is an important part in administering criminal justice.
(C) People with the ability to detect lies are far fewer than usually expected.
(D) Advanced technology now available enables us to detect lies with confidence.

5-6 **spot** v. 찾아내다 **gaze** n. 응시 **squirm** v. 꿈틀거리다, 몸부림치다 **stutter** v. 말을 더듬다 **a dead giveaway** n. 확실한 증거 **sniff** v. 냄새를 맡다 **deception** n. 속임, 사기 **chance** n. 우연 **flip a coin** v. 동전을 던지다 **cause** n. 대의명분 **polygraph** n. 거짓말 탐지기

10분 모의고사 08 문제편

1 제시문과 가장 가까운 의미의 영문은?

> A surprising number of parents are either unaware that the problem exists or reluctant to face up to it.

(A) Some parents do not actually understand the problem and solve it.
(B) A lot of parents neither want to know the problem nor like to face it.
(C) A surprising number of parents evidently neglect both the problem and its full meaning.
(D) An amazing number of parents are both aware of the existing problem and take full cognizance of it.

---

1 **surprising** a. 놀랄만한 **unaware** a. 인식하지 못하는 **exist** v. 존재하다 **reluctant** a. 마음 내키지 않는, 꺼리는 **face up to** v. 직면하다 **evidently** ad. 분명하게 **amazing** a. 놀랄 정도의, 어처구니없는, 굉장한 **take cognizance of** v. 인지하다

2 주제로 적절한 것은?

Numerous companies have embraced the open office and by most accounts, very few have moved back into traditional spaces with offices and doors. But research findings that we're 15% less productive, we have immense trouble concentrating and we're twice as likely to get sick in open working spaces, have contributed to a growing backlash against open offices. There's one big reason we'd all love a space with four walls and a door that shuts: focus. The truth is, we can't multi-task, and small distractions can cause us to lose focus for upwards of 20 minutes. What's more, certain open spaces can negatively impact our memory. We retain more information when we sit in one spot without distractions. It's not so obvious to us each day, but we offload memories into our surroundings in the open spaces.

(A) The Pros and Cons of the Open Office
(B) The Myth of the Open Office Now Being Challenged
(C) The Open Office: the Hub of Collaboration and Bond
(D) The Rationale behind the Open Office

---

2 **embrace** v. 받아들이다 **finding** n. (조사·연구 등의) 결과 **immense** a. 거대한 **backlash** n. 심한 반발 **multitask** v. 한꺼번에 여러 일을 처리하다 **distraction** n. 주의산만, 기분전환 **retain** v. 유지[간직]하다 **spot** n. 장소, 자리 **pros and cons** n. 장단점 **myth** n. (근거 없는) 사회통념, 그릇된 통념 **hub** n. 중심지 **collaboration** n. 협업, 공동작업 **bond** n. 유대감 **rationale** n. 정당화, 이유 **offload** v. 잃어버리다, 없애다

3 주어진 문장이 들어가기에 가장 적절한 곳은?

In the end, however, I chose this college because of its convenience.

I found myself in the difficult position of having to choose between not just two but five colleges, all offering fine programs in my field of study. Three of them offered great financial aid, while two of them promised an exciting campus life. (A) I was at a loss. (B) First of all, I could live at home while attending classes, since the campus is located near my neighborhood. (C) Although I did not have a car, taking the bus to my college was not too much trouble. (D) And sometimes, when the weather was nice, I could even ride my bike to the campus.

3 aid n. 조력, 원조 at a loss ad. 어찌할 바를 모르는 convenience n. 편리함, 편의 locate v. 설치하다 financial a. 재정적인

4 제시문들을 논리적으로 나열한 것은?

[A] Here is what had happened. The pressure of the air had popped the back window out of Johns's fast-moving car. Wind rushed in through the wide opening. The force of the wind propelled the car through the air. The car sailed more than sixty feet before it came down and stopped. Johns was not injured, but he was scared. He couldn't finish the race.

[B] Johns was leading the 1960 Daytona 500-mile race. He was far ahead of his opponents. There were only four miles to go. Everyone thought Johns would easily achieve victory. Johns's car was going more than 130 miles an hour. Suddenly, the car was elevated off the ground. The car spun in the air and landed off the track. Everyone, including Johns, was astounded.

[C] Race-car drivers are used to going at high speed on the ground. But what do you do if your car totally leaves the ground? That is what happened to Bobby Johns. An unscheduled flight made him lose a big race.

(A) [C] - [B] - [A] (B) [C] - [A] - [B]
(C) [B] - [A] - [C] (D) [A] - [C] - [B]

4 pop v. 갑자기 튀어나오게 하다 propel v. 추진하다 opponent n. 적, 상대방 elevate v. 상승시키다 spin v. 돌다, 회전하다
astounded a. 깜짝 놀란

[5-6]

IQ testing has had momentous consequences in our century. In this light, we should investigate Binet's motives, if only to appreciate how the tragedies of misuse might have been avoided if its founder had lived and his concerns been heeded. For American psychologists perverted Binet's intention and invented the hereditarian theory of IQ. They reified Binet's scores, and took them as measures of an entity called intelligence. They assumed that intelligence was largely inherited and developed a series of specious arguments confusing cultural differences with innate properties. They believed that inherited IQ scores marked persons, people and groups for an inevitable station in life. And they assumed that average differences in intelligence were largely the products of heredity, despite manifest and profound variation in quality of life.

5 Choose the one which is not implied in the passage.

(A) American psychologists believed that IQ scores were inherited.
(B) Binet's intention was different from that of American psychologists.
(C) American psychologists used Binet's scores as measures of intelligence.
(D) American psychologists thought that differences in IQ were the products of the environment.

6 According to the passage, Binet's IQ testing _____.

(A) was only concerned with heredity theory
(B) was wrongly used by American psychologists
(C) was originated from the station in life of people
(D) was indifferent to manifest and profound variation in quality of life

10분 모의고사 09 문제편

1 제시문과 가장 가까운 의미의 영문은?

> The atomic reactor, people have begun to realize, may be a solution to our energy problem, but it also constitutes a hazard which must be taken into consideration.

(A) It dawned on people that the atomic reactor solved the energy problem but that there was a danger in assuming this.
(B) Now, people criticize the atomic reactor for being harmful although it is an ideal means of producing energy.
(C) People recognized the dangers of using an atomic reactor but condoned its use anyway.
(D) People now know that the atomic reactor not only can be beneficial but also can be detrimental.

---

1 atomic reactor n. 원자로 constitute v. 구성하다 hazard n. 위험 take into consideration v. 고려하다
  dawn on v. (생각)분명해 지다 detrimental a. 유해한 condone v. 용납하다

2. What does the author predict to be likely to occur?

> The science of evolution is taught in all advanced academies. That in another generation evolution will be regarded as uncontradictable as the Copernican system of astronomy, or the Newtonian doctrine of gravitation, can scarcely be doubted. Each of these passed through the same contradiction by theologians. They were charged by the church, as is evolution now, with fostering materialism and atheism.

(A) Evolution will never be accepted by the church.
(B) The heliocentric theory of Copernicus will contradict the Newtonian doctrine of gravitation.
(C) Evolution will universally be accepted as has been the heliocentric theory of Copernicus.
(D) The Church will forbid people to accept evolution.

3 주어진 문장이 들어가기에 가장 적절한 곳은?

So when it's time for a break on TV, everyone who likes her turns up the volume.

It must be an amazing feeling to go on a concert tour of the world. And it is really so especially if the people who come to see you are enthusiastic about your songs. (A) It takes a special genius to be able to write and sing songs that everyone in the world can listen to and understand. (B) It is not simple to get attention, but once a singer is seen on the air, she has a real chance for success. (C) Some popular singer, like Fergie, now does commercials for Pepsi. (D) This is how she becomes more famous as she meets more people. In conclusion, media is important to success for singers.

3 **turn up** v. 소리를 높이다, 불을 밝히다 **amazing** a. 놀랄 만한 **commercial** n. 상업 광고 **in conclusion** ad. 결론적으로 **medium** n. 수단, 매개, 매체 (pl : media) **Fergie** n. (가수) 퍼기 (블랙 아이드 피스)

4 제시문들을 논리적으로 나열한 것은?

[A] One focus of this medical research is on practices of healers in other cultures — they might know something that we don't, something that would be useful in developing our medical culture. The traditions of doctors and healers in one place on this planet can be very dramatically different from the practices of doctors and healers in another part of the world. One report on a doctor's experience below illustrates this point clearly.

[B] How much do we really know about medicine and healing? In hospitals, doctors remove diseased parts, repair injuries, and cure millions of people every year. In those hospitals, research continues daily for better techniques of curing, better medicines, and improved procedures. As a result, the term "modern medicine" is constantly being revised.

[C] The physician, Marlo Morgan, describes her journey in the Australian desert with the people called "the real people." During this hike, one member of the tribe fell and badly broke his leg: the bone had broken into two pieces and one end had broken through the skin. Morgan watched as the real people's healers pulled the foot gently just one and the bone slipped right back into place, and also saw the man get up the next morning and walk the whole day. To Morgan, it was a miracle. To the real people, it is the way they have always practiced medicine, through the wisdom of their culture.

(A) [A] - [B] - [C]
(B) [C] - [B] - [A]
(C) [B] - [A] - [C]
(D) [B] - [C] - [A]

4 injury n. 상처 revise v. 교정(정정, 수정)하다 practice n. 실습 physician n. 내과 의사 barbarous a. 야만스러운, 미개한 procedure n. 절차, 과정 gently ad. 부드럽게 slip v. 미끄러지다

5 빈칸에 가장 적절한 표현은?

> _____; even within an individual patient, tumors may change over time. And doctors are learning that a melanoma growth might have more in common with a lung cancer or a brain cancer than another melanoma. "We are moving away from the concept that all lung cancers are the same and all breast cancers are the same and all colon cancers are the same," says Dr. David Solit, director of the Kravis Center for Molecular Oncology at MSKCC.

(A) Hospitals should give every cancer patient equal care
(B) Tumors come back even after treatment
(C) No two cancers are alike
(D) All cancers are fundamentally the same

6 빈칸에 가장 적절한 표현은?

Rooted in romanticism and derived from the idea of natural human rights, European laws have mostly sought to protect creators. America's notion of copyright, ①_____, sees culture more as a commodity. The constitution of the United States frames copyright as a reward that is granted to authors for a limited time to encourage them to be creative. ②_____ recently America has followed Europe's lead in extending the term of copyright to 70 years after a creator's death — not so much in belated recognition of authors' rights as in a concession to Hollywood and other important rights-holders, which had lobbied for the changes. In 1998 Disney and other studios even pushed through legislation that extended the copyright on films to 95 years; it became known as the "Mickey Mouse Bill".

(A) ① however — ② Consequently
(B) ① similarly — ② Nevertheless
(C) ① on the other hand — ② Yet
(D) ① therefore — ② As a result

---

6 derive v. 유래하다 natural human rights n. 천부인권 commodity n. 상품 belated a. 뒤늦은 not so much A as B con. A라기보다는 B이다 concession n. 굴복, 양보 bill n. 지폐, 계산서, 법안 right-holder n. 권리자 lobby v. 노력하여 통과시키다

10분 모의고사 10 문제편

1 제시문과 가장 가까운 의미의 영문은?

> Whether a policy which is "good" in the aggregate sense is also "good" for a particular person is a different matter.

(A) In a collective sense, a "good" policy can be generalized to include any kind of individual.
(B) It does not matter whether a policy which is "good" can be "good" for all individuals.
(C) It is wrong to assume that a "good" policy in general will also be "good" for a specific individual.
(D) What is considered "good" for individuals does not necessarily have to be considered when making a policy.

---

1 **aggregate** a. 집합적인, 종합적인 **collective** a. 전체적인 **generalize** v. 일반화하다
not necessarily v. 반드시 ~ 것은 아니다(부분부정)

2 주제로 적절한 것은?

We all fear tossing something out only to regret it later on. But if that's your one reason for hanging on to something, it isn't enough. Ask yourself why you're not using it now. The answer can offer clues about whether your possession is worth saving. Take scrapbooking. If you see yourself turning to the hobby in the near future — not 10 years from now when you think you might have more free time, store the supplies. But if you never really enjoyed the activity, or it's been eclipsed by knitting or painting, donate the materials — especially if they're eating up valuable closet space or making you feel guilty. As for the money you spent on them, think of it as a worthy gift to a local Girl Scouts troop, Boys & Girls Club or school art department.

(A) Donation Makes a Difference
(B) Tips for Having Good Hobbies
(C) Doing Activities Leads to a Healthy Life
(D) Don't Regret: Throwing Is a Virtue

2 **toss out** v. (불필요한 것을) 버리다 **regret** v. 후회하다 **hang on to** v. (불필요 한 것이지만) 계속 보관하다 **clue** n. 실마리, 단서 **scrapbooking** n. 스크랩북 만들기 **eclipse** v. 빛을 잃게 하다 **donate** v. 기증하다 **material** n. 재료, 원료 **closet** n. 벽장, 옷장 **troop** n. 무리, 군대 **as for** pre. ~ 관해서 말하면

3 주어진 문장이 들어가기에 가장 적절한 곳은?

> But new words show an awareness in today's society that differences are good and that everyone deserves respect.

Changes in attitude affect language. As people become more sensitive to the right and needs of individuals, it becomes necessary to change the words we use to describe them. (A) The elderly are now called "senior citizens" and the handicapped are described as "physically challenged." (B) Many of the words we once used had negative feelings attached to them. (C) Even the names of certain jobs have changed so that workers can be proud of what they do. (D) The trashman, for example, is now called a sanitation worker, a doorman is an attendant, and a janitor is a custodian.

4 가장 적절한 논리적 순서는?

[A] Diana was a clerk in a company. One day she went into Russell's office. She noticed that he looked very tired. In fact, he looked awful. She knew it was not a good time to ask for a raise, but she felt she had to. She tried to think of something casual to say first. It was always best to begin such conversations casually.

[B] "You needn't bother. I can go there myself," he said. "Oh, but I'm going to the store anyway. It's no trouble," she protested. Russell thanked her and gave her some money for the aspirins. She left. It was only after she had closed the door behind her that she remembered the real reason why she had come to see Russell.

[C] "Uh... you're looking a bit tired," she said. "Yes, I have just seen the Financial Controller. It wasn't a very pleasant conversation. I feel burned out today," Russell sighed. Then he mentioned that he had a terrible headache. Diana began to feel sorry for him. She offered to get some aspirins for him from the company store.

(A) [A] - [B] - [C] (B) [A] - [C] - [B]
(C) [B] - [A] - [C] (D) [B] - [C] - [A]

---

4 **ask for a raise** v. 봉급 인상을 요구하다 **burned out** a. 기진맥진한, 탈진한 **protest** v. 단언하다, 강력하게 주장하다 **casually** ad. 우연히

5 빈칸에 가장 적절한 표현은?

> Sound waves from an object moving away from you have a lower frequency. So do light waves. The different colors in the spectrum have different frequencies. Violet has light waves of the highest frequency. Red light waves have the lowest frequency. Scientists studied the motion of the stars in distant galaxies. They discovered that the light from these distant galaxies shifted slightly towards the red end of the spectrum and had a lower frequency. Astronomers concluded that these galaxies _____.

(A) are getting brighter and brighter
(B) are moving away from the earth
(C) do not allow even light to escape
(D) send light in different directions

5 sound wave n. 음파 frequency n. 주파수 light wave n. 광파 spectrum n. 스펙트럼, 분광 galaxy n. 은하계

6 글의 내용과 일치하지 않는 것을 고르시오.

> What an Indian eats depends on his region, religion, community, and caste. It also depends on his wealth. A vast proportion of the Indian population is made up of the rural poor who subsist on a diet that meets only about 80 percent of their nutritional requirements. Many of the poor, unable to find work all year round, and therefore unable to buy food everyday, have to manage their hunger by fasting on alternate days. In Bengal, the meals of the poor are made up of rice, a little dhal flavored with salt, chillies, and a few spices, some potatoes or green vegetables, tea and paan. Paan, which is an areca nut mixed with spices and rolled up in a betel leaf, is chewed after the meal. Although it seems a luxury, in fact, the poor use it to stave off hunger.

(A) Indians' diets vary across their religion and wealth.
(B) The food the rural poor in India take doesn't meet their nutritional requirements.
(C) Many poor Indians go without food every other day.
(D) In Bengal, paan is luxurious food for the poor.

---

6 region n. 지역, 영역 caste n. 카스트 제도(인도의 계급제도) vast a. 큰, 광대한 proportion n. 비율, 균형, 크기 v. 적합하게 하다 be made up 구성되다 rural a. 시골의 subsist v. 생존하다, 존속하다 diet n. 식단, 일상음식 nutritional a. 영양의 requirement n. 필요조건, 필수품 fast a. 빠른 v. 단식하다 fasting n. 단식 alternate a. 번갈아가며 meal n. 식사 dhal n. 콩요리 flavored a. 양념이 가미된 flavor n. 맛, 향미 v. 맛을 들이다 spice n. 양념 potato n. 감자 areca n. 빈랑나무(야자나무) nut n. 견과, 핵심 mixed a. 섞여있는 rolled up a. 말아 올린 betel n. 구장나무 leaf n. 잎, 잎사귀 chew v. 씹다 stave off v. 지연시키다, 피하다 vary v. 바꾸다, 다양하다

10분 모의고사 11 문제편

1 주어진 문장이 들어가기에 가장 적절한 곳은?

If a person knows 5,000 of the most commonly used characters, he can read a newspaper.

Chinese is one of the most remarkable pieces of art in language that humankind has ever made. In elementary school, Chinese teachers ask their students to write not only correctly but beautifully. (A) Chinese is different from Western languages such as German, French, or English because it has no alphabet. (B) Instead, it contains 50,000 characters. (C) How many characters a person knows indicates how intellectual that person is. Chinese is one of the world's oldest languages and its written form as in most languages, developed from the pictograph. (D)

1 elementary a. 초보의, 기본(원리)의 indicate v. 지시[지적]하다 intellectual a. 지적인, 지성을 지닌
pictograph n. 그림문자, 상형문자 character n. 문자(글자)

2 제시문과 가장 가까운 의미의 영문은?

> I hope to organize a political force to protect the pollution-free environment in the city.

(A) I am willing to form a government which would stop air pollution.
(B) By organizing the environment to stop pollution, I want to establish the necessary force.
(C) I want to guard the environment against pollution by establishing a political organization.
(D) A political force is to protect the environment from air pollution.

3 빈칸에 가장 적절한 표현은?

> I was four, playing outside in the humid Kentucky air. I saw my grandfather's truck and thought, "Granddad shouldn't have to drive such an ugly truck." Then I spied a gallon of paint. Idea! I got a brush and painted white polka dots all over the truck. I was on the roof finishing the job when he walked up, looking as if he were in a trance. "Angela, that's the prettiest truck I've ever seen!" Sometimes I think adults don't stop to see things through a child's eyes. He could have crushed me. _____.

(A) Instead, he lifted my little soul
(B) My dreams, however, came true
(C) He thus turned a deaf ear to my wishes
(D) In the end, I blossomed into a renowned artist

---

2 **political force** n. 정치단체 **pollution-free** a. 무공해의 **guard** v. 지키다
3 **humid** a. 습기 있는, 눅눅한 **spy** v. 조사하다, 발견하다 **polka dot** n. 물방울무늬 **in a trance** ad. 무아지경에 있는 **trance** n. 최면상태 **blossom** v. 개화하다, 발전하다 **renowned** a. 유명한 **crush** v. 박살내다, 화를 내다 **turn a deaf ear to** v. 무시하다

4 도입부 이후에 논리적 순서는?

In 2005, C. K Prahalad, a University of Michigan Business School professor, wrote a book 'The Fortune at the Bottom of the Pyramid'. He shows how private firms can sometimes find it in their own interest to help solve some of the problems of the poor that are traditionally addressed by aid agencies.

[A] Getting people to use soap, however, is not as easy as it sounds. Poor people are not well informed about the science of disease transmission. Most poor people wash their hands only if they are visibly dirty, not when their hands are covered with invisible germs after using the latrine or changing a baby's diaper. HLL had to change behavior.

[B] Prahalad gives the example of HLL, a subsidiary of the giant-multinational Unilever. HLL sold a very simple product, soap, which it realized could find a larger market if it was tied to preventing diarrheal diseases of the poor. Hand washing with soap is critical to preventing the spread of the viruses and bacteria that cause diarrhea HLL realized that if it could promote increased awareness among the poor of the benefits of antibacterial soap, it could significantly increase sales.

[C] To realize this market potential, HLL had to find ways of gaining the poor's trust in its health-promoting product. Working with the government and aid agencies, it started educational programs, including a program called Lifebuoy Glowing Health, which sent out two-person teams to show schoolchildren how they could avoid infections by washing with Lifebuoy soap. The teams also enlisted the village doctors to speak to the children's parents about how hand washing with soap could prevent diarrhea and other health complications.

(A) [B] - [C] - [A]   (B) [B] - [A] - [C]
(C) [A] - [B] - [C]   (D) [C] - [B] - [A]

4 address v. (어려운 문제 등을) 다루다, 처리하다 aid agency n. 구호단체 transmission n. 전염, 전파 latrine n. 임시 변소 diaper n. 기저귀 subsidiary n. 자회사 giant-multinational n. 거대 다국적기업 diarrhea n. 설사 infection n. 감염 complications n. 합병증 antibiotic a. 항균의 eradicate v. 뿌리뽑다

5 이 글의 내용과 일치하는 것은?

Jim Belushi comes to network television as a loving family man in this show. Happily married with three kids, Jim is an all-American guy's guy, not quick to admit fault, but a softie underneath. He's a contractor in a design firm with his younger, architect brother-in-law, Andy, yet he still finds time to hang out with his six-man garage blues band. Jim's wife, Cheryl, gave up dating corporate guys for a life with a simpler man who makes her laugh. She is champagne and strawberries while Jim is beer, nuts and bratwurst but they're in love. Dana is Cheryl's sister, who works as a VP in an ad agency. She's single and gorgeous, but emotionally short-sighted and self-centered. She gets lots of first dates, not too many second ones. But she adores her two nieces and her baby nephew and she loves verbally sparring with Jim. So that's Jim Belushi, a husband who knows that the key to a good marriage is nodding when your wife talks.

(A) Jim is a workaholic.
(B) Jim's wife met some guys before she married him.
(C) Jim and his wife are a perfect match in personality.
(D) Jim works with his sister-in-law in the same company.

5 guy's guy n. 전통적인 남성 underneath n. 저면, 하부 hang out with v. 함께 어울리다 bratwurst n. 소시지 종류
  goregous a. 매우 매력적인 short-sighted a. 근시안적인 spar v. 말다툼하다 perfect match n. 찰떡궁합

6 글의 요지로 가장 적절한 것은?

It is so difficult for human beings to live together; it is difficult for them to associate, however transitorily, and even under the most favorable conditions, without some shadow of mutual offense. Consider the differences of task and of habit, the conflict of prejudices, and the divergence of opinions, which quickly reveal themselves between any two persons and see how much self-control is implicit whenever, for more than an hour or two, they co-exist in seeming harmony. Man is not made for peaceful intercourse with his fellows; he is by nature self-assertive, commonly aggressive, and always critical toward any characteristic which seems strange to him.

(A) It is not easy for us to get on peacefully with our fellows.
(B) By instinct man is a peace-seeking creature.
(C) Human beings do not offend one another in a favorable situation.
(D) The differences of task and of habit often lead to close friendship.

6 transitory a. 일시적인 offense n. 범죄, 공격 divergence n. 일탈 casual contact n. 일상적인 만남 implicit a. 은연중에 intercourse n. 친교, 거래 by nature ad. 천성적으로 self-assertive a. 독단적인 get on with v. 해나가다

CHAPTER 2   10분 모의고사 12   문제편

1 제시문과 가장 가까운 의미의 영문은?

> Because of its efficacy in treating many ailments, penicillin has become an important addition to a druggist's stock.

(A) Penicillin has become indispensable to druggists because it can treat many different illnesses.
(B) Druggists have found penicillin to be the most effective medicine they know.
(C) Druggists were forced to add effective medicines such as penicillin to their drug stores.
(D) Penicillin was necessary to druggists because it could boost their store profits.

---

1 **efficacy** n. 효율성 **treat** v. 치료하다 **ailment** n. 질병 **penicillin** n. 페니실린 **stock** n. 저장품 **indispensable** a. 필수 불가결한 **boost** v. 상승시키다

2 빈칸에 가장 적절한 표현은?

The best exercise is one that you enjoy and will do. But otherwise, it's probably running. Running is cheap, easy, as you go out of your house and just do it, and you can't fake it - it's always energetic. Even a jog counts as moderately vigorous exercise. _____, you need run for only half the time to get the same benefits as other sports. Angelique Brellenthin, of the department of kinesiology at Iowa State University, says it takes 105 minutes of walking to yield the same benefits as a 25-minute run.

(A) If you want to speed up your running
(B) If you are time poor
(C) With good running shoes
(D) In order to avoid knee pain

2 energetic a. 정력적인, 활기있는 jog n. 조깅 count as v. 간주되다 vigorous a. 활발한, 격렬한 kinesiology n. 신체 운동학 time poor a. (일에 쫓겨서) 자유 시간이 없는

3 제시된 문장의 적절한 위치는?

> These essays were then evaluated according to the criteria of purity, truthfulness, elegance, and propriety.

To pass the civil service examinations in ancient China was no easy matter. Preparation took years, since candidates were required to know thousands of logo-graphs merely to read the classics. (A) Furthermore, they had to memorize whole texts. (B) On the examinations, they wrote essays about particular questions on particular texts. (C) These criteria were, however, so vague that candidates had little choice but to try to detect the literary preferences of the examiners. (D)

---

3 **criterion** n. 표준, 척도 **purity** n. 순수성 **elegance** n. 우아, 간결함 **propriety** n. 예의 바름, 적당함 **candidate** n. 후보자 **logo-graph** n. 기호, 한자 **vague** a. 막연한 **detect** v. 탐지하다 **literary** a. 문학의 **preference** n. 애호, 우위 **have little choice but to 동사원형** v. ~하지 않을 수 없다.

4 주어진 글 다음에 이어질 글의 순서로 가장 적절한 것은?

"I'm a company man." This was something many workers were accustomed to saying with pride for most of this century.

[A] But with the loss of thousands of manufacturing jobs in the 1960s and 1970s and of thousands more white collar jobs in 1980s and 1990s, this expression has become a memory.

[B] It meant that the worker was proud of working for a particular company throughout adulthood. Both blue collar workers and white collar workers often felt loyal to a company and the company returned this loyalty.

[C] In the late 1990s, employees felt it was foolish to be loyal to a company that could fire them at any moment.

(A) [A] - [B] - [C]   (B) [B] - [A] - [C]
(C) [B] - [C] - [A]   (D) [C] - [A] - [B]

4 company man n. 회사원 be accustomed to v. 익숙하다 white collar job n. 사무직 blue collar job n. 노동직
  loyal a. 충성스런 fire v. 해고하다

5 이 글의 제목으로 가장 적절한 것을 고르시오.

Image processing techniques originally developed by space scientists to analyze pictures taken by spacecraft are being turned to the detection of skin cancer. Researchers at NASA's Jet Propulsion Laboratory, working with dermatologists at Beth Israel Hospital, have adapted the imaging technology to detect the onset of melanoma, a type of cancer that can be treated if detected early enough. The work was initiated by Robert Selzer of JPL's biomedical image processing laboratory in collaboration with Kenneth Arndt, head of the department of dermatology at Beth Israel. Some patients at risk of developing melanoma have so many lesions on their skin that it is difficult for dermatologists to detect and track all changes and thus evaluate treatment. Under the system, photos of patients taken at intervals are sent to the biomedical image processing laboratory where they are scanned into a personal computer and then analyzed by imaging software to indicate changes.

(A) Space Technology on Cancer
(B) The Origin and History of Dermatology
(C) Image Processing and Home Computer
(D) Skin Cancer Causes Death in Deep Space

6 글의 내용과 일치하는 것은?

The Wildfoods Festival takes place in the old mining town of Hokitika on the west coast of the South Island. This year, the organizers are preparing for more than 23,000 curious visitors from all over the world, a 10 percent increase in attendance over last year's crowd. Each year, the chefs invent more and more exotic dishes, and you may need to have a strong stomach and be open-minded to try them. This year they are offering new dishes such as insect eggs, scorpions, and venison tongue. Last year's favorites are still available: kangaroo and emu steaks fresh from neighboring Australia, and of course, earthworms and snails. It's a country full of sheep, but don't expect to eat any of them here!

(A) The Wildfoods Festival takes place in Australia.
(B) More than 20,000 visitors attended last year's festival.
(C) Kangaroo steak is one of this year's new dishes.
(D) Sheep steak is one of last year's favorites.

6 wildfood n. 야생음식 take place v. 열리다, 일어나다 mining n. 채광, 광산업 organizer n. 주최자 attendance n. 참여, 출석 crowd n. 대중, 군중 chef n. 요리사, 주방장 exotic a. 이국적인, 외래적인 dish n. 큰 접시, 요리, 음식 stomach n. 위, 복부, 식욕 v. 소화하다 open-minded a. 개방적인 scorpion n. 전갈 venison n. 사슴 고기 emu n. 에뮤(타조과의 큰 새) earthworm n. 지렁이 snail n. 달팽이 sheep n. 양, 유순한 사람

10분 모의고사 13

1 제시문과 가장 가까운 의미의 영문은?

> Subsequent changes to an original invention do not represent new concepts at all, but rather extensions of the original innovative idea.

(A) Nothing that is done to an original invention is completely new.
(B) Originality is essentially lost in the innovation of products.
(C) When an original invention changes, so do the perceptions towards it.
(D) New ideas about original inventions are continuously being generated.

---

1 **subsequent** a. 이어지는 **represent** v. 표현하다 **extension** n. 확장 **innovative** a. 혁신적인 **perception** n. 인식, 지각 **generate** v. 발생시키다

2 문맥상 다음 문장이 위치할 곳을 고르시오.

This apathy of the wealthy caused the poor to resort to violence to attract attention to their complaints.

Although the last days of the Roman Empire may at first appear very different from those of the United States today, there are ominous likenesses. Ancient Rome possessed tremendous military strength, not of the magnitude of our air power, true, but enough to maintain its control over almost all of the known world. (A) Because of the vast expanse of its rule, however, much of its strength was devoted to maintaining order in areas other than within its own borders. Just as in the United States today, Rome was so intensely occupied with establishing and maintaining its political principles in areas other than those within its own borders, its rulers were blind to the full significance of the ominous changes taking place at home. (B) Much of this change consisted of internal conflict induced by the indifference of the affluent Roman to the suffering of the less fortunate. (C) This is not unlike our own time when dissenters shoot someone of renown to penetrate the stone wall of indifference. (D)

2 **apathy** n. 무관심 **resort** v. 의존하다 **ominous** a. 암울한 **likenesses** n. 유사성 **tremendous** a. 엄청난 **magnitude** n. 규모 **vast** a. 방대한 **expanse** n. 영역 **take place** v. 발생하다 **at home** ad. 국내에서 **induce** v. 유발하다 **dissenter** n. 반대자 **renown** a. 유명한 **penetrate** v. 관통하다

3 빈칸에 적절한 표현은?

Earlier this month, Facebook announced it would be using facial recognition to let users know every time a photo of them had been uploaded to the site. Such a feature would be extremely useful to one man - public-relations professional Jonathan Hirshon, who has managed to _____ for the past 20 years. He has more than 3,000 friends on Facebook and regularly updates his profile with persona information - where he is going on holiday, what he has cooked for dinner and the state of his health. But what he has never shared on the social network, or anywhere else online, is a picture of himself. It is, he said, his way of "screaming my privacy to the world".

(A) share a picture of himself on social media
(B) stay anonymous online
(C) keep a secret of himself
(D) leave traces of himself online

3 persona n. 모습 recognition n. 인지, 인식 feature n. 특색 public-relations n. 홍보 professional n. 전문가 update v. 가장 최근의 정보를 알려주다 state n. 상태 scream v. 소리 지르다

4 다음 글의 주제로 가장 적절한 것은?

> The inventor of the first written tablets may have realized the advantage these pieces of clay had over holding memories in the brain: first, the amount of information storable on tablets was endless - one could go on producing tablets again and again in the same way, while the brain's remembering capacity is limited; second, tablets did not require the presence of the memory-holder to retrieve information. Suddenly, something intangible - a number, an item of news, a thought, an order - could be acquired without the physical presence of the message-giver; magically, it could be imagined, noted and passed on across space and beyond time. Since the earliest phases of prehistoric civilization, human society had tried to overcome the obstacles of geography, the finality of death, the erosion of oblivion. With a single act - the incision of a figure on a clay tablet - that first anonymous writer suddenly succeeded in all these seemingly impossible feats.

(A) remarkable results of storing information on tablets
(B) expansion of knowledge in various fields
(C) different types of memory and storage devices
(D) training necessary for improving memory capacity

4 intangible a. 무형의 oblivion n. 망각 tablet n. 서판 storable a. 저장할 수 있는 capacity n. 용량 retrieve v. 회수하다, 상기하다 phase n. 단계 prehistoric a. 선사시대의 finality n. 최후 erosion n. 침식, 쇠퇴 incision n. (칼로) 새김 figure n. 형상, 모습 anonymous a. 익명의 feat n. 위업

5 Albert Bruce Sabin에 관한 다음 글의 내용과 일치하지 않는 것은?

Albert Bruce Sabin was born in Bialystok, Poland. His family settled in New Jersey, USA in 1921. Sabin received his medical degree from New York University in 1931. During World War II, he served in the U.S. Army Medical Corps, where he was involved with the development of a vaccine against dengue fever and the successful vaccination of 65,000 military personnel against the Japanese type of polio. While Jonas Salk developed a vaccine using dead virus, Sabin devised one that used live virus. He later produced a pill vaccine and, in 1955, conducted experiments with prisoners who had volunteered. From 1957 to 1959, the Soviet Union and the other Eastern Bloc nations administered Sabin's pill, with its advantages of oral administration and long-term immunity. It was subsequently accepted in the United States.

(A) 폴란드에서 출생하여 미국으로 이주했다.
(B) 제2차 세계대전 동안 미군 의무부대에서 복무했다.
(C) 죽은 바이러스를 이용하여 백신을 고안했다.
(D) 자원한 재소자들을 대상으로 실험을 실시하였다.

6 도입문 뒤에 이어질 순서로 적절한 것은?

> Milton Keynes is a dream researcher in Miami, Florida.

[A] Clearly, dreams can have harmful or beneficial effects.
[B] He also found that after having a good dream, people feel more optimistic.
[C] He found that people wake up very discouraged after having a bad dream.
[D] As a result, he believes that we need to learn how to change our bad dreams.

(A) [A] — [C] — [B] — [D]
(B) [C] — [D] — [B] — [A]
(C) [C] — [B] — [A] — [D]
(D) [B] — [C] — [D] — [A]

6 dream researcher n. 꿈 연구가 beneficial a. 유익한 optimistic a. 낙천적인 wake up v. 잠에서 깨다 discouraged a. 낙담한

10분 모의고사 14

1 제시문과 가장 가까운 의미의 영문은?

> Science does not seek to enforce a moral code of behavior in its practitioners, as much as ancient philosophy did.

(A) Like ancient philosophers, practitioners of science should be held accountable for their moral behavior.
(B) Ancient philosophy placed more pressure on its practitioners to adhere to moral rules regarding behavior than science currently does.
(C) How a moral code of behavior is contested in science differs from how it was done in ancient philosophy.
(D) Science is more rigorous about regulating its practitioners through a moral code of behavior than in ancient philosophy.

1 enforce v. 강요하다 moral code n. 도덕적 원칙 practitioner n. 행위자 accountable a. 책임지는 contest v. 경쟁하다

2 다음 글의 제목으로 가장 적절한 것은?

It may sound counterintuitive, but excessive freedom of thought leads to "idea anarchy" and a poor level of inventiveness. Most of us have had a firsthand or secondhand experience of a brilliant solution devised by improvising with scant materials at hand. In many cases, a lack of an essential substance or tool requires resourcefulness. If you've ever communicated a big idea concisely on a napkin or managed to score tickets to a soldout concert (without paying a ticket scalper), you can consider yourself resourceful — that is, using existing resources extremely efficiently. Using this same logic, when we place enough constraints around resources, we can prevent ideation anarchy and focus productive thinking into that limited space where the creative solutions are frequently hiding.

(A) Enjoy Unrestricted Freedom of Ideas
(B) Lack of Resources Leads to Creativity
(C) The More Materials, the More Inspiration
(D) Small Ideas: The Best Source of Big Ideas

2 anarchy n. 혼란, 무질서 ticket scalper n. 암표 장수 counterintuitive a. 직관에 어긋나는 excessive a. 지나친, 과도한 devise v. 고안하다 improvise v. 임시변통으로 만들다 scant a. 부족한, 거의 없는 resourcefulness n. 풍요로운 자원, 뛰어난 지략 concisely ad. 간결하게 score v. 얻다, 손에 넣다 constraint n. 제한 ideation n. 관념 작용, 관념화

3 제시문에 이어질 가장 적절한 순서는?

> The ability to detect potential toxins in foods via taste is just one adaptation humans have to protect themselves against food-related illness. Food neophobia is one such proposed adaptation humans share with other animals that may prevent the ingestion of dangerous substances.

[A] Then, when possible, some amount of time is allowed to pass before a final judgment is made. If the food does not taste bad and the time following its ingestion is not marred by illness, the food may be considered potentially safe and edible.

[B] Many animals, including humans, have an immediate distrust of new foods. Especially as children, people avoid unfamiliar foods and, when encouraged to try them, do so only in small amounts. Typically, when people taste something that has never been eaten before, the first bite is small and carefully evaluated.

[C] If, however, the food tastes bad or is associated with sickness, the food may be considered inedible and avoided. This combination of an aversion to new foods and a sensitivity to the association between food and illness provides some protection against potential poisons.

(A) [A] - [C] - [B]
(B) [B] - [A] - [C]
(C) [B] - [C] - [A]
(D) [C] - [A] - [B]

3 toxin n. 독소 via pre. 거쳐서 adaptation n. 적응 ingestion n. 섭취 distrust n. 불신 bite n. 한입 먹음 inedible a. 먹을 수 없는 combination n. 조합 neophobia n. 새것 싫어하기 mar v. 손상하다 aversion n. 혐오감

4 빈칸에 적절한 표현은?

What controls the number of times cells divide? The answer may lie with our telomeres, the protective tips on the ends of our chromosomes (a bit like the protective tips on the ends of shoestrings). These tips become shorter each time cells divide. Eventually, when the telomeres have nearly disappeared, the cells stop dividing, causing the cells to age and deteriorate. You might be inclined to think this means that the body has a built-in clock that controls the length of life by _____.

(A) isolating defective cells
(B) limiting cell reproduction
(C) allowing for cell expansion
(D) preventing the binding of cells

4 cell divide n. 세포 분열 telomere n. (생물) 말단소립 chromosome n. 염색체 shoestring n. 신발끈 a bit like prep. 다소 유사한 deteriorate v. 악화되다 isolate v. 고립시키다 defective a. 결함이 있는 expansion n. 확장 tumor n. 종양

5 peaberry에 관한 다음 글의 내용과 일치하지 않는 것은?

Coffee beans are seeds that grow inside a coffee plant's fruit, known as a cherry. Normally, two beans are found inside each cherry. However, about 5% of the time there is only one bean. When this happens, it is called a "peaberry." Peaberries are smaller and denser than normal coffee beans. Many people find coffee made from peaberries to be sweeter and more flavorful. But peaberries aren't easy to sort. The problem is that there is no way to tell which cherries contain peaberries just by looking at them. Because of this, they are usually sold mixed in with other coffee beans. Some coffee growers will remove peaberries by hand and sell them separately. However, because of the extra labor required, they are quite expensive.

(A) 커피콩 수확량의 약 5퍼센트를 차지한다.
(B) 일반 커피콩보다 크기가 더 작다.
(C) 어느 체리 안에 들어있는지 육안으로 식별이 가능하다.
(D) 보통 다른 커피콩과 섞여서 판매된다.

6 다음 글에서 전체 흐름과 관계없는 문장은?

Each geographical region and each cultural group of persons has its own pottery fashions that rapidly go through short-lived generations. (A) Pottery is easily broken but the resulting fragments are nearly indestructible and leave valuable clues for archaeologists. (B) Fragments enable them to determine the time, place, and size of cultural areas and the changes in these areas. (C) There are hundreds of volumes describing the sequences of pottery styles throughout the world, including both the location and date at which each existed. (D) In the strictest of terms antique pottery is pottery that is at least 100 years old, but today anything that simply looks antique will pass the grade regardless of age. For example, if a farming village was occupied for just a generation or two then its pottery would allow the village site to be dated because it would consist of styles from that period in time.

6 geographical a. 지리적인, 지리학의 pottery n. 도기, 도기 제조법 region n. 지역 fragment n. 파편, 조각 indestructible a. 파괴할 수 없는 archaeologist n. 고고학자 sequence n. 순서, 연속 term n. 용어, 말 antique a. 골동품의, 오래된 occupy v. 거주하다, 점유하다 date v. 연대를 추정하다

10분 모의고사 15

1 제시문과 가장 가까운 의미의 영문은?

> Despite its purported neutrality, the study will be compelled to produce results favorable to its sponsors.

(A) The results of the study will be unbiased though the people who fund it do not want them to be.

(B) Some say the research is biased, but really it will only do exactly what people ordered it to do.

(C) The research claims to be fair, but it will be forced to say good things about the people who paid for it.

(D) Even though people say it has to be fair, the report will be supported by financial backers.

---

1 purported a. 알려져 있는 neutrality n. 중립성 favorable a. 우호적인 sponsor n. 후원자 unbiased a. 중립적인 backer n. 후원자

2 Creative writing can help release dormant tensions because _____.

> Creative writing may serve many purposes for the writer. Above all, it is a means of self-expression. It is the individual's way of saying, "These are my thoughts and they are uniquely experienced by me." But creative writing can also serve as a safety valve for dormant tensions. This implies that a period of time has evolved in which the child gave an idea some deep thought and that the message on paper is revealing of this deep inner thought. Finally, a worthwhile by-product of creative writing is the stimulus it gives students to be an ardent reader of good literature.

(A) the writer will usually write something autobiographical
(B) creative writing can be attractive to readers.
(C) creative writing can express what the writer has long held within
(D) understanding literature means understanding the tensions of the characters

3 빈칸에 적절한 내용은?

We are programmed to be together. Even when we think we are being most individual in the way we present ourselves through the fashions we wear and the way we cut our hair, we are conforming to this truth. Exactitudes is an ongoing photo project started by Dutch photographer Arie Versluis and stylist Elly Yttenbroek in 1995. The two tour the world taking pictures of individuals from social groups wherever they are to be found and get individuals to pose in identical poses. They then display shorts of these individuals in grids of 4×3, so that the similarities are clear. The tattoo section shows that even when we think of the most individualist of fashions — having someone draw on your body — the individuals are clearly doing what other individuals are doing and not being 'different' and unique. _____.

(A) Fashions are the best way to present ourselves
(B) Our efforts to be individual are ultimately in vain
(C) The common frames that held us together are crashing
(D) We are destined to be an 'I-species' rather than a 'we-species'

4 다음 글의 주제로 가장 적절한 것은?

Suppose you wish to determine which brand of microwave popcorn leaves the fewest unpopped kernels. You will need a supply of various brands of microwave popcorn to test, and you will need a microwave oven. If you used different brands of microwave ovens with different brands of popcorn, the percentage of unpopped kernels could be caused by the different brands of popcorn or by the different brands of ovens. Under such circumstances, the experimenter would be unable to conclude confidently whether the popcorn or the oven caused the difference. To eliminate this problem, you must use the same microwave oven for every test. In order to reasonably conclude that the change in one variable was caused by the change in another specific variable, there must be no other variables in the experiment. By using the same microwave oven, you control the number of variables in the experiment.

(A) importance of safety in experimental work
(B) need for controlling variables in experiments
(C) influence of prior knowledge on experiments
(D) benefits of combining experimental methods

5 글의 흐름으로 보아, 주어진 문장이 들어가기에 가장 적절한 곳은?

> The human brain, on the other hand, is incredibly poor at arithmetic.

What a computer is designed to do is, essentially, arithmetic. (A) Any problem, however complex, can somehow be broken down into a well-defined series of arithmetical operations that can be solved by a computer. (B) The computer is amazing not because of its capability to handle arithmetical operations, but because of the fact that it can perform these operations in one billionth of a second without error. (C) Unlike computers, it needs and has always needed outside help to solve the simplest problems. (D) We began by counting on our fingers, and have moved on to better things only with the help of pen and paper, Arabic numerals, mechanical calculators and eventually computers.

6 제시문 뒤에 이어질 적절한 글의 순서는?

Whenever anything goes wrong on this globe of ours, it is human tendency for someone, anyone, or all of us to point a long finger of blame at someone or anyone besides ourselves, of course. This finger pointing has certainly been seen with regard to energy shortages and energy-derived pollution problems.

[A] Although it is true that environmental regulations have caused some increased energy demand and have restricted supply to some extent, it is important to recognize that other factors have been considerably more significant.

[B] These include rapidly escalating demand for energy, energy pricing policies, oil import quotas, lack of incentives to invest in domestic energy facilities, and depletion of domestic oil and gas reserves.

[C] In particular, many critics point the finger of blame for our current and pending shortage of liquid fuels at the environmentalists; however, the U.S. Environmental Protection Agency suggested that a finger of blame pointed at the environmental movement is misdirected.

(A) [A] - [C] - [B]
(B) [C] - [B] - [A]
(C) [B] - [C] - [A]
(D) [C] - [A] - [B]

10분 모의고사 16 문제편

1 제시문과 가장 가까운 의미의 영문은?

> Managers in commerce and industry must increase efficiency to help get us out of the economic slump, and the same applies to public-service managers.

(A) In order to overcome the economic slump, managers in commerce and industry and public-service managers need to boost efficiency.

(B) To maintain the current economic state, efficiency should be increased by managers in commerce and industry and public-service managers.

(C) Managers in commerce and industry need to negotiate with public-service managers to assist in improving the economy.

(D) Unlike public-service managers, managers in commerce and industry must do their share for the economy.

1 efficiency n. 효율성 apply to v. 적용되다 boost v. 증진시키다 negotiate v. 협상하다 economic slump n. 경기침체

2 다음 글에서 전체 흐름과 관계 없는 문장은?

For a long time psychoanalysis was the only psychotherapy practiced in Western society, and it is based on the theories of Sigmund Freud. According to Freud's views, psychological disturbances are due to anxiety about hidden conflicts in the unconscious parts of one's personality. (A) One job of the psychoanalyst, therefore, is to help make the patients aware of the unconscious impulses and desires that are causing the anxiety. (B) However, some symbols in dreams seem to be universal; in other words, they appear to have the same meaning to people everywhere. (C) Psychoanalysts believe that understanding these unconscious motives is very important. (D) If patients can have that kind of understanding, called insight, they have taken the first step toward gaining control over their behavior and freeing themselves of their problems.

2 psychoanalysis n. 정신분석학 psychotherapy n. 심리치료 disturbance n. 장애, 혼란 unconscious a. 무의식적인 impulse n. 충동 take the first step v. 첫 걸음을 내딛다

3 글의 요지로 가장 적절한 것은?

The ad hominem fallacy is one of the most common mistakes in reasoning. The fallacy rests on a confusion between the qualities of the person making a claim and the qualities of the claim itself. Let's say my friend, Parker, is an ingenious fellow. It follows that Parker's opinion on some subject, whatever it is, is the opinion of an ingenious person. But it does not follow that Parker's opinion itself is ingenious. To think that, it is would be to confuse the content of Parker's claim with Parker himself. Or let's suppose you are listening to your teacher whom you regard as a bit strange or maybe even weird. Would it follow that the car your teacher drives is strange or weird? Obviously not. Similarly, it would not follow that some specific proposal that the teacher has put forth is strange or weird. A proposal made by an oddball is an oddball's proposal, but it does not follow that it is an oddball proposal.

(A) It is ingenious to suppose that a teacher who owns a strange car also does weird things.
(B) We must accept the reasoning that the qualities of a person determine the qualities of the claim he makes.
(C) It is odd to claim that common mistakes we make result from confusion between truth and fallacy.
(D) We must not confuse the qualities of the person making a claim with the qualities of the claim itself.

3 **ad hominem** a. 인신공격의 **impression** n. 인상 **suppose** v. 가정하다 **evaluation** n. 평가, 판단 **groundless** a. 근거 없는 **saint** n. 성인, 성자 **status** n. 신분, 상태 **prejudice** n. 선입견 **fallacy** n. 오류 **ingenious** a. 현명한, 영리한, 독창적인 **oddball** n. 괴짜 **weird** a. 이상한

4 주어진 글 다음에 이어질 글의 순서로 가장 적절한 것은?

> Nowadays, most people use passwords and government ID numbers on the Web. They think they are safe, but that may not be true. A new kind of attack is being used by dishonest people to steal IDs and credit card numbers from innocent websurfers.

[A] In addition, they imitate well-known banks, online sellers. and credit card companies. Successful phishers may convince as many as 5 percent of the people they contact to respond and give away their personal information.

[B] Like real fishermen, they use bait in the form of great online deals or services. For example, phishers might use fake e-mails and false web-sites to cheat people into revealing credit card numbers, and passwords.

[C] This new kind of attack is called "phishing." phishing sounds the same as the word "fishing," and it implies a thief is trying to lure people giving away valuable information. How can fishers lure people to do this?

(A) [A] - [C] - [B]
(B) [C] - [B] - [A]
(C) [B] - [C] - [A]
(D) [C] - [A] - [B]

---

4 phishing n. 피싱사기 websurfer n. 인터넷 사용자 convince v. 설득하다 give away v. 주다 lure v. 꼬시다

5 빈칸에 가장 적절한 표현은?

It is important to understand the impact of wide-scale implementation of digital tools because many of the systems are adopted by many people. This is why organizations must spend some amount of time preparing and researching the process of technology implementation before deciding to add new tools to a system. A good starting point for the implementation of new digital technologies is to anticipate who the users will be and to understand the specific needs of the users. For example, an institution might decide to offer special cell phones to all of its employees, so it must spend some time contemplating who would use the phones, and for what purpose. If the phones are to be used only to stay in touch with the main office, then the phones do not require a built-in camera. The _____ of the technology needs to be the most important criteria before introducing new digital tools.

(A) expected use
(B) introduction cost
(C) security system
(D) overall performance

6 다음 글에서 전체 흐름과 관계없는 문장은?

People name their children using all sorts of rules and approaches. (A) Sometimes they borrow names from historical or literary heroes, sometimes they follow ancestral naming traditions, and sometimes they just like how a name sounds. (B) In all cases, though, the otherwise meaningless name acquires meaning because it's associated with other concepts that are themselves meaningful. (C) The power of association explains why Adolf, a common boy's name once associated with Swedish and Luxembourger kings, declined in popularity during and after World War II. (D) Most people have a tendency to trust individuals with names that they could easily pronounce. Meanwhile, the name Donald fell from favor when Donald Duck appeared in the 1930s, and parents stopped naming their sons Ebenezer in the 1840s when Charles Dickens's newly published book, A Christmas Carol, featured the miserly Ebenezer Scrooge.

10분 모의고사 17

1 제시문과 가장 가까운 의미의 영문은?

> Considering all your options means more than taking stock of the pros and cons of any given choice.

(A) In decision-making, you need to explore all the options available and moreover the pros and cons of a choice.
(B) Striking a balance between the pros and cons of a situation is the key to making a wise choice.
(C) You have to go beyond just reviewing what the pros and cons are regarding a decision, when you think over what options are available.
(D) If the pros outweigh the cons of a decision, then you should reconsider what alternatives are available.

---

1 take stock of v. 살펴보다 pros and cons n. 찬반양론 strike a balance v. 균형을 맞추다 outweigh v. 능가하다 alternative n. 대안 reconsider v. 재고하다

2 다음 글에서 필자가 주장하는 바로 가장 적절한 것은?

Poems can be taken apart from time to time, like any well-made objects, but it is important to remember to put them back together properly at the end and check that they still work. Looking at how a poem has built up sound patterns through rhythm, rhyme, alliteration, and other devices, or how word pictures have been built up through images, or meanings made through wordplay, can add a different sort of enjoyment as well as understanding of poems. But poems should not be used just as excuses for feature-spotting, for example hunting down metaphors and similes for the sake of naming the parts. Poems are often left in pieces after this kind of activity as the lesson moves on to another text with the same feature or topic. It should be a rule to read the poem aloud again after any form of analysis, savoring its sounds and images anew.

(A) 문학 수업에서 운문과 산문을 골고루 다루어야 한다.
(B) 깊이 있는 감상을 위해 시 형식에 대한 이해가 필수적이다.
(C) 시인은 언어적 기교보다는 삶의 진실을 표현하려 해야 한다.
(D) 시를 분석한 후에는 다시 한 번 감상하는 시간을 가져야 한다.

2 **alliteration** n. 두운(법) **simile** n. 직유법 **take apart** v. 분해하다 **rhyme** n. 각운, 운(음조가 비슷한 글자) **word picture** n. 그림을 보는 듯한 생생한 서술 **feature-spotting** n. 특징 찾아내기 **metaphor** n. 은유 **analysis** n. 분석 **savor** v. 음미하다, 감상하다

3 다음 빈칸에 들어갈 말로 가장 적절한 것은?

Scientific experiments should be designed to show that your hypothesis is wrong, and should be conducted completely objectively with no possible subjective influence on the outcome. Unfortunately few, if any, scientists are truly objective. They have often decided long before the experiment is begun what they would like the result to be. This means that very often bias is (unintentionally) introduced into the experiment, the experimental procedure or the interpretation of results. It is all too easy to justify to yourself why an experiment which does not fit with your expectations should be ignored, and why one which provides the results you 'hoped for' is the right one. This can be partly avoided by conducting experiments '_____' and by asking others to check your data or repeat experiments.

(A) isolated
(B) blinded
(C) deceived
(D) informed

4 다음 주어진 문장이 들어가기에 가장 적절한 곳은?

For a good half hour, individuals held their respective posts, tracing wide circles in silence, until one finally let out a piercing shriek.

A naturalist named Syevertsoff documented nearly a dozen white-tailed eagles acting as a survey team. (A) Spread across the sky at a considerable distance apart, they were together scanning an estimated twenty-five square miles. (B) Its cry was soon answered by another eagle approaching, followed by a third, a fourth, and so on, till nine or ten eagles came together and soon disappeared. (C) Later that afternoon, Syevertsoff arrived at the place where he had seen the group descend into the gently rolling grasslands hours earlier. (D) There he discovered the birds gathered around the corpse of a horse. Some of the eagles, probably the older ones, who had eaten first, were perched nearby keeping watch while the youngsters dined in safety, surrounded by bands of crows.

5 주어진 글 다음에 이어질 글의 순서로 가장 적절한 것은?

Social stereotypes are often formed initially from some specific experience, or from observations of one or more individuals. These specific impressions become a stereotype when this information is then generalized to apply to *all* members of a group, regardless of circumstances.

[A] The teacher had asked the children to 'draw a picture of your father relaxing.' When the teacher saw the boy drawing a picture of a man chopping wood, she said, "No, I said draw him relaxing." Bursting into tears, the 6-year-old exclaimed, "But my Daddy *does* chop wood to relax!"

[B] This creates difficulties when circumstances change, but the stereotype does not, or when a stereotype is used as a substitute for gathering accurate information about a person. For example, a friend once reported an experience that his 6-year-old son had at school.

[C] By contrast, his father's 'work' involved sitting at a desk all day. The teacher's stereotype, not the boy's drawing, was the problem. Stereotypes, as mental schemata, can lead us to prejudge others — and *all* schemata carry this risk of distorting reality.

(A) [A] - [C] - [B]
(B) [B] - [A] - [C]
(C) [B] - [C] - [A]
(D) [C] - [A] - [B]

6 글의 내용과 일치하지 않는 것은?

> Tipping is rarely required in Korea. The one exception is in Western-style hotels, restaurants, bars, and nightclubs where a 10% service charge and 10% value added tax will be added automatically to the bill. It is not necessary to tip taxi drivers. From time to time, it might be prudent to offer a small gift to someone who has provided especially good service. In these special circumstances, no doubt that the gift will be received with great appreciation and will help secure future assistance.

(A) The service charge is one form of indirect tipping in Korea.
(B) Tipping is required in some Korean establishments.
(C) Korean taxi drivers do not expect to be tipped.
(D) Tipping almost always leads to adverse consequences in Korea.

6 exception n. 예외 automatically ad. 자동적으로 prudent a. 세심한 circumstance n. 상황, 환경 assure v. 확실하게 하다 appreciation n. 평가, 감사 secure v. 보증하다 assistance n. 도움

10분 모의고사 18 문제편

1 제시문과 가장 가까운 의미의 영문은?

> Any recovery of the natural world will require not only extensive financial funding but conversion deep in the psychic structure of the human.

(A) It will be impossible to save the natural world unless humans change their attitudes about investing a vast amount of money in conservation.
(B) The natural world can be restored with substantial amounts of money and a change in the minds of humans.
(C) Humans recognized that a great amount of funding is necessary to sustain the natural world, which resulted in a shift in mentality.
(D) Saving the environment depends more on the consciousness-raising of humans than on the amount of money spent.

---

1 **extensive** a. 광범위한 **conversion** n. 변환, 개종 **psychic** a. 정신의 **shift** n. 변화 **mentality** n. 정신 **consciousness-raising** a. 의식을 고양하는 **substantial** a. 실질적인, 상당한

2 다음 빈칸에 들어갈 말로 가장 적절한 것은?

Throughout the centuries, immigrant groups coming to America have attempted to _____. Often, however, the needed ingredients are unavailable or too expensive. Moreover, in the early-20th century, dietitians and reformers frequently looked upon the food choices and dishes of immigrants with alarm and disdain. Dietitian Bertha M. Wood wrote a cookbook that conveyed many of the then prominent beliefs and stereotypes about immigrants to the United States. Yet she also expressed some sympathy toward the various groups of people who arrived, often penniless, in America. For example, in contrast to the opinion often given by other Americans that immigrants "should learn to eat American food if they are to live here," she countered, "When a person is ill and needs a special diet, it is no time to teach him to eat new foods. It is like hitting a person when he is down. Our milk soups are nutritious, but so are theirs; why not learn what they are and prescribe them? The same is true of other foods."

(A) develop new kinds of dishes
(B) re-create the dishes of their homelands
(C) accept and learn traditional American dishes
(D) change the ingredients of their own traditional dishes

2 **dietitian** n. 영양사 **disdain** n. 경멸 **ingredient** n. 재료, 구성물 **unavailable** a. 이용할 수 없는 **convey** v. 전달하다 **prominent** a. 두드러진, 유명한 **stereotype** n. 고정관념 **sympathy** n. 동정 **penniless** a. 빈털터리의 **counter** v. 반박하다 **nutritious** a. 영양가가 있는 **prescribe** v. 처방하다

3 글의 내용과 일치하는 것은?

Most people feel lonely sometimes, but it usually only lasts between a few minutes and a few hours. For some people, though, loneliness can last for years. Psychologists are studying this complex phenomenon. The most common type of loneliness is temporary. It usually disappears quickly and does not require any special attention. The second kind, situational loneliness, is a natural result of a particular situation - for example, a divorce, the death of a loved one, or moving to a new place. Although this kind of loneliness can cause physical problems, such as headaches and sleeplessness, it usually does not last for more than a year. Situational loneliness is easy to understand and to predict. The third kind of loneliness is the most severe. Unlike the second type, chronic loneliness usually lasts more than two years and has no specific cause. People who experience habitual loneliness have problems socializing and becoming close to others. Many chronically lonely people think there is little or nothing they can do to improve their condition.

(A) Chronic loneliness is the most severe.
(B) Situational loneliness usually lasts for two years.
(C) Habitually lonely people experience sleepless nights.
(D) Temporary loneliness does not have a specific cause.

3 lonely a. 외로운, 고독한 last v. 지속되다 psychologist n. 심리학자 complex a. 복잡한 phenomenon n. 현상 temporary a. 일시적인 particular a. 특정한, 특유의 n. 상세한 사항 severe a. 심각한 chronic a. 만성적인 specific a. 특정한, 구체적인 habitual a. 습관적인 socialize v. 사회화하다 improve v. 향상시키다

4 주어진 글 다음에 이어질 순서로 가장 적절한 것은?

Elizabeth Gibson was walking down a street on Manhattan's Upper West Side and spied a piece of art squeezed between two garbage bags.

[A] So Gibson took it home, where she hung it on her wall. Years later she discovered that the painting was "Three People," which had been painted by the celebrated 20th-century Mexican artist Rufino Tamayo. The painting had been stolen and later thrown away.

[B] Had Gibson come along twenty minutes later, it would have already been picked up by garbage collectors. Instead, the painting was returned to the original owners and auctioned by Sotheby's for over a million dollars.

[C] She was tempted to walk away, but then she stopped to reflect about the art. She had a real debate with herself. It had a cheap frame, but she felt it was so overpowering.

(A) [A] - [C] - [B] (B) [C] - [A] - [B]
(C) [C] - [B] - [A] (D) [B] - [A] - [C]

---

4 **spy** v. 보다, 알아채다 **squeeze** v. 밀어 넣다, 비집고 들어가다 **celebrated** a. 유명한 **reflect** v. 깊이 생각하다
have a debate with oneself v. 숙고하다, 곰곰이 생각하다 **overpowering** a. 압도적인, 아주 강한

5 다음 글의 요지로 가장 적절한 것은?

People define themselves to the rest of the world by the things they wear, the objects they use, and the things they do. Clothing, jewelry, makeup, and hairstyles help to define the self. In addition, jobs, houses, cars, and recreational and other activities play a role in creating the persona that the world sees. As people go about defining themselves and the world around them, shopping plays a huge role. The things we wear, the goods we use, and the activities in which we engage are all part of our personalities. All of these involve shopping. From this perspective, shopping becomes much more than an activity we carry out in order to acquire goods and services. In fact, it becomes the most central event in people's efforts to define themselves as human beings. Self-definition is one of the most pivotal functions of shopping.

(A) 사람은 자신의 경제 사정에 맞게 쇼핑을 한다.
(B) 사람은 쇼핑을 통하여 세상에 자신을 규정한다.
(C) 사람은 정신보다 물질에 더 많은 애착을 느낀다.
(D) 겉모습으로 사람들을 규정하는 데는 한계가 있다.

5 **persona** n. (다른 사람의 눈에 비치는) 개인의 모습 **pivotal** a. 중추적인, 중요한 **define** v. 규정하다, 정의하다
go about -ing v. ~하기 시작하다 **engage in** v. ~에 참여하다, 종사하다 **personality** n. 개성, 인격 **perspective** n. 관점, 원근법
carry out v. ~을 수행하다 **self-definition** n. 자아 규정

6 다음 글의 빈칸 (A), (B)에 들어갈 말로 가장 적절한 것은?

More and more today, English is used by Korean professionals on business in Brazil, by Polish hotel staff welcoming tourists from around the world, or by Indian workers who have taken up jobs in the Gulf States. When the role of a language is to be a tool for communication between non-native speakers, we cannot rationally call it a 'foreign' language. Who is the foreigner, (A), when a speaker from Chile interacts with a colleague from Kazakhstan, using English? In a situation like this, the concept of 'foreigner' and of 'foreign language' is not applicable. Instead, we have a situation where English is acting as a lingua franca. (B), it is acting as the common language for speakers whose mother tongues are different.

	(A)	(B)
(A)	in addition	By contrast
(B)	however	In conclusion
(C)	for example	That is to say
(D)	by contrast	As a result

6 take up job v. 일자리를 얻다 rational a. 이성적으로 interact v. 교류하다 applicable a. 적용될 수 있는
lingua franca n. 국제 공용어 mother tongue n. 모국어

10분 모의고사 19

1 제시문과 가장 가까운 의미의 영문은?

> There has never been a period of human history altogether free from war, and seldom one of more than a generation which has not witnessed a major conflict.

(A) Most periods in human history have been war-free but some generations have experienced war in a significant way.
(B) War has dominated human history, so that every generation has always been in war-like circumstances.
(C) There has rarely been a time in human history when it was carefree from war and when there was no major conflict for generations.
(D) Human history is practically based on war and every other generation has seen at least one major battle.

---

1 **free from** a. 빠져 있는, 자유로운 **war-free** a. 전쟁 없는 **carefree** a. 걱정 없는 **dominate** v. 지배하다

2 제목으로 가장 적절한 것은?

Plug-in hybrids have the potential to make a huge leap over current hybrids. They were first made available to the public in 2010 and were initially quite expensive. It is hoped, though, that models will be available within a few years that will be cost competitive with regular cars. They get 100 miles per gallon or more, but the advantages go way beyond fuel efficiency. It is not an exaggeration to say that plug-in hybrids could help save us from oil dependence, air pollution, and a deteriorating atmosphere. By doing without 80 to 90 percent of the gasoline used by conventional cars, these vehicles could play a key role in our getting unhooked from fossil fuels.

(A) How Hybrid Cars Work
(B) The History of Hybrid Cars
(C) Plug-in Hybrids: The Next Wave
(D) Benefits of Doing Without Your Car

2 deteriorate v. 악화되다 plug-in hybrid n. 플러그인 하이브리드 자동차 leap n. 도약 current a. 현재의
cost competitive a. 가격 경쟁력이 있는 go way beyond v. ~을 훨씬 넘어서다 exaggeration n. 과장
do without v. ~없이 지내다 conventional a. 관습적인 get unhooked from v. ~로부터 벗어나다

3 다음 빈칸 (A), (B)에 들어갈 말로 가장 적절한 것은?

The historian of philosophy, whether primarily interested in philosophy or primarily interested in history, cannot help being both a philosopher and a historian. A historian of painting does not have to be a painter; a historian of medicine does not practise medicine. (A), a historian of philosophy cannot help doing philosophy in the very writing of history. The link between philosophy and its history is a far closer one. The historical task itself forces historians of philosophy to paraphrase their subjects' opinions, to offer reasons why past thinkers held the opinions they did, to speculate on the premises left tacit in their arguments, and to evaluate the coherence of the inferences they drew. But the supplying of reasons for philosophical conclusions, the detection of hidden premises in philosophical arguments, and the logical evaluation of philosophical inferences are themselves full-blooded philosophical activities. (B), any serious history of philosophy must itself be an exercise in philosophy as well as in history.

	(A)	(B)
(A)	However	For example
(B)	However	Consequently
(C)	That is	Likewise
(D)	Moreover	Nevertheless

3 tacit a. 암묵적인 paraphrase v. 다른 말로 표현하다 speculate on v. 추측하다 premise n. 전제 coherence n. 일관성, 통일성 inference n. 추론 detection n. 발견 full-blooded a. 순수 혈통의

4. 다음 글에서 전체 흐름과 관계없는 문장은?

Despite the very real problems in the traditional society and the equally real improvements brought about by development, things look different when one examines the important relationships: to the land, to other people, and to oneself. (A) Viewed from this broader perspective, the differences between the old and the new become obvious and disturbing — almost black-and-white. (B) It becomes clear that the traditional nature-based society, with all its flaws and limitations, was more sustainable, both socially and environmentally. (C) It was the result of a dialogue between human beings and their surroundings, a continuing dialogue that meant that, over two thousand years of trial and error, the culture kept changing. (D) The need for wild and undisturbed nature and the need to design nature and the environment are deeply rooted in humans; both must be valued. The traditional Tibetan world view emphasized change, but change within a framework of compassion and a profound understanding of the interconnectedness of all phenomena.

5 다음 주어진 문장이 들어가기에 가장 적절한 곳은?

> They then cast shade on neighboring, shorter plants, depriving them of energy and tending to impoverish them.

Although plankton live near the surface, they don't live on the surface. The ocean surface itself is generally pretty clear. (A) Looking down at the water, one usually sees mostly water, not a plant covering. (B) Thus, the competition for sunlight that often seems to characterize plant life on land seems not to be as important in the oceans. (C) This is due to dissolved nutrients being present only in dilute form, as well as the action of currents, waves, and wind. On land, plants that shoot up the fastest and tallest get more precious sunlight, solar energy that they use for growth. (D) That seems to be why trees are tall and why rainforests grow as high as they do.

6 빈칸에 적절한 것은?

Any time you use another writer's words or even a close paraphrase of his or her words, you must give that writer credit. If you don't, you've committed the crime of plagiarism. Simply out, plagiarism is using somebody else's words and claiming or pretending that the words are your own. A simple rule of thumb for avoiding plagiarism is: When in doubt, give the original writer credit. If you're applying common information, you do not have to worry about plagiarism. If you say the Earth is round, nobody will accuse you of plagiarism. On the other hand, if you write a research paper stating that 16.5 percent of all merchant marines get seasick, chances are some poor researcher spent months of his or her life to determine that fact. In this case, _____.

(A) nobody will claim his or her right
(B) the researcher deserves the credit
(C) you don't have to worry about plagiarism
(D) the readers would accuse the original writer

10분 모의고사 20

1 제시문과 가장 가까운 의미의 영문은?

> Jenny said to a waiter, "What's this fly doing in my soup?"

(A) Jenny asked a waiter what action the fly was taking in her soup.
(B) Jenny asked a waiter what the fly was doing in my soup.
(C) Jenny told a waiter that she didn't know what a fly was doing in my soup.
(D) Jenny complained to a waiter that there was a fly in her soup.

---

1 **fly** n. 파리 **take action** v. 행동하다 **complain** v. 불평하다

2 주어진 글 다음에 이어질 순서로 가장 적절한 것은?

A toy shop selling teddy bears and a range of soft toys wanted to encourage more families with children to visit their shop. They wanted to communicate fun and excitement and to drive the right people to their door.

[A] To enter the competition, families had to complete an entry form that requested contact details. The competition involved correctly matching the named bears with a location. All correct entries were entered into a draw to win the bear of their choice.

[B] They came up with the idea of running a hunt-the-bears competition. They took pictures of all their top bears and gave them all a special name. They arranged to put pictures of the bears up in different places in the town centre.

[C] Competition entry forms had to be delivered to the shop where entrants were given a special gift voucher. This creative marketing idea generated a lot of fun and attracted a crowd of excited kids who all wanted a bear.

(A) [A] - [C] - [B]
(B) [B] - [A] - [C]
(C) [B] - [C] - [A]
(D) [C] - [A] - [B]

2 **a range of** a. 다양한 **soft toy** n. 봉제완구 **entry form** n. 응모 신청서 **contact details** n. 상세한 연락처 **draw** n. 추첨 **come up with** v. 제시하다 **run** v. 개최하다, 운영하다 **arrange to** v. ~하기로 정하다 **deliver** v. 전달하다, 배달하다 **entrant** n. 참가자 **gift voucher** n. 상품권 **generate** v. 생산하다 **put up** v. 배치하다

3 제목으로 적절한 것은?

Over the years I have asked thousands of people to do a simple exercise of stating how they intend to influence others every day. I am always both amazed and inspired by the answers people give. A receptionist in a law firm, for example, told me that her intention was that every person who met her all day long got a "shot of friendliness" so that they felt the world was a friendlier place because they encountered her. The list of intentions is inspiring. Some say they want to bring kindness, others goodness, compassion, energy, courage, or hope. Your position does not limit the way you can influence others. This woman was only a receptionist, but she could influence others in a profound way by holding that intention.

(A) Your Intention to Influence People Can Make a Difference
(B) Don't Impose Your Thoughts on Others
(C) Facial Expressions Reveal Hidden Intentions
(D) Good Intentions Don't Always Lead to Good Results

3 state v. 진술하다 intend to v. 의도하다 amazed a. 깜짝 놀란 receptionist n. 접수계원 get a shot v. 주사를 맞다 friendliness n. 다정함, 친절함 goodness n. 선량함 compassion n. 온정, 동정, 연민 profound a. 심오한

4 글의 흐름으로 보아 주어진 문장이 들어가기에 가장 적절한 곳은?

However, being socially responsible does not mean that a company must abandon its primary economic mission.

Corporate social responsibility means that a corporation should be held accountable for any of its actions that affect people. (A) It implies that negative business impacts on people and society should be corrected if at all possible. (B) It may require a company to give up some profits if its social impacts are seriously harmful to some of the corporation's investors. (C) This also doesn't suggest that socially responsible firms cannot be as profitable as other less socially responsible firms. (D)

4 abandon v. 버리다 corporation n. 회사 accountable a. 책임있는 impact n. 영향 profitable a. 이익이 되는

5 빈칸에 적절한 것은?

The Internet and communication technologies play an ever-increasing role in the social lives of young people in developed societies. Adolescents have been quick to immerse themselves in technology with most using the Internet to communicate. Young people treat the mobile phone as an essential necessity of life and often prefer to use text messages to communicate with their friends. Young people also increasingly access social networking websites. As technology and the Internet are a familiar resource for young people, it is logical that they _____. This has been shown by the increase in websites that provide therapeutic information for young people. A number of 'youth friendly' mental health websites have been developed. The information presented often takes the form of Frequently Asked Questions, fact sheets and suggested links. It would seem therefore logical to provide online counselling for young people.

(A) might be the victim of identity theft
(B) would seek assistance from this source
(C) might enjoy themselves with online games
(D) could be satisfied with relationships in real life

5 ever-increasing a. 계속 증가하는 adolescent n. 청소년 immerse oneself in v. ~에 몰두하다 necessity n. 필수품 access v. 접근하다 resource n. 수단, 자원 therapeutic a. 치료(법)의 Frequently Asked Questions n. FAQ 자주 묻는 질문들 fact sheet n. 자료표

6 다음 글의 제목으로 가장 적절한 것은?

　　An additional trend in consumer behaviour is what is referred to as 'time deepening' in which the individual is involved in more than one activity at the same time. Many people in the home will combine activities such as watching television while ironing, or reading while listening to music; but there are similar trends in travel business contexts as well. An increasing number of people are seeking holidays during which they can focus on an activity such as painting or wine tasting while still enjoying conventional attributes such as climate, scenery and culture. 'Edutainment,' in which entertainment is combined with educational learning, is also apparent in theme parks, heritage centres and contemporary museums and other facilities that are incorporating educational benefits into their service package, such as Chessington World of Adventures and Techniquest.

(A) Edutainment: An Outdated Travel Option
(B) A Complete Guide to World Heritage Sites
(C) Contemporary Need for Multi-Purpose Travel
(D) Why Multitasking May Make You Less Productive

6 **time deepening** n. 시간 심화 **conventional** a. 관습적인 **attribute** n. 속성, 특성 **edutainment** n. 에듀테인먼트(오락성을 겸비한 교육용 상품) **theme park** n. 놀이공원 **heritage** n. 유산 **incorporate** v. 통합하다 **contemporary** a. 현대의, 당대의 **affordable** a. (가격이) 알맞은

10분 모의고사 21 문제편

1 제시문과 가장 가까운 의미의 영문은?

> Based on their school experiences, many students view writing as limited to utilitarian ends : writing to please a teacher or to pass a composition course.

(A) Students learn at school that writing is a short-cut to obtaining good grades in a composition course or showing what they can do to a teacher.

(B) Through schooling, many students learn to consider writing as a means to please the teacher and to obtain a passing grade in a writing course.

(C) Many students attain the perspective from school that writing is to make their teacher happy or obtain a passing grade in a writing course.

(D) The school instills in students the notion that they can pass a composition course by pleasing their teacher.

---

1 **utilitarian** a. 실용적인 **instill** v. 주입시키다 **please** v. 기쁘게 하다 **short-cut** n. 지름길 **perspective** n. 관점, 견해
honorable a. 명예로운

2 다음 글의 주제로 가장 적절한 것은?

Competitive debate is an activity as consuming and, in its own way, as brutal as football. Students spend their days preparing for tournaments in which they will debate a major issue of public policy. These tournaments require them to argue in support of a resolution in one round and then against it in the next. The practical emphasis in debate is on tying logical knots, sounding persuasive, and even speaking so quickly that an opponent cannot respond to all of one's arguments. The point is not to arrive at a fuller understanding of the question at hand or to form genuine convictions. Debaters develop considerable expertise as a result of their preparations, but this is only a means to victory. As for convictions, a premium is placed on not having any; believing in something could interfere with one's ability to win on both sides of the issue. This arrangement may force participants to see both points of view, but it does so in a way that promotes a kind of cynical relativism: no position is better than any other since any position can be successfully defended.

(A) basic rules for resolving a heated debate
(B) various controversial topics for a debate
(C) attempts to use debate as a learning tool
(D) potential problems of competitive debates

3 다음 글에서 전체 흐름과 관계없는 문장은?

In an attempt to make packaging less harmful to the environment, one company has created a new green packaging material that looks like plastic but turns into compost once it's thrown away. (A) Some grocery stores are already using the material to package their products, and customers are encouraged to return the packaging to the stores later. (B) From there, it is shipped to a recycling facility and processed into organic soil. (C) One current drawback is that this material is much more expensive than traditional plastics, but its cost should come down soon. (D) Plastic substitutes had also been used in products such as mattresses, rugs, and pillows to help the environment. When it does, experts believe green packaging production will become a major industry in the U.S.

3 attempt v. 시도하다 green a. 환경보호의 packaging n. 포장 throw away v. 던지다, 버리다 process v. 가공[처리]하다 organic a. 유기체의, 생물의 drawback n. 약점, 결점 come down v. (값이)하락하다 subsitute n. 대체재 rug n. 깔개

4 다음 빈칸에 들어갈 말로 가장 적절한 것은?

In a famous experiment, participants were asked to watch a video of six people passing a pair of basketballs to one another. Their instructions were to count how many times the people wearing white shirts passed the ball. Halfway through the video, a man in a gorilla costume walks through the players. Surprisingly, only half of the participants saw him. The others were so focused on the basketballs that they didn't notice. This experiment suggests that _____. The researchers believe this is because there is only a certain amount of information the brain can handle. Once this amount is reached, it stops noticing other things. This is one of the reasons activities like driving while talking on a cell phone are considered dangerous.

(A) we react differently to the same event
(B) we have a hard time paying attention for a long time
(C) our limited knowledge can cause us to make mistakes
(D) our ability to concentrate on multiple tasks at once is limited

4 experiment n. 실험 participant n. 참가자 instruction n. 설명, 지시 halfway a. 중간[가운데쯤]에 costume n. 의상 suggest v. 제안하다, 시사하다 handle v. 처리하다, 감당하다

5 다음 주어진 문장이 들어가기에 가장 적절한 곳은?

> However, that is not the whole story because speakers also make those gestures in different situations.

When two people have a conversation, the person who is speaking generally makes various gestures coordinated in timing and in meaning with the words being spoken. (A) It is natural to assume that these gestures serve a communicative function by providing visual cues that make the speaker's message easier for the listener to understand. (B) As you may have noticed, speakers often gesture during telephone conversations, even though these gestures are not visible to the listener. (C) Bavelas, Gerwing, Sutton, and Prevost found that speakers make more gestures while talking to someone face-to-face than over the telephone, which suggests that gestures are often used for communication purposes. (D) Why do speakers make any gestures when on the telephone? Perhaps it has become habitual for them to use gestures while speaking, and they maintain this habit even when it is not useful.

---

5 **coordinate** v. 조화시키다 **assume** v. 추정하다 **communicative** a. 의사 전달의, 말을 잘하는 **face-to-face** a. 정면으로 맞서서 **maintain** v. 유지하다

6 주어진 글 다음에 이어질 글의 순서로 가장 적절한 것은?

Ecosystems are generally very efficient in cycling matter, in that most matter is cycled over and over within the ecosystem itself. For example, the carbon atoms in a plant will be incorporated into a deer.

[A] Nevertheless, a small amount of matter will be lost from the ecosystem over time. Leaching from rainfall will carry off carbon from decaying organic matter, leaves, and so on. In undisturbed ecosystems, this output loss is roughly balanced by an equal input gain of similar materials.

[B] These, in turn, will be incorporated into the tissue of a wolf that eats the deer. When the wolf dies, decomposers will incorporate the same carbon atoms. All of these changes take place within the ecosystem.

[C] For instance, carbon enters the ecosystem via weathering of rocks and is carried out of the ecosystem by rainwater. In undisturbed natural ecosystems, both the input and the output are small relative to the amount of matter locked up and recycled within the biomass of the ecosystem itself.

(A) [A] - [C] - [B]
(B) [B] - [A] - [C]
(C) [B] - [C] - [A]
(D) [C] - [A] - [B]

10분 모의고사 22

1 제시문과 가장 가까운 의미의 영문은?

> It is no easier for Americans to just listen during a conversation than it is for Korean students to just relax when speaking with foreigners.

(A) It is not easier for Americans to keep silent during a conversation than it is for Korean students to get excited when speaking with foreigners.

(B) It is as difficult for Americans not to speak during a conversation as it is for Korean students not to be nervous when speaking with foreigners.

(C) It is slightly more difficult for Americans to just listen during a conversation than it is for Korean students to get excited when speaking with foreigners.

(D) It is not so difficult for Korean students not to be nervous when speaking with foreigners as it is for Americans not to talk during a conversation.

---

1 **relax** v. 긴장을 풀다 **slightly** ad. 약간 **nervous** a. 긴장한

2 글의 흐름으로 보아, 주어진 문장의 적절한 위치는?

It was part of the economy drive in preparation for Hate Week.

The hallway smelt of boiled cabbage and old rag mats. At one end of it a colored poster, too large for indoor display, had been tacked to the wall. It depicted simply an enormous face, more than a meter wide : the face of a man of about forty-five, with a heavy black moustache and ruggedly handsome features. (A) Winston made for the stairs. It was no use trying the lift. (B) Even at the best of times it was seldom working, and at present the electric current was cut off during daylight hours. (C) The flat was seven flights up, and Winston, who was thirty-nine, and had a varicose ulcer above his right ankle, went slowly, resting several times on the way. (D) On each landing, opposite the lift shaft, the poster with the enormous face gazed from the wall. It was one of those pictures which are so contrived that the eyes follow you about when you move.

2 smell of v. 냄새가 나다 cabbage n. 양배추 rag mat n. 양탄자 tack v. 벽에 걸다 depict v. 그리다 moustache n. 턱수염 ruggedly ad. 거칠게 make for v. 전진하다 cut off v. 단절되다 varicose a. 정맥류의 ulcer n. 궤양 contrive v. 만들다

3 다음 글의 주제로 가장 적절한 것은?

When a person watches a television movie or listens to a compact disc, it is reasonably clear that the prime purpose of the communication is entertainment. Television news shows might be watched to gain information, but the television stations are well aware of the importance of presenting news in an entertaining fashion. Are television news and newspaper reporting really just other forms of entertainment? You might argue that listening to the radio in the morning to check traffic conditions is information gathering. Calling a travel agent to make an airline reservation clearly is an example of using the telephone as an information tool. But talking by telephone for hours with a distant friend is an entertaining way to keep in contact and exchange information of what is happening.

(A) multi-purpose nature of communication
(B) various ways of gaining new information
(C) telephone as a primary means of communication
(D) role of mass media in providing entertainment

---

3 **reasonably** ad. 상당히, 꽤 **prime** a. 가장 중요한 **entertainment** n. 오락 **be aware of** v. ~을 알고 있다
   entertaining a. 즐겁게 하는 **fashion** n. 유행, 방식 **multi-purpose** a. 다목적의 **side effect** n. 부작용

4 다음 글에서 전체 흐름과 관계없는 문장은?

We can see the occasional clash between compassion and morality in the lab. (A) Experiments by the psychologist C. Daniel Batson and his colleagues find that being asked to adopt someone else's perspective makes participants more likely to favor that person over others. (B) For example, they are more prone to move a suffering girl ahead of everyone else on a waiting list for a lifesaving procedure. (C) This is compassionate, but it's not moral, since this sort of decision should be based on objective and fair procedures, not on who causes the most intense emotional reaction. (D) Morality is an end in itself, and without humanity, there would be no morality. Part of being a good person, then, involves overriding one's compassion, not cultivating it.

5 주어진 글 다음에 이어질 글의 순서로 가장 적절한 것은?

Why did Columbus not immediately realize he was not in Asia? Surely the plants and animals and people he discovered were nothing at all like what Marco Polo had reported from his travels eastward from Europe where he had met the Great Khan and absorbed Asian culture.

[A] Marco Polo's reports of Asia were imperfect at best, allowing huge amounts of wiggle room for interpreting New World data as Old World facts.

[B] The answer can be found in the twofold problem of data and theory. What made Columbus confused was poor-quality data coupled with incorrect theory.

[C] Plus, there was no theory of a New World, so in Columbus's mind when he made first contact with the New World on that fateful day in October 1492, where else could he be but in Asia?

(A) [A] - [C] - [B] (B) [B] - [C] - [A]
(C) [C] - [B] - [A] (D) [B] - [A] - [C]

6 Which of the following is NOT true according to the passage?

> Philosophical questions do not get "solved," as empirical questions do. The empirical question "How many pages are in this book?" has a single, correct answer; all others are wrong. But a philosophical question like "Is abortion wrong?" has more than one plausible answer. Depending on the positions taken on such debatable issues as "life," "personhood," and "rights," we can find even completely opposing arguments that are reasonable and believable. Similarly, we can make a plausible case for saying that we're free to choose anything we want whenever we want to. It is simply a characteristic of philosophical issues that we fall short of absolute certainty.

(A) Philosophical questions are mostly equivocal.
(B) Various answers can be drawn from philosophical questions.
(C) Questions as to what is right or wrong are not philosophical.
(D) Empirical questions are not ambiguous.

6 philosophical a. 철학의 empirical a. 경험의 plausible a. 그럴듯한 debatable a. 논쟁의 여지가 있는 personhood n. 개성 oppose v. 반대하다 believable a. 믿을 수 있는 characteristic n. 특질, 특색 punishment n. 벌, 형벌 equivocal a. 애매한 as to prep. ~관한 make a case v. 정당성을 입증하다

10분 모의고사 23 문제편

1 제시문과 가장 가까운 의미의 영문은?

> A world heritage site may be in danger because a country does not have the technical or scientific expertise to salvage an historic building or protect a particular habitat that is home to endangered species.

(A) Because a country lacks things that can protect an endangered species or the skills to look after an old building, a world heritage site is at risk of being destroyed.
(B) A country that wants to have a world heritage site must improve its knowledge and skills in order to get one.
(C) World heritage sites around the world are in danger because countries do not want to allot resources that take care of their upkeep.
(D) Habitats that support endangered species need to be protected just as much as old buildings are protected as world heritage sites.

1 **heritage** n. 유산 **expertise** n. 전문성 **salvage** v. 구조하다 **habitat** n. 서식지 **upkeep** n. 유지

2 다음 글에서 전체 흐름과 관계없는 문장은?

Children of Native American parents are traditionally socialized through an extensive network of relatives. (A) Along with grandparents, uncles and aunts participate with parents in child care, supervision of children, and assurance of love, and cousins are thus considered as close as siblings. (B) Members of this extended family also teach children their tribal values and beliefs along with traditions and rituals. (C) Reflecting a group-oriented culture, the values of cooperation and sharing are emphasized, while competitive behavior is discouraged. (D) As a result, one-third of all Native Americans who marry outside their ethnic group have adopted either white values completely or a mixture of white and traditional values. Children and adolescents are further encouraged to participate in tribal ceremonies and develop an appreciation for their cultural heritage.

2 **socialize** v. 사회화하다 **extensive** a. 넓은 **supervision** n. 관리, 감독 **assurance** n. 보장 **sibling** n. 형제자매 **extended family** n. 대가족 **ritual** n. 의례, 의식 절차 **group-oriented** a. 집단 지향적인 **ethnic** a. 종족의, 민족의 **mixture** n. 혼합물 **appreciation** n. 이해, 평가 **heritage** 유산

3 다음 빈칸에 들어갈 말로 가장 적절한 것은?

An edge that happy people have for building physical resources is how well they deal with unexpected, difficult events. How long can you hold your hand in a bucket of ice water? The average duration before the pain gets to be too much is between sixty and ninety seconds. Rick Snyder, a professor at Kansas and one of the fathers of Positive Psychology, used this test on Good Morning America to demonstrate the effects of positive emotion on _____. He first gave a test of positive emotion to the regular cast. By quite a margin, Charles Gibson, host of Good Morning America, outscored everybody. Then, before live cameras, each member of the cast put his or her hand in ice water. Everyone, except Gibson, pulled their hands out before ninety seconds had passed. Gibson, though, just sat there grinning, and still had his hand in the bucket when a commercial break was finally called.

(A) coping with difficulty
(B) cooperating with others
(C) promoting physical fitness
(D) coming up with new ideas

4 주어진 글 다음에 이어질 글의 순서로 가장 적절한 것은?

Today in a highly competitive sporting world where one mistake or one slow reaction can ruin a sporting career, good vision is as important to sporting performance as good physical conditioning and consistent mental concentration.

[A] It has also been observed that athletes with excellent vision perform better than other athletes. In fact, today at the elite levels, vision is the one thing that makes a difference between a good athlete and an exceptional one.

[B] As physical conditioning has already proved its worth, more and more athletes will find value in visual conditioning. Many studies show that athletes have better visual abilities than the normal population.

[C] They are better at focus flexibility, and reveal greater depth perception or better eye-hand coordination, as well as many other excellent visual skills. Their visual system is fine-tuned to aim, anticipate, and respond more quickly to complete a visual task.

(A) [A] - [C] - [B]
(B) [B] - [A] - [C]
(C) [B] - [C] - [A]
(D) [C] - [A] - [B]

4 competitive a. 경쟁하는, 경쟁력 있는 consistent a. 지속적인 exceptional a. 탁월한, 예외적인 flexibility n. 유연성 depth perception n. 원근감 eye-hand coordination n. 눈과 손의 조화 tune v. 조정하다, 맞추다 anticipate v. 예측하다

5 다음 글의 제목으로 가장 적절한 것은?

Think of your DNA as an ongoing instruction manual for how to build and maintain your body, which remains in use every moment of every day. The cells and enzymes responsible for helping the body to grow, replenish, and repair, continuously refer to those instructions. The manual itself rarely changes, but how it's read does. Nutrients, microbes, and synthetics that enter our bodies — largely but not exclusively through food — can signal which sets of instructions our cells should follow. It's like putting sticky notes on some pages of the manual, while leaving others unread. So you might carry the genetic predisposition for things like cancer, mental illness, ADHD, or obesity, but it's by no means a sure thing that those portions of your DNA will be expressed. Nutrients flag important areas at certain times; thus many "on" and "off" labels come from food.

(A) What Is It That Affects How DNA Operates?
(B) How to Prevent Genetic Diseases in Advance
(C) Food: An Important Factor for Repairing DNA
(D) Why Are We Forced to Follow a DNA Manual?

5 **instruction manual** n. 사용설명서 **enzyme** n. 효소 **replenish** v. 보충하다 **microbe** n. 미생물 **synthetic** n. 화학합성물 **exclusively** ad. 전적으로 **genetic predisposition** n. 유전적 소인(요소) **obesity** n. 비만 **by no means** ad. 결코 ~ 아닌 **flag** v. 표시를 하다

6 글의 흐름으로 보아, 주어진 문장이 들어가기에 가장 적절한 곳은?

If you keep up the sleep-depriving behavior, you appear to accelerate parts of the aging process.

Recent research has begun to shed light on important functions that do not at first glance seem associated with sleep. (A) When people become sleep-deprived, for example, their ability to utilize the food they are consuming falls by about one-third. (B) The ability to make insulin and to extract energy from the brain's favorite dessert, glucose, begins to fail miserably. (C) At the same time, you find a marked need to have more insulin because the body's stress hormone levels begin to rise in an increasingly deregulated fashion. (D) For example, if healthy 30-year-olds are sleep-deprived for six days, parts of their body chemistry soon turn to that of a 60-year-old. And if they are allowed to recover, it will take them almost a week to get back to their 30-year-old systems.

---

6 **keep up** v. ~을 계속하다 **accelerate** v. 촉진하다 **aging** n. 노화 **shed light on** v. 빛을 밝히다 **at first glance** ad. 언뜻 보기에 **sleep-deprived** a. 잠이 부족한 **consume** v. 먹다, 소모하다 **extract** v. 뽑다, 얻다 **miserably** ad. 형편없이, 비참하게 **marked** a. 뚜렷한, 두드러진 **deregulated** a. 통제가 해제된 **chemistry** n. 화학 작용, 화학 반응 **glucose** n. 포도당

CHAPTER 2 — 10분 모의고사 24 (문제편)

1 제시문과 가장 가까운 의미의 영문은?

> The gradations of the moral faculties in the higher animals and man are so imperceptible that to deny to the first a certain sense of consciousness would certainly be an exaggeration of the difference between animals and man.

(A) The differences between higher animals and man are so vast that it is possible to claim that they are truly different.

(B) It would be far-fetched to say that higher animals are not inferior to man because they have the same consciousness.

(C) Higher animals and man have similar moral faculties, so it would wrong be imply that higher animals do not have consciousness.

(D) To claim that higher animals are not as conscious as man is to refuse to acknowledge many differences between them.

---

1 **gradation** n. 등급, 계급 **faculty** n. 능력 **imperceptible** a. 인식할 수 없는 **consciousness** n. 의식 **exaggeration** n. 과장 **far-fetched** a. 설득력 없는

2 다음 빈칸에 들어갈 말로 가장 적절한 것은?

In 1859, a man released 24 European wild rabbits into a park in Australia. Less than 70 years later, the population had exploded to more than 10 billion rabbits across the nation. Although this number has since decreased to about 300 million, these rabbits are _____. The primary reason is that rabbits eat the same vegetation as Australia's native animals. Rabbits also reproduce more quickly than these native species, and they tend to eat the roots of plants rather than just the leaves, meaning the plants cannot regrow. With less food available, more than 20 species of Australian mammals have gone extinct, as have a number of native plants. What's worse, a lack of plants and grass causes once green areas to turn into lifeless deserts.

(A) the national animal of Australia
(B) an endangered species in Australia
(C) the most popular animal in Australia
(D) a danger to the ecosystem of Australia

3 다음 글의 주제로 가장 적절한 것은?

> The human body shows various responses to stress. When a person experiences stress, the brain releases stress hormones. The hormones signal blood to move to the heart and other organs. People experiencing stress might suddenly feel hot. Their heart may beat faster and their muscles may tense. Their hands and feet might feel cold. Their senses may become sharper. People might feel like they can smell, see, and taste things more clearly. Once the factor causing stress disappears, the stress hormones quiet down. The body gradually goes back to normal.

(A) direct effects of stress on memory
(B) physical reactions caused by stress
(C) key factors causing stress hormones
(D) ways to overcome stressful situations

3 response n. 반응 signal v. 신호를 보내다 go back v. 회귀하다 key factor n. 핵심요소 overcome v. 극복하다

4 글의 흐름으로 보아, 주어진 문장이 들어가기에 가장 적절한 곳은?

Although fear can encourage a negative attitude and even an intention to change, such feelings tend to disappear over time and when faced with a real decision-making situation.

Many health education campaigns have attempted to motivate people to change their behavior through fear or guilt. (A) Anti-drinking and driving campaigns at Christmas show the devastating effects on families of road accident victims; smoking prevention posters urge parents not to 'teach your children how to smoke.' (B) Increasingly hard-hitting campaigns are used amongst others to raise awareness of the consequences of heavy drinking, smoking and drug use. (C) Whether such campaigns do succeed in shocking people to change their behavior is the subject of ongoing debate. (D) Being very frightened can also lead people to deny and avoid the message. Protection Motivation theory suggests that fear only works if the threat is perceived as serious and likely to occur if the person does not follow the recommended advice.

4 devastating a. 엄청난 충격을 주는 guilt n. 죄책감 urge v. 촉구하다 hard hitting a. 강력한, 직설적인 awareness n. 인식, 의식 consequence n. 결과 ongoing a. 계속 진행 중인 frightened a. 겁먹은, 무서워하는 deny v. 거부하다, 부인하다 perceive v. 인식하다, 감지하다

5 주어진 글 다음에 이어질 순서로 가장 적절한 것은?

> Products will no longer be bought and used, but jointly bought, used or rented. Instead of more possessions, people born after the year 1980 (the so-called Generation Y) prefer to have more time for experiences.

[A] Nonetheless, this generation doesn't want to forego pleasure, so those who cannot afford to buy everything tend to swap products instead. In view of the useful lives of objects, the changed mindset initiated by Generation Y seems to make sense.

[B] Possessing as many items as possible is no longer regarded as an indication of status for them, but is instead seen as a burden. From this perspective, each possession hinders mobility and restricts one's freedom.

[C] For example, a power drill is typically used for only 11 minutes a year, and lawn mowers are used only for a few hours every summer in many parts of the world. In a sharing economy, payment is still made using money — or at least digital money — but mutual trust may well turn out to be a kind of new currency.

(A) [A] - [C] - [B]　　　　　　(B) [B] - [A] - [C]
(C) [B] - [C] - [A]　　　　　　(D) [C] - [A] - [B]

5 forego v. 포기하다 afford v. 여유가 있다 swap v. 교환하다 mindset n. 사고방식 indication n. 징표, 상징 perspective n. 관점 hinder v. 방해하다 lawn mover n. 잔디 깎기 currency n. 통화, 화폐

6 다음 글에서 전체 흐름과 관계없는 문장은?

When photography came along in the nineteenth century, painting was put in crisis. The photograph, it seemed, did the work of imitating nature better than the painter ever could. Some painters made practical use of the invention. (A) There were Impressionist painters who used a photograph in place of the model or landscape they were painting. (B) But by and large, the photograph was a challenge to painting and was one cause of painting's moving away from direct representation and reproduction to the abstract painting of the twentieth century. (C) Therefore, the painters of that century put more focus on expressing nature, people, and cities as they were in reality. (D) Since photographs did such a good job of representing things as they existed in the world, painters were freed to look inward and represent things as they were in their imagination, rendering emotion in the color, volume, line, and spatial configurations native to the painter's art.

10분 모의고사 25

1 제시문과 가장 가까운 의미의 영문은?

> No matter which piece of art or architecture you see, there were personal, political, sociological and religious factors behind its creation.

(A) If you have personal, political, sociological or religious feelings inside of you, there is also the ability to create art or architecture.
(B) The thought that goes into creating art or architecture can be traced back to the origins of personal, political, sociological or religious ideas.
(C) Creating something for personal, political, sociological or religious motivations is just what the art and architecture world needs its aficionados to do.
(D) All art and architecture was made because somebody wanted to create something on personal, political, sociological or religious grounds.

---

1 architecture n. 건축학, 건축물 be traced back v. 거슬러 올라가다 aficionado n. 애호자

2 다음 빈칸에 들어갈 말로 가장 적절한 것은?

Many cultures of the world see arguing as _____. Americans in Greece often get the feeling that they are witnessing an argument when they are overhearing a friendly conversation that is more heated than such a conversation would be if Americans were having it. Linguist Sarah Tannen showed that in the conversations of working class Eastern European Jewish speakers — both male and female — in Philadelphia, a friendly argument was a means of being on good terms with someone. Linguist Jane Frank analyzed the conversation of a Jewish couple who tended to polarize and take argumentative positions in social situations. But they were not fighting. They were staging a kind of public sparring, where both fighters were on the same side.

(A) a pleasurable sign of intimacy
(B) an effective tool to educate students
(C) a major cause of couples breaking up
(D) an inevitable process in drawing conclusions

2 polarize v. 양극화하다 overhear v. 우연히 듣다, 엿듣다 linguist n. 언어학자 working class n. 노동자 계급 Jewish a. 유대인의 be on good terms with v. ~와 친한 관계를 유지하다 argumentative a. 논쟁적인 stage v. 연출하다, 상연하다 sparring n. 말다툼, 스파링

3 다음 주어진 문장이 들어가기에 가장 적절한 곳은?

> Nonhuman infant primates take a shorter time to produce adult-like calls, but never progress beyond the use of a fairly limited vocabulary or surpass the single-call level.

One reason why humans take much longer than other species to produce their species-specific "calls" is that at birth the vocal tract of the human infant is disproportionately short compared to the rest of the articulatory system. (A) The oral cavity is broader, the larynx is higher, and the tongue is more forward. (B) This significantly limits the infant's ability to vocalize. (C) It is only at around six months that the vocal tract will become more adult-like and allow the baby to begin babbling language-like sounds. So in humans, the physical capacity to produce language is not present at birth. (D) Human infants, in contrast, show sophisticated sensitivity to language structure prior to production and quickly surpass their primate cousins at every level once production begins.

3 surpass v. 넘어서다, 능가하다 **vocal tract** n. 성도(성대에서 입술 또는 콧구멍에 이르는 통로) **larynx** n. 후두(구강기관)
disproportionately ad. 불균형적으로 **articulatory** a. 발성의, 조음의 **oral cavity** n. 구강 **cavity** n. 구멍
significantly ad. 상당히, 의미 있게 **vocalize** v. 발성하다 **babble** v. 옹알이하다

4 다음 글의 요지로 가장 적절한 것은?

Efficiency in solving new problems tends to be assumed as a measure of the individual level of intelligence. The more intelligent a person is considered, the quicker he is in his thinking (with other factors held constant). In intelligence testing, a great (and perhaps excessive) emphasis is placed on the time in which test items are accomplished. Most tests demand completion within a certain time-limit; consequently, a slow-thinking subject is bound to solve fewer problems and will therefore rate low on the intelligence scale, though he may be superior to quick thinkers in accuracy. Admittedly, there are numerous practical situations demanding swift solutions (e.g. in combat, in face of technical breakdown), but the ingenuity of the solution is often a more distinct sign of intelligence, though it need not coincide with speed. Intelligence is the antithesis of instinct and habit — the two stereotyped kinds of behavior. The ability to devise new solutions creatively is the principal domain, and hence also the basic criterion of intelligence.

(A) 지능에 있어서 속도와 창의성 모두 중요한 지표이다.
(B) 새로운 문제를 빠르게 해결하는 능력은 매우 중요한 지능의 척도이다.
(C) 지능 측정 검사는 인간의 다양한 측면을 고려해야만 한다.
(D) 지능의 척도는 문제 해결 속도가 아니라 해결책의 창의성이다.

4 **antithesis** n. 정반대 **be superior to** v. ~보다 우수한 **admittedly** ad. 명백하게, 틀림없이 **swift** a. 신속한 **breakdown** n. 고장 **ingenuity** n. 독창성 **coincide with** v. ~일치하다 **stereotyped** a. 판에 박힌, 진부한 **devise** v. 고안하다 **domain** n. 영역 **criterion** n. 기준(pl. criteria)

5 다음 글에서 전체 흐름과 관계없는 문장은?

Many governments have instituted regulations concerning the humane treatment of animals on fur farms; however, the regulation and methods of enforcement vary widely across the world. (A) For example, European Union legislation includes guidelines for the humane treatment and slaughter of agricultural animals raised for food as well as clothing, including fur. (B) While these guidelines are enforced by routine monitoring carried out by state-authorized agencies, observers find variable results in many countries. (C) Some people say that with so many attractive and sensible alternatives available, animal fur is simply unnecessary, and even purchasing the tiniest bit of fur trim supports a cruel industry. (D) In China, a major supplier of farmed fur, minimal regulatory oversight exists regarding fur farms. Total bans on fur farming are in effect in the United Kingdom and Austria; in the Netherlands, Croatia, and Switzerland, heavy restrictions or partial bans have been established.

6 주어진 글 다음에 이어질 글의 순서로 가장 적절한 것은?

René Descartes is the French philosopher who wrote the famous line "I think, therefore I am." Fortunately for psychology, this was not his only contribution.

[A] Thus, Descartes' notion of mind-body dualism proposes that some human behaviors are automatic reactions that are driven by external stimulation, while other behaviors are freely chosen and controlled by the mind.

[B] On the one hand, he claimed, we have a body that functions like a machine and produces automatic, involuntary behaviors in response to external stimulation (such as coughing in response to dust). On the other hand, we have a mind that has free will and produces behaviors that we regard as voluntary (such as choosing what to eat for dinner).

[C] In Descartes' time, many people assumed that human behavior was governed entirely by free will or "reason." Descartes disputed this notion and proposed a dualistic model of human nature.

(A) [A] - [C] - [B] (B) [C] - [B] - [A]
(C) [B] - [C] - [A] (D) [C] - [A] - [B]

6 **dualism** n. 이원론 **stimulation** n. 자극 **function** v. 작동하다, 기능하다 **cough** v. 기침하다 **free will** n. 자유 의지 **reason** n. 이성 **dispute** v. 반박하다 **dualistic** a. 이원론적인 **human nature** n. 인간의 본성

10분 모의고사 26

1 제시문과 가장 가까운 의미의 영문은?

> Like language itself, a technology predisposed us to favor and value certain perspectives and accomplishments and to subordinate others.

(A) Language and technology are similar in that they both highly consider some views and accomplishments but trivialize others.//
(B) Both technology and language use the same means to rank certain views and assess results on a relative scale.//
(C) Compared to language, technology is more discriminatory of certain views and results.//
(D) Technology judges particular views and accomplishments differently than language does.

---

1 **predispose** v. ~하게 만들다 **value** v. 높이 평가하다 **subordinate** v. 낮게 평가하다 **in that** con. ~라는 점에 있어서 **trivialize** v. 과소평가하다 **rank** v. 평가하다 **scale** n. 기준, 규모 **discriminatory** a. 차별적인

2 다음 글의 제목으로 가장 적절한 것은?

Most people could be forgiven for thinking that human beings are, generation by generation, growing inexorably taller. After all, that certainly seems to be the case with our waistlines. But measurements of human skeletal remains from across the ages made by Richard Steckel, at Ohio State University, tell a different story. Far from gradual evolution from short to tall, Steckel finds that Northern European men living in the Early Middle Ages (9th to 11th centuries AD) were several centimeters taller than their counterparts at the start of the Industrial Revolution around 1750 — and almost as tall as modern humans today. Steckel believes that the height of a population is an indicator of the overall prosperity of the region. He speculates that the differences may be due to a period of warm climate during the Early Middle Ages, which made food plentiful, followed by the Little Ice Age between the 16th and 19th centuries when it would have been scarce.

(A) Height Is Affected by Ethnic Origins
(B) Taller Humans Are Not Good for the Earth
(C) Prosperous Regions May Have Tall Residents
(D) Positive Effects of Humans' Height Increase throughout the history.

2 forgive v. 용서하다 inexorably ad. 멈추지 않고 skeletal a. 골격의 remains n. 유해 counterpart n. 대응되는 사람[물건]
the Industrial Revolution n. 산업혁명 indicator n. 지표 prosperity n. 번영, 번성 speculate v. 추측[짐작]하다

3 다음 중 글의 내용과 일치하지 않는 것은?

> Often people who hold higher positions in a given group overestimate their performance, while people in the lowest levels of the group underestimate theirs. While this may not always be true, it does indicate that often the actual position in the group has much to do with the feeling of personal confidence a person may have. Thus, members who hold higher positions in a group or feel that they have an important part to play in the group will probably have more confidence in their own performance.

(A) People who hold high positions have more self-confidence than those who don't.
(B) If we let people know they are an important part of a group, they will probably become more self-confident.
(C) People who hold low positions in a group often overestimate their performance.
(D) People in positions of power in a group may feel they do better work than they really do.

4 다음 빈칸에 들어갈 말로 가장 적절한 것은?

Making judgments will stop the creative process — that is, stop synthesis. People with strong opinions often have difficulty being creative because they are inclined to short-circuit the creative process by making premature judgments. Langer has identified premature judgments as a cause or characteristic of mindlessness. Hobson has suggested that to dream (which is a kind of creative storytelling), people need to set aside their self-reflection systems. Some researchers have suggested that being introspective or self-focused can interfere with making good decisions. We need to learn to _____ long enough for the creative process to run its course.

(A) take risks
(B) activate debate
(C) control emotions
(D) suspend judgment

5 글의 흐름으로 보아, 주어진 문장이 들어가기에 가장 적절한 곳은?

> Until recent times, psychology was unimportant philosophical verbiage — the academic stuff that I learnt in youth was not worth learning.

The power of physics has been due to the fact that it is a very definite science, which has profoundly altered daily life. But this alteration has been proceeded by operating on the environment, not on man himself. (A) Given a science equally definite, and capable of altering man directly, physics would be put in the shade. (B) This is what psychology may become. (C) But now there are two ways of approaching psychology which are obviously important: one that of the physiologists, and the other that of psychoanalysis. (D) As the results in these two directions become more definite and more certain, it is clear that psychology will increasingly dominate man's perspective.

6 주어진 글 다음에 이어질 글의 순서로 가장 적절한 것은?

Affirmations are a way of turning negative self-talk, which leads to stress, into positive, life-affirming statements. They are always stated in the present tense — 'I am', 'I have' and 'I choose' — and they reflect what you wish to experience, not what you should or could.

[A] But with regular practice, you will notice a change. The inner world of your thoughts and feelings will be in line with the outer world of your experience. Your mind and body will work together to produce a positive result.

[B] They are negative and focus on what you do not want to happen. More positive and effective statements are, "I feel energetic and healthy," or "I am relaxed and have plenty of time to do what needs to be done." At first it may feel silly to state over and over the exact opposite of what you are feeling.

[C] Think back to what you say when you might be getting sick or feeling tired: "I don't feel sick," or "I don't have time to be sick." What do both of these statements have in common?

(A) [C] - [B] - [A]   (B) [B] - [A] - [C]
(C) [B] - [C] - [A]   (D) [C] - [A] - [B]

6 **Affirmation** n. 긍정 **lead to** v. 초래하다 **life-affirming** a. 긍정적인 **have in common** v. 공통점을 갖다 **state** v. 진술하다 **present tense** n. 현재시제 **over and over** ad. 반복해서

10분 모의고사 27

1 제시문과 가장 가까운 의미의 영문은?

> Put differently, an average American can speak the equivalent of two novels per day, although he reads less than three books per year.

(A) There are many people in America who do not read anywhere near what they should and speak too much.
(B) Americans, though capable of speaking enormous amounts in a day, tend to read only a fraction of that amount each year.
(C) In American society people are relying too much on the spoken word and not enough on the written.
(D) There is a great void in the level of written versus spoken English in America, and it must change.

---

1 **put differently** ad. 달리 말하면 **equivalent** a. 동등한 **enormous** a. 엄청난 **fraction** n. 부분, 단편 **void** n. 공백 **versus** prep. ~대한

2 Which is true according to the passage?

> Until the nineteenth century, when steamships and transcontinental trains made long distance travel possible for large number of people, only a few adventurers, mainly sailors and traders, traveled out of their own countries. "Abroad" was a truly foreign place about which the vast majority of people knew very little indeed. Early map makers therefore had little fear of being accused of mistakes, even though they were often wildly inaccurate. When they compiled maps, imagination was as important as geographic reality. Nowhere is this more evident than in old maps illustrated with mythical creatures and strange humans.

(A) Despite their unusual illustrations, maps made before the nineteenth century were remarkably accurate.
(B) Old maps often included pictures of imaginary animals.
(C) Until the nineteenth century, map makers could draw imaginative animals.
(D) Early map makers were afraid of traveling abroad.

2 steamship n. 증기선 transcontinental a. 대륙횡단의 be accused of v. ~고발당하다 compile v. 편집하다
  geographic a. 지리적인 illustrate v. 삽화를 넣다 mythical a. 신화적인

3 다음 글의 주제로 가장 적절한 것은?

Although we normally think of floods as destructive events, flood plain ecosystems depend on floods. For example, cottonwood tree seeds only develop after a flood, and waterfowl depend on flood plain wetlands. Many species of fish gradually lose out to stronger competitors during normal flows but have adapted better to floods, so their populations increase as a result of flooding. Thus species diversity is maintained by interchanging periods of flooding and normal flow. Deltas are created and expanded by floods. At normal times, when rivers are confined within their banks, the flowing water transports sediment out to sea and deposits it on the ocean floor. But during floods, river water rises above the stream banks and covers the delta land. When the flood waters slow down, they deposit sediment, thus expanding the delta.

(A) importance of preserving water resources
(B) beneficial impacts of floods on ecosystems
(C) how to prevent floods using simple measures
(D) devastating floods that changed world geography

3 sediment n. 퇴적물 flood plain n. 범람원 cottonwood n. 미루나무 waterfowl n. 물새 lose out to v. ~에게 밀리다 diversity n. 다양성 interchange v. 교환하다 delta n. 삼각주 confine v. 가두다, 한정하다 deposit v. 침전시키다 stream bank n. 강둑, 개울둑 devastating a. 파괴적인

4 다음 빈칸에 들어갈 말로 가장 적절한 것은?

> Campaign officials want to encourage their supporters to vote. How can they do that? One obvious method is to emphasize the stakes; another is to decrease the cost and burdens, by making it easier for people to get to the polls. But there is another way. It turns out that if you ask people, the day before the election, whether they intend to vote, you can increase the probability of their voting by as much as 25 percent! Or suppose that the goal is to increase new purchases of a certain product, such as cell phones or automobiles. A study of a nationally representative sample of more than forty thousand people asked a simple question: Do you intend to buy a new car in the next six months? The very question increased purchase rates by 35 percent. Or suppose that an official wants to encourage people to take steps to improve their own health. With respect to health-related behavior, significant changes have been produced by _____.

(A) offering a variety of options
(B) improving the service quality
(C) measuring people's intentions
(D) giving people equal opportunities

5 글의 흐름으로 보아, 주어진 문장이 들어가기에 가장 적절한 곳은?

During the 1960s and 1970s, automation also reached the office, with the same results.

Technology influenced and even rearranged the traditional divisions between professions and the workforce. The introduction of automation in manufacturing allowed many manufacturing processes to be done by less skilled workers. Also, the new, more complicated technology associated with automated manufacturing required more know-how. (A) Technical know-how became the domain of an increasingly powerful but small group of people. (B) For example, when the first computers appeared in management, banking, and administration, they were completely puzzling to the average worker, and the few computer "specialists" gained considerable earning power. (C) Meanwhile, some of the tasks secretaries and bookkeepers normally do could now be handled by word-processing and spreadsheet programs that a manager could use himself or herself. (D)

5 automation n. 자동화 rearrange v. 재정리[재배열]하다 division n. 구분, 분할 profession n. (전문적인) 직종, 직업 manufacturing n. 제조업 be associated with v. ~와 관련된 considerable a. 상당한 earning power n. 수익능력 bookkeeper n. 회계장부 담당자

6 주어진 글 다음에 이어질 순서로 가장 적절한 것은?

A perceptually subjective view gives the audience a closer awareness of what a character is experiencing. Filmmakers may use this technique if they want the audience to feel a stronger sense of connection with a character.

[A] The entire screen goes black as the lead character, Tom Reagan, is knocked unconscious, so that the audience is effectively 'blacked out' as well. The rest of the scene is not shown until Tom comes around.

[B] For example, in Joel and Ethan Coen's gangster drama Miller's Crossing, creative editing makes the audience experience the sudden disorientation of being knocked out and then waking up in a confused state.

[C] The audience therefore has a degree of perceptual subjectivity in this scene because it sees only what Tom sees and not the events that occur while he is unconscious.

(A) [A] - [C] - [B]
(B) [B] - [A] - [C]
(C) [B] - [C] - [A]
(D) [C] - [A] - [B]

10분 모의고사 28 문제편

1 제시문과 가장 가까운 의미의 영문은?

> Business investment in Britain is weak by the standards of other rich countries - one reason why its recovery has been so sluggish.

(A) As other rich countries received business investment from far and wide, Britain's slow recovery scared all potential investors off.
(B) On seeing the lack of business investment in Britain, other rich countries were deterred from helping the recovery.
(C) Business investment in Britain remains low as a direct result of its slow recovery as other rich countries see furtive investment.
(D) As a result of the lack of business investment in Britain compared to other rich countries, its recovery has been lethargic.

1 **sluggish** a. 느린, 부진한 **scare off** v. 겁을 주어 쫓아 버리다 **deter** v. 단념시키다 **lethargic** a. 무기력한 **furtive** a. 은밀한

2 Which of the following is NOT the purpose of genetic study?

> Genes are part of the center of every living cell. In the form of DNA, this biological genetic material determines the characteristics of every living thing. Medical geneticists are scientists that study DNA and genes for many purposes. First, they study to learn how living things such as viruses and bacteria cause illness. Second, they try to find the gene that cause certain diseases to pass from parents to their children. Third, they try to prevent or repair birth defects. Fourth, they expect to change gene structure to improve health and increase longevity. Fifth, they want to change the biological characteristics of humans in ways that are beneficial to society.

(A) to lengthen human life-span
(B) to discover the relationship between virus and diseases
(C) to lower the birthrate of human babies
(D) to cure genetically transmitted diseases

2 **gene** n. 유전자 **cell** n. 세포 **biological** a. 생물학(상)의 **genetic** a. 유전학적인 **birth defect** n. 선천적 기형 **longevity** n. 장수, 수명 **lengthen** v. 길게 하다, 늘이다 **life-span** n. 수명 **birthrate** n. 출생률 **transmit** v. 보내다, 전달하다

3. 다음 글의 제목으로 적절한 것은?

For many years, behavioral scientists believed a sharp distinction existed between such instinctive behaviors and acquired behaviors, which they classified as learning. To many, a behavior had to be either instinctive or learned. Ethologists, viewing behavior from an evolutionary perspective, emphasized the importance of instinctive behaviors to survival in nature. Behavioral psychologists, interested in mechanisms of learning under controlled conditions, believed that all complex behaviors are acquired by a nervous system that starts off at birth as a clean slate. To some, instinct seemed nearly irrelevant.

This philosophical conflict between the importance of genes (or "nature") and the significance of environmental factors and learning during development (or "nurture") raged fiercely for many years. We now know that both nature and nurture are important in shaping many complex behaviors. Genetic instructions guide the growth of the neurons and synapses that make behavior possible; however, individual experience can change both the structure and the function of cells and synapses. The behaviors that mature animals display, like many other visible characteristics, depend on both genes and environment. To understand this still-controversial area, we must look closely at both instinctive behaviors and learned responses.

(A) Evolutionary Aspects of Human Behaviors
(B) The Significance of Environmental Factors for Humans
(C) The Making-up of Behaviors: Instinct vs. Learning
(D) Various Ways of Survival in Nature

---

3 **distinction** n. 구분, 차이 **ethologist** n. 생태학자 **start off** v. 시작되다 **clean slate** n. 백지 **rage** v. 화를 내다, 맹렬히 계속되다 **neuron** n. 뉴런, 신경세포 **synapses** n. 시냅스 (신경접합부)

4 주어진 글 다음에 이어질 글의 순서로 가장 적절한 것은?

Let's move on to the concept of how we create our own reality. A good example is exam tension. This is a very common stress that has a clear cause: mild tension or anxiety is normal during an exam.

[A] This can in turn have a severe impact on performance. For some, the fear will become real and they will indeed fail the exam and thus confirm their negative beliefs. In other words, fear can create precisely what we don't want.

[B] These thoughts can often create physical symptom such as fear, sleep loss, lack of appetite, nausea, restlessness, frequent urination, headaches, aggression, irritability and dizziness.

[C] It helps students improve their focus and pace. But when this stress is severe, students may experience negative thoughts or beliefs such as 'I will fail' or 'I can't remember anything.'

(A) [C] - [B] - [A]
(B) [B] - [A] - [C]
(C) [B] - [C] - [A]
(D) [C] - [A] - [B]

---

4 nausea n. 메스꺼움 urination n. 배뇨 tension n. 긴장(감) confirm v. 확인하다 symptom n. 증상 restlessness n. 안절부절 aggression n. 공격성 irritability n. 신경과민, 화를 잘 냄 dizziness n. 어지러움, 현기증

5 글의 흐름으로 보아, 주어진 문장이 들어가기에 가장 적절한 곳은?

Our growing environmental awareness casts a colder light on these accomplishments, however.

The United States was founded on a spirit of dominion over nature. "My family, I believe, have cut down more trees in America than any other name!" boasted John Adams. (A) Benjamin Lincoln, a Revolutionary War general, spoke for most Americans of his day when he observed in 1792, "Civilization directs us to remove as fast as possible that natural growth from the lands." (B) The Adams-Lincoln mode of thought did make possible America's rapid expansion to the Pacific, the Chicago school of architecture, and Henry Ford's assembly line. (C) Since 1950 more than 25 percent of the remaining forests on the planet have been cut down. (D) Recognizing that trees are the lungs of the planet, few people still think that this represents progress.

6 다음 빈칸에 들어갈 말로 가장 적절한 것은?

Mark Twain observed, "We are all ignorant, but about different things." One mistake technical professionals make when writing for non-technical readers is assuming their readers are as knowledgeable as they are about the subject. This is a fatal assumption that will only result in confusion and frustration for your reader. Also, a great deal of your time will be spent generating additional messages to the reader trying to explain what should have been clear the first time. Just because it's clear to you does not make it clear to your reader. If you are an engineer or accountant writing to others in your field, then perhaps there will be less need to explain all aspects of your message. If you're writing to the senior vice president of marketing, who is not familiar with software applications, then you will need to "walk" that reader through your message. Remember that when it comes to technical knowledge, _____.

(A) good readers can be good writers
(B) writers and readers are hardly equal
(C) readers don't necessarily trust writers
(D) writers and readers have the same purpose

10분 모의고사 29 문제편

1 제시문과 가장 가까운 의미의 영문은?

> Commonly found in architecture and design, the art nouveau style can be seen in many of the world's cities and perhaps most famously in the Parisian Metro stations.

(A) The architecture and design of many of the world's cities is a direct imitation of the art nouveau style intended to be unique to Paris' Metro stations.

(B) The Metro stations in Paris were created in the art nouveau style that had already become popular in the architecture and design of cities around the world.

(C) As the world's cities begin to understand the effect the art nouveau style can have on architecture and design, the Parisian Metro stations become more popular.

(D) All over the world's cities, especially the Metro stations in Paris, the art nouveau style can be seen in architecture and design.

---

1 **architecture** n. 건축물 **art nouveau** n. 아르누보 (곡선을 강조했던 건축양식) **imitation** n. 모방

2 이 글의 내용과 일치하지 않는 것은?

Cialdini is an expert in the field of influence. The book is a comprehensive study on the psychology of influence. It is an indispensible tool for professionals involved in sales and marketing and negotiations, but it has practical applications for everyday social interactions as well. Cialdini explains techniques, a.k.a. weapons of influence, that can be used to gain compliance from others. These techniques are drawn from real-life situations. While he constantly cites academic sources and laboratory experiments, the book remains accessible to the casual, non-academic reader. Illustrations, cartoons, and "reader's reports" are sprinkled throughout, which helps the book stay firmly grounded in practicality. The study questions at the end of the chapter help to pull each chapter's ideas together. To critics of the book many of the ideas presented are seen as common sense, but I really think that everyone can benefit from reading this book.

(A) Cialdini is the author of the new book.
(B) Critics regard the book as too academic.
(C) Some practical techniques are introduced in the book.
(D) The book is written for readers of general backgrounds.

2 comprehensive a. 포괄적인 practical a. 실제의, 실용적인 application n. 적용, 응용 interaction n. 상호작용[영향] a.k.a. a. 별칭은 (=also known as) compliance n. 승낙, 동의 sprinkle v. 뿌리다, 끼얹다 practicality n. 실용주의 dissertation n. 논설, 학위논문 abstract n. 요약 book review n. 서평 letter of reference n. 추천서

3 다음 빈칸에 들어갈 말로 가장 적절한 것은?

Sugar's effects are ironic; that is, they have the opposite effect from the one you intended. You wanted to feel less hungry and nasty, and you ended up feeling more hungry and nasty. TV has a similar effect, but on happiness instead of hungriness. You watch TV because you want to be entertained, relaxed, involved — you want to feel happy. Unfortunately, although TV can be relaxing, it is only occasionally entertaining and very rarely involving. So, you end up bored, which makes you think you should watch more TV, and you can guess the consequences. Everyone needs a little time to watch TV or just do nothing, just like everyone needs a little sugar now and then. A problem arises when you assume that _____. I guarantee that prolonged periods of sitting in front of the TV and eating sugary snacks will not make you happy in the long run.

(A) if a little is good, then more must be better
(B) happiness can be achieved in a few easy ways
(C) when sugar is consumed, your body energy increases
(D) there is an interaction between happiness and health

4 다음 빈칸 (A), (B)에 들어갈 말로 가장 적절한 것은?

Most modern nations contain a lot of cultural diversity within their boundaries. This is especially true for nations with a history of colonialism.   (A) , the internationally recognized national borders of most African and South Asian countries are a product of their history as colonies, not of their indigenous cultural or ethnic identities. That is, more often than not, colonizing nations created boundaries between "their" colonies to further their own interests rather than to reflect cultural distinctions and ethnic divisions.   (B) , modern India has dozens of languages and cultural identities, as do most sub-Saharan African nations like Kenya and Tanzania. The government of the People's Republic of China recognizes 56 minority peoples, some of whom theoretically have traditional homelands labeled autonomous regions on maps.

	(A)	(B)
(A)	For example	Thus
(B)	For example	Instead
(C)	As a result	However
(D)	In contrast	Instead

5 주어진 글 다음에 이어질 글의 순서로 가장 적절한 것은?

> To produce the distinctive sounds of laughter, we make use of a number of muscles that control our breathing and vocal apparatus. The normal human breathing cycle consists of inspiration, inspiration pause, expiration, and expiration pause.

[A] This is followed by a sustained sequence of repeated, rapid, and shallow expirations, which, when accompanied by phonation, produce the "ha-ha-ha" of laughter. By the end of this expiratory laugh bout, the lungs reach the air volume remaining in the lungs after maximal expiration.

[B] Regardless of where the person happens to be in this cycle, laughter typically begins with an initial forced exhalation, which brings the lung volume down to around functional residual capacity (i.e., the volume that remains after a normal expiration).

[C] Thus, laughter typically occurs at a low lung volume, forcing out more air from the lungs than occurs during normal breathing. Following a laughter bout, a quick inhalation occurs, filling the lungs once again to normal capacity. Another laughter bout may then follow.

(A) [A] - [C] - [B]
(B) [B] - [A] - [C]
(C) [B] - [C] - [A]
(D) [C] - [A] - [B]

6 다음 글의 제목으로 가장 적절한 것을 고르시오.

Has your creativity ground to a stop? Instead of letting frustration get the better of you, try to sit back and take a few deep breaths. Did you know that drawing a deep breath gives your creativity a boost by increasing the negative ions in oxygen? The negatively charged oxygen circulates throughout the brain, refreshing the neurons and, because these negative ions promote alpha waves of longer amplitude in the brain, which are associated with creative thinking, suddenly your creativity receives a boost. So, next time your creative spirit feels burdened, spend two minutes taking deep breaths, breathing in and out every five seconds, and repeat the cycle at least 12 times.

(A) Breathe Deep for Inspiration
(B) Frustration Makes Hope
(C) Can Memory Be Boosted?
(D) Don't Fear Ridiculous Ideas

6 **boost** n. 활력 **amplitude** n. 진폭 **grind to a stop** v. 천천히 멈추다 **frustration** n. 좌절감 **get the better of** v. ~을 이기다 **draw a deep breath** v. 심호흡을 하다 **negative ion** n. 음이온 **negatively charged** a. 음전하를 띤 **circulate** v. 순환하다 **refresh** v. 생기를 찾아주다 **neuron** n. 신경세포, 뉴런

CHAPTER 2

10분 모의고사 30   문제편

1 제시문과 가장 가까운 의미의 영문은?

> After thousands of years of studying and treating every aspect of it, there are still many facets of the brain that remain mysterious.

(A) Despite having spent many years trying to work out what goes on in the brain, much of it still remains a mystery.
(B) Understanding the brain has been at the forefront of medical advances for years and years, and finally we are close to understanding its true origins.
(C) Although it has taken many years to get to this point, it seems the inner workings of the brain have at last been untangled.
(D) Even though we have spent so long studying the brain, to this day we are no closer to understanding it than before.

---

1 facet n. 측면 work out v. 해결하다 forefront n. 선두 untangle v. 풀다 be close to v. ~하기 직전이다

2 다음 중 본문의 내용과 일치하는 것은?

Of all the mystic places, the most enigmatic - and the source of many of the rest, in the view of some people - is the lost island of Atlantis. The subject of more than 2,000 books and countless articles and poems, Atlantis has been traced to a long list of sites and regions in the world. Thousands of years after it supposedly sank into the cold and gloomy depths of the Atlantic Ocean, the island continent of Atlantis lives on as one of history's most tantalizing puzzles. If indeed such a place existed, it was a civilization unequaled before or since. Yet its chroniclers say that it vanished in little more than a single day, leaving not a trace behind. Plato described Atlantis as an idyllic land with beautiful gardens and a balmy climate - a place where people lived lives of cultivated leisure in magnificent mansions.

(A) Atlantis is believed to have declined gradually.
(B) Atlantis was the place where savages used to live.
(C) The existence of Atlantis has been unconfirmed.
(D) The idea of paradise has nothing to do with Atlantis.

2 enigmatic a. 수수께끼의 Atlantis n. 아틀란티스 섬 tantalizing a. 애타게 하는 chronicler n. 연대기 작가 vanish v. 사라지다 little more than av. ~ 마찬가지인 idyllic a. 멋진 balmy a. 온화한, 향기로운 cultivated a. 우아한, 교양 있는 magnificent a. 훌륭한 mansion n. 저택 unconfirmed a. 확인되지 않은 have nothing to do with v. 관계없다

3 다음 빈칸에 들어갈 말로 가장 적절한 것은?

> I would like to introduce what I've come to call the lasagna principle — the notion that our capacity to enjoy different activities is limited and unique. Lasagna is my favorite food, and every time I visit my parents, my mother prepares a tray of it. This does not, however, mean that I want to eat lasagna all day and every day. The same principle applies to my favorite activities, such as writing and watching movies, as well as to my favorite people. The mere fact that my family is the most meaningful thing in my life does not mean that spending eight hours a day with them is what would make me happiest; and not wanting to spend all my waking hours with them does not imply that I love them any less. I derive a great deal of pleasure and meaning from being with other people, but I also need my daily quota of solitude. _____ leads to the highest quality of life.

(A) Striving and struggling for a worthwhile goal
(B) Protecting myself from external forces that I can't control
(C) Staying positive and constructive, and focusing on favorite activities
(D) Identifying the right activity, and then the right quantity for each activity

---

3 **imply** v. 암시[시사]하다, 의미하다 **derive** v. 얻다, 끌어내다 **a great deal of** a. 많은 **quota** n. 할당량 **solitude** n. 고독
strive v. 애쓰다, 노력하다 **constructive** a. 건설적인 **compassion** n. 연민

4 다음 글의 주제로 가장 적절한 것은?

　Small children have smaller stomachs. They need concentrated foods, high in calories but low in volume. This is one of the main causes of infant malnutrition. In many countries, children are poorly fed but adults are not. It would be a mistake to believe that adults eat everything and leave nothing for the children. Parents (and especially mothers) watch out for their children. They would happily give up their own food in order to feed their children. The problem is that many times the only food available to families consists of vegetables and roots high in fibre but low in calories. Adults can eat all they need, as their stomachs are big enough. And in enough quantity, any food will fatten a person. Small children, as hard as they try, cannot eat the amount of vegetables needed, because they don't have enough room in their stomach.

(A) types of foods that are good for small eaters
(B) simple ways to lose weight in the healthy way
(C) development of eating habits among children
(D) reasons that small children may not get enough calories

4 malnutrition n. 영양실조 stomach n. 위 volume n. 양, 부피 infant n. 유아 fibre n. 섬유소[질] fatten v. 살찌우다

5 글의 흐름으로 보아, 주어진 문장이 들어가기에 가장 적절한 곳은?

> This fact evidently caused the reason of headaches as Barry's career unfolded.

Barry Mazur, one of the world's leading mathematicians, has always been a prodigy. He left the Bronx High School of science after his junior year in order to go directly to MIT. (A) He left MIT after his sophomore year to go to Princeton for graduate studies. (B) Barry told me that he also left Princeton after one year to go study in England. (C) To make a long story short, the only degree that Mazur ever got was the PhD from Princeton. (D) When he would submit his NSF grant proposals, they would invariably be returned with a request for information about his high school diploma and college degree. The Administrative Assistant, Mary McQuillen, would write back and say, "This is not an omission; PhD is Professor Mazur's only degree."

6 제시문 뒤에 이어질 순서로 적절한 것은?

In the 19th century, the UK government nearly surrendered to a powerful foe - the smell of human excrement. By that summer, the River Thames had become such a large repository of human waste that the stench drove all of London to its knees.

[A] Then came the great heat wave of 1858. That summer was a scorcher in England. It boiled the waste in the Thames, which released noxious odors of increasing pungency. The situation grew so desperate that everyone agreed that something had to be done. Figuring out the solution was the next challenge, and after debates and arguments, Disraeli finally passed a bill in July 1858 authorizing the construction of a system of embankments and tunnels that would lead the sewage out of the city.

[B] For all the suffering it caused, the Great Stink of 1858 eventually became a blessing for London. Not only was the Thames cleansed over the next decade but the whole city was infrastructurally and visibly improved by Thames embankments, which carried the sewage while at the same time easing road traffic from the congested thoroughfare, embracing the new underground railway system and enhancing the look of London above ground.

[C] The problem had been decades in the making. Since experts at the time believed the spread of contagious disease was solely airborne, little thought was given to the dangers of disposing of London's sewage in the Thames. Media outlets like the Times had editorialized for years about the need to clean up the river, but nothing changed.

[D] As work got underway, Joseph Bazalgette, the chief engineer who led the project, spoke publicly about its problems. "It was tremendously hard work," Bazalgette said. Despite the difficulties, the embankment project gradually became part of the crafting of a more modern city. A new underground-railway system was also built as part of the effort. The embankment wasn't completed until 1874, but by 1861 residents were raving about the transformation.

(A) [C] - [A] - [B] - [D] (B) [B] - [C] - [A] - [D]
(C) [C] - [A] - [D] - [B] (D) [A] - [C] - [D] - [B]

---

5 unfold v. 전개되다 graduate a. 대학원의 PhD n. 박사 (학위) submit v. 제출하다 grant n. 보조금 proposal n. 제안(서) invariably ad. 예외[변함] 없이 diploma n. 졸업 증서 administrative a. 행정의 assistant n. 조교, 조수 omission n. 누락
6 foe n. 적군 excrement n. 배설물 repository n. 매장지 stench n. 악취 heat wave n. 폭염 scorcher n. 매우 더운 날 noxious a. 유독한 odor n. 냄새 pungency n. (코가) 얼얼함 figure out v. 생각해내다 bill n. 법안 embankment n. 둑 stink n. 악취 congested a. 밀집한 thoroughfare n. 주요(간선)도로 contagious disease n. (접촉) 전염병 airborne a. 공기로 운반되는 sewage n. 하수, 오물 editorialize v. 입장을 밝히다 get underway v. 진행 중이다 craft v. 만들다 rave about v. 격찬[극찬]하다 a blessing in disguise n. 뜻밖의 좋은 결과, 전화위복

EPILOGUE

Thoughts are things.
by Rudy Jeon

EPILOGUE 에필로그

Thoughts are things

Whenever I start something, I always see it to the end.
Although, at times I fall into the spell of laziness, thinking that life doesn't always go the way you want it to, I understand and forgive myself.
However, I will see things to the end, telling myself never to give up.

I strongly want to keep the conviction in my heart that it is never ever too late for realizing my dream, when I am an old man looking back at the past smilingly.

On snowy days, I want to climb the mountain that has wonderful night scenery and atop I could oversee the lights of city below.
On hot summer days, I want to take a plane with a thin shirt and take off to a place where I could put on a heavy coat.
While flying the small plane to the North Pole, I want to stay up all night long with crazy anticipation of the aurora.

Although I surely can put the blame to others, I strongly hope to possess the wisdom to distinguish between the person and the blame. So I want to be the kind of person who has nobody to hate.

I believe that human beings could not be perfect, so I want to be who I am rather than who I am expected to be.
I want to be a narrow-minded person, while having generosity.

When I see the weak and the unfortunate, tears falling from my heart, I sincerely want to help the person in need in practical ways.
I really want to enjoy the solitude of loneliness while sincerely always longing for someone.
Although it could be good to meet someone through a blind date, I really want to find someone whom I fell in love with at first sight by blind fate.
I wish she would be a kind of person who is humorous, warm hearted and able to drink together.

Finally, I want to be a kind of person who always thinks broadly and is never in a rush, bearing in mind the fact that the end of my days will come.
While loving myself who faithfully believe that there would be another day, I want to be a kind of person who realizes deeply that today will never come again.

나는 무엇인가를 시작했을 때 포기하지 않고, 끝까지 가보고 싶다. 잠깐의 나태함에 파묻혀도 좋으며, 인생이란 원래 다 생각처럼 되는 건 아니야 라는 스스로의 합리성에 몸을 담그는 나 자신을 이해해 주고도 싶다.
하지만 그런 자신과 끊임없이 대화하고 타협하며 끝까지는 가보고 싶다.

60이 되어도 열아홉에 꾸었던 꿈을 되돌아보고, 추억에 잠겨도 좋지만, 언제나 늦은 건 없어 라는 신념 또한 간직하고 싶다.

눈 오는 날에는 야경이 아름다운 산 정상에 올라 도시를 내려다보고 싶다.
뜨거운 여름날에는 얇은 옷차림으로 비행기에 올라, 두툼한 털 코트를 입을 수 있는 곳에 가보고도 싶다.
경비행기를 몰고 극지방을 횡단하고, 설레는 눈망울로 밤을 새워 오로라에 미쳐 보고도 싶다.

누군가의 잘못을 탓할 수도 있지만, 잘못과 사람은 구분할 수 있는 지혜로움을 가지고 싶으며, 그래서 누군가를 미워하지 않는 사람이 되고 싶다.

사람은 완전치 못한 존재라는 것을 알기에, 완전한 사람이 되기보단, 나다운 사람이 되고 싶다.
다소 편협한 생각을 갖고 싶기도 하고, 한 편으론 끝없이 자애로운 사람이 되고 싶다.

약하고 힘없는 사람들을 대할 때, 진심 어린 눈물을 흘려도 좋지만, 현실적으로 도움이 되는 일을 해 주고 싶다.
언제나 사람을 그리워하는 사람이 되고 싶지만, 혼자 있음의 외로움도 즐길 수 있는 사람이 되고 싶다.
누군가의 소개로 만나도 좋지만, 운명적으로 첫 눈에 반하는 그런 사람을 만나고 싶다.
많이 쾌활하고, 술 한 잔쯤은 할 수 있어야 하며, 정이 많은 착한 사람이었으면 싶다.

무엇보다 나에게도, 이 세상의 삶이 끝나는 날이 있다는 것을 기억하며, 삶을 더 큰 견지에서 바라다 보고, 조급해 하지 않는 사람이 되고 싶다.
또 다른 내일이 있다는 믿음을 갖는 나 자신도 사랑하지만, 오늘이란 시간은 영원히 다시 오지 않는다는 절실함 또한 느끼는 사람이 되고 싶다.

전경식 독한독해 3.0

초판인쇄	2020년 08월 26일
초판발행	2020년 09월 02일
2쇄 발행	2021년 02월 03일
편 저 자	전경식
발 행 인	최창호
등 록	제2016-000065호
발 행 처	주식회사 좋은책
주 소	서울시 관악구 관악로12길 10, 3층
교재문의	TEL) 02-871-7720 / FAX) 02-871-7721
I S B N	979-11-6348-214-7 (13740)

본서의 무단 전재·복제 행위는 저작권법에 의거하여 5년 이하의 징역 또는 5천만원 이하의 벌금에 처하거나 이를 병과할 수 있습니다.

저자와의 협의하에 인지를 생략합니다.

정가 25,000원

이 도서의 국립중앙도서관 출판시도서목록(CIP)은 서지정보유통지원시스템 홈페이지(http://seoji.nl.go.kr)와 국가자료공동목록시스템(http://www.nl.go.kr/kolisnet)에서 이용하실 수 있습니다. (CIP제어번호 : CIP2020035961)

독한독해 3.0 해설집

문제 뽀개기

| 저자 전경식 |

EXPLANATION+

▸ 네이버 카페 '맨발의 청춘 영어'
http://cafe.naver.com/rudyenglish

▸ 동영상 강의
www.withstars.co.kr | www.eduwill.net

CONTENTS

이 책의 목차

Chapter 01 파트별 전략 / 5

UNIT 01 문제 분석 ·· 6

UNIT 02 PARAPHRASE ·· 16

UNIT 03 TOPIC ··· 20

UNIT 04 내용일치 ·· 25

UNIT 05 빈칸 추론(Blank) ·· 31

UNIT 06 순삽탈(순서배열 문장삽입 논지일탈) ·· 36

Chapter 02 10분 모의고사 / 49

CHAPTER 1

파트별 전략

Unit 01 문제 분석

02 텍스트 의존성 Practice

01 The above passage suggests that in order to fully understand the literary excellence of the English Bible, we should first _____.
영문 성경의 문학적 우수성을 완전하게 이해하기 위해서 우리는 먼저 ____ 해야만 한다.

02 How have we been able to learn about the mummification process?
어떻게 해서 우리는 미라처리 과정을 알 수 있게 되었는가?

03 Which of the following is true about the ceremonies at Gettysburg during the Civil War?
남북 전쟁 동안 Gettysburg에서의 의식 행사에 대해서 사실이 아닌 것은?

04 When did Lincoln's Gettysburg Address begin to receive public acclaim?
언제 링컨의 Gettysburg 연설이 대중의 호응을 받기 시작했는가?

05 What is the main reason city officials created official spots for the locks?
시 공무원들이 자물쇠를 위한 공공장소를 만든 이유는 무엇인가?

06 According to the advisory, what is one possible consequence of misuse of the equipment?
조언자들에 따르면, 장비 남용의 가능한 결과는 무엇인가?

07 According to the passage, what can make cycling in traffic less perilous?
글에 따르면, 무엇이 교통 체증 속에서 자전거를 덜 위험하게 만드는가?

08 What prompted Briggs to alter its asthma medication?
무엇이 브리그스가 천식약을 변경하도록 했는가?

09 What is a requirement of the reception desk agent job?
접수 담당자의 일에 필요한 조건은 무엇인가?

10 Which of the following is a social science discipline that the author mentions as being possibly over-utilized?
남용될 소지가 있는 것으로 작가가 언급한 사회과학 분야가 다음 중 어느 것인가?

11 According to the passage, which one is not correct as a possible cause of the end of the Earth?
글에 따르면, 지구 멸망의 가능한 원인으로 정확하지 않은 것은 어느 것인가?

12 According to the passage, which of the following transformed the men from a mob of individual fighters into an army?
글에 따르면, 개별적인 전사들의 무리를 군대로 변화시키는 것은 무엇인가?

13 Why did some critics doubt the antiquity of the inscriptions?
왜 전문가들은 비문이 오래되었다는 것은 의심했는가?

14 What does the writer think of the heedlessness of children?
아이들의 부주의함을 작가는 무엇으로 생각하는가?

15 Why were X-rays given to older women more than younger women?
왜 엑스레이 촬영은 젊은 여성들보다 나이 든 여성들에게 이루어졌는가?

16 What will probably be the first stage of change as the Sun becomes a red giant?
태양이 적색 거성이 될 때 변화의 첫 번째 단계는 무엇인가?

17 It can be inferred from the passage that the author believes which of the following about the current state of public awareness concerning nuclear power?
글을 통해서 추론해 볼 수 있다. 작가는 원자력에 대한 대중의 현재 인식 수준을 어떤 것이라고 믿는가?

18 According to the passage, short stories are popular in the United States today primarily because they _____.

글에 따르면, 오늘날 단편소설은 미국에서 인기가 많다. 주로 _____ 때문이다.

19 Mathematical laws explaining the movement of the planets according to the Copernican theory were made by _____.

코페르니쿠스 이론에 따른 행성들의 움직임을 설명하는 수학 법칙들은 _____ 의해서 만들어졌다.

20 Why did the people of Macondo decide not to return to the movies?

왜 마콘도 사람들은 극장으로 돌아가지 않기로 결심했는가?

21 Which design principle does this passage focus on as most important for dashboard visualizations?

이 글은 계기판 시각화를 위해 가장 중요한 것으로 어떤 디자인 원칙을 강조하고 있는가?

22 Rosa Parks usually didn't take the bus home from work, because _____.

로사 파크는 보통 버스를 타고 귀가하지 않는다. 왜냐하면 _____ 때문이다.

23 According to the passage, blue monkeys of different groups can live together as long as _____.

글에 따르면, 다른 집단들의 파란색 원숭이들은 함께 살 수 있다. _____ 하는 한.

24 According to the passage, why did the Census Bureau revise the definition of urban in 1950?

글에 따르면, 왜 인구 조사국은 1950년대 도시에 대한 정의를 수정했는가?

25 According to the passage, what kind of difficulty would the astronauts have?

글에 따르면, 우주 비행사들은 어떤 어려움을 가지고 있는가?

26. According to the passage, what is the most comprehensive explanation for the success of Asian immigrants in the US?

글에 따르면, 미국에서 아시아 이민자들의 성공에 대한 가장 포괄적인 설명은 무엇인가?

27. According to the passage, which of the following is not a reason for travel becoming increasingly unnecessary?

글에 따르면, 여행이 점점 불필요해지는 이유가 아닌 것은 다음 중 어느 것인가?

28. which of the following best describes the relation between physical exercise and brain exercise?

신체 운동과 두뇌 운동 사이의 관계를 가장 잘 설명한 것은 어느 것인가?

29. According to the passage, why are architects taking into account of the environment in designing buildings?

글에 따르면, 왜 건축가들은 건물을 설계할 때 환경을 고려하는가?

30. For a company registering a business in Delaware what is not necessary?

델라웨어 주에서 사업을 신청하는 회사에게는 무엇이 필요하지 않은가?

04 보기 문항 Practice

01 ① How to Protect the Wild Life 야생 동물 보호 방안
    ② The Life of the Passenger Pigeon 나그네 비둘기의 생활
    ③ Hunting in Nineteenth-Century America 19세기 미국에서의 사냥
    ④ How Passenger Pigeon Became Extinct 어떻게 나그네 비둘기가 멸종되었는지

02 ① Climate Changes in Recent Years 최근의 기후 변화
    ② Why Americans Move to the South 미국인들이 남부로 이동하는 이유
    ③ What caused Stress of Modern People 현대인들에게 스트레스를 일으키는 것
    ④ The Increase of Living Cost in America 미국에서 생활비의 상승

03 ① Sharing of Our Problems 문제들을 공유하는 것
    ② The Importance of Job 일의 중요성
    ③ Types of Family Business 가족 사업의 유형들
    ④ How to Cope with Crisis 위기에 대처하는 법

04 ① How Can We Make Snow? 눈을 만드는 방법
    ② Two Sides of Artificial Snow 인공 눈의 2가지 특성들
    ③ The Importance of 'Safety First' 안전우선의 중요성
    ④ The Increasing Number of Skiers 스키어들의 증가하는 수

05 ① Harmful Effects of Computer 컴퓨터의 해로운 측면
    ② Increasing Needs for Computer 컴퓨터에 대한 증대되는 요구들
    ③ Computer: A Useful Tool of Art 컴퓨터, 예술의 인공 도구
    ④ Various History of Computer Graphics 컴퓨터 그래픽의 다양한 역사

06 ① Effects of the Sun's Heat 태양열의 영향들
    ② Causes of Weather Changes 기후 변화의 원인들
    ③ Mysteries of the Solar System 태양계의 신비들
    ④ Results of the Earth's Movement 지각 이동의 결과들

07 ① Advantage of Small Family 소가족의 이점
② Importance of Family Bond 가족유대감의 중요성
③ Nuclear and Extended Family 핵가족과 대가족
④ Element of Family Organization 가족 구성의 요소

08 ① Greatness of Barack Obama 버락 오바마의 위대함
② Barack Obama : the 44th US President 버락 오바마 : 44대 미국 대통령
③ Possible Threat to the Inauguration 취임식에 대한 가능성 있는 위협
④ Public safety plan for Obama Inauguration 오바마 취임식을 위한 시민 안전 대책

09 ① To Get a Job, Be a Pleasant Person 직업을 얻기 위해서는 호감이 가는 사람이 되어라
② More Qualifications Bring Better Chances 더 많은 자격조건들이 더 좋은 기회를 가져다준다
③ It Is Ability That Counts, Not Personality 성격이 아니라 능력이 중요하다
④ Show Yourself As You Are at an Interview 면접에서 자기의 참모습을 보여줘라

10 ① The restaurant presents a culinary performance.
그 레스토랑은 요리 퍼포먼스를 제공한다.
② The restaurant is highly praised in Beijing.
그 레스토랑은 베이징에서 상당히 찬사를 받는다.
③ The restaurant features a special champagne bar.
그 레스토랑은 특별한 샴페인 바를 특징으로 한다.
④ The restaurant only serves dishes from the Beijing region.
그 레스토랑은 오로지 베이징 지역의 음식만 제공한다.

11 ① Time your feedback well. 당신의 피드백을 잘 조절하라.
② Customize negative feedback. 부정적인 피드백을 (상대에 맞게) 맞춰라.
③ Tailor feedback to the person. 사람마다 피드백을 조정하라.
④ Avoid goal-oriented feedback. 목적 지향적인 피드백을 피하라

12 ① the development of legal names 법적 이름의 발전
② the concept of attractive names 매력적인 이름의 개념
③ the benefit of simple names 단순한 이름의 혜택
④ the roots of foreign names 외국 이름의 뿌리들

13 ① In the past, the study of history required disenchantment from science
  과거에 역사 연구는 과학으로부터의 각성을 요구했다
② Recently, science has given us lots of clever tricks and meanings
  최근에 과학은 우리에게 영리한 속임수들과 의미들을 제공해 왔다
③ Today, we teach and learn about our world in fragments
  오늘날 우리는 단편적으로 세상을 가르치고 배운다
④ Lately, history has been divided into several categories
  최근에 역사는 몇 가지 항목으로 나누어졌다.

14 ① The increase in the number of working women boosted the expansion of food service programs. 일하는 여성의 수의 증가가 급식 프로그램의 확대를 신장시켰다.
② The US government began to feed poor children during the Great Depression despite the food shortage. 미국 정부는 식량 부족에도 불구하고 대공황 동안 가난한 아이들에게 급식하기 시작했다.
③ The US school food service system presently helps to feed children of poor families.
  미국 학교의 급식 시스템은 현재 빈곤 가정의 아이들에게 급식하는 것을 돕는다.
④ The function of providing lunch has been shifted from the family to schools.
  점심을 제공하는 기능은 가정에서 학교로 이동되었다.

15 ① What effects does worry have on life? 걱정이 삶에 미치는 영향은 무엇인가?
② Where does worry originate from? 걱정은 어디서부터 비롯되는 것인가?
③ When should we worry? 우리는 언제 걱정해야 하는가?
④ How do we cope with worrying? 우리는 어떻게 걱정에 대처하는가?

16 ① Insomnia can be classified according to its duration.
  불면증은 그것의 지속 기간에 따라 분류될 수 있다.
② Transient insomnia occurs solely due to an inadequate sleep environment.
  일시적인 불면증은 단지 부적절한 수면 환경에 의해서만 발생한다.
③ Acute insomnia is generally known to be related to stress.
  급성 불면증은 보통 스트레스와 관련있는 것으로 알려져 있다.
④ Chronic insomnia patients may suffer from hallucinations.
  만성 불면증 환자들은 환영의 고통을 겪을 수 있다.

17 ① to improve the quality of teacher training facilities 교사 양성 시설의 질을 향상시키기 위해
② to bridge the gap through virtual classrooms 가상의 교실을 통해 그 격차를 메우기 위해
③ to get students familiarized with digital technology 학생들을 디지털 기술에 친숙하게 만들기 위해
④ to locate qualified instructors across the nation 나라 전체에 거쳐 질 좋은 교사들을 배치시키기 위해

18 ① Governments must control the flow of trade to revive the economy.
정부는 경제를 회복시키기 위해 무역의 흐름을 통제해야 한다.

② Globalization can be beneficial regardless of one's economic status.
세계화는 경제적 지위와 관계없이 유익할 수 있다.

③ The global economy grows at the expense of the poor.
세계 경제는 빈곤층을 희생시켜 성장한다.

④ Globalization deepens conflicts between rich and poor.
세계화는 부자와 가난한 자의 충돌을 심화시킨다.

19 ① There was an increase in the knowledge of the Earth and heavens in the early 17th century. 17세기 초반에 천지만물에 대한 지식에서의 발전이 있었다.

② Dependence on the philosophy of Aristotle was on the decline in universities in the 17th century. 아리스토텔레스 철학에의 의존은 17세기 대학에서 쇠퇴하고 있었다.

③ Natural philosophy proposed four elements to explain the movements of bodies.
자연 철학은 물체의 운동을 설명하기 위해 네 가지 원소를 제시하였다.

④ In natural philosophy, numbers were routinely put to use for measurable external quantities. 자연 철학에서, 측정 가능한 외부 수량을 위해 언제나 숫자가 사용되었다.

20 ① Your grandfather's stress when he was an adolescent might make you more anxious.
당신의 할아버지가 청소년이었을 때 겪었던 스트레스는 당신을 더 불안하게 만들 수도 있다.

② Early stressful experiences alleviate anxiety later in life.
초기의 스트레스를 일으키는 경험들은 삶의 후반 불안을 완화시킨다.

③ Constant moving from one place to another can benefit offspring.
한 장소에서 다른 장소로의 지속적인 이동은 자손들에게 이득을 줄 수 있다.

④ Chronic social stress cannot be caused by relocation.
만성적인 사회적 스트레스는 재배치로 인해 유발될 수 없다.

21 ① Sponsorship is necessary for a successful career.
성공적인 커리어를 위해서 후원은 필수적이다.

② Building a good network starts from your accomplishments.
좋은 네트워크를 형성하는 것은 당신의 성과로부터 시작된다.

③ A powerful network is a prerequisite for your achievement.
강력한 인맥은 당신의 성공을 위한 전제조건이다.

④ Your insights and outputs grow as you become an expert at networking.
당신이 네트워크 전문가가 됨에 따라 당신의 통찰력과 결과는 성장한다.

22 ① Some writers struggle for teaching positions to teach creative writing courses.
일부 작가들은 창작 작문 강좌를 가르치는 강사자리를 위해 고군분투한다.

② As a doctor, William Carlos Williams tried to find the time to write.
의사로서 William Carlos Williams는 글을 쓸 시간을 찾기 위해 노력했다.

③ Teaching is a common way for writers to make a living today.
작가들이 오늘날 생계를 유지하기 위해 가르치는 일을 하는 것은 흔한 일이다.

④ Salman Rushdie worked briefly in advertising with great triumph.
Salman Rushdie는 광고업에서 큰 성공을 하면서 잠시 일했었다.

23 ① Public adoption agencies are better than private ones.
공공 입양 기관들이 사설 기관들보다 더 낫다.

② Parents pay huge fees to adopt a child from a foster home.
부모들은 위탁 양육 가정으로부터 아이를 입양하는 데 큰 비용을 지불한다.

③ Children in need cannot be adopted through public agencies.
도움이 필요한 아이들은 공공 기관을 통해 입양될 수 없다.

④ Private agencies can be contacted for international adoption.
국제 입양을 위해서 사설 기관들에 연락할 수 있다.

24 ① the better world that is within our reach 우리의 능력(도달) 범위 안에 있는 더 나은 세상
② the accumulation of wealth in fewer pockets 소수 주머니 속의 부 축적
③ an effective response to climate change 기후 변화에 대한 효과적인 반응
④ a burning desire for a more viable future 더욱 가능성 있는 미래를 위한 불타는 욕구

25 ① children's identification with teachers at school
학교에서 아이들의 교사와의 동일성

② low intelligence of primary school children
초등학교 아이들의 낮은 지능

③ influence of poor working memory on primary school children
초등학생들에게 미치는 부진한 작동 기억의 영향

④ teachers' efforts to solve children's working-memory problem
아이들의 작동 기억 문제를 해결하기 위한 교사들의 노력들

26 ① The Brookfield Zoo ran a program that supports free admission for low-income families.
브룩필드 동물원은 저소득 가정에게 무료 입장을 후원하는 프로그램을 운영했다.

② The Brookfield Zoo assisted African-American kids in tracing their family history.
브룩필드 동물원은 아프리카계 미국인 아이들이 가족사를 추적하는 데 도움을 주었다.

③ The Newberry Library and the Brookfield Zoo won a $10,000 award respectively.
뉴버리 도서관과 브룩필드 동물원은 각각 10,000달러의 상금을 받았다.

④ The Newberry Library was awarded the medal for an extensive number of maps.
　뉴버리 도서관은 방대한 수의 지도에 대해 상을 받았다.

27　① Science is very helpful in modern society.
　　　현대 사회에서 과학은 매우 도움이 된다.
　　② Science and technology are developing quickly.
　　　과학과 기술이 빠르게 발전하고 있다.
　　③ The absolute belief in science is weakening.
　　　과학에 대한 절대적인 믿음이 약해지고 있다.
　　④ Scientific research is getting more funds from private sectors.
　　　과학적 연구는 민간 부문으로부터 더 많은 자금을 얻고 있다.

28　① Movie and concert schedules will be notified twice a month.
　　　영화와 콘서트 일정이 한 달에 두 번 공지될 것이다.
　　② During the weekdays, the cafeteria and the library will open at noon.
　　　주중에, 구내식당과 도서관은 정오에 문을 열 것이다.
　　③ Campus buses will run every hour and make all of the regular stops.
　　　교내 버스들은 1시간마다 운행될 것이고, 모든 정규 정류장에 정차할 것이다.
　　④ A valid identification card is required to use the athletic and entertainment facilities during the summer session.
　　　여름학기 중에 운동 및 오락 시설을 이용하는 데에 유효한 신분증이 필요하다.

29　① In the nineteenth century, opening windows was irrelevant to the density of miasma.
　　　19세기에, 창문을 여는 것은 나쁜 공기의 농도와는 무관했다.
　　② In the nineteenth century, it was believed that gentlemen did not live in places with bad air. 19세기에, 귀족들은 나쁜 공기가 있는 곳에서 살지 않는다고 믿어졌다.
　　③ Vaccines were invented after people realized that microbes and bacteria were the real cause of diseases. 미생물과 박테리아가 질병의 진짜 원인임을 사람들이 깨달은 후 백신들이 발명되었다.
　　④ Cleaning cuts and scrapes could help people to stay healthy.
　　　찰과상을 소독하는 것은 사람들이 건강을 유지하는 것을 도울 수 있다.

30　① People tend to explain behavior in terms of individual personality.
　　　사람들은 개인의 개성이라는 관점에서 행동을 설명하려는 경향이 있다.
　　② Individual behaviors in a given situation are determined by the objective conditions.
　　　특정한 상황에서 개인의 행동들은 객관적 조건에 의해서 결정된다.
　　③ The social environment shapes the thoughts, feelings, and behaviors of the individual.
　　　사회적 환경이 개인의 생각, 느낌, 행동들을 결정한다.
　　④ People often distort reality in order to view themselves favorably.
　　　사람들은 자주 자신을 긍정적으로 평가하기 위해서 현실을 왜곡한다.

Unit 02 PARAPHRASE

Case Study 1　　　　　　　　　　　　　　　　　　　　　　　　정답 (D)

He **couldn't care less** that his neighbors were **moving**.
그는 자신의 이웃들이 이사 가는 것에 대해서 전혀 신경쓰지 않는다.

(A) He was very disappointed that his neighbors were **going away**.
　　그는 이웃들이 떠나는 것에 대해 매우 실망했다.

(B) He had mixed feelings about his neighbors' **leaving**.
　　그는 이웃들이 떠나는 것에 대해 복합적인 감정을 가지고 있었다.

(C) He secretly wished that his neighbors would stay.
　　그는 마음속으로 이웃들이 머물기를 원했다.

(D) He was **indifferent** to his neighbors' **moving**.
　　그는 이웃들이 이주하는 것에 관심이 없었다.

Rudy's Tip 제시문의 'not care less'와 'moving'과 동일한 표현이 있는 문항이 정답이다. 또한 A와 C는 이웃들이 그대로 있어주기를 바라는 점에서 동일한 내용으로 볼 수 있기에, 정답이 될 가능성이 매우 적다는 것을 유추할 수 있다.

Case Study 2　　　　　　　　　　　　　　　　　　　　　　　　정답 (D)

We have to deal **not so much** with actual facts **as** with **various questions concerning the origins**.
우리는 실제 사실보다는 그 기원과 관련한 다양한 질문들을 다루어야 한다.

(A) We have to deal with more **questions about actual facts** than about the origins.
　　우리는 기원보다 실제 문제들에 대한 질문들을 좀 더 다루어야만 한다.

(B) **Actual facts are more urgent issues** to be addressed than questions concerning the origins.
　　실제 문제들이 기원에 관련된 질문들보다 다루어야 할 더 긴급한 문제들이다.

(C) We are **as much** concerned with actual facts **as** with diverse issues surrounding the origins.
　　우리는 기원에 관련된 다양한 문제들만큼이나 실제 사실에 관해서 관심이 있다.

(D) Our discussion should be more focused on questions about the origins than on actual facts.
우리 논의는 실제 사실들보다 기원에 관련된 문제들에 좀 더 집중되어야 한다.

Rudy's Tip 'not so much A as B'는 B에 강조가 있기에, origins를 강조하는 내용이 제일 적절하다.

Case Study 3
정답 (A)

The enduring values of freedom of thought outweigh any particular advantages that demand its violation.
사상의 자유가 지니는 지속적인 가치는 사상의 자유를 침해(무시)하는 것을 요구하는 어떤 이점들보다도 크다.

(A) The long-held merits of freedom of thought are greater than benefits gained from restricting it.
사상의 자유의 장기적인 이점들은 사상의 자유를 제한한대서 생기는 이점들보다 더 크다.

(B) Freedom of thought endured long persecution and it gives advantages even when it is partially violated.
사상의 자유는 오랜 박해를 견디었다. 그래서 부분적으로 침해받을 때에도 그것은 이점들을 준다.

(C) Advantages coming from the breach of freedom of thought are often greater than those from upholding it.
사상의 자유를 침범(무시)하는데서 오는 이점들은 그것을 지키는 데서 오는 이점들보다 흔히 더 크다.

(D) The values of freedom of thought are so great that its violation must be tolerated only when warranted.
사상의 자유의 가치들은 너무 위대하다. 그래서 정당한 경우에만 그것의 침해는 수용되어야만 한다.

Rudy's Tip 제시문은 outweigh을 통해서 사상의 자유를 강조한다. 따라서 사상의 자유를 강조하는 문항이 제일 적절하다.

Case Study 4

정답 (B)

Most people consider it discourteous to arrive at an appointment later than the time agreed upon. 대부분 사람은 약속 시각보다 늦게 도착하는 것을 예의에 어긋난다고 생각한다.

(A) As a general rule, one needs to obtain advance permission to arrive late.
일반적으로, 우리는 늦는 것에 대해 미리 양해를 얻을 필요가 있다.

(B) Being tardy for an appointment is generally regarded as unmannerly.
약속에 늦는 것은 일반적으로 비매너적인 것으로 받아들여진다.

(C) Arriving after the prearranged time is not considered rude.
정해진 시간 이후에 도착하는 것은 예의가 없는 것은 아니다.

(D) Most people do not take timely arrival for an appointment too seriously.
대부분 사람은 약속시간에 맞게 도착하는 것을 크게 중요한 것으로 여기지는 않는다.

Rudy's Tip 가진목적어 구문으로 discourteous = appointment later 동일한 의미를 선별한다.

Case Study 5

정답 (D)

It was the man's flamboyant self-indulgence that allowed himself to become an election issue at the expense of his own achievements.
자신의 업적들을 희생하면서 선거 이슈가 되게 한 것은 바로 그 남자의 눈에 띄는 자기방종(오만함)이었다.

(A) The man attempted to mask his personal behavior in the election through emphasizing his achievements.
선거에서 자신의 업적들을 부각해서 그는 개인적인 행동을 숨기려고 시도했다.

(B) The man's self-centeredness caused attention to be focused on his achievements and not on himself.
자기 중심성(이기심)이 사람들이 그가 아니라 그의 업적들에 집중하게 만들었다.

(C) In the election, the man's achievements received less attention than his character because he was generous.
성격이 관대했기 때문에 선거에서 그 남자의 업적들이 성격보다 더 적은 관심을 받았다.

(D) Because of the man's conceitedness, he himself became an election issue rather than his achievements.
그 남자의 자만심 때문에 그의 업적들 보다 자신이 선거의 이슈가 되었다.

Rudy's Tip it ~ that 강조용법으로 자만함을 강조하는 내용이다. 따라서 보기에서도 자만함을 강조하는 문항이 적절하다.

Case Study 6

정답 (B)

If your teammates had shown the same level of devotion and diligence as you have shown, the project could not have been concluded so satisfactorily.

만일 당신의 팀 동료들이 당신이 보여준 것과 같은 수준의 헌신과 근면을 보여주었다면 프로젝트가 그렇게 만족스럽게 끝나지 않았을 수도 있다.

(A) Your teammates should have followed your example in completing the project successfully.
  당신의 팀 동료들은 프로젝트를 성공적으로 완성하는 데 있어서 당신의 본보기를 따랐어야 했다.

(B) The team project was successful despite your lack of effort and care.
  팀 프로젝트는 당신의 노력과 관심이 부족했음에도 불구하고 성공적이었다.

(C) Despite your diligence and devotion, the project could not be completed satisfactorily.
  당신의 근면과 헌신에도 불구하고 프로젝트는 만족스럽게 끝나지 않을 수도 있었다.

(D) Without your input, the team could not have successfully completed the project.
  당신의 조언이 없이, 팀은 프로젝트를 성공적으로 마무리할 수 없었을 것이다.

Rudy's Tip 가정법은 사실과 반대로 표현하는 것으로, 제시문의 의도는 상대가 성실하지 못했다는 것을 비판하는 내용이다. 따라서 상대가 노력하지 않았다는 내용이 가장 적절하다.

Unit 03 TOPIC

Case Study 1
정답 (D)

Some people become blind because a part of the eye called the cornea doesn't let in enough light. The cornea becomes clouded over. These people can be made to see again, however, if they are able to get clear corneas to let in the light. The blind must get the corneas from people with healthy eyes — people who agree to let blind people use their eyes after they die.

어떤 이들은 각막이라고 불리는 눈의 일부분이 충분한 빛을 들여보내지 못하기 때문에 앞을 못 보게 된다. 즉, 각막이 온통 흐려지게 된다. 그러나 이들은 만일 빛을 들여보낼 수 있는 깨끗한 각막을 얻을 수 있게 된다면 다시 앞을 보게 될 수 있다. 앞을 못 보는 사람들은 이들에게 사망 후에 자신의 눈을 사용하게 하는 데에 동의한 건강한 눈을 가진 사람들로부터 각막을 기증받아야 한다.

(A) Why corneas get clouded over. 각막이 흐릿해지는 이유
(B) Why healthy eyes need more light. 건강한 눈이 더 많은 빛이 필요한 이유
(C) How people can see better. 사람들이 더 잘 볼 수 있는 방법
(D) How clear corneas can help the blind. 깨끗한 각막이 보이지 않는 사람들에게 도움이 되는 방법

Rudy's Tip 반복적인 cornea에 주목하자. ST 구성으로 각막의 역할을 서술하고 있다. 지문에서 반복적으로 등장하는 표현(단어)들은 keyword가 될 가능성이 매우 높기에, 언제나 문항에서 해당 keyword가 있는 문항을 중심으로 정답을 선별해 보자.

Case Study 2
정답 (D)

There are those who say: "War is part of human nature, and human nature cannot be changed. If war means the end of man, we must sigh and submit." But they forget that what is called "human nature" is, in the main, the result of custom and tradition and education, and in civilized men, only a very tiny fraction is due to primitive instinct. If the world could live for a few generations without war, war would come to seem as absurd as dueling has come to seem to us.

"전쟁은 인간 본성의 일부이며, 인간 본성이란 바뀔 수 없는 것이다. 만일 전쟁이 인간의 종말을 뜻한다면, 우리는 한숨 쉬며 그에 굴복해야 한다."라고 말하는 이들이 있다. 그러나 그들은 소위 "인간 본성"이 주로 관습, 전통, 교육의 소산물이며, 문명인에게 있어 원시적 본능에 기인하는 것은 아주 적은 부분에 불과하다는 사실을 망각하고 있다. 만약 이 세상이 전쟁 없이 몇 세대를 살아갈 수 있다면, 두 사람 간의 결투가 우리에게 어리석게 여겨지게 된 것만큼이나 전쟁 또한 불합리한 것으로 여겨지게 될 것이다.

(A) War means the end of man. 전쟁은 인류의 종말을 의미한다.
(B) Man is selfish by nature. 인간은 본질적으로 이기적이다.
(C) War is part of human nature. 전쟁은 인간 본능의 일부이다.
(D) Man can avoid war. 인간은 전쟁을 피할 수 있다.

Rudy's Tip MT 구성으로 전쟁이 인간의 본성이라는 것을 반박하는 구조이다. 문항분석에서 C와 D가 대립되는 문항이다. 이처럼 대립되는 문항이 등장하는 경우에는, 양자 사이에 하나가 정답이 될 가능성이 크다.

Case Study 3 　　　　　　　　　　　　　　　　　　　　　정답 (C)

There is an enormous difference in the ways various public officials respond to public pressures, and in the means and methods they employ to deal with them. The best possess understanding of the forces that must be taken into account, determination not to be swerved from the path of public interest, a willingness to make enemies along with a gift for avoiding them, and faith that public support will be forthcoming for the correct course. The poorest are over-hesitant, evasive and preoccupied with their relationships with their colleagues, superiors, the press or the political support on which they lean. They will make no move unless the gallery is packed. They confront all embarrassment with a stale general formula.

여러 공무원들이 대중으로부터 받게 되는 압력에 반응하는 방식과 그 압력을 처리하기 위해 채택하는 수단과 방법 사이에는 엄청난 차이가 있다. 최고의 공무원들은 고려되어야 할 압력에 대한 이해, 대중의 관심의 경로에서 벗어나지 않는 결단력, 적을 피하는 재능과 함께 적을 만들 수도 있는 의지, 그리고 올바른 길을 개척하면 대중의 지지가 있으리라는 신념을 가지고 있다. 가장 형편없는 공무원들은 우유부단하고 회피적이며, 자신의 동료, 상관, 언론과의 관계 또는 그들이 의존하고 있는 정치적 지지에 몰두하고 있다. 만약 관객이 꽉 차지 않는다면(감시하는 사람이 많지 않으면), 그들은 어떠한 행동도 하지 않는다. 그들은 난처한 일에 봉착하면 진부한 보편적 방식으로 대응한다.

(A) Political Pressure Groups 정치 압력 단체들
(B) Mistakes for Public Officials to Avoid 공무원들이 회피하는 위험들
(C) Characteristics of Public Officials 공무원들의 유형들(특징들)
(D) Gaining Political Support 대중의 지지를 얻는 것

Rudy's Tip G진술로 시작한 첫 문장에 'enormous difference'를 통해서 대조구조임을 알 수 있다. 첫 문항부터 본문 전체에 걸쳐 'public official'에 관련한 내용임을 알 수 있다. 따라서 B와 C로 선지를 좁힌 상태에서 키워드 분석을 통해서 정답을 선별할 수 있다.

Case Study 4

정답 (B)

All living languages are characterized by sound changes that have occurred and will continue to occur in the course of their history. Some linguists choose to consider the sound change as something that operates with the regularity of physical laws. "Sound law" is a term devised by linguist August Leskien to describe the supposed absolute regularity of this kind of structural change in language. The term "Sound law" means that, in a given area and at a given period of a sound change, the change will be universal and will gave no exceptions. This rule loses some of its inflexibility by amendments to the effect that, if apparent exceptions are found, they are due to some extraneous factor, such as foreign or dialectal borrowing.

모든 살아있는 언어는 자신의 역사 속에서 발생해 왔고, 앞으로 지속적으로 발생할 음운 변화로 특징지어진다. 어떤 언어학자들은 음운 변화를 물리적 법칙의 규칙성을 가지고 작용하는 그 무엇으로 여기기로 정했다. "음운 규칙"은 언어에 있어 이러한 종류의 구조적 변화의 가설적인 절대 규칙성을 설명하기 위해 언어학자인 어거스트 레스킨이 만든 용어. "음운 규칙"이라는 용어가 의미하는 것은 주어진 지역에서, 주어진 기간에 만약 어떤 소리가 변화하면, 그 변화는 일반적이며 예외가 없다는 것이다. 이러한 규칙은 만약 분명한 예외가 발견된다면 불가변적 특성의 일정 부분을 상실하게 된다. 만약 예외가 발견된다면, 외국어 또는 방언의 차용 같은.

(A) The history of languages 언어들의 역사
(B) A theory of sound change 음운변화 이론
(C) Some exceptions to the rule of sound change 음운변화 규칙의 몇몇 예외들
(D) Some reasons for sound change 음운변화가 생기는 이유들

Rudy's Tip ST 방식으로 모든 언어들은 음운변화를 통해 규정된다는 서론에 이어서 sound change에 대한 정의와 예외들을 설명하고 있다. 이런 본문의 내용을 포괄할 수 있는 표현은 'theory'가 가장 적절하다.

Case Study 5

정답 (C)

An essay which appeals chiefly to the intellect is France Bacon's 'Of Studies.' His careful tripartite division of studies expressed succinctly in aphoristic prose demands the complete attention of the mind of the reader. He considers studies as they should be: for pleasure, for self-improvement, for business. He considers the evils of excess study; laziness, affectation, and precocity. Bacon divides books into three categories; those to be read in part, those to be read cursorily, and those to be read with care. Studies should include reading, which gives depth; and writing, which trains in preciseness. The author ascribes certain virtues to individual fields of study: wisdom to history, wit to poetry, subtlety to mathematics, and depth to natural philosophy. Bacon's four-hundred-word essay, studded with Latin phrases and highly compressed in thought, has intellectual appeal indeed.

프란시스 베이컨의 '연구에 대하여'는 주로 지성인에게 호소하는 수필이다. 금언적 산문체로 간결하게 표현된 철저한 그의 연구 3부작은 이성을 완전히 집중시킬 것을 독자에게 요구한다. 그는 연구를 기쁨을 위해, 자기 향상을 위해, 그리고 일을 위해 마땅히 있어야 할 것으로 생각한다. 그는 과잉연구의 병폐, 가령 게으름, 허식, 그리고 조숙을 염두에 두고 있다. 베이컨은 책을 세 개의 범주, 즉 부분적으로 읽어야 할 책, 대강 읽어야 할 책, 주의해서 읽어야 할 책으로 구분한다. 연구에는 깊이를 주는 읽기, 정확성을 키워주는 쓰기가 포함되어야 한다. 저자는 특정 가치를 개인의 연구 분야라고 생각하는데, 가령 지혜를 역사에게, 기지를 시에게, 예민함을 수학에게, 그리고 깊이를 자연 철학에게로 돌리고 있다. 라틴 문구와 고도로 압축된 사고로 채워진 베이컨의 4백 단어로 된 에세이는 참으로 지적 호소력을 갖고 있다.

(A) Francis Bacon 프란시스 베이컨
(B) 'Of Studies': A Tripartite Division 학문에 대하여: 3단 구성
(C) An Intellectual Exercise: Francis Bacon's 'Of Studies' 지적 훈련 : 프란시스 베이컨의 '학문에 대하여'
(D) The Categorization of Books According to Bacon 베이컨에 따른 책들의 분류

Rudy's Tip GS 구성의 영문으로 첫 문장과 마지막 문장이 동일하다. 본문은 책의 구성과 내용에 대한 설명으로 다소 난이도 높은 구문으로 이루어져 있다. 본문의 전반적인 내용을 이해하려고 하기보다, 본문의 모든 내용은 책의 지적인 측면을 부각시키기 위한 의도라는 것을 파악하자. 그러면 쉽게 정답을 선별할 수 있다.

Case Study 6

정답 (C)

Many of the scientific achievements that we take for granted today have reached far beyond the dreams of scientists and science fiction writers of just seventy-five years ago. One of the most spectacular of these scientific accomplishments was the splitting of the atom. Life has never been the same since that event. From microwave ovens to electrical power and nuclear medicine, to ships that can sail the seas for as long as twelve years without refueling, the atom provides a better life for many of the inhabitants of the earth. Yet, this same power that is used today to detect genetic disorders in unborn children or to destroy a malignant cancer cell was the destructive, for that killed over one hundred thousand people in Hiroshima and Nagasaki at the end of World War II. The splitting of the atom, the unleashing of its terrific power, poses the greatest single threat known to humanity. We now have the power to destroy in a matter of minutes a civilization that has taken centuries to develop. Never before has the power for such potential good or such total destruction existed.

오늘날 우리가 당연하게 여기는 많은 과학적인 성과들은 75년 전 과학자들과 공상과학 소설가들의 상상을 넘어서는 수준에 도달해 있다. 이러한 대단한 과학적 성과들 중의 한 가지는 원자 분열이었다. 그 사건 (원자분열) 이후 인류의 삶은 결코 그 전과 같지 않았다. 전자레인지에서부터 전력과 핵의학에 이르기까지, 그리고 12년 동안 연료의 재공급 없이 바다를 항해할 수 있는 선박에 이르기까지 원자는 지구상의 많은 사람들에게 더 나은 삶을 제공하고 있다. 그러나 태어나지 않은 아기의 유전병을 감지해내거나 악성 암세포를 파괴시키기 위해 사용되는 이 동일한 힘(원자력)은 제2차 세계대전이 끝날 무렵 히로시마와 나가사키에서 10만 명 이상의 사람들을 죽게 한 파괴적인 힘이었다. 엄청난 힘을 방출하는 원자의 분열은 인류에게 알려져 있는 가장 크고 유일한 위협이 되고 있다. 우리는 이제 수세기에 걸쳐 발전되어 온 문명을 몇 분 만에 파괴시킬 힘을 갖고 있다. 이전에는 그러한 잠재적인 이로움이나 완전한 파괴력이 존재했던 적이 결코 없었다.

(A) examples of scientific achievements 과학 업적들의 예시들
(B) examples of destructive power 파괴적인 힘(권력)의 예시들
(C) powers resulting from splitting of the atom 원자 분열에서 등장하는 힘(에너지)
(D) potentially good and destructive powers 잠재적으로 좋고 파괴적인 힘

Rudy's Tip GS 구성으로 'one of the 최상급'은 주제가 빈출하는 문장 형식이다. 과학에서 가장 눈에 띄는 발전 중 하나로 '원자 분열'을 제시하고, 이것에 대한 긍정적, 부정적 예시들을 열거하고 있다.

Unit 04 내용일치

Case Study 1 정답 (D)

The self-serving bias is the tendency for us to attribute positive events to ourselves and negative ones to external factors. For example, a star athlete interviewed after winning a big game attributes his success to his hard work. The same athlete interviewed a few weeks later after losing a game explains, "Today just wasn't my day." Psychologists say it is human nature to think this way in order to protect our self-esteem and reputation. The advantages of the self-serving bias are: it prevents us from getting depressed in the face of failure, and it allows us to remain confident about the future. However, blaming negative outcomes on external sources robs us of opportunities to learn from our mistakes and become better people. If we continue to avoid looking honestly at how we contributed to a negative outcome, we will remain stagnant.

확증 편향은 긍정적인 사건은 자신 때문으로, 부정적인 사건은 외부적인 요인이라고 생각하는 경향이다. 예를 들면, 큰 경기에서 승리한 후에 인터뷰를 한 유명 운동선수는 그의 성공을 자신이 열심히 훈련한 결과라고 생각한다. 몇 주 후에 경기에서 지고 나서 한 인터뷰에서 그 운동선수는 "오늘은 운이 없네요."라고 이유를 댄다. 심리학자들은 자존심과 평판을 지키기 위해서 이런 방식으로 생각하는 것이 인간의 본성이라고 말한다. 확증 편향 이점은 우리가 실패에 직면했을 때 우울해지지 않도록 해주며 우리가 미래에 대해 자신감을 유지하게 해준다. 그러나 부정적인 결과를 외부적인 요인 탓으로 돌리는 것은 실수로부터 배워 더 나은 사람이 될 수 있는 기회를 우리에게서 앗아간다. 만약 우리가 어떻게 해서 부정적인 결과를 초래했는지 솔직히 살펴보는 것을 계속해서 회피한다면, 우리는 정체된 채로 있을 것이다.

According to the passage, what do we usually do after experiencing a negative event?
글에 따르면, 우리는 부정적인 사건을 경험한 후에 무엇을 하는가?

(A) Think of ourselves as responsible 우리 자신에게 책임이 있다고 생각한다.
(B) Listen to critique from other people 타인의 비평에 귀 기울이다.
(C) Try to learn from our mistakes 실수들로부터 배우려고 노력한다.
(D) Blame things other than ourselves 자신이 아니라 다른 것을 탓한다.

Rudy's Tip 문제의 '부정적인 사건'을 키워드로 본문에서 동일한 표현을 찾아본다. 첫 문장의 external factors와 중반부의 external sources를 통해 정답을 선별할 수 있다.

Case Study 2

정답 (B)

How on earth will it help the poor if governments try to strangle globalization by stemming the flow of trade, information, and capital — the three components of the global economy? That disparities between rich and poor are still too great is undeniable. But it is just not true that economic growth benefits only the rich and leaves out the poor, as the opponents of globalization and the market economy would have us believe. A recent World Bank study entitled "Growth Is Good for the Poor" reveals a one-for-one relationship between income of the bottom fifth of the population and per capita GDP. In other words, incomes of all sectors grow proportionately at the same rate. The study notes that openness to foreign trade benefits the poor to the same extent that it benefits the whole economy.

정부가 세계 경제의 세 가지 요소인 무역, 정보 및 자본의 흐름을 막음으로써 세계화를 묵살하려 한다면 도대체 어떻게 가난한 자들을 도울 것인가? 부자와 가난한 사람 사이의 격차가 여전히 아주 크다는 것은 부인 할 수 없는 일이다. 그러나 경제 성장이 부유층에게만 이익을 주고 가난한 사람들은 배제하는 것은 사실이 아니다. 왜냐하면 세계화와 시장 경제에 반대하는 사람들이 우리를 (그렇게) 믿게 만들기 때문이다. 최근 세계은행의 "성장은 가난한 사람들에게 좋다"라는 제목의 연구는 인구의 하위 5%의 소득 과 1인당 GDP 간의 일대일 관계를 보여준다. 즉, 모든 부문의 소득은 동일한 비율로 비례하여 증가한다. 이 연구는 대외 교역에 대한 개방성이 전체 경제 에 혜택을 주는 것과 같은 정도로 빈곤층에게 혜택을 준다고 지적한다.

(A) Governments must control the flow of trade to revive the economy. (−)
    정부는 경제를 회복시키기 위해 무역의 흐름을 통제해야 한다.

(B) Globalization can be beneficial regardless of one's economic status. (+)
    세계화는 경제적 지위와 관계없이 유익할 수 있다.

(C) The global economy grows at the expense of the poor. (−)
    세계 경제는 빈곤층을 희생시켜 성장한다.

(D) Globalization deepens conflicts between rich and poor. (−)
    세계화는 부자와 가난한 자의 충돌을 심화시킨다.

Rudy's Tip 세계화에 대한 태도를 중심으로 문항들을 2분법으로 나눌 수 있다. 긍정 (B) − 부정 (A), (C), (D). 따라서 긍정 문항이 단일문항 (B)뿐이기 때문에 정답을 선별하는데 있어서 매우 유익한 구분법이 된다. 언제나 보기 문항들이 긍부정/장단점... 등의 이분법으로 분류될 수 있는지 유의하자.

Case Study 3

정답 (D)

Electric cars were always environmentally friendly, quiet, clean – but definitely not sexy. The Speedking has changed all that. A battery-powered sports car that sells for $120,000 and has a top speed of 125m.p.h., the Speedking has excited the clean-tech crowd since it was first announced. Some Hollywood celebrities also joined a long waiting list for the Speedking; magazines like Wired drooled over it. After years of setbacks and shake-ups, the first Speedkings were delivered to customers this year. Reviews have been ecstatic, but Sesta Motors has been hit hard by the financial crisis. Plans to develop an affordable electric sedan have been put on hold, and Sesta is laying off employees. But even if the Speedking turns out to be a one-hit wonder, it's been an exciting electric ride.

전기차들은 항상 환경친화적이고 조용하며 쾌적하지만 확실히 섹시하진 않다. Speedking은 이 모든 것을 바꾸어 놓았다. 120,000달러에 팔리고 시속 125마일(시속 200km)의 최고 속력을 내며 배터리로 동력을 내는 스포츠카인 Speedking은 처음 발표되었을 때부터 친환경 기술을 선호하는 사람들을 흥분시켰다. 또한 일부 할리우드 연예인들도 Speedking의 긴 대기 줄에 동참했다. Wired와 같은 잡지사들도 침을 흘렸다(극찬하다). 수년간의 실패와 대개편 후에 올해 첫 Speedking이 고객들에게 배송되었다. 후기들은 열광적이었다. 그러나 Sesta Motors는 재정적 위기로 심한 타격을 받았다. 저렴한 전기 세단을 만들려는 계획들은 중지되었고 Sesta는 직원들을 일시 해고했다. 비록 Speedking이 반짝하고 사라지는 제품이 되었지만 그것은 감동적인 전기차였다.

(A) Speedking is a new electric sedan. Speedking은 새로운 세단형 전기 자동차이다.
　　함정 포인트 sedan이 아니라 sports car이다.
(B) Speedking has received negative feedback. Speedking은 부정적인 반응을 얻었다.
(C) Sesta is hiring more employees. Sesta는 직원을 더 채용하고 있다.
(D) Sesta has suspended a new car project. Sesta는 신차 프로젝트를 중지시켰다.

Rudy's Tip 보기문항을 speedking과 sesta를 중심으로 나누고, 본문에서 해당 표현이 등장하는 문장을 스키밍해서 해결하자.

Case Study 4   정답 (D)

Langston Hughes was born in Joplin, Missouri, and graduated from Lincoln University, in which many African-American students have pursued their academic disciplines. At the age of eighteen, Hughes published one of his most well-known poems, "Negro Speaks of Rivers." Creative and experimental, Hughes incorporated authentic dialect in his work, adapted traditional poetic forms to embrace the cadences and moods of blues and jazz, and created characters and themes that reflected elements of lower-class black culture. With his ability to fuse serious content with humorous style, Hughes attacked racial prejudice in a way that was natural and witty.

Langston Hughes는 미주리 주 Joplin에서 태어나 많은 아프리카계 미국 학생들이 학업을 추구한 Lincoln 대학교를 졸업했다. Hughes는 열여덟 살 때 가장 잘 알려진 시 중 하나인 "Negro Speaks of Rivers"를 출간했다. 창의적이고 실험적인 Hughes는 작품에 진정한 사투리를 접목시켰고, 블루스와 재즈의 억양과 분위기를 수용하기 위해 전통적인 시적 형식을 조정했으며, 하류 흑인 문화의 요소를 반영하는 인물과 주제를 창조했다. 진지한 내용과 재미있는 문체를 결합시키는 능력으로, Hughes는 자연스럽고 재치 있는 방법으로 인종적 편견을 공격했다.

(A) Hughes는 많은 미국 흑인들이 다녔던 대학교를 졸업하였다.
(B) Hughes는 실제 사투리를 그의 작품에 반영하였다.
(C) Hughes는 하층 계급 흑인들의 문화적 요소를 반영한 인물을 만들었다.
(D) Hughes는 인종편견을 엄숙한 문체로 공격하였다.

함정 포인트 humorous를 통해서 틀린 문항이라는 것을 알 수 있다.

Rudy's Tip 문항이 한글인 경우에는 상대적인 난이도가 매우 낮은 문제이다. 본문을 빠르게 스캔하면서 반복적인 표현과 키워드 등을 통해서 본문의 내용을 미리 예측하고 스키밍하자.

Case Study 5   정답 (D)

In the U.S., 80% of people ages 65 and older are now living in metropolitan areas, and according to the World Health Organization, by 2030, an estimated 60% of all people will live in cities — many of them over age 60. Cities increasingly rank high on both doctors' and seniors' lists of the best places to age gracefully.

Every year, the Milken Institute Center for the Future of Aging (CFA) ranks the best metropolitan places for successful aging, and most years, major cities sweep the top 10 spots. No wonder: cities tend to have strong health systems, opportunities for continued learning, widespread public transportation, and an abundance of arts and culture. That's not to say that people can't feel isolated or lonely in cities, but you can get lonely in a country cottage too. In cities, the cure can be just outside your door.

"We all long to bump into each other," says Paul Irving, the chairman of the Milken Institute

CFA. "The ranges of places where this can happen in cities tend to create more options and opportunities." They tend to be alone especially as we age and families disperse. But there are answers: a 2017 study in the journal Personal Relationships found that it can be friends, not family, who matter most. The study looked at 270,000 people in nearly 100 countries and found that while both family and friends are associated with happiness and better health, as people aged, the health link remained only for people with strong friendship.

"While in a lot of ways, relationships with friends had a similar effect as those with family," says William Chopik, assistant professor of psychology at Michigan State University and the author of the study, "in others, they surpassed them."

현재 미국에서는 65세 이상의 사람들 중 80%가 대도시 지역에 살고 있는데, 세계보건기구(WHO)에 따르면, 2030년까지 모든 사람들의 약 60%가 도시에서 살 것이며 이들 중 대다수의 나이는 60세가 넘을 것이라고 한다. 의사와 연장자 모두가 선정한 우아하게 늙기에 가장 좋은 장소 목록에서 도시는 점점 더 상위에 오르고 있다.

밀큰 고령화 미래 연구소(CFA)는 성공적인 노후를 위한 최고의 대도시 지역의 순위를 매년 평가하는데, 대부분의 연도에 주요 도시들이 상위 10위권을 휩쓴다. 그것은 놀랄 일이 아니다. 도시들은 강력한 의료체계, 지속적인 학습 기회, 광범위한 대중교통, 〈심각한 범죄와 공해〉, 그리고 풍부한 예술과 문화를 갖고 있는 경향이 있기 때문이다. 그렇다고 도시의 사람들이 소외감 또는 외로움을 느끼지 않는다는 말은 아니지만, 당신은 시골의 오두막에서도 외로움을 느낄 수 있다. 도시에서는, 당신이 문만 열면 바로 앞에 치유책이 있을 수 있다.

"우리는 모두 서로 우연히 마주치기를 갈망합니다. 도시에서는 이러한 일이 일어날 수 있는 장소의 범위가 넓기 때문에 더 많은 선택권과 기회를 만들어 내는 경향이 있습니다."라고 밀큰 고령화 미래 연구소(CFA)의 회장인 폴 어빙(Paul Irving)은 말한다. 특히 우리가 늙고 가족이 뿔뿔이 흩어지게 되면서 사람들은 외로워집니다. 그러나 이에 대한 해답이 있는데, 『인간관계(Personal Relationships)』라는 저널에서 발표된 2017년의 한 연구는 가장 중요한 것은 가족이 아니라 친구일 수 있다는 것을 밝혔다. 그 연구는 약 100개의 국가에서 27만 명을 살펴보았는데, 가족과 친구 모두 행복과 더 나은 건강과 연관되어 있지만, 사람들이 늙으면서 건강과의 연관성이 우정이 두터운 사람들에게만 여전히 있다는 것을 알게 되었다.

"많은 면에서 친구들과의 관계는 가족들과의 관계와 비슷한 효과를 가졌지만, 어떤 사람들의 경우, 친구들과의 관계는 가족들과의 관계를 능가했습니다."라고 미시간 주립대학교의 심리학과 조교수이자 이 연구의 저자인 윌리엄 초피(William Chopik)은 말한다.

(A) Four fifths of Americans at 65 and over are now living in metropolitan areas.
65세 이상의 미국인들 중 5분의 4는 현재 대도시에 살고 있다.

(B) Cities are increasingly favored by doctors as the best places to live gracefully in old age.
도시들은 노령에 우아하게 살기에 가장 좋은 장소로서 의사로부터 점점 더 많은 사랑을 받고 있다.

(C) The finding of the 2017 study in Personal Relationships was based on the subjects from around 100 countries.
대인관계에 대한 2017년 연구는 100개국의 참가자들을 토대로 하고 있다.

(D) Paul Irving is the author of the 2017 study published in Personal Relationships.
폴 어빙은 2017 『인간관계』에 발표된 연구의 저자이다.
함정 포인트 폴 어빙은 CFA 회장이고, 2017 연구는 인간관계라는 저널에 등재된 기사이다.

Rudy's Tip 문항에 명확한 S포인트가 등장하는 경우에는 해결의 실마리가 한결 수월해진다. 각 문항에서 S포인트를 표시하고, 본문에서 해당 S포인트를 찾아 스키밍하자.

Case Study 6

정답 (D)

When the gong sounds, almost every diner at Beijing restaurant Duck de Chine turns around. That's because one of the city's greatest culinary shows is about to begin — the slicing of a Peking duck. Often voted by local guides in China as the best Peking duck in the city, the skin on Duck de Chine's birds is crispy and caramelized, its meat tender and juicy. "Our roasted duck is a little different than elsewhere," says An Ding, manager of Duck de Chine. "We use jujube wood, which is over 60 years old, and has a strong fruit scent, giving the duck especially crispy skin and a delicious flavor." The sweet hoisin sauce, drizzled over sliced spring onions and cucumbers and encased with the duck skin in a thin pancake, is another highlight. "The goal of our service is to focus on the details," says Ding. "It includes both how we present the roasted duck, and the custom sauces made for our guests." Even the plates and the chopsticks holders are duck-shaped. Duck de chine also boasts China's first Bollinger Champagne Bar. Though Peking duck is the star, there are plenty of other worthy dishes on the menu. The restaurant serves both Cantonese and Beijing cuisine with a touch of French influence.

그 종이 울릴 때, 베이징 레스토랑 Duck de Chine의 거의 모든 손님들은 몸을 돌린다. 그 도시의 가장 위대한 요리 쇼인 베이징덕 썰기가 시작되기 때문이다. 종종 중국의 지역 가이드들 사이에서 그 도시의 최고의 베이징덕으로 꼽히는 Duck de Chine의 오리 껍질은 바삭하고 설탕으로 덮이고, 고기는 부드럽고 육즙이 많다. "우리 구운 오리는 다른 곳과는 살짝 달라요." Duck de Chine의 매니저 An Ding은 말한다. "60년 넘는 것으로, 특히 고기에 바삭바삭한 껍질과 맛있는 풍미를 제공하는 강한 과일 향을 풍기는 대추나무를 사용합니다." 얇게 썬 봄양파와 오이 위에 뿌려지고 얇은 팬 케이크 안에 오리 껍질에 싸여있는, 달콤한 해선장 소스는 또 다른 하이라이트이다. "우리 서비스의 목적은 디테일에 집중하는 것입니다."라고 Ding은 말한다. "우리가 구운 오리를 제공하는 방식과 고객을 위한 맞춤 소스 모두를 포함합니다." 심지어 접시와 젓가락 받침까지도 오리 모양이다. Duck de Chine는 또한 중국의 첫 번째 볼랑저 샴페인 바를 자랑한다. 베이징덕이 최고 인기이긴 하지만, 메뉴에는 다른 맛있는 음식들도 많다. 그 레스토랑은 프랑스 풍미가 살짝 가미된 광둥 요리와 베이징 요리를 모두 제공한다.

(A) The restaurant presents a culinary performance.
그 레스토랑은 요리 퍼포먼스를 제공한다.

(B) The restaurant is highly praised in Beijing.
그 레스토랑은 베이징에서 상당히 찬사를 받는다.

(C) The restaurant features a special champagne bar.
그 레스토랑은 특별한 샴페인 바를 특징으로 한다.

(D) The restaurant only serves dishes from the Beijing region.
그 레스토랑은 오로지 베이징 지역의 음식만 제공한다.

> **함정 포인트** 마지막 문장을 통해서 광둥어 음식도 제공된다는 것을 알 수 있다. 언제나 문항에 only가 있다면 함정문항임을 의심하자.

Rudy's Tip 문항에서 S 포인트를 확보하고, 본문을 스키밍할 때, 문항과 관련없는 내용은 빠르게 skip하는 것이 중요하다. 특히 단순 내용일치 문제의 경우에는 문맥적, 내포적 의미를 묻는 경우가 없기에 S 포인트를 중심으로 해당 표현이 등장하는 지점에만 집중하는 것이 요령이다.

Unit 05 빈칸추론

Case Study 1

정답 (B)

Many prophets of information technology (IT) believe that the next big movement in their field will be the "_____." This, they hope, will connect objects hitherto beyond the reach of IT's tendrils so that, for example, your sofa can buzz your phone to tell you that you have left your wallet behind, or your refrigerator can order your groceries without you having to make a shopping list. That, though, will mean putting chips in your sofa, your wallet and your fridge to enable them to talk to the rest of the world.

정보 기술(IT)을 예측하는 많은 사람들은 이 분야에서 다음으로 이어질 큰 진전은 "사물 인터넷"이 될 것이라고 믿는다. 그들은 이것이 지금까지는 IT가 미치는 범위 밖에 있던 사물들을 서로 연결하게 되기를 희망하는데, 예를 들면 당신의 소파가 당신에게 전화를 걸어 지갑을 두고 갔다는 것을 알려줄 수 있다. 또는 당신이 쇼핑 목록을 만들지 않아도 당신의 냉장고가 당신의 식료품을 주문할 수 있다. 그러나 그것은 소파와 지갑과 냉장고에 칩을 넣어 이것들이 세상과 대화할 수 있게 하는 것을 의미할 것이다.

(A) artificial intelligence 인공지능
  함정 포인트 냉장고나 소파가 인간의 편의성을 높여준다는 것으로, 물건과 연결되어 있는 사물인터넷이 더 적절하다.
(B) internet of things 사물인터넷
(C) driverless vehicle 무인자동차
(D) big data 빅데이터

Rudy's Tip 빈칸 뒤의 'This'는 빈칸을 의미한다. 따라서 재진술 구조를 파악하고, 뒤에 등장하는 예시들을 중심으로 정답을 선별할 수 있다.

Case Study 2

정답 (B)

The attitude toward _____ is seen in many aspects of American life. One is invited to dinner at a home that is not only comfortably but even luxuriously furnished. Yet the hostess probably will cook the dinner herself, will serve it herself, and will wash the dishes afterward. Furthermore, the dinner will not consist merely of something quickly and easily assembled from the contents of various cans and a cake or pie bought at the nearby bakery. On the contrary, the hostess usually takes pride in her own careful preparation of special dishes.

육체노동에 대한 태도는 미국 생활의 여러 가지 면에서 볼 수 있다. 쾌적할 뿐만 아니라 호화스럽게 장식된 집에 저녁 식사 초대를 받는다. 그런데도 여주인은 아마도 자신이 직접 저녁 식사를 요리하고 직접 나르며 나중에는 설거지까지 한다. 게다가 저녁 식사는 여러 가지 깡통에 든 내용물이나 근처 빵집에서 사 온 케이크이나 파이 같은 쉽고 빠르게 구할 수 있는 것만으로 만들어지지는 않을 것이다. 그와는 정반대로 여주인은 대개 자신이 특별한 요리를 직접 준비하는 데서 자부심을 느낀다.

(A) family tie 가족관계
(B) manual labor 육체 노동
(C) social activity 사회적 활동
(D) public relations 홍보(선전)

Rudy's Tip 첫 문장에 빈칸이 위치하면 대부분 첫 문장이 주제문인 GS구조이다. 따라서 빈칸뒤에는 재진술, 특히 예시가 등장하는 경우가 빈번하다. 본문의 'herself'를 통해 직접 음식을 하고, 청소를 하고, 대접한다는 내용을 통해 정답을 선별할 수 있다.

Case Study 3

정답 (B)

Researchers placed "lost" applications to graduate school at an airport and studied how frequently people who found the application helped by putting it in the mail. Results showed that people were more likely to send in the application if the person in the photo, whether male or female, was attractive. On overage, 52 percent of the applications of good-looking people were returned, compared to 35 percent of the applications of less attractive people. In this anonymous situation, willingness to help was affected by _____.

연구 조사자들은 잃어버린 (실제로 잃어버린 것은 아니지만 잃어버린 것처럼 보이는)대학원 지원서를 공항에 놓고 그 지원서를 발견한 사람들이 그것을 우편함에 넣음으로써 얼마나 자주 도와주느냐를 조사했다. 사람들은 사진에 들어 있는 사람이 남자이건 여자이건 간에 잘생겼으면 그 지원서를 더 보내 주는 경향이 있다는 결과가 나왔다. 평균적으로 덜 매력적으로 생긴 사람들의 지원서의 35퍼센트가 되돌아온 것에 비해 잘생긴 사람들의 지원서의 52 퍼센트가 되돌아 왔다. 이 익명의 상황에서 남을 기꺼이 도와주느냐는 신체적 외모의 영향을 받았다.

(A) environmental conditions 환경적 조건들
(B) physical appearance 신체적 외모
(C) the number of witnesses 목격자의 수
(D) social responsibility 사회적 책임

Rudy's Tip 빈칸이 마지막에 등장하는 구조는 ST 구조일 가능성이 크다. 이런 ST 구조의 SSG 구조에서는 본문의 SS진술들이 대체로 예시로 등장하기에, 본문의 예시들을 스키밍해서 종합적인 진술을 선별하는 것이 요령이다.

Case Study 4

정답 (C)

"Let's Uber." Few companies offer something so popular that their name becomes a verb. But that is one of the many achievements of Uber, a company founded in 2009 which is now the world's most valuable startup, worth around $70 billion. But Uber's ambitions extend much further: using self-driving vehicles, it wants to make ride-hailing so cheap and convenient that people forgo car ownership altogether. Not satisfied with shaking up the $100-billion-a-year taxi business, it has its eye on the far bigger market for personal transport, worth as much as $10 trillion a year globally. _____. Companies big and small have recognized the transformative potential of electric, self-driving cars, summoned on demand. Technology firms including Apple, Google and Tesla are investing heavily in autonomous vehicles.

"우버(Uber) 택시를 이용하자" 회사 이름이 동사가 될 정도로 인기가 많은 것을 제공하는 회사는 거의 없다. 그러나 이는 2009년 설립되어 현재 세계에서 가장 가치 있는 신생 기업이 된, 약 700억 달러의 가치를 가지고 있는 우버가 이뤄 낸 많은 성과 가운데 하나이다. 그러나 우버의 야망은 한층 더 확대되고 있는데 우버는 자율주행 자동차를 이용하여 사람들이 자동차 소유를 완전히 포기하도록 라이드헤일링(ride-hailing: 이동을 원하는 소비자와 이동 서비스를 제공하는 사업자를 실시간 연결해주는) 서비스를 매우 저렴하고 편리하게 만들기 원한다. 연간 1천억 달러 규모의 택시업계를 뒤흔들어 놓은 것에 만족하지 않고, 우버는 전 세계적으로 연간 10조 달러 규모의 가치를 지닌 훨씬 규모가 큰 사장인 개인 수송 시장을 눈여겨 보고 있다. 이러한 야망을 품고 있는 것은 비단 우버만이 아니다. 크고 작은 기업들이 요청에 따라 호출되는 전기 자율 주행 자동차가 가진 변화 잠재력을 깨달았다. 애플, 구글, 테슬라와 같은 첨단 기술회사들은 자율주행 자동차에 대규모 투자를 하고 있다.

(A) Uber is getting bigger and bigger. 우버는 점점 더 커지고 있다.
(B) That was a mistake. 그것은 실수였다.
(C) Uber is not alone in this ambition. 우버만이 이런 야망을 품고 있는 것은 아니다.
(D) That's not the way it goes. 세상이 그렇게 돌아가지는 않는다.

Rudy's Tip 빈칸 앞에 보다 큰 시장에 눈을 돌린다는 것과, 빈칸 뒤에 작고 큰 회사들이 잠재력을 알고 있다는 전후 문맥을 통해 우버 외에도 다른 회사들이 관심을 가지고 있다는 것을 유추할 수 있다.

Case Study 5

정답 (A)

Like most patriotic Americans, my father was forever buying gizmos that proved to be disastrous — clothes steamers that failed to take the wrinkles out of suits but had wallpaper falling off the walls in whole sheets, an electric pencil sharpener that could consume an entire pencil in less than a second, a water pick that was so lively it required two people to hold and left the bathroom looking like the inside of a car wash, and much else. But all of this was nothing compared with the situation today. We are now surrounded with items that do things for us to an almost absurd degree — automatic cat food dispensers, electric juicers and can openers, refrigerators that make their own ice cubes, automatic car windows, disposable toothbrushes that come with the toothpaste already loaded. People are so addicted to convenience that they have become trapped in _____: The more labor-saving appliances they acquire, the harder they need to work; the harder they work, the more labor-saving appliances they feel they need to acquire.

애국심이 강한 대부분의 미국인들처럼, 나의 아버지는 형편없는 것으로 드러난 장치들을 계속해서 구매해 왔다. 그 장치들에는 양복의 주름은 없애지 못하지만 벽지를 벽에서 몽땅 떨어지게 하는 다리미, 일초도 안 되어 연필 전체를 다 깎아 버릴 수 있는 전기연필깎이, 너무 수압이 강해서 두 사람이 잡고 있어야 하고, 욕실을 자동차 세차장의 내부처럼 보이게 만드는 워터마크(구강 세척기) 등이 있었다. 그러나 이런 모든 기계들은 오늘날의 상황과 비교하면 아무것도 아니다. 우리는 현재 우리를 위해 너무 터무니없는 일을 하는 물건 – 자동 고양이 먹이 배급기, 전기 과즙기와 전기 캔 오프너, 얼음 조각을 만들어 주는 냉장고, 자동 차창, 치약이 들어 있는 1회용 칫솔 등 – 에 둘러싸여 있다. 사람들이 편리함에 너무 중독되어 있어서 이들은 악순환에 빠져 있다. 사람들이 노동을 덜어주는 기기를 많이 구입할수록, 더 열심히 일해야 하고, 더 열심히 일할수록, 더 많은 노동 절감 기기를 구입해야 한다고 느끼게 된다.

(A) a vicious circle 악순환
(B) a dilemma 진퇴양난
(C) a balloon effect 풍선효과(한 곳의 문제를 해결하면 그 부작용으로 다른 문제가 발생하는 것)
(D) a domino effect 도미노 효과(하나의 사건이 단초가 되어 이후에 비슷한 사건들이 연속적으로 발생하는 것)

Rudy's Tip 빈칸 뒤에 문장부호는 재진술 신호이다. 물건을 구입하면 할수록, 그 물건을 구입하기 위해 일을 더 해야 하고, 일을 더 할수록 물건이 더 필요한 상황은 전형적인 악순환이다.

Case Study 6

정답 (B)

The Nobel Prize in Literature may be the world's most important literary award, but not everyone who wins can make it to the ceremony. Among the reasons given by past laureates for failing to travel to Stockholm to accept the award: being gravely ill and in a wheelchair (Harold Pinter, 2005); and being a Soviet dissident terrified to leave the country because you might not be allowed back in (Aleksandr Solzhenitsyn, 1970). Over the years, some literature prize winners seem to have delighted in making things difficult for the academy by reacting to news of their win with _____. In 1964, Jean-Paul Sartre turned the award down. As for V. S. Naipaul, when the academy telephoned him at home to let him know that he'd won the 2001 prize, he refused to come to the phone.

노벨문학상은 세계에서 가장 중요한 문학상일 수도 있지만, 수상자 모두가 시상식에 참석할 수 있는 것은 아니다. 과거 수상자들이 상을 받으러 (노벨상 시상식이 열리는) 스톡홀름으로 여행을 떠날 수 없는 이유로 든 것들에는 중한 병이 들어 휠체어를 타고 있다는 것 (2005년 수상자 해롤드 핀터), 귀국이 허용되지 않을지 몰라 출국하기를 두려워하는 소련의 반체제 인사라는 것 (1970년 수상자 알렉산드르 솔제니친) 등이 있었다. 여러 해 동안, 일부 노벨문학상 수상자들은 자신들의 수상 소식에 시큰둥한 반응을 보임으로써 한림원의 입장을 난처하게 만드는 것을 즐긴 것처럼 보인다. 1964년, 장 폴 사르트르 (Jean-Paul Sartre)는 노벨문학상을 거부했다. 네이폴(V. S. Naipaul)의 경우, 한림원이 2001년 노벨문학상 수상자임을 알리기 위해 그의 집으로 전화했을 때, 그는 전화받기를 거부했다.

(A) welcoming gestures 환영의 몸짓들
(B) less than complete enthusiasm 시큰둥한 (부족한 열정)
(C) fear of public recognition 대중의 인정에 대한 두려움
(D) expressions of excitement 기쁨의 표현들

Rudy's Tip 빈칸 뒤에 수상을 거부한 구체적인 예시들을 통해서 적절한 표현을 선별할 수 있다. 언제나 빈칸 뒤에 S진술이 등장한다면, S진술을 포괄하는 표현이 빈칸에 적절하다.

Unit 06 순삽탈(순서배열 문장삽입 논지일탈)

Case Study 1
정답 (A)

[I] Music has long been appreciated for its calming effects, but new research shows it also may have the power to restore and keep us healthy.

[II] Soothing sounds, from Tibetan chants to Beethoven symphonies, are being given scientific credit for preventing colds, easing labor pain and even boosting anti-aging hormones. One recent study found that surgery patients who listened to comforting music recovered more quickly and felt less pain than those who did not.

[III] Sound therapy goes beyond recorded music: The International Journal of Arts Medicine reports that infants in intensive care unit go home three days sooner, eat better and gain more weight if the staff talks and sings to them.

[I] 음악이 마음을 안정시키는 효과가 있다는 것은 오랫동안 인정되어왔지만, 새 연구 결과에 의하면, 원기를 회복시켜주고 건강을 유지시켜주는 효과를 가지고 있을 수도 있다고 한다.

[II] 티벳의 성가에서부터 베토벤의 교향곡에 이르기까지, 사람의 마음을 진정시켜주는 소리는 감기를 예방하고, 산고(産苦)를 덜어주며, 심지어는 노화를 방지하는 호르몬까지 나오게 하는 것으로 과학적으로 인정을 받고 있다. 최근 한 연구에서 편안한 음악을 들었던 수술 환자들이 좀더 빨리 회복되고, 음악을 듣지 않은 환자들보다 고통을 덜 느꼈다는 것이 밝혀졌다.

[III] 소리를 이용한 치료방법은 녹음된 음악을 능가한다. The international journal of arts medicine는 직원이 말을 건네고 노래를 해주면, 중환자실의 유아들이 3일 빨리 퇴원하고, 더 잘 먹고, 몸무게도 더 늘어난다는 사실을 전했다.

Rudy's Tip 첫 문항으로 music이 G로 적절하다. 또한 [I]의 healthy가 [II]의 preventing으로 연결된다.

Case Study 2

정답 (B)

(a) For the past two years, I have been studying cancer survivors at the university, trying to find out why it is that some people respond much better to their treatment than do others.

(f) At first I thought that some patients did well because their illnesses were not as severe as the illnesses of others.

(d) On closer scrutiny, however, I discovered that severity of the illness was only one of a number of factors that accounted for the difference between those who get well and those who don't.

(c) The patients I am talking about here received upon diagnosis whatever therapy — medication, radiation, surgery — their individual cases demanded.

(e) Yet the response to such treatments was hardly uniform.

(b) Some patients fared much better in their therapies than others.

(a) 지난 2년간 나는 대학에서 암 생존자들에 관한 연구를 수행하면서 왜 어떤 환자들은 다른 환자들에 비해 치료에서 더 나은 반응을 보이는가를 밝히려 했다.
(f) 처음에 나는 어떤 환자들은 그들의 질병이 다른 환자들의 질병만큼 심하지 않기 때문에 치료가 더 빠르다고 생각했다.
(d) 그러나 좀 더 정밀히 살펴본 결과 나는 질병의 증세 정도는 빨리 회복되는 환자와 그렇지 않은 환자들 간의 차이를 설명하는 많은 요인들 중 하나에 불과하다는 것을 알게 되었다.
(c) 지금 내가 말하고 있는 환자들은 진단에 따라 그들의 개별 상태가 요구하는 모든 치료 즉, 약물, 방사선, 수술 등을 받았다.
(e) 그러나 그러한 치료에 대한 반응은 거의 천차만별이었다.
(b) 어떤 환자들은 다른 환자들에 비해 치료가 훨씬 더 잘 진행되었다.

Rudy's Tip 시간표시 부사가 첫 문항으로 적절하기에 (a)가 첫 문항으로 적절하다. 또한 (a)의 much better가 (f)의 did well로 연결된다.

Case Study 3

정답 (B)

[II] A study conducted by the University of Queensland's School of Pharmacy involving more than 12,000 Australians revealed that the benefits of a fresh produce-rich diet extend beyond physical health.

[III] With every added daily portion of fruits or vegetables (up to eight), the subjects' happiness levels rose slightly.

[IV] The researchers calculated that if someone were to switch from a diet free of fruit and vegetables to eight servings per day, he or she would theoretically gain as much life satisfaction as someone who transitioned from unemployment to a job.

[I] The exact reason is unclear, but it may be related to the effect of carotenoid levels in the blood.

[II] 퀸즈랜드(Queensland)대학교 약학대학에서 12,000명 이상의 호주 국민들을 대상으로 실시한 한 연구에 따르면, 신선한 농산물이 풍부한 식단이 가져다주는 이점은 신체적인 건강 이상인 것으로 나타났다.
[III] 하루에 과일이나 채소를 먹는 횟수가 매일 늘어날 때마다 (최대 8회까지) 피험자의 행복 수준은 약간씩 상승했다.
[IV] 연구원들은 누군가가 과일과 채소가 전혀 없는 식단으로부터 하루 8차례 과일과 채소를 먹는 것으로 바꾸는 경우, 이론적으로 그 사람은 실직상태에서 일자리를 얻게 된 사람만큼의 삶의 만족도를 얻게 될 것이라고 추정했다.
[I] 정확한 이유는 분명하지 않지만, 혈중 카로티노이드 수준이 미치는 영향과 관련이 있을지 모른다.

Rudy's Tip 'A study conducted'가 실험의 개요를 의미하기에 첫 문항으로 가장 적절하다. 실험에 관련된 내용은 언제나 실험의 장소, 참가자, 시간, 이유, 연구자, 목적 등의 개요가 등장하는 문항이 첫 문항으로 적절하다.

Case Study 4

정답 (B)

Thunderstorms are extremely common in many parts of the world, for example, throughout most of North America. Updrafts of warm air set off these storms.

[B] An updraft may start over ground that is more intensely heated by the sun than the land surrounding the area. Bare, rocky, or paved areas, for example, usually have updrafts above them. The air in contact with the ground heats up and thus becomes lighter, more buoyant, than the air surrounding it.

[A] This more buoyant air then rises and carries water vapor to higher altitudes. The air cools as it rises, and the water vapor condenses and starts to drop as rain. As the rain falls, it pulls air along with it and turns part of the draft downward.

[C] The draft may turn upward again and send the rain churning around in the cloud. Some of it may freeze to hail. Sooner or later, the water droplets grow heavy enough to resist the updrafts and fall to the ground, pulling air in the form of downdrafts with them.

폭풍우는 전 세계 많은 지역에서 예를 들면 북미 전역에서 매우 흔한 것이다. 따뜻한 공기의 상승기류가 이런 폭풍을 시작하게 한다.

[B] 태양에 의해 주변보다 집중적으로 가열된 지역의 땅 위에서 상승기류가 시작할 수 있다. 예를 들어 노출되고, 돌이 많고, 포장된 지역 위에서 보통 상승기류가 나타난다. 그 땅과 접촉한 공기는 가열되고 그 주변의 공기보다 더 가벼워지고, 더 부력을 갖게 된다.

[A] 더 부력을 가진 이 공기는 상승하고 더 높은 고도로 수증기를 운반한다. 그 공기는 상승하면서 차가워지고, 수증기는 응축되고, 비로 떨어지기 시작한다. 비가 내리면서, 비는 공기를 끌어당겨 일부 기류를 아래로 회전시킨다.

[C] 이 기류는 다시 상승할 수 있으며 구름 속에서 마구 휘젓고 다니면서 비를 내릴지도 모른다. 이들 중 일부가 얼어서 우박이 될 수도 있다. 이내 곧 빗방울이 상승기류에 저항할 만큼 무거워지고 그들과 함께 하강기류의 형태로 공기를 빨아들이며 땅으로 떨어진다.

Rudy's Tip 도입문의 updrafts - (B) An updraft 연결, (B)의 buoyant - (A)의 buoyant air로 연결된다.

Case Study 5

정답 (D)

ⓓ There is nothing new about people cutting down trees. In ancient times, Greece, Italy, and Great Britain were covered with forests. Over the centuries those forests were gradually cut back. Until now almost nothing is left.

ⓐ Today, however, trees are being cut down far more rapidly. Each year, about 2 million acres of forests are cut down. That is more than equal to the area of the whole of Great Britain.

ⓒ While there are important reasons for cutting down trees, there are also dangerous consequences for life on earth. A major cause of the present destruction is the worldwide demand for wood. In industrialized countries, people are using more and more wood for paper.

ⓑ There is not enough wood in these countries to satisfy the demand. Wood companies, therefore, have begun taking wood from the forests of Asia, Africa, South America, and even Siberia.

ⓓ 사람들이 벌목을 하는 데는 새로운 것이 없다. 고대에, 그리스, 이탈리아, 영국은 숲으로 덮여 있었다. 수세기 동안, 그 숲들은 점차적으로 벌목되었다. 지금은 거의 남은 것이 없다.
ⓐ 그러나 오늘날 나무는 훨씬 더 빨리 베어지고 있다. 매년, 대략 200만 에이커의 숲이 베어진다. 이것은 영국 전체의 면적보다 더 크다.
ⓒ 벌목을 하는 중요한 이유들이 있기는 하지만, 지구상의 생명체에 위험한 영향 또한 있다. 현재 삼림 파괴의 주요 원인은 전 세계적인 목재에 대한 수요이다. 선진국에서는, 사람들이 종이를 위해 점점 더 많은 나무를 사용하고 있다.
ⓑ 이 국가들에서는 그 수요를 충족시킬 만큼 충분한 나무가 없다. 따라서 목재 회사들은 아시아, 아프리카, 남아메리카, 그리고 심지어 시베리아의 숲에서 나무를 가지고 오기 시작했다.

Rudy's Tip (a)는 however, (b)는 these countries가 있기에 첫 문항으로 적절하지 않다. 첫 문항에 역접의 접속사, 대명사는 등장할 수 없기 때문이다.

Case Study 6

정답 (D)

Many people dream of being celebrities, but they might change their minds if they considered all the disadvantages there are to being famous. For one thing, celebrities have to look perfect all the time. There's always a photographer ready to take an unflattering picture of a famous person looking dumpy in old clothes. Celebrities also sacrifice their private lives. Their personal struggles, divorces, or family tragedies all end up as front-page news. Most frighteningly, celebrities are in constant danger of the wrong kind of attention. Threatening letters and even physical attacks from crazy fans are things the celebrity must contend with.

많은 사람들은 셀럽(유명인)이 되기를 꿈꾸지만 유명하게 됨으로써 받는 모든 불이익을 고려한다면 마음을 달리 먹을 것이다. 먼저, 셀럽은 항상 완벽하게 보여야만 한다. 낡은 옷을 입어 땅딸막하게 보이는 유명한 사람을 있는 그대로 촬영하기 위해서 파파라치가 항상 모든 준비를 갖추고 있다. 유명 인사는 또한 사적인 삶도 희생한다. 그들의 개인적인 갈등, 이혼, 또는 가족에게 일어난 비극적 사건들은 모두 1면 기사로 오르게 된다. 가장 놀라운 것은 셀럽들은 그릇된 관심의 위험에 항상 처해있다는 점이다. 열광적인 팬들의 협박 편지와 심지어 신체적인 가해는 유명 인사가 맞서 싸워야 하는 것들이다.

Rudy's Tip 'also sacrifice'를 통해 부정적인 내용 뒤에, private lives 앞에 등장해야 한다.

Case Study 7

정답 (A)

Frequent beatings. Water torture. Being dragged around by the neck, and forced to eat crumbs off the floor. Sound like the abuses committed by some soldiers on suspected terrorists in a certain country? No, these are what two middle-school boys have subjected a classmate to for the past nine months. The victim leapt to his death lately, leaving a note of painful recollections of his ordeals. The word shock hardly suffices to describe the huge impact this incident has had on society. Even more astounding, however, is most experts agree these kinds of grim episodes can happen anytime, anywhere in the present educational and social environment of Korea. This shows why the nation must waste no more time to drive out bullying in and outside of campus, immediately and fundamentally.

빈번한 매질, 물고문, 목을 질질 끌고 다니고, 바닥의 빵 부스러기 주워 먹게 하기. 미국 군인들이 어떤 나라의 테러 용의자들에게 저지르는 학대처럼 들리는가? 아니다. 이들은 두 명의 중학생들이 지난 9개월 동안에 걸쳐 그들의 급우에게 저질렀던 일들이다. 피해자는 최근 투신자살을 하며, 그의 시련에 관한 고통스런 기억을 담은 노트를 남겨 놓았다. 충격이라는 말은 이 사건이 사회에 미친 영향을 기술하는 데 충분치 못하다. 하지만 더욱 놀라운 것은, 이러한 종류의 무서운 일들이 지금 한국의 교육·사회적 환경 모든 곳에서 언제라도 일어날 수 있다는 것에 대부분의 전문가들이 동의하고 있다는 사실이다. 이는 우리나라가 학교 안팎의 학원 폭력을 즉시, 그리고 근본적으로 몰아내야 하는 이유를 보여주고 있다.

Rudy's Tip 삽입문의 'NO'라는 대답과 대명사 these를 통해서 위치를 찾을 수 있다.

Case Study 8

정답 (B)

At around 8 months of age, infants begin to use gestures such as pointing and showing in a communicative manner. It is not easy to determine whether a behavior is meant to communicate something or is simply a behavior that an infant enjoys. However, psychologists have developed criteria to determine whether a behavior reveals an intent to communicate. The major criteria are waiting, persistence, and development of alternative plans. For example, suppose an infant pulls his or her parent's leg, waits for the parent to look down, and then points at a toy. The fact that the infant waited for the adult to pay attention suggests that the infant was operating on the assumption that we first have to get an adult's attention and then we point out what we want.

대략 8개월쯤 되면, 유아들은 가리키기와 보여주기와 같은 제스처들을 의사소통을 위한 방식으로 사용하기 시작한다. 어떤 행동이 어떤 것을 전달하기 위한 것인지, 혹은 단지 유아가 즐기는 행동인지를 구별하는 것은 쉽지 않은 일이다. 하지만 심리학자들은 어떤 행동이 의사소통의 의도를 보여주는 것인지를 판단하는 기준을 만들었다. 주요 기준은 기다리기, 인내하기, 대안 계획의 개발이다. 예를 들어, 유아가 부모의 다리를 잡아당기고, 부모가 내려다 봐주길 기다린 다음, 장난감을 가리킨다고 하자. 어른이 주의를 기울여 주기를 유아가 기다린다는 사실은 유아가 먼저 어른의 주의를 얻은 다음 원하는 것을 가리켜야겠다는 가정을 가지고 행동하고 있다는 것을 보여준다.

Rudy's Tip 삽입문의 'criteria to determine'를 통해 적절한 자리를 알 수 있다.

Case Study 9

정답 (D)

Different ways of speaking are part of gender. As adults, men and women sometimes face difficulties in their communication with each other. Studies of communication show that if a woman tells her husband about a problem, she will expect him to listen and offer sympathy. She may be annoyed when he simply tells her how to solve the problem. Similarly, a husband may be annoyed when his wife wants to stop and ask a stranger for directions to a park or restaurant. Unlike his wife, he would rather use a map and find his way by himself. Language is also part of the different ways that men and women think about friendship. Most American men believe that friendship means doing things together such as camping or playing tennis. Talking is not an important part of friendship for most of them. American women, on the other hand, usually identify their best friend as someone with whom they talk frequently.

성별에 따라 말하는 방식이 다르다. 성인으로서 남자와 여자는 때때로 서로 그들의 의사를 전달하는데 있어서 어려움에 직면한다. 의사소통에 관한 연구에 따르면 만약 여자가 그녀의 남편에게 어떤 문제에 관해 말한다면 그녀는 그가 귀담아 듣고 공감해 주기를 기대할 것이라는 사실을 보여준다. 그녀는 남편이 그저 그 문제를 해결하는 방법을 말할 때는 화를 낼 수도 있다. 이와 비슷하게 남편은 그의 아내가 멈춰 서서 공원이나 음식점으로 가는 길을 낯선 사람에게 묻고 싶어 할 때 화를 낼 수도 있다. 아내와 달리 그는 지도를 보고 혼자서 가는 길을 알아낼 것이다. 언어는 또한 남자와 여자가 우정에 관해 생각하는 다른 방식들의 부분이다. 대부분의 미국 남성들은 우정은 이를테면 캠핑이나 테니스를 치는 것과 같이 함께 무언가를 하는 것을 의미한다고 생각한다. 대부분의 남성들에게 있어서 대화는 우정의 중요한 부분이 아니다. 반면 미국 여성들은 보통 그들이 자주 함께 이야기하는 누군가를 자기가 가장 좋아하는 친구라고 생각한다.

Rudy's Tip 삽입문의 'most of them'의 선행사를 찾는 것이 요점이다. 문맥상 'American men'이 적절하다. 또한 [III]에 들어가게 된다면 선행사가 'men and women'이 되기 때문에 적절하지 않다.

Case Study 10 정답 (D)

One of the challenges we face in the world today is that a lot of the information we get about other people and places comes from the advertising and entertainment we see in the media. You can't always trust these types of information. To the people who make television programs and advertisements, true facts and honest opinions aren't as important as keeping you interested long enough to sell you something! In the past, the messages we received from television programs, advertisements, and movies were full of stereotypes. For example, some cultural groups were often portrayed as gangsters, while others were usually shown as the 'good guys' who arrested them. Even places were presented as stereotypes : European cities, such as Paris and Venice, were usually shown as beautiful and romantic, but cities in Africa and Asia, such as Cairo and Calcutta, were often shown as poor and overcrowded.

우리가 세상에서 접하는 어려움 중 하나는 다른 사람들과 장소에 대해 우리가 얻는 많은 정보가 언론에서 보는 광고와 오락물에서 나온다는 것이다. 이런 유형의 정보를 항상 신뢰할 수 있는 것은 아니다. TV 프로그램과 광고를 만드는 사람들에게 진정한 사실과 정직한 의견은 당신에게 무언가 팔 수 있도록 오랫동안 관심을 갖도록 하는 것만큼 중요하지는 않다. 과거에 우리가 TV 프로그램, 광고 그리고 영화에서 우리가 얻는 정보는 고정관념으로 가득 차 있었다. 예를 들면 어떤 집단의 사람들은 흔히 악당으로 묘사되고, 이에 반해 그들을 체포하는 사람들은 흔히 좋은 사람들로 표현되었다. 심지어 장소도 고정관념으로 표현되기도 했다. 파리와 베니스 같은 유럽의 도시는 대개 아름답고 낭만적인 곳으로 묘사되었지만 카이로와 캘커타 같은 아프리카와 아시아의 도시들은 가난하고 인구가 넘쳐나는 곳으로 표현되기도 했다.

Rudy's Tip (D)를 기준으로 G진술 stereotypes이 앞에 등장했기에 구체적인 예시에 해당하는 삽입문이 뒤에 위치해야 한다.

Case Study 11

정답 (C)

Depression is one of the most common mental illnesses. (A) At least 8% of adults in the United States experience serious depression at some point during their lives, and estimates range as high as 17%. (B) The illness affects all people, regardless of sex, race, ethnicity, or socioeconomic standing. (C) People commonly view depression as a sign of personal weakness, but psychiatrists and psychologists view it as a real illness. (D) However, women are two to three times more likely than men to suffer from depression.

우울증은 가장 흔한 정신 질환 중 하나이다. (A) 적어도 미국 성인의 8%가 살면서 한번 정도는 심각한 우울을 경험하는데, 높게는 17%까지 추산된다. (B) 이 질병은 성별, 인종, 민족, 사회 경제적인 신분에 관계없이 모든 사람에게 영향을 미친다. (C) 사람들은 우울증을 개인적인 허약함의 징후로 보는 경향이 있지만, 정신과 의사들과 심리학자들은 우울증을 실제 질병으로 여긴다. (D) 그러나 남자보다 여자가 우울증에 걸릴 확률이 두 세배나 높다.

Rudy's Tip 첫 문장이 G진술로 Topic이다. 따라서 본문의 내용들 또한 주제문에 대한 재진술이 되어야 한다. (C)를 제외하고는 모두 정신질환의 발병에 대한 내용이고, (C)는 정신질환의 평가에 대한 진술로 흐름상 적절하지 않다.

Case Study 12

정답 (B)

In any science, a good general theory is the handiest tool possible. (A) Not only does it link many seemingly random facts into one coherent framework, but it also acts as a powerful aid to prediction. (B) Making predictions has become one of the leading growth industries of the twentieth century. (C) For instance, if you wanted to find out whether there is a planet beyond the known series, you could ask several hundred astronomers to keep their eyes open at night. (D) However, it would be more fruitful to turn to gravitational theory, which predicts that if there was a further planet out there it would cause detectable movements in the orbit of some other known planets. Indeed that is exactly how Leverrier predicted in 1846 that a planet would be discovered: Uranus.

어떠한 과학 분야에서건 훌륭한 일반 이론은 가장 편리한 도구이다. 그것은 겉으로 보기에 아무런 연관성도 없는 많은 사실들을 하나의 일관성 있는 틀 안에 묶어줄 뿐 아니라, 예측에도 효과적인 도움을 준다. 미래를 예측하는 것은 20세기의 주도적인 성장 산업의 하나가 되고 있다. 예를 들어 이미 알려진 것 이상으로 행성이 있는지 알고 싶다면 당신은 수백 명의 천문학자들에게 밤 하늘을 지켜봐달라고 부탁할 수도 있다. 그러나 중력이론 쪽으로 방향을 돌리는 것이 더 효과적일 것이다. 왜냐하면 그것(중력이론)은 우주에 알려진 것보다 더 많은 행성이 있다면 그것은 어떤 다른 이미 알려져 있는 행성의 궤도에 감지할 수 있는 운동을 야기할 것이라는 것을 예측할 수 있기 때문이다. 실제로 1846년에 르베리에(Leverrier)는 바로 이러한 방법을 사용해서 어떤 행성, 즉 천왕성(Uranus)이 발견될 것이라는 것을 예측했던 것이다.

Rudy's Tip (B)의 'industries'를 통해서 prediction은 과학적 예측이 아니라, 역술(사주) 사업임을 알 수 있다.

Case Study 13

정답 (C)

Before the Industrial Revolution, most goods were produced by hand in rural homes or urban workshops. (A) Merchants, known as entrepreneurs, distributed the raw materials to workers, collected the finished products, paid for the work, then sold them. (B) Growing demand for consumer products, together with a shortage of labour, placed pressure on entrepreneurs to find new, more efficient methods of production. (C) The great era of European exploration that began in the 15th century arose primarily out of a desire to seek out new trade routes and partners. (D) With the development of power-driven machines, it made economic sense to bring workers, materials and machines together in one place, giving rise to the first factories. For added efficiency, the production process was broken down into basic individual tasks that a worker could specialize in, a system known as the division of labour.

산업혁명 이전에는 대부분의 상품이 시골의 가정이나 도시의 작업장에서 수작업으로 생산됐다. 기업가로 알려져 있던 상인들은 원자재를 노동자들에게 배급하고, 완제품을 모은 다음, 그 일에 대해 돈을 지불한 후에 그 완제품들을 내다 팔았다. 소비재에 대한 수요가 점차 늘어나고 이와 함께 노동력이 부족해 짐에 따라 기업가들은 새롭고 보다 효율적인 생산 방법을 찾아야 한다는 압박을 받았다. 15세기에 시작된 유럽의 위대한 탐험 시대는 주로 새로운 교역로와 파트너를 찾고자 하는 욕구에서 비롯되었다. 동력 기계가 개발됨에 따라, 노동자, 자재, 기계를 한 곳에서 모으는 것이 경제적으로 타당하게 되었고, 최초의 공장이 생겨나게 되었다. 효율성을 더 높이기 위해, 생산과정은 노동자가 전문적으로 할 수 있었던 기본적인 개별 작업들로 나뉘어졌는데, 이것은 분업으로 알려져 있는 시스템이다.

Rudy's Tip 첫 문장의 제품 생산에 대한 흐름은 finished products, production, factories로 그대로 연결되고 있다. 따라서 (C)의 대탐험 이야기는 흐름상 매우 어색하다.

Case Study 14

정답 (D)

The earth is a planet full of life. One of the reasons for this is that our sun is the kind of star that can support life on a planet. All the time the sun continues to send out a steady supply of heat and light. For our sun is a stable star. (A) This means that it stays the same size. And its output of energy (heat and light) does not change much. (B) Some stars are not stable. They grow bigger and hotter and then smaller and cooler. (C) The heat and light they send out vary greatly. If our sun behaved like that, the earth would boil and freeze repeatedly. (D) Life could exist under these great changes. We are here because a steady amount of energy pours forth from our sun.

지구는 생명체로 가득한 행성이다. 이것이 가능한 이유 중의 하나는 태양은 행성의 생명체를 유지해 줄 수 있는 유형의 별이기 때문이다. 태양은 계속해서 열과 빛을 일정하게 발산하고 있다. 우리 태양은 안정된 별이기 때문이다. 이것은 태양이 동일한 크기로 존재한다는 것을 뜻한다. 태양의 에너지(빛과 열) 분출은 큰 변화가 없다. 어떤 별들은 안정적이지 않다. 이 별들은 점점 커지고 뜨거워지며 그러다 더 작아지고 더 추워진다. 이 별들이 내뿜는 열과 빛은 상당히 다르다. 만일 우리의 태양이 그와 같다면, 지구는 반복적으로 끓고 얼어버릴 것이다. 생명체는 이런 상당한 변화에서 존재할 수 있다. 우리는 일정한 양의 에너지가 우리의 태양에서 뿜어져 나오기 때문에 이곳에 있는 것이다.

Rudy's Tip 각 문장들은 모두 태양, 별과 관련된 내용이다. 마지막 문장만 생명체에 관련된 문장이기에 흐름상 어색하다.

Case Study 15  (C)

Children's book awards have proliferated in recent years; today, there are well over 100 different awards and prizes by a variety of organizations. (A) The awards may be given for books of a specific genre or simply for the best of all children's books published within a given time period. An award may honor a particular book or an author for a lifetime contribution to the world of children's literature. (B) Most children's book awards are chosen by adults, but now a growing number of children's choice book awards exist. The larger national awards given in most countries are the most influential and have helped considerably to raise public awareness about the fine books being published for young readers. (C) An award ceremony for outstanding services to the publishing industry is put on hold. (D) Of course, readers are wise not to put too much faith in award-winning books. An award doesn't necessarily mean a good reading experience, but it does provide a starting place when choosing books.

최근 수년간 어린이 도서상이 증가했다. 즉, 오늘날 다양한 조직에서 주는 100가지가 넘는 다양한 상이 존재한다. 상은 특정 장르의 책에 대해 주어지거나 또는 단순히 주어진 기간 내에 출판된 모든 아동 도서 중 최고에게 주어진다. 상은 세계 어린이 문학에 대한 평생 공헌에 대해 특정 책이나 저자에게 수여될 수도 있다. 대부분의 아동 도서상은 성인이 선택하지만, 현재는 어린이가 선택한 도서상도 늘고 있다. 대부분의 국가에서 제공되는 더 큰 국가상은 가장 영향력이 크며, 젊은 독자들을 위해 발간되는 훌륭한 책에 대한 대중의 인식을 높이는 데 큰 도움을 주어왔다. 출판 산업에서 뛰어난 서비스에 대한 시상식이 연기된다. 물론, 독자는 수상을 한 도서에 너무 많은 믿음을 두지 않는 것이 현명하다. 상은 꼭 좋은 독서 경험을 의미하는 것은 아니지만, 책을 선택할 때 분명히 시작점을 제공해준다.

Rudy's Tip 밑줄 친 문장들은 연결해 보면, 모두 'book award'에 관련된 내용들이지만, (C)만 'ceremony'에 관련된 내용으로 어색하다. 또한 뒤에 이어지는 내용 또한 (C)와 호응하지 않는다.

CHAPTER 2
10분 모의고사

10분 모의고사 01 해설편

1
정답 (D)

American uniformity is an **axiom** for the European **beyond any experience**.
미국인의 동질성은 유럽들에게 어떤 경험을 뛰어넘는 자명한 이치이다.
(경험과 상관없이 유럽인들에게 미국인들은 똑같아 보인다는 의미)

(A) Europeans do not believe in American uniformity until they come to America.
유럽인들이 미국에 가보기 전에는 미국의 동질성을 믿지 않는다.

(B) Europeans are more convinced of American uniformity after they have been to America.
유럽인들은 미국을 방문하고 나서 그들의 동질성에 대해 더 확고해 졌다.

(C) Europeans have never believed in American uniformity due to their experience in America.
유럽인들은 미국에서의 경험들 때문에 미국인들의 동질성에 대해 믿지 않는다.

(D) Europeans **believe so strongly** in American uniformity that **no experience can alter their belief**.
유럽인들은 미국의 동질성을 강력히 믿으며 그 어떤 경험도 그들의 믿음을 바꿀 수 없다.

Rudy's Tip axiom = believe so strongly
beyond any experience = no experience can alter their belief

2
정답 (C)

Sometimes things change without appearing to have changed at all. Let's take a pebble lying on a beach as an example. During the day the pebble is heated by the sun's rays. At night it cools down. To anyone who did not touch the pebble at both times it would **not seem to have changed**. However, to an insect walking across the pebble during the day and again at night, the pebble would **seem to have changed a great deal**. So to some extent, change is **relative**.

때때로 사물들이 전혀 변한 것처럼 보이지 않게 변한다. 해변에 있는 자갈을 예로 들어보자. 낮 동안에 자갈은 태양 빛에 의해 뜨거워진다. 자갈은 밤에 식는다. 뜨거웠을 때와 식었을 때 둘 다 자갈을 만지지 않았던 사람은 누구에게든지 자갈에 변화가 없었던 것처럼 보일 것이다. 그러나 낮에 그리고 밤에 다시 자갈을 걸어갔던 곤충에게는 그 자갈이 대단히 변한 것처럼 보일 것이다. 따라서 변화란 어느 정도 상대적인 것이다.

Rudy's Tip 빈칸 앞에 대조적인 예시를 통해 빈칸을 추론할 수 있다. 조약돌의 예시를 통해 사람은 변화를 느끼지 못하지만 곤충은 변화를 느끼는 것은 변화에 대해서 '상대적'인 상황이다.

독독 1.0 청킹

Sometimes things change/without appearing/to have changed at all.
때때로 사물들은 변한다/보이지 않게/전혀 변한 것처럼

3   정답 (A)

If we want to describe our society in terms of age, we may come up with four age groups — childhood, adolescence, maturity, and old age. We take it for granted that people of different ages behave differently. For example, we feel that a man in his thirties should act his age and not behave like an adolescent or an old man. Equally, we expect that, as they go through life, people of the same age will in some ways understand each other better than people of different ages. All this is part of expected ways of behaving in our social life, but it is not something that we can apply to formal institutions governed by hard-and-fast rules.

나이를 기준으로 사회집단을 설명하고자 한다면 우리는 유년기, 청년기, 장년기, 노년기라는 4개의 연령집단을 생각할 것이다. 우리는 사람들의 행동방식이 나이에 따라 다르다는 것을 당연한 것으로 간주한다. 예를 들어, 30대의 남자는 자신의 나이답게 행동해야 하며 청년이나 노인처럼 행동해서는 안 된다고 느낀다. 같은 맥락에서, 우리는 같은 연령대의 사람들은 삶을 살아가는 동안 몇 가지 면에서 다른 연령대의 사람들보다는 서로를 더 많이 이해할 거라고 기대한다. 이 모든 것은 사회생활에서 기대되는 행동방식의 일부이지만, 엄격한 규칙에 의해 지배되는 정형화된 제도에 적용할 수 있는 것은 아니다.

(A) Age Groups : Their Expected Behavior
  연령별 집단 : 나이에 적절한 행동
(B) Secrets of Aging : Myth and Truth
  노화의 비밀 : 신화와 진실
(C) Formal Institutions : Their Social Rules
  공식적인 기관들 : 그들의 사회적 역할들
(D) Teens' Behavior : Respected or Neglected?
  10대들의 행동 : 존중할 것이냐 무시할 것이냐?

Rudy's Tip GS 구조이다.

독독 1.0 청킹

people of the same age will/in some ways/understand each other better/than people of different ages.
같은 나이의 사람들은/어떤 면에서는/서로를 더 잘 이해한다/다른 나이의 사람들보다

4

정답 (B)

Footwear has a history which goes back thousands of years, and it has long been an article of necessity.

[A] The earliest footwear was undoubtedly born of the necessity to provide some protection when moving over rough ground in varying weather conditions. In ancient times, as today, the basic type of shoes worn depended on the climate.

[C] For instance, in warmer areas the sandal was, and still is, the most popular form of footwear, whereas the modern moccasin derives from the original shoes adopted in cold climates by races such as Eskimos and Siberians.

[B] Shoes have not always served such a purely functional purpose, however, and the requirements of fashion have dictated some curious designs, not all of which made walking easy.

신발은 그 역사가 수천 년 거슬러 올라가며, 오랫동안 필수적인 물건이 되어왔다.
[A] 가장 오래된 신발은 변화하는 날씨 여건에서 험한 길로 이동할 때 어느 정도의 보호를 제공할 필요성 때문에 생겨난 것임에 틀림없다. 오늘날과 마찬가지로 옛날에는 착용된 신발의 기본적 형태는 기후에 따라 결정되었다.
[C] 예를 들면, 따뜻한 지역에서는 샌들이 예전에도 지금도 가장 인기가 있는 신발의 형태인 반면, 현대의 모카신(moccasin)이라는 신발은 에스키모와 시베리아인과 같은 종족들이 추운 기후에서 사용했던 신발을 원형으로 하여 파생된 것이다.
[B] 하지만 신발은 항상 그러한 순수하게 기능적인 목적만 충족시킨 것은 아니었고, 유행을 끌기 위한 필요 때문에 몇몇 호기심을 끄는 디자인이 등장했지만 그러한 디자인들 모두가 걷기에 편한 것은 아니었다.

Rudy's Tip [A] climate 예시로 [C]가 연결된다. 또한 [B]의 such가 대명사 역할을 하기에 [C] 뒤에 위치해야 한다.

5

정답 (D)

Our nursing professor gave us a quiz. I had easily answered all the questions until I read the last one: "What is the name of the woman who cleans the school?". I knew she was tall, short-haired, and in her fifties, but how would I know her name? I handed in my paper, leaving the question blank. Collecting the papers, the professor said the last question would count. Then she added, "In your careers you will meet many people. All are significant. They deserve your attention and care, even if all you do is smile and say hello." I've never forgotten that lesson. I also learned that her name was Dorothy.

간호학 교수가 우리에게 퀴즈를 냈다. "학교 청소를 하는 여자 분의 이름은 무엇인가?"라는 마지막 한 문제를 읽기 전까지 나는 모든 문제에 쉽게 답을 했다. 나는 그녀가 단발에 키가 크고, 50대라는 사실을 알고 있었지만, 어떻게 그녀의 이름을 알겠는가? 마지막 문제를 빈칸으로 남겨둔 채 답지를 제출했다. 답안을 모으던 교수는 마지막 문제가 중요하다고 했다. "여러분의 직무에 있어서, 여러분은 많은 사람을 만날 것입니다. 그들은 모두 중요한 사람들이에요. 비록 여러분이 미소 짓고, 인사를 건네는 것이 전부라 해도, 그분들 모두는 여러분의 관심과 보살핌을 받을 자격이 있습니다."라고 덧붙였다. 나는 절대로 그 교훈을 잊지 않았다. 또한 그녀의 이름이 Dorothy라는 것도 알게 되었다.

Rudy's Tip that lesson에 이어서 '이름을 알았다'는 내용이 연결되어야 적절하다.

6

정답 (A)

According to a new paper by Paola Acevedo of Tilburg University and Steven Ongena of the University of Zurich, the trauma affects how bankers subsequently do business. The authors look at bank lending after heists in Colombia, a country where 835 bank robberies took place between 2003 and 2011. They find that loan officers treat would-be borrowers differently in the aftermath of an armed robbery. Loan volumes did not change, but the duration of loans issued in the first 90 days after a stickup was 70% longer. The average Colombian loan matures in 5.4 months, but a newly burgled branch typically lends for 8.7 months. The traumatized loan officers also demand more collateral, but offer slightly lower interest rates than normal. All of these changes reduce the need to deal with new customers in person. Lending for longer periods pushes repayment meetings further into the future. Taking more collateral reduces the need to vet customers thoroughly. And the lower interest rates suggest that loan officers spend less time haggling. This behaviour is a classic symptom of post-traumatic stress disorder.

Tilburg 대학의 Paola Acevedo와 Zurich 대학의 Steven Ongena가 발표한 새로운 논문에 따르면, 트라우마는 이후에 어떻게 은행가들이 사업을 진행할지에 영향을 미친다. 저자들은, 2003년부터 2011년 사이 835차례에 걸쳐 은행 강도사건이 발생했던 콜롬비아에서 은행 강도 사건 이후의 은행 대출을 살펴보았다. 저자들은 무장 강도 이후에 대출담당직원이 대출을 희망하는 사람들을 다르게 대우한다는 것을 발견한다. 대출의 규모는 변하지 않았지만, 권총강도 사건이후 처음 90일 동안 이루어진 대출기간은 70% 정도 길어진다. 콜롬비아의 평균적인 대출 기간은 5.4개월이지만, 은행 강도를 당한 지점은 일반적으로 8.7개월 동안 대출을 해 준다. 트라우마에 사로잡힌 대출 직원은 더 자주, 더 많은 담보를 요구하지만 평소보다 약간 낮은 금리를 제시한다. 이 모든 변화들은 새로운 고객과 직접적으로 소통해야 하는 필요성을 감소시킨다. 더 길어진 대출 기간은 대출금 상환을 위해 고객과 만나는 미팅을 미래 속으로 밀어 넣는다. 더 많은 담보물을 설정하는 것은 고객들을 철저하게 심사할 필요성을 줄어들게 한다. 그리고 낮은 금리는 대출직원이 고객과 언쟁을 벌이는 시간이 줄어들었다는 것을 의미한다. 이러한 행동은 전형적인 외상 후 스트레스 장애 증상이다.

(A) give out loans on better terms
　　더 나은 조건의 대출을 제공하다.
(B) tend to reduce the duration of loans
　　대출 상환 기간을 단축하는 경향이 있다.
(C) would not give out loans to new customers
　　신규 고객에게는 대출하지 않는다.
(D) do not require any collateral
　　어떤 담보물도 요구하지 않는다.

Rudy's Tip 대출기간이 길어지고, 금리가 낮아진 것은 대출조건이 좋아졌다는 의미이다.

독독 1.0 청킹

the duration of loans/issued in the first 90 days/after a stickup/was 70% longer
대출 상환기간/처음 90일동안 발행된/총기사건 이후에/70% 길어졌다

10분 모의고사 02 해설편

1
정답 (C)

It is unlikely that the city subway system will be able to continue its present level of service without a price increase.
도시철도 시스템이 요금 인상 없이 현재의 서비스 수준을 유지한다는 것은 불가능할 것 같다.

(A) In order to increase the level of service, the city subway system will have to raise the subway fare.
서비스 수준을 높이기 위해서 도시 지하철공사는 요금을 인상해야 할 것이다.

(B) The level of service will probably not increase because of the present subway fares.
현재 지하철 요금 때문에 서비스의 수준은 아마도 향상되지 않을 것이다.

(C) The city subway system will probably have to raise subway fares in order to continue similar service.
도시 지하철공사는 비슷한 서비스를 유지하기 위해 요금을 인상해야 할 것이다.

(D) The city subway system will probably face a financial crisis.
아마도 도시 지하철 공사는 재정적인 위기를 직면할 것이다.

Rudy's Tip 제시문의 unlikely와 without을 종합하면 요금 인상이 있어야 현재의 서비스가 가능하다는 내용이다.

2
정답 (C)

As children enter the educational system, traditional expectations for boys and girls continue. In the past, much research focused on how teachers were shortchanging girls in the classroom. Teachers would focus on boys, calling on them more and challenging them. Because boys were believed to be more analytical, teachers assumed they would excel in math and science. Teachers encouraged them to go into careers, such as computer science or engineering.

아이들이 교육제도 속으로 편입되게 되면, 소년들과 소녀들에 대한 전통적인 기대치들은 계속 된다. 과거에 많은 연구들은 어떻게 교사들이 소녀들을 부당하게 교육했던가에 초점을 맞추었다. 교사들은 소년들에게 초점을 맞추고, 더 많은 것을 요구하고, 도전적 과제를 제시했었다. 소년들이 더 분석적이라고 믿었기 때문에, 교사들은 소년들이 수학과 과학에서 더 뛰어나다고 생각했다. 교사들은 소년들이 컴퓨터 과학이나 공학과 같은 분야의 직업을 갖도록 소년들을 격려했다.

Rudy's Tip Because boys were believed to be more _____, teachers assumed they would excel in math and science. 전형적인 인과구조로 '원인 – 결과'의 구조이다. 결과에 해당하는 수학과 과학을 통해서 정답을 유추할 수 있다.

> 독독 3.0 분석독해
> **much research focused on/how teachers were shortchanging girls /in the classroom**
> 많은 연구들은 초점을 맞추었다/어떻게 선생님들이 여학생들을 부당하게 대우했는지/교실에서

3-4

정답 (B), (C)

The poor talker sometimes surprises us by being a good writer. Such a one is usually of the Cerebral type. He likes to think out every phase of a thing and put it into just the right words before giving it to the world. So, many a Cerebral does little talking outside; his intimate circle does a good deal of surreptitious writing. It may be only the keeping of a diary, jotting down memoranda or writing long letters to his friends, but he will write something. Some of the world's greatest ideas have come to light first in the forgotten manuscripts of people of this type who died without showing their writings to anyone. Evidently they did not consider them as sufficient importance or did not care as much about publishing them as about putting them down.

말을 잘 못하는 사람은 때로 글을 훌륭하게 써서 우리를 놀라게 한다. 이러한 사람은 일반적으로 사색적 타입에 속한다. 이런 사람은 사물의 모든 측면을 깊이 생각하고, 세상에 이것을 알리 전에 정확한 말로 표현하는 것을 좋아한다. 그리고 밖에서 말을 거의 안하는 대부분의 사색가들은 그의 개인적인 영역에서 많은 은밀한 글쓰기를 한다. 이것은 단지 일기가 될 수 있고, 비망록을 적는 수준 또는 친구에게 보내는 장문의 편지가 될 수 있지만, 여하튼 그는 무언가를 쓴다. 세상에서 가장 위대한 사상 중 몇몇은 다른 누군가에서 자신의 글을 보이지 않고 죽은 이런 종류의 사람들이 쓴 잊혀진 원고에서 세상에 처음 알려진 것이다. 분명 이들은 자신들의 글을 아주 중요하게 생각하지 않았거나 글로 표현하는 것만큼 출판하는 데에는 별 관심이 없었던 사람들이다.

03 글의 중심내용으로 가장 적절한 것은?

(A) Actions speak louder than words.
   말보다 행동이 중요하다.
(B) There are people who write better than they talk.
   말보다 글을 잘 쓰는 사람들이 있다.
(C) Some of the greatest ideas remain in the dark because of public ignorance.
   어떤 위대한 사상들은 대중의 무지 때문에 알려지지 않는다.
(D) Speaking does a thousand things while writing does not get you anywhere.
   웅변은 많은 것을 할 수 있지만 글은 어떤 효과도 발휘하지 못한다.

Rudy's Tip GS 구조로 말 보다는 글을 잘 쓰는 사람들에 대한 글이다.

04 사색적인 사람에 대한 것으로 올바른 것은?

(A) He knows how to make bad ideas sound plausible.
그릇된 생각을 그럴듯하게 만드는 법을 알고 있다.
(B) He's reluctant to share his ideas with others.
자신의 생각을 타인들과 마지못해 공유한다.
(C) He's not so interested in delivering his ideas to the public.
대중에게 자신의 생각을 전달하는데 별 관심이 없다.
(D) His thoughts are more creative than those of ordinary people.
그의 생각은 보통 사람들의 생각보다 더 창의적이다.

Rudy's Tip 본문의 'not care as much about publishing them'을 통해서 알 수 있다.

독독 3.0 분석독해

Some of the world's greatest ideas /have come to light first /in the forgotten manuscripts of people of this type /who died without showing their writings to anyone.
위대한 사상들 중 몇몇은/처음 세상에 등장한다/이런 유형의 사람들의 잊혀진 원고 속에서/다른 이들에게 자신들의 글을 보이지 않고 사망한

---

5 정답 (C)

Most people like to talk, but few people like to listen, yet listening well is a rare talent that everyone should treasure. Because they hear more, good listeners tend to know more and to be more sensitive to what is going on around them than most people. In addition, good listeners are inclined to accept or tolerate rather than to judge and criticize. Therefore, they have fewer enemies than most people, and they are probably the most loved of people. However, there are exceptions to that generality. For example, John Steinbeck is said to have been an excellent listener, yet he was hated by some people. No doubt his ability to listen contributed to his capacity to write, but the results of his listening did not make him popular.

대부분의 사람들은 말하기를 좋아하고 듣기를 좋아하는 사람은 거의 없는데, 잘 듣는 것은 누구나 소중히 해야 할 드문 재능이다. 잘 듣는 사람들은 더 많이 듣기 때문에 그들은 대부분의 사람보다 그들 주위에 일어나는 일을 더 잘 알고 더 민감한 경향이 있다. 게다가 잘 듣는 사람들은 판단하고 비판하기보다 받아들이고 참는 경향이 있다. 따라서 그들은 대부분의 사람들보다 적이 더 적고, 사람들 중 가장 사랑을 받는 사람들일 것이다. 그러나 그런 일반성에는 예외가 있다. 예를 들어, John Steinbeck은 매우 잘 듣는 사람이었으나 몇몇 사람에 의해 미움을 받았다. 틀림없이 잘 듣는 그의 능력은 그의 글쓰기 능력에 공헌했지만, 잘 듣는 결과는 그를 인기있게 만들어 주지는 못했다.

Rudy's Tip 삽입문은 잘 듣는 것에 대한 플러스 진술이다. 따라서 however 앞에, 즉 예외적인 내용 앞에 위치해야 적절하다.

6

정답 (D)

[C] Infrasound is a low-pitched sound, whose frequency is far below the range of human ears. Scientists, however, have been able to discover the existence of infrasound by using special technologies. These new technologies have revealed that many things can produce infrasound, from earthquakes and thunderstorms to trains and underground explosions, thus making possible the warning of earthquakes and the monitoring of underground nuclear-explosion tests.

[A] These new technologies have another benefit for biologists by allowing them to gain access to the unknown world of communication between animals. For centuries, biologists believed giraffes were the silent giants of Africa. In recent years, however, biologists have been able to listen more carefully by means of these technologies and have realized that giraffes may talk, though not in a way that we can hear.

[B] Communication through infrasound is not limited to giraffes. Over the last few decades, biologists have found that whales, elephants, and some other animals also use this extremely low-pitched sound to communicate. This infrasound, as a means of communication, has special merit: It can travel a greater distance than higher-pitched noise. Such long-distance communication is a must for animals such as giraffes or elephants that roam over wide areas.

[C] 초저주파 음은 저음의 소리를 말하는데, 그 주파수는 인간의 귀에 들리는 범위를 벗어난다. 그러나 과학자들은 특수한 기술을 사용함으로써 초저주파 음이 존재함을 발견할 수 있었다. 이러한 새로운 기술은 지진과 천둥에서부터 기차와 지하 폭발에 이르기까지, 많은 것들이 초저주파 음을 만들어 낼 수 있음을 밝혀냈다. 그래서 지진 경고와 지하 핵폭발 실험의 탐지까지 가능한 것이다.

[A] 이러한 새로운 기술은 생물학자들로 하여금 미지의 세계인 동물 간의 의사소통에 접근하게 함으로써 또 다른 이점을 갖는다. 수세기 동안, 생물학자들은 기린이 아프리카에 있는 조용한 거인이라고 믿었다. 그러나 최근에 생물학자들은 이러한 기술로 인해 더 주의 깊게 들을 수 있게 되었고, 비록 우리가 들을 수 있는 방식으로는 아니지만, 기린이 말을 할 수 있음을 알게 되었다.

[B] 초저주파 음을 통한 의사소통은 기린에게만 해당되는 것이 아니다. 지난 수십 년에 걸쳐, 생물학자들은 고래, 코끼리, 그리고 몇몇 다른 동물들도 의사소통을 하기 위해 초저음을 사용한다는 것을 알게 되었다. 의사소통의 수단으로서의 이 초저주파 음은 특별한 장점을 가지고 있는데, 그 소리는 고음의 소리보다 훨씬 더 먼 거리를 간다. 그런 원거리 의사소통은 넓은 지역을 돌아다니는 기린이나 코끼리 같은 동물에겐 필수적이다.

Rudy's Tip C의 첫 문장이 G이다. C의 끝부분과 A의 첫 문장이 연결되고, A의 기린과 B의 기린이 서로 연결된다.

10분 모의고사 03 해설편

1 정답 (B)

The future, as we stand on the threshold of 2012, looks bleaker than it did during the past few years.
우리는 2012년의 경계에 있으면서, 미래는 더 어두워 보인다, 과거 수년간 보다.

(A) The future only seems bleaker; however, in reality that is because the past few years were great.
  미래는 암울해 보이기만 한다. 그러나 실제로 그것은 지난 몇 년 동안 상황이 매우 좋았기 때문이다.

(B) As we enter 2012, we are more pessimistic than we have been over the past few years.
  우리가 2012년으로 들어가면서, 우리는 지난 몇 년 동안 그랬던 것보다도 더 비관적이다.

(C) From the vantage point of 2012, the situation has no hope of improvement.
  2012년이라는 시점에서 볼 때, 상황은 개선될 희망이 전혀 없다.

(D) Although the future from 2012 looks bleak, it is because we only have the past for perspective.
  2012년부터 미래가 암울해 보이긴 하지만, 그것은 우리가 과거의 관점(기준)만을 가지고 있기 때문이다.

Rudy's Tip 다른 문항들도 미래에 대한 부정적 예상은 동일하지만, 제시문에 없는 정보들이 등장했기에 적절하지 않다. 언제나 제시문을 벗어나는 추가적인 정보는 오답일 가능성이 높다.

2 정답 (D)

It's important to remember that you must take pride in the work you do. It's like learning how to use a computer. The first time, the computer is intimidating and not very user-friendly: Files are deleted, screens freeze, and software doesn't install. But you don't give up. You read the owner's manual, ask friends for help and call the manufacturer for assistance. After a few weeks, you begin to master the intricacies of using a computer and begin to wonder how you ever lived without one. If you didn't take pride in learning how to use a computer, it would probably end up gathering dust instead of making your life more efficient and productive.

자신이 하는 일에 자부심을 가져야 한다는 것을 기억하는 것이 중요하다. 이는 컴퓨터를 사용하는 방법을 배우는 것과도 같다. 처음에 컴퓨터는 위협적이고 사용하기 쉽지 않다. 즉 파일은 날아가고 화면은 정지되며, 소프트웨어는 설치가 되지 않는다. 하지만 당신은 포기하지 말라. 입문서를 읽고, 친구에게 도와 달라고 하며 제조업자에게 전화를 걸어 도움을 청하라. 몇 주 지나면 컴퓨터 사용의 복잡한 원리들을 습득하게 되고 컴퓨터 없이 어떻게 살아왔나 의아하게 생각하게 된다. 컴퓨터 사용 방법을 배우는 데 대한 자부심이 없다면 컴퓨터는 당신의 생활을 보다 효율적이고 생산적으로 만들지 못하고 먼지나 쌓이는 것으로 끝나고 말 것이다.

Rudy's Tip 포기하지 말라는 것과 컴퓨터에 능숙해 진다는 것은 내용상 공백이 존재한다. 즉, 중간에 구체적인 해결방안이 등장해야 자연스럽다.

3
정답 (B)

[C] Everyone makes decisions every day. What clothes should you wear? Should you go out tonight or stay home and study? Most of the decisions people make are based on what they feel will be the best solution. Feelings and judgments of how others feel toward you play a major role in how you choose to solve your day-to-day problems.

[B] True problem solving, however, goes beyond feelings. To solve a problem, you must look beyond how you feel and combine information that you already know with new observations. Then, on the basis of your knowledge of the situation, you can evaluate the problem and come up with the best way to solve it. An example will make this point clear.

[A] Imagine that it's Saturday and you are to meet your friends at the mall at 12:00. You've been busy all morning, and suddenly you notice it is 11:45. You hurry to get ready and then jump in the car. What route is probably the fastest? You know where the mall is, and you choose the best route based on what you know about the distance, the number of stop lights, and the amount of traffic. In short, you make observations and make your best guesses based on what you know and have observed.

[C] 모든 사람들은 매일매일 결정을 내린다. 어떤 옷을 입어야 할까? 오늘밤 외출을 할 것인가? 집에서 공부를 할 것인가? 사람들이 내리는 결정의 대부분은 그들이 느끼기에 그것이 최상의 해결책일 것이라는 것에 기초한다. 다른 사람들이 당신에 대해 어떻게 느낄 것인가에 대한 감정과 판단은 당신이 자신의 일상적인 문제들을 어떻게 선택할 것인가 하는 데에 있어 중요한 역할을 한다.
[B] 그러나 진정한 문제 해결은 감정의 영역 밖이다. 문제를 해결하기 위해서는 여러분이 어떻게 느끼는가 하는 것을 뛰어넘어야 하고 새로운 관찰로 이미 인지하고 있는 정보를 연결시켜야 한다. 그 다음, 그 상황에 대한 당신의 지식에 기초하여, 당신은 그 문제를 평가할 수 있고, 그것을 해결할 수 있는 최선의 방법에 근접할 수 있다. 이러한 점을 명백히 해줄 하나의 예를 들어보자.
[A] 토요일이고 12시에 쇼핑가에서 친구를 만난다고 상상해 보아라. 아침내내 분주한 당신이 갑자기 11시 45분임을 알아챈다. 당신은 급하게 준비하고 차에 올라탄다. 어떤 길이 가장 빠를까? 당신은 상가가 어디인지를 알고, 거리, 신호등 수, 교통량 등에 대해 당신이 인지하고 있는 것에 기초하여 최상의 길을 선택한다. 간단히 말해, 당신은 자신이 인지하고 관찰하는 것에 기초해서 인지하고 최고의 추측을 한다.

Rudy's Tip C의 첫 문장이 G이기에 첫 문항으로 적절하고, C 마지막 to solve가 B의 첫 문장과 연결된다. B 마지막의 example로서 A가 이어지고 있다.

4

정답 (D)

A wealthy individual, whose basic survival needs are met many times over, buys his pets gourmet, organic food that costs more per week than the weekly earnings of a minimum-wage worker. He is proud that he is able to take such good care of his animals and insists that it's the right thing to do if one really loves one's pets. After all, his vet was the one who recommended that he buy that brand. A minimum-wage worker who loads that food into the rich person's car might feel anger when he realizes how much money this individual spends on his pets. The minimum-wage worker might fume that this man's pets eat better than he does. He might wonder whether this rich man has any concept of reality.

부유한 개인은, 기본 생계에 필요한 것들보다 더 많은 것들을 버는, 애완동물을 위해 미식가용 유기농 식품을 구입한다. 최저임금 노동자의 주급보다 많은 비용이 드는. 그는 자신의 애완동물을 잘 돌봐줄 수 있다는 것을 자랑스럽게 여기고 이것이 애완동물을 사랑한다면 당연한 것이라고 생각한다. 무엇보다. 그가 브랜드 제품을 구입하도록 추천하는 사람은 수의사다. 브랜드 음식을 부유한 사람의 차에 실어주는 최저임금 노동자는 분노할 것이다. 얼마나 많은 돈을 이 부유한 사람이 애완동물을 위해 지출하는지를 알게 될 때. 최저임금 노동자는 이 부유한 사람의 애완동물이 자신보다 비싼 음식을 먹는다는 사실에 화를 낼 것이다. 최저임금 노동자는 부유한 사람이 현실에 대한 개념을 가지고 있는지 의아해 할지도 모른다.

Rudy's Tip 빈칸을 위해서 마지막 2~3문장에 집중하자. 최저임금 노동자들이 애완동물이 자신들보다 비싼 음식을 먹는다는 것을 알게 되었을 때 느끼는 감정이 빈칸의 내용이다.

5

정답 (B)

"Heaven helps those who help themselves" is a well-tried maxim, embodying in a small compass the results of vast human experience. The spirit of self-help is the root of all genuine growth in the individual, and as exhibited in the lives of many, it constitutes the true source of national vigor and strength. Help from without is often enfeebling in its effects, but help from within invariably invigorates. Whatever is done for men or classes to a certain extent takes away the stimulus and necessity of doing for themselves. And where men are subjected to overgovernment, the inevitable tendency is to render them comparatively helpless.

"하늘은 스스로 돕는 자를 돕는다"는 말은 충분히 입증되어온 격언으로, 광범위한 인간의 경험을 통한 결과를 간결하게 나타낸다. 스스로 해보겠다는 정신은 개인의 모든 진정한 성장의 뿌리이고, 많은 이들의 삶에서 볼 수 있듯이 국가적 활기와 힘의 진정한 원천이 된다. 외부로부터의 원조는 종종 그 효과가 약화되지만 내부로부터의 원조는 항상 활기를 북돋운다. 사람들 혹은 계층을 위해 하는 일은 그것이 무엇이든 간에 어느 정도는 자립적인 추진력과 필요성을 앗아가 버린다. 그리고 인간이 지나친 통제를 받는 곳에서는, 인간을 상대적으로 무력하게 만드는 필연적 경향이 존재한다.

(A) Too much intervention goes against the spirit of self-help.
너무나 많은 간섭은 자립정신에 도움이 되지 않는다.
(B) "Heaven helps those who help themselves" is now an obsolete aphorism.
'하늘은 스스로 돕는 자를 돕는다'는 격언은 한물 갔다.
(C) Self-help is an essential requirement to achieve a real progress in the individual.
자립은 개인의 진정한 발전을 위해서 필수적인 조건이다.
(D) Selfish motives are generally more stimulating than altruistic ones.
이기적인(개인주의적인) 동기가 이타적인 동기보다 더 활력을 제공한다.
ⓡ selfish motives = the spirit of self-help

Rudy's Tip GS 구조의 영문으로 '자립성'을 강조하는 글이다. B는 자립성을 부정하는 내용으로 적절하지 않다. 또한 B와 C는 대조적인 문항으로 둘 중 하나가 틀릴 가능성이 큰 관계이다.

독독 3.0 분석독해

Whatever is done for men or classes/to a certain extent/takes away the stimulus and necessity /of doing for themselves.
사람이나 계층을 위해서 이루어진 것은 무엇이든/어느 정도는/자극과 필요성을 빼앗는다/스스로 하려는

6
정답 (B)

In its effort at social engineering to build the perfect society, Singapore has, among other things, banned chewing gum, run campaigns encouraging people to smile, and passed edicts to stop children from climbing trees. Since 1984 the Social Development Unit, a government agency, has even attempted to create smarter Singaporeans. The forum was launched to redress a vexing imbalance: too few bright Singaporean men and women seemed interested in marrying each other, preferring either to wed intellectual inferiors or not to marry at all. Fearing the trend pointed in the direction of dullardism, the government decided to play Cupid by organizing dances for eligible college graduates. The SDU, though, quickly earned a reputation among critics as the port of last resort for the "Single, Desperate and Ugly." But the government's efforts have become effective: more than half of Singapore's graduate men now marry graduate women — an increase of nearly 25% since 1984.

완벽한 사회를 건설하기 위한 사회적 조정의 노력 속에서, 싱가포르는 다른 무엇보다도 껌을 금지시키고, 사람들이 미소 짓는 것을 격려하는 캠페인을 벌였고, 아이들이 나무에 오르는 것을 금지하는 법령을 통과시켰다. 1984년 이래 정부기관인 사회개발부는 보다 더 똑똑한 싱가포르인들을 만들어 내는 시도를 하고 있다. 걱정스런 불균형을 바로잡고자 토론회가 개최되었다. 즉, 대다수의 똑똑한 싱가포르 남자들과 여자들이 서로가 결혼하는 것에 관심이 적고, 그들보다 지적으로 열등한 상대와 결혼을 하거나 아예 결혼하지 않는 것을 선호한다는 것이다. 정부는 멍청함(대중의 우민화)으로 향하는 추세를 두려워하면서, 결혼적령기 대학졸업자들을 위한 무도회를 조직해서 중매자 역할을 하기로 결정하였다. 그럼에도 불구하고 SDU(사회개발부)는 비판가들 사이에서 빠르게 "독신자들, 절망하는 자들, 그리고 추악한 자들"을 위한 최후의 안식처라는 평판을 얻었다. 그러나 정부의 노력은 효과가 있었다. 현재 싱가포르 대졸자 남성의 절반 이상이 대졸자 여성과 결혼하고 있다. 이것은 1984년 이후 거의 25% 증가한 것이다.

(A) Civilized Wedding 선진화된 결혼
(B) State Matchmaking 국가의 중매
(C) Social Welfare Policy 사회 복지정책
(D) Common Law Marriage 결혼 관습법

Rudy's Tip ST 구조의 영문이다. 정부의 중매 노력과 이에 따른 결실이 주제로 적절하다.

독독 3.0 분석독해

Singapore has, among other things, ①banned chewing gum, ②run campaigns encouraging people to smile, and ③passed edicts to stop children from climbing trees.
①+②+③ 모두 has에 연결되는 공통관계 구조이다.
has banned + has run + has passed

10분 모의고사 04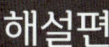

1
정답 (C)

A number of studies showed the relationship between population density and the rates of disease, crime, and mental illness.

[C] The results of these studies were confusing, because they sometimes didn't support the idea of the existence of the relationship.

[B] Hong Kong, for instance, has a population density 4 times as great as even the most crowded American cities.

[A] But it has lower rates of hospitalization for mental illness and criminal violence than American cities.

많은 연구가 인구 밀도와 질병, 범죄 그리고 정신병의 비율과의 관련성을 보여주었다.
[C] 가끔 그러한 관계가 존재한다는 생각을 뒷받침하지 않는 경우가 있었기 때문에, 이 연구 결과는 혼란스러웠다.
[B] 예를 들어, Hong Kong의 밀도는 심지어 가장 과밀한 미국 도시의 네 배이다.
[A] 하지만, Hong Kong은 미국의 도시들보다 정신병 입원율과 강력 범죄율이 더 낮다.

Rudy's Tip C의 these studies 가 도입문의 a number of studies 연결된다. A의 it은 B의 홍콩을 의미한다.

2

정답 (B)

Among their possible uses, smartphones can be used to mobilize individuals for political as well as social purposes.
스마트폰을 활용하는데 있어서, 스마트폰은 사회적 목적뿐 아니라 정치적 목적을 위해서 개인들을 동원하는 데 사용될 수 있다.

(A) Smartphones make it easy for individuals to track changes in politics and society.
스마트폰은 개인들이 정치와 사회 변화를 추적하기 쉽게 해준다.

(B) Smartphones enable people to unite to achieve political goals in addition to enabling social achievement.
스마트폰은 사람들이 사회적 업적(목적)을 가능하게 해줄 뿐 아니라 정치적 목적을 달성하기 위해 연합할 수 있게 해준다.

(C) Smartphones enable the integration of political and social agendas through a common technology.
스마트폰은 공통적인 기술을 통해 정치적 사회적 의제들의 통합을 가능하게 해준다.

(D) Smartphones are blurring lines between diverse political and social trends by causing individuals to merge into one group.
스마트폰은 개인들을 한 집단으로 통합해서 다양한 정치적, 사회적 경향 사이의 경계를 허물고 있다.

Rudy's Tip to mobilize individuals for political purposes = enable people to unite to achieve political goals
정치적 목적을 위해서 개인들을 동원한다는 의미는 정치적 목적을 이루기 위해 개인들을 통합할 수 있다는 의미와 동일하다.

3

정답 (B)

The average human pulse rate is around seventy beats per minute. This is also the average tempo of most Western music. In fact, it's said that the slow parts of Baroque music induce mental and emotional integration. Concentrating on the rhythm of music affects the rate of breathing, making it more regular, and faster or slower depending on the piece. There are interesting developments involving music. People are making "bioelectric" music, recording the sounds made by the electric impulses that result from brain activity or muscle movement. The sounds are processed through a computerized gadget for the use of composers, musicians, and even handicapped people who can be taught this means of self-expression. It's possible that by studying the "music" made by cells, microscopic creatures, and plants, we will understand biology much better.

보통 사람의 맥박 속도는 1분에 약 70회이다. 이것은 대부분의 서양 음악의 평균 박자이기도 하다. 실제로, 바로크 음악의 느린 부분은 정신과 감정의 통합을 이끌어낸다고들 한다. 음악의 리듬에 집중하는 것은 호흡의 속도에도 영향을 미쳐서, 호흡을 더욱 규칙적이게 하고, 곡에 따라 호흡은 더 빨라지거나 느려진다. 음악과 관련된 흥미 있는 사실이 있다. 사람들은 뇌의 활동이나 근육 움직임에 의해 생겨나는 전기적인 파장에 의해서 만들어진 소리를 녹음하여 '생물 조직의 전기 에너지' 음악을 만든다. 그 소리는 컴퓨터 장비를 통해 가공되어 작곡가들, 음악가들이 사용할 수 있고, 심지어 장애인들은 이를 배워 자기표현의 수단으로 이용할 수 있다. 세포, 미세 생물, 식물의 '음악'을 연구하여 생물을 훨씬 더 잘 이해하는 것이 가능하게 되었다.

(A) New Developments in Music 음악에서 새로운 발전들
(B) Relation of Music to Biology 음악과 생물학의 관계
(C) Use of Biology to Music 음악을 대상으로 생물학을 이용하는 것
   ⓡ 음악과 생물학이 매우 밀접하다는 내용으로 음악을 활용하여 생물학에 접목시킬 수도 있다는 내용이다. C는 생물학이 중심이 되어 음악에 적용한다는 의미로 다른 의미이다.
(D) Ways to Understand Biology 생물학을 이해하는 방법

Rudy's Tip ST 구성으로 지문의 처음과 마지막이 동일한 것에 유의하자. 음악과 생물학이 매우 밀접하다는 것이 주제이다.

독독 3.0 분석독해
The sounds are processed/through a computerized gadget /for the use of composers, musicians, /and even handicapped people /who can be taught this means of self-expression.
이 소리들은 가공된다/컴퓨터 장비들을 통해서/작곡가들, 음악가들이 사용할 수 있도록/그리고 심지어 장애인들이 사용할 수 있도록/자기표현의 수단으로 배울 수 있는

4   정답 (A)

The migrant question is a more serious threat to Europe's future than anything in recent memory, because it can't be resolved by a promise from a central bank or an infusion of someone else's cash. This is a question of Europe's identity – whether it means as much to European voters as it did a generation ago. All the while, the refugees will keep coming, and it will become harder for governments to make sacrifices to welcome them.

최근에 이민 문제는 그 어떤 것보다 유럽의 미래에 더 심각한 위협이다. 이민 문제가 유럽 중앙은행의 약속이나 누군가의 현금을 투입하는 것을 통해서 해결될 수 없기 때문이다. 이민 문제는 유럽의 정체성에 관한 문제이다. 이것이 한 세대 전만큼이나 현재 유럽의 유권자들에게도 많은 것을 의미하든 안 하든 간에. 그러는 동안 난민들은 계속해서 지속적으로 몰려올 것이다. 그리고 유럽 정부들이 난민들을 받아들이는 희생을 감수하는 일은 점점 더 어려워질 것이다.

(A) All the while 그러는 동안 (동시성으로 전후 관계의 논리적 연관성이 존재하지 않는다)
(B) On the one hand 한편으로는
   ℝ on the one hand & on the other hand - 한 편 & 다른 한편으로는
(C) In conclusion 결론적으로
(D) On the other hand 다른 한편으로는

Rudy's Tip 빈칸을 중심으로 전후 관계에 어떤 연계성이 존재하지 않는다. 즉, 이민문제에 대해서 어떤 정체성을 갖는 것과 난민들이 계속해서 증가한다는 것은 별개의 사건이다. 따라서 아무런 논리적 연결성이 필요없는 연결어가 적절하다.

독독 3.0 분석독해
it means as much to European voters /as it did a generation ago.
= it means as much to European voters /as it meant much to European voters a generation ago.
그것은 유럽 유권자들에게 많은 것을 의미한다 /한세대전에 유럽 유권자들에게 많은 것을 의미했던 것처럼.

5   정답 (D)

During a momentous battle, a Chinese general decided to attack even though his army was greatly inferior in numbers. He was confident they would win, but his men were filled with doubt. On the way to the battle, they stopped at a religious shrine. After praying with the men, the general took out a coin and said, "I shall now toss this coin. If it is heads, we shall win. If it is tails we shall lose." He threw the coin into the air and all watched intently it landed. It was heads. The soldiers were so overjoyed and filled with confidence that they vigorously attacked the enemy and were victorious. After the battle, a lieutenant remarked to the general, "No one can change destiny." "Quite right," the general replied as he showed the lieutenant the coin, which had heads on both sides.

아주 중요한 전투를 치르는 동안에 중국의 한 장수가 비록 그의 군대가 수적으로 훨씬 열세였지만 공격을 하기로 마음을 먹었다. 그는 그의 군대가 이길 것이라는 것을 확신했지만 그의 부하들은 회의가 많았다. 전투를 하러 가는 도중에 그들은 한 사당에 멈추었다. 부하들과 함께 기도를 한 다음에 장수는 동전을 꺼내고 말했다. "이제 이 동전을 던지겠다. 만약 동전의 앞면이 나오면 우리가 이길 것이고 뒷면이 나오면 우리가 질 것이다." 그는 동전을 공중으로 던졌고 동전이 떨어질 때 모든 사람들이 열중하여 지켜보았다. 앞면이었다. 군사들은 너무 기뻤고 너무 자신감에 찼기 때문에 힘차게 적을 공격했고 승리했다. 전투가 끝난 다음에 부관이 장수에게 말했다. "어느 누구도 운명을 바꿀 수 없습니다." "자네 말이 맞네." 장수가 대답을 하며 부관에게 동전을 보여 주었는데 그 동전은 양쪽에 앞면이 있었다.

Rudy's Tip coin이 키워드로 동전을 던진 결과가 등장하는 (D)가 적절하다.

6

정답 (D)

An abbreviation is a shortened form of a word or phrase that is used to save space in written form. Certain types of abbreviations, such as some acronyms, may also facilitate memory and are spoken, if easily pronounced, as well as written. The use of abbreviations dates back to ancient times, but the proliferation of abbreviations has been most acute in the 20th century. This is directly related to the vast increase in information, especially in science and technology, and to the ever-burgeoning number of agencies and organizations, both private and governmental.

약어(줄임말)란 글을 쓸 때 공간을 줄이기 위해 낱말이나 구를 단축시킨 형태이다. 약어의 유형들 중 몇몇 두문자어의 경우에는 기억하기 쉽게 만들어 주기도 하는데, 쉽게 발음할 수 있다면 그대로 쓰여 지거나 말하여지기도 한다. 약어의 사용은 고대까지 거슬러 올라간다. 그러나 약어는 20세기 들어 가장 널리 사용되고 있다. 이는 정보, 그 중에서도 특히 과학과 기술에서의 정보의 증가, 그리고 사립, 정부기관과 조직이 계속 늘어나고 있는 것과 직접적인 관련이 있다.

(A) most acronyms are fairly easy to pronounce and remember
대부분의 두문자는 발음하거나 기억하기가 상당히 쉽다.
(B) the use of abbreviations has been steady throughout history
약어의 활용은 역사를 통틀어 안정적이다. (과거부터 점진적으로 활용되어 왔다는 의미)
(C) abbreviations did not appear in ancient times
고대에는 약어들이 등장하지 않았다.
(D) proliferation of acronyms may not cease
두문자의 확산은 멈추지 않을 것이다.

Rudy's Tip 본문의 ever-burgeoning 통해서 향후에도 증가할 것이라고 예상할 수 있다.

독독 3.0 분석독해

This is directly related /to the vast increase in information, especially in science and technology, /and to the ever-burgeoning number of agencies and organizations, both private and governmental.

Ⓡ be related to + be related to 병렬구조.

10분 모의고사 05 해설편

1
정답 (C)

Nowadays religion gets less credit for its staple function of patching up the moral fabric of society.
요즘 종교는 사회의 도덕적 구조를 연결시켜주는 주요한 기능에 있어 신뢰를 별로 받지 못한다.

(A) Religion's heavy task of revising the moral criteria of society is becoming less trustworthy.
사회의 도덕적 범주를 개정하는 종교의 어려운 직무는 점차 신뢰할 수 없게 되었다.

(B) Religion is believed to perform an insignificant task in supporting moral standards of society.
종교는 사회의 도덕적 기준을 뒷받침하는 사소한 직무를 담당한다고 사람들은 생각한다.

(C) Religion's principal role in sustaining moral cohesion of society is not acknowledged as much.
사회의 도덕적 화합을 유지하는 종교의 주요한 역할은 그다지 인정되지 않는다.

(D) Religion does not recognize its traditional role in creating moral principles of society.
종교는 사회의 도덕적 원칙을 창조하는 종교의 전통적인 역할을 알지 못한다.

Rudy's Tip get less credit = not acknowledged
patching up the moral fabric = sustaining moral cohesion

2

정답 (D)

Since the Hawaiian Islands have never been connected to other land masses, the great variety of plants in Hawaii must be a result of the long-distance dispersal of seeds, a process that requires both a method of transport and equivalence between the ecology of the source area and that of the recipient area. There is some of dispute about the method of transport involved. Some biologists argue that ocean and air currents are responsible for the transport of plant seeds to Hawaii. Yet the results of flotation experiments and the low temperatures of air currents cast doubt on these hypotheses. More probable is bird transport, rather externally, by accidental attachment of the seeds to feathers, or internally, by the swallowing of fruit and subsequent excretion of the seeds. While it is likely that fewer varieties of plant seeds have reached Hawaii externally than internally, more varieties are known to be adapted to external than to internal transport.

하와이의 섬들은 결코 다른 땅덩어리와 연결되었던 적이 없어서, 많은 종류의 하와이 식물들은 씨가 먼 거리까지 퍼져나간 결과임이 틀림없는데, 이렇게 씨가 퍼져나가는 것은 어떠한 수송 방법이 있어야 하는 동시에 씨의 원천지의 생태와 수령지의 생태가 비슷할 것을 요구한다. 관련된 수송 방법에 대해서는 약간의 논란이 있다. 몇몇 생물학자들은 해류와 대류가 하와이까지 식물 씨앗을 옮긴 원인이라고 주장한다. 그러나 부양 실험의 결과와 대기의 낮은 온도로 볼 때 이런 가설은 의심의 여지가 있다. 보다 설득력 있는 것은, 외적으로 씨가 우연히 깃털에 묻어서, 또는 내적으로 열매를 삼키고 뒤이어 그것을 배설함으로써, 새가 씨앗을 옮겨왔다는 것이다. 외적으로 하와이에 도착한 식물 씨앗의 종류가 내적으로 도착한 것보다 적을 것 같지만, 더 많은 종류가 내적 수송보다는 외적 수송에 보다 알맞은 것으로 알려져 있다.

The author mentions the results of flotation experiments on plants seeds in order to _____.

작가는 식물 씨앗의 부양 실험 결과들을 설명하고 있다. _____ 위해서.

(A) support the claim that the distribution of plants in Hawaii is the result of the long-distance dispersal of seeds
하와이 식물들 분포는 씨앗들의 장거리 확산의 결과라는 주장을 뒷받침하기 위해서
(B) lend credibility to the thesis that air currents provide a method of transport for plant seeds to Hawaii
대류가 하와이로 씨앗들이 운송된 방법을 제공했다는 이론을 뒷받침하기 위해서
(C) suggest that the long-distance dispersal seeds is a process that requires long periods of time
씨앗의 장거리 확산은 장시간이 걸리는 과정이라는 것을 보여주기 위해서
(D) challenge the claim that ocean currents are responsible for the transport of plant seeds to Hawaii
해류가 하와이로 씨앗을 운반한다는 주장에 이의를 제기하기 위해서

Rudy's Tip 문제의 형식은 빈칸 채우기이지만, 문제 의도는 내용일치에 해당한다. 기존 학설에 문제가 있다는 것을 제시하는 것이 이 글의 목적으로, 기존 학설에 대한 이의를 제기하는 문항이 적절하다.

3

정답 (A)

(a) In March 1979 Wertheimer and physicist Ed Beeper, Ph. D. published this ominous finding in the American Journal of Epidemiology, one of the foremost epidemiological journals in the world.

(e) They wrote that power lines "are taken for granted and generally assumed to be harmless," but that assumption had "never been adequately tested."

(d) Their article noted that certain household appliances — hair dryers, toasters, and electric drills — can also produce strong magnetic fields.

(c) They pointed out, however, that unlike the magnetic fields given off by power lines, the fields from most household appliances fall off sharply with distance from the appliance.

(b) In addition, appliances tend to be used sporadically and therefore do not constitute sources of chronic, or continuous, magnetic-field exposure.

(a) 1979년 3월 Wertheimer와 물리학자 Ed Leeper 박사는 세계에서 가장 권위 있는 전염병학 학술지 중 하나인 전미 전염병학 학술지에 이 불길한 연구결과를 발표했다.
(e) 그들은 전선들이 "당연한 것으로 여겨지고 일반적으로 무해한 것으로 생각되어지고 있지만 그러한 생각은 "충분히 검토된 바 없다"고 밝혔다.
(d) 그들의 연구는 헤어드라이어, 토스트기, 전기 드릴과 같은 특정 가전제품들 또한 강력한 자기장을 만들 수 있다는 사실에 주목했다
(c) 그러나 그들은 전선에 의해 형성되는 자기장과는 달리 대부분의 가전제품들로부터 발생되는 자기장은 전기제품과 거리를 두면 급격히 약화된다는 점을 지적했다.
(b) 더욱이 가전제품들은 간헐적으로 사용되는 경향이 있어 상습적인 즉, 지속적인 자기장에의 노출 대상이 되지는 못한다.

Rudy's Tip (a) 시간 표시 부사구가 있기에 첫 문항으로 적절하다. (c) 와 (e)는 둘다 they가 있어서 첫 문항으로 적절하지 않다. (a)의 'ominous finding'이 (e)의 내용으로 연결된다.

4 정답 (D)

The intelligence of the elephant is widely known. We say, "the elephant never forgets," in honor of its excellent memory. An Indian farmer who kept elephants discovered this fact. He had noticed that his elephants were eating his bananas at night. No fence could keep out the elephants, of course, so he decided to tie bells on them. Then he would hear them when they come to eat the bananas and he could chase them away. A few mornings later, however, the bananas were all gone, though he had heard nothing at night. When he checked the elephants he found that they had played a trick on him. They had filled the bells with mud so that they would not make any noise!

코끼리의 지능은 널리 알려져 있다. 우리는 코끼리의 뛰어난 기억력에 경의를 표하여 "코끼리는 결코 잊지 않는다."고 말한다. 코끼리들을 기르는 한 인디언 농부가 이런 사실을 발견했다. 그는 자기 코끼리들이 밤에 자기 바나나를 먹는다는 것을 알아차렸다. 물론 어떤 담장도 코끼리들을 막을 수 없어서, 그는 코끼리들에게 종을 매달기로 결심했다. 그러면 코끼리들이 바나나를 먹기 위해서 왔을 때 벨 소리를 듣고, 코끼리들을 쫓아 버릴 수 있었다. 그러나 그가 밤에 아무것도 못 들었음에도, 며칠 후 아침에 바나나는 모두 없어졌다. 코끼리들을 확인해 봤을 때 그는 그것들이 자신을 속였다는 것을 알았다. 코끼리들은 종에서 아무 소리도 나지 않도록 진흙으로 종을 꽉 채웠던 것이었다!

Rudy's Tip 삽입문 'them'의 선행사는 bells 이다. 대명사는 선행사 뒤에 위치하는 것이 논리적이다.

5-6

정답 (C), (D)

While computer scientists would prefer that our passwords be a hard-to-crack jumble, precisely what makes passwords so flawed is also what computer scientist Joseph Bonneau finds uplifting. "People take a nonnatural requirement imposed on them, like memorizing a password," he said, "and make it a meaningful human experience." Here is a good example. In 1993, when she was 22, Maria T. Allen used for her password a combination of the name of her summer crush, J. D. and the name of a mythological female deity to whom he had compared her when they'd first met. The fling ended, and they went their separate ways. But the password endured. Eleven years later, out of the blue, Maria received a message through "classmates.com" from J. D. himself. They dated a few years, then decided to marry. Before the wedding, J. D. asked Maria if she had ever thought of him during that interim decade. "About every time I logged in to my Yahoo! account," she replied, before recounting to him her secret. He had the password inscribed on the inside of his wedding ring.

컴퓨터 과학자들은 우리의 비밀번호를 깨기 어렵게 뒤죽박죽 섞인 것을 선호하는 반면, 비밀번호를 약점이 있는 것으로 만드는 것 또한 컴퓨터 과학자 Joseph Bonneau를 들뜨게 만든다. "사람들은 비밀번호를 암기하는 것과 같은 불편한 요구 조건을 받아들입니다. 그리고 그것을 중요한 삶의 경험으로 만듭니다."라고, 그는 말한다. 적절한 예가 있다. 1993년, 그녀의 나이 22살이었을 때 Maria T. Allen은 그녀가 여름에 반한 상대 J.D.의 이름과 그들이 처음 만났을 때 J.D.가 그녀와 비교했던 신화 속의 여신의 이름을 조합해서 비밀번호로 사용하게 되었다. 짧은 연애는 끝났다. 그리고 그들은 각자 자신의 길을 갔다. 그러나 비밀번호는 남았다. 11년 후, 난데없이, Maria는 J. D.로부터 "classmates.com"을 통해서 메시지를 받았다. 그들은 몇 년 동안 교제를 했고 결혼하기로 했다. 결혼 전 J. D.는 Maria에게 그들이 헤어져 있었던 10년 동안 자신에 대해서 생각해 본 적이 있었느냐고 물었다. 자신의 비밀번호 비밀을 설명하기 전에 그녀는 "내 야후에 로그인할 때마다 거의 매번 생각했어."라고 답했다. 그는 그 비밀번호를 그의 결혼반지 안쪽에 새겨 넣었다.

5 빈칸에 적절한 표현을 고르세요.

(A) a true story 실제 이야기
(B) a code of conduct 행동규범
(C) a meaningful human experience 의미 있는 삶의 경험
(D) a means of encoding a password 비밀번호를 부호화하는 수단

Rudy's Tip 패스워드를 빈칸으로 만든다는 내용으로, 빈칸 이후의 재진술을 통해서 일반적으로 패스워드는 개인에게 의미 있는 사건, 사람과 관련해서 만든다는 것을 알 수 있다.

6 다음 중 맞지 않는 것은?

(A) Maria's Yahoo! account password had an emotional edge.
   마리아의 야후 계정 비밀번호는 감성적 강렬함(특성)을 가지고 있었다.
(B) J. D. once praised Maria's beauty by likening it to that of a goddess.
   J. D. 는 마리아의 아름다움을 여신의 아름다움에 비유했었다.
(C) It was in 2004 that Maria received a message again from J. D. after the breakup.
   헤어진 후 2004년에 마리아는 J. D에게서 메시지를 받았다.
   ℛ 93년에 만나 헤어지고, 10년 후에 다시 만났기에 맞는 문항이다.
(D) Maria stopped using all passwords associated with J. D. right after the breakup.
   마리아는 헤어진 직후에 J. D와 관련된 모든 비밀번호 사용을 중지했다.

Rudy's Tip D는 본문의 내용과 완전히 상반되는 문항이다.

10분 모의고사 06 해설편

1
정답 (A)

It would have been an ideal location for a waste incineration facility except for the opposition of the people in a nearby town.
근처 마을 주민들의 반대만 없었다면 그곳은 쓰레기 소각시설을 설치하기에 이상적인 장소가 되었을 것이다.

(A) The people interfered with the construction of a waste incineration facility.
주민들은 쓰레기 소각시설의 건설에 대해 반대하였다.
(B) A waste incineration facility was built in spite of the opposition of the people.
주민들의 반대에도 불구하고 쓰레기 소각시설이 지어졌다.
(C) The opposition of the people did not prevent the construction of a waste incineration facility.
주민들의 반대는 쓰레기 소각시설 건설을 막지 못했다.
(D) People have always raised objections to a waste incineration facility even in ideal locations.
이상적인 장소일지라도 주민들은 쓰레기 소각시설에 대해서는 언제나 반대한다.

Rudy's Tip 제시문의 'it would have pp'는 가정법 과거완료로 실현되지 못한 과거 사실을 의미한다. 따라서 주민들의 반대로 소각장 건설이 이루어지지 못했다는 내용이 적절하다.

2
정답 (B)

(e) Most people probably spend more time thinking about weather than about climate.
(d) Although weather and climate are closely related, climate is different from weather.
(c) Weather refers to the temperature and amount of rain, wind, sun, and snow during a specific time.
(b) On the other hand, climate refers to the typical weather patterns of an area over many years.
(a) So, climate is a long view of weather.

(e) 대부분의 사람들은 아마도 기후에 대해서보다 날씨에 대해서 생각하는데 더 많은 시간을 보낼 것이다.
(d) 비록 날씨와 기후는 밀접하게 관련되어 있지만 기후는 날씨와 다른 것이다.
(c) 날씨란 특정 시간 동안의 온도나 비, 바람, 태양 그리고 눈의 양을 말하는 것이다.
(b) 반면, 기후란 수년간에 걸친 특정 지역의 대표적인 날씨의 패턴을 가리키는 것이다.
(a) 따라서 기후란 날씨에 대한 장기적인 관찰인 것이다.

Rudy's Tip 첫 문항으로 적합한 것은 c와 e가 될 수 있는데, c는 날씨에 대한 정의를, e는 날씨에 대한 언급이기 때문에 e가 더 G에 가깝다. 따라서 첫 문항으로 e가 더 적절하다.

3   정답 (B)

The advance of technology is a key force behind economic growth. What drives technology? Scientific advances make new technologies possible. To take the most spectacular example in today's world, the semiconductor chip — which is the basis for all modern information technology — could not have been developed without the theory of quantum mechanics in physics. But science alone is not enough: scientific knowledge must be translated into useful products and processes. And that often requires devoting a lot of resources to research and development, or R&D, spending to create new technologies and prepare them for practical use. Although some research and development is conducted by governments, much R&D is paid for by the private sector. The United States became the world's leading economy in large part because American businesses were among the first to make systematic research and development a part of their operations.

기술 발전은 경제 성장의 원동력이다. 기술을 이끌어나가는 것은 무엇일까? 과학 발전은 새로운 기술을 가능하게 만든다. 오늘날의 세계에서 가장 극적인 예를 들면, 모든 현대 정보기술의 토대가 되고 있는 반도체칩은 물리학의 양자역학 이론이 없었다면 개발될 수 없었을 것이다. 그러나 과학만으로는 충분하지 않다. 과학적 지식은 유용한 제품과 과정들로 바뀌어져야 한다. 그리고 그렇게 하기 위해서는 종종 새로운 기술 개발과 그 기술을 실용적인 용도에 쓸 수 있게 준비하기 위한 연구 개발(R&D) 지출에 많은 자원을 쏟아부어야 한다. 정부에서도 연구와 개발을 일부 수행하고 있긴 하지만, R&D의 상당 부분은 민간 분야에서 자금을 대고 있다. 미국이 세계 제일의 경제대국이 된 것은 대체로 미국 기업들이 가장 먼저 체계적인 연구와 개발을 기업 경영의 일부로 삼았기 때문이다.

Rudy's Tip (B) 뒤에 등장하는 지시대명사 'that'의 선행사가 필요하다. that = useful products and processes를 파악하는 것이 요점이다.

4   정답 (D)

Scientists with the National Oceanic and Atmospheric Administration say that with the sun now moving toward solar maximum, power outages, computer problems, and communication failures are likely to increase during 2018 and 2019. Solar max refers to the sun reaching the most active stage of its 11-year cycle where the number and intensity of solar events increase. During solar max, the surface of the sun spews electrically charged particles into space. Depending on the movement of the particles, they could head towards Earth. Since the last solar max in 1999, most nations have increased their dependency on wireless and satellite services, making them even more vulnerable.

국립 해양 대기연구소 과학자들은 현재 태양이 활동 극대점으로 이동하고 있음에 따라 2018년과 2019년 중에 정전, 컴퓨터 장애, 통신 장애가 증가할 가능성이 있다고 이야기한다. 솔라맥스란 태양이 11년 주기 중 가장 활동적인 단계에 이른 때를 일컬으며, 이 단계에서 태양 활동의 수와 강도는 증가한다. 솔라맥스 중에 태양 표면은 전기적으로 충전된 입자들을 우주 공간에 쏟아낸다. 입자 운동에 따라 이들은 지구 쪽으로 향할 수도 있다. 1999년의 마지막 솔라맥스 이후로 대부분의 국가는 무선 및 위성서비스에 대한 의존도를 높여왔으며, 따라서 영향을 받을 가능성이 훨씬 더 높아지게 된 것이다.

(A) Solar max increases our dependency on science.
솔라맥스는 과학에 대한 우리의 의존도를 높인다.
(B) We can prevent solar max from activating sooner or later.
조만간 우리는 솔라맥스가 활성화되는 것을 예방할 수 있다.
(C) The sun moves toward solar max.
태양이 솔라맥스로 이동하고 있다.
(D) Scientists anticipate solar max problems.
과학자들은 솔라맥스 문제들을 예상하고 있다.

Rudy's Tip GS 구조의 영문으로 'failures are likely to increase = more vulnerable' 동일한 의미이다. 즉, 솔라맥스 때문에 피해가 증가하리라는 것이 지문의 요지이다.

5
정답 (D), (A)

How do you feel about sending women into combat? I'm a woman who will be going through Army basic training in a few months. I think it would be foolish of me to say that I want to go into battle, but I think it's totally unfair to exclude women from combat duty when they can handle it as well as men. Women should be expected to do the same work as men in the military and in wartime. When are the people going to realize that women are a viable source of our national defense? Canadian law has been revised, and now women are allowed to serve in all military positions – except on submarines – in the Canadian armed forces. There are plenty of men out there who would gladly give up their combat positions to women, and plenty of women who would jump at the chance to prove themselves in a battle.

여성들을 전투에 보내는 것을 어떻게 생각하는가? 나는 몇 달 동안 육군의 기본 훈련을 받을 여성이다. 나는 내가 전투에 참여하기를 원한다고 말하는 것이 어리석다고 생각한다. 그러나 나는 여성이 남성만큼 전투를 잘 할 수 있을 때, 여성을 전투에서 배제하는 것은 전적으로 공정하지 않다고 생각한다. 여성들은 군대나 전투에서 남성들과 동일한 일을 수행해야만 한다. 언제쯤 사람들은 국토수호에 있어서 여성이 유용한 자원이라는 것을 알게 될까? 캐나다의 법이 개정되었다. 그래서 이제는 여성들도 잠수함을 제외한 모든 군대의 직책에서 근무할 수 있게 되었다. 여성들에게 전투 직책을 양보할 많은 남성들이 있고 많은 여성들은 전투에서 스스로를 증명할 수 있는 기회를 얻고자 한다.

5 글에 따르면 작가는 _____ 믿고 있다.

(A) all women are eager to go into combat
모든 여성들은 전투에 참가하기를 원한다.
(B) it is fair to exclude women from combat duty
국방의무에서 여성을 제외하는 것은 공정하다.
(C) men are unwilling to yield their positions to women
남성들은 여성들에게 자신의 지위를 양보하려 하지 않는다.
(D) women can play an important role in national defense
여성들은 국토방위에서 중요한 역할을 담당할 수 있다.

Rudy's Tip 본문의 'women are a viable source of our national defense'를 통해서 정답을 선별할 수 있다.

6 빈칸에 적절한 것은?

(A) jump at the chance to prove themselves
자신들을 입증하기 위해서 기회를 잡다.
(B) be likely to be missing in action
전투 중에 실종될 가능성이 높다.
(C) be afraid to substantially participate
실질적으로 참여하는 것을 두려워하다.
(D) fight fiercely against women's rights
여성의 권리를 강하게 반대하다.

Rudy's Tip 'and'를 통해서 두 개의 절이 연결되어 있다. and는 유사한 내용을 병렬적으로 열거하거나 '원인-결과'의 구조를 이끈다. 많은 남성들이 여성들에게 양보할 수 있다는 진술 뒤에는 여성들 역시도 기꺼이 참여한다는 내용이 적절하다.

독독 3.0 분석독해

I think ① <u>it</u> would be foolish ① <u>of me to say</u> that I want to go into battle, but I think ② <u>it</u>'s totally unfair ② <u>to exclude</u> women from combat duty when they can handle it as well as men.
①, ② 모두 '가-진주어' 구문이다. ①에서 of me to say = I say 구조이다.

10분 모의고사 07 해설편

1
정답 (C)

Your persistence in being chronically late is only matched by your inability to recognize the inconvenience it causes to those it affects.

습관적으로 지각하는 것을 반복하는 것은 지각이 영향을 미치는 사람들에게 야기시키는 불편을 인식하지 못하는 것과 어울릴 뿐이다.

(A) Your lateness is causing you to become stubborn towards people you know.
당신의 지각은 당신이 아는 사람들에게 당신을 고집스러워지게 만든다.
(B) Your chronic lateness makes you unable to recognize its inconvenience.
당신의 만성적인 지각은 당신이 지각의 불편함을 인식하지 못하게 한다.
(C) You do not realize the problems your constant lateness causes.
당신은 계속되는 지각이 초래하는 문제를 알아차리지 못하고 있다.
(D) You are aware of your lateness though you criticize others for being inconsiderate.
당신은 자신이 지각한다는 것을 인식하면서도 다른 이들이 배려가 없다고 비난한다.

Rudy's Tip Your persistence in being chronically late = your constant lateness inability to recognize = not realize

2

정답 (C)

How can you recognize a quack? Sometimes it's easy because he or she offers something we know is impossible. A drink to keep you young is an example of this. But many times, these people lie, saying that their product was made because of a recent scientific discovery. This makes it more difficult to know if the person is real or a fraud. Another way to recognize quackery is that many quacks will say their product is good for many different illnesses, not just for one thing. They usually like to offer money-back guarantees if their treatment doesn't work. "Unfortunately, the guarantee is often also a lie." Finally, the fraudulent clinic will often be in another country. Laws in the United States will not allow a quack to have a clinic in the United States because the quack doesn't have the proper medical training.

어떻게 당신이 돌팔이 의사를 알아낼 수 있을까? 때로 돌팔이 의사는 우리가 아는 바로 실행 불가능한 어떤 것들을 제시하기 때문에 그들을 알아보는 것이 어렵지 않다. 당신을 젊게 해준다는 음료수가 예가 된다. 그러나 자주 이런 사람들은 그들의 상품이 최근의 과학적인 발견으로 만들어졌다고 말하면서 거짓말을 한다. 이 때문에 그 사람이 진짜인지 사기꾼인지를 아는 것이 더 어려워진다. 엉터리 치료를 알아낼 수 있는 또 다른 방법은 많은 돌팔이 의사들은 그들의 상품이 단지 하나의 질병을 위해서가 아니라 많은 다른 질병에도 좋다고 말할 것이라는 점이다. 대개 그들은 그들의 치료약이 효과가 없으면 환불을 보장한다고 한다. 불행하게도 그 보증도 또한 종종 거짓말이다. 결국, 무허가 진료소도 다른 나라에서는 종종 있을 것이다. 미국 법에서는 돌팔이 의사들은 정규 의료 교육을 받지 않았기 때문에 미국 내에 진료소를 열 수 없도록 하고 있다.

Rudy's Tip 동일어구 the guarantee와 also를 통해서 위치를 알 수 있다.

독독 3.0 분석독해

Another way /to recognize quackery/ is that many quacks will say /their product is good for many different illnesses, not just for one thing.
또 다른 방법은/돌팔이를 알아보는/많은 돌팔이 의사들은 말할 것이다/그들의 제품들은 다양한 질병에 효과가 있다고/하나의 질병이 아니라

3

정답 (C)

For decades, doctors have been intrigued by the apparent health benefits of the so-called Mediterranean diet, which is not really a diet the way most people think of one. It's more of a dietary pattern or rather, several complementary dietary patterns that have existed around the Mediterranean basin for centuries.

[B] Typical Mediterranean diets emphasize lots of fruits, cooked vegetables and legumes, grains and, in moderation, wine, nuts, fish and dairy products, particularly yogurt and cheese.

[A] But most people tend to focus on one component of these diets — olive oil — as if it were a magical potion that you could drizzle over any meal to make it healthy.

[C] According to the most rigorously controlled study of a Mediterranean diet, people with the most Mediterranean-like eating habits seem to have a reduced risk of dying from heart disease. But the study was unable to link the health benefits to any one ingredient, not even olive oil.

수십 년 동안 의사들은 소위 지중해식 식단이 건강에 미치는 이로운 점에 관해 관심을 보여왔는데, 지중해식 식단은 대부분의 사람들이 일반적으로 생각하고 있는 식단이 아니다. 그것은 식이(食餌)요법에 가깝고, 혹은 수세기 동안 지중해 연안주변에서 이용된 여러 가지 보충적인 식이 요법에 가깝다.

[B] 전형적인 지중해식 식단에서는 많은 과일 조리된 야채와 콩류, 곡물, 적당한 포도주, 견과, 생선 그리고 특히 요구르트나 치즈 같은 유제품 등을 강조한다.
[A] 그러나 대부분의 사람들은 이러한 식단들 중에서 한 가지 성분인 올리브유에 주목한다. 마치 어느 식단에든 넣기만 하면 건강에 좋은 식단이 되는 마법의 약처럼 여기면서.
[C] 지중해식 식단에 대하여 가장 철저하게 실시된 연구에 따르면 지중해식 식단으로 먹는 습관을 들인 사람들은 심장병으로 사망하는 위험을 줄일 수 있는 것으로 보인다. 그러나 이 연구는 올리브유는 물론 어떤 하나의 성분이 건강상의 혜택을 준다고 결론짓지는 못했다.

Rudy's Tip [A]는 but으로 시작하기에 첫 문항으로 적절하지 않다. 또한 [A]의 'these diets'의 선행사는 [B]에 제시된 식단들이기 때문에 [B]—[A]의 순서가 적절하다.

4

정답 (B)

The best poetry seems to be fully appreciated only by the few and to be beyond the comprehension of the many. The best advertising, however, is thought about, laughed over, and acted upon by multitudes. Poetry is, in the general apprehension, something special to be studied in schools, to be enjoyed by cultivated people who have time for that sort of thing and to be read on solemn or momentous occasions. By contrast, advertising is part of everyday life.

최고의 시는 소수의 사람들에 의해서만 제대로 이해되고, 많은 사람들의 이해는 벗어나 있는 것처럼 보인다. 그러나 최고의 광고는 대중들에 의해 생각되고, 웃음의 대상이 되고, 대중들에 근거해서 만들어진다. 일반적인 관점에서 시는 특별한 것이다. 학교에서 연구되고, 시에 대해서 시간을 낼 수 있는 교양 있는 사람들이 즐기고, 진지하거나 중요한 순간에 읽히는. 대조적으로 광고는 일상생활의 일부분이다.

(A) for example 예를들어   However 그러나
(B) however 그러나   By contrast 대조적으로
(C) however 그러나   In short 요컨대
(D) therefore 그러므로   Otherwise 그렇지 않다면

Rudy's Tip by the few – by multitudes를 통해 처음 빈칸에는 역접의 연결어가 적절하다. something special – part of everyday life를 통해 빈칸에는 대조의 연결어가 적절하다.

독독 3.0 분석독해

Poetry is, in the general apprehension, something special ① to be studied in schools, ② to be enjoyed by cultivated people who have time for that sort of thing and ③ to be read on solemn or momentous occasions.

①+②+③ 모두 something을 수식하는 형용사구들이다. 전형적인 후치수식의 구조이다.

5-6

정답 (A), (C)

The idea that liars are easy to spot is still with us. Just last month, Charles Bond, a psychologist at Texas Christian University, reported that among 2,520 adults surveyed in 63 countries, more than 70 percent believe that liars avert their gazes. The majority believe that liars squirm, stutter, touch or scratch themselves or tell longer stories than usual. The liar stereotype exists in just about every culture, Bond wrote, and its persistence "would be less puzzling if we had more reason to imagine that it was true." What is true, instead, is that there are as many ways to lie as there are liars; there's no such thing as a dead giveaway. Most people think they are good at spotting liars, but studies show otherwise. A very small minority of people, probably fewer than 5 percent, seem to have some innate ability to sniff out deception with accuracy. But, in general, even professional lie-catchers, like judges and customs officials, perform, when tested, at a level not much better than chance. In other words, even the experts would have been right as if they had just flipped a coin. Most of mechanical devices now available, like the polygraph, detect not the lie but anxiety about the lie. So it can miss the most dangerous liars: the ones who don't care that they are lying or have been trained to lie. It can also miss liars with nothing to lose if they are detected, the true believers willing to die for the cause.

거짓말쟁이는 쉽게 발각될 것이라는 생각을 우리는 가지고 있다. 바로 지난 달, 텍사스 크리스천 대학의 심리학자 찰스 본드는 세계 63개국 2,520명의 성인을 대상으로 한 실험에서, 대략 70% 사람들은 거짓말쟁이들은 자신들의 시선을 피할 것이라고 믿는다는 보고를 했다. 대대수의 사람들은 거짓말쟁이들이 몸을 비틀고, 말을 더듬거리고, 자신의 몸을 만지거나 긁어대고, 평소보다 더 길게 이야기 한다고 믿고 있다. 본드는 거짓말쟁이에 대한 이러한 고정관념이 거의 모든 문화권에 존재하며, "그것이 사실이라고 믿을 수 있는 이유가 있다면 이런 고정관념이 지속되는 것이 당연한 것이다"라고 쓰고 있다. 그러나 진실은 거짓말쟁이들만큼 많은 거짓말을 하는 방법이 존재하며, 거짓말을 하고 있다는 사실을 알려줄 결정적인 증거는 없다는 것이다.

사람들은 거짓말쟁이들을 잘 간파할 수 있다고 생각하지만, 연구결과는 상반된 사실을 보여준다. 아마도 5% 미만인, 소수의 사람들만이 속임수를 정확히 간파하는 타고난 능력을 가지고 있는 것처럼 보인다. 그러나 일반적으로, 판사와 세관원처럼 전문적으로 거짓말쟁이를 찾아내는 사람들조차, 테스트를 해보면, 우연보다 더 나은 수준의 능력을 보여주지 못한다. 다시 말해서 심지어 전문가들도 동전던지기를 하는 것처럼 거짓말쟁이를 맞힐 수 있을 뿐이다. 거짓말 탐지기 등과 같은 이용 가능한 많은 기계적 장비들은 거짓말이 아니라 거짓말에 대한 불안을 찾아낸다. 따라서 거짓말 탐지기는 가장 위험한 종류의 거짓말쟁이들을 놓친다. 즉, 거짓말하는 것에 대해 개의치 않거나 거짓말을 하도록 훈련을 받은 사람을 잡지 못한다. 거짓말 탐지기는 발각된다 해도 더 이상 잃을 것이 없는 거짓말쟁이들, 즉 대의명분을 위해서 기꺼이 죽을 각오가 되어 있는 확신범들 또한 놓칠 수 있다.

5

(A) ① they are good at spotting liars 거짓말쟁이들을 잘 간파할 수 있다
　　② with nothing to lose if they are detected 발각된다 해도 더 이상 잃을 것이 없는
(B) ① liars cannot but be detected 거짓말쟁이는 걸릴 수밖에 없다.
　　② who believe the machine can detect the lie 기계가 거짓말을 감지할 수 있다고 믿는 사람들
(C) ① experts are not reliable in spotting liars 전문가들이 거짓말쟁이를 찾는다고 믿을 수 없다
　　② who believe they are innocent 그들이 무죄라고 믿는
(D) ① beliefs about lying are plentiful and contradictory 거짓말에 대한 믿음들은 다양하고 모순적이다
　　② with unusual sensitivity to conscientiousness 성실성에 극도로 민감한

Rudy's Tip ① 빈칸 뒤에 otherwise를 통해서 실험 결과와는 상반되는 내용이 적절하다는 것을 추론할 수 있다.
② 거짓말 탐지기가 잡을 수 없는 거짓말쟁이에 관한 내용이 적절하다.

6

(A) Most people can spot deception by paying sufficient attention to liars' physical signals.
　　대부분의 사람들은 거짓말쟁이의 신체적 신호를 통해서 거짓말을 알 수 있다.
(B) Learning to detect serious lies is an important part in administering criminal justice.
　　중대한 거짓말들을 알아채는 것을 배우는 것은 형사사법제도를 수행하는데 중요한 부분이다.
(C) People with the ability to detect lies are far fewer than usually expected.
　　거짓말을 알아차리는 능력을 가진 사람들은 예상보다 적다.
(D) Advanced technology now available enables us to detect lies with confidence.
　　현재 활용할 수 있는 발전된 기술은 확실하게 거짓말을 탐지할 수 있다.

Rudy's Tip 본문의 'very small minority of people, probably fewer than 5 percent'를 통해 정답을 선별할 수 있다.

10분 모의고사 08　해설편

1
정답 (B)

A surprising number of parents are either unaware that the problem exists or reluctant to face up to it.
놀랄 만큼 많은 부모가 문제가 있다는 것을 모르고 있거나 문제에 직면하기를 꺼리고 있다.

(A) Some parents do not actually understand the problem and solve it.
　몇몇 부모들은 사실문제를 이해하지 못하며 해결하지 못하고 있다.
(B) A lot of parents neither want to know the problem nor like to face it.
　많은 부모가 문제를 알고 싶어 하지 않으며 또 문제를 직면하려고 하지도 않는다.
(C) A surprising number of parents evidently neglect both the problem and its full meaning.
　놀랄 만큼 많은 부모가 분명 문제와 그것이 지닌 충분한 의미를 모두 무시하고 있다.
(D) An amazing number of parents are both aware of the existing problem and take full cognizance of it.
　놀랄 정도로 많은 부모가 현재의 문제를 알고 있으며 충분히 인지하고 있다.

Rudy's Tip A surprising number of parents = An amazing number of parents
unaware = not aware

2
정답 (B)

Numerous companies have embraced the open office and by most accounts, very few have moved back into traditional spaces with offices and doors. But research findings that we're 15% less productive, we have immense trouble concentrating and we're twice as likely to get sick in open working spaces, have contributed to a growing backlash against open offices. There's one big reason we'd all love a space with four walls and a door that shuts: focus. The truth is, we can't multi-task, and small distractions can cause us to lose focus for upwards of 20 minutes. What's more, certain open spaces can negatively impact our memory. We retain more information when we sit in one spot without distractions. It's not so obvious to us each day, but we offload memories into our surroundings in the open spaces.

많은 기업들이 개방형 사무실을 선택해왔으며 대부분의 평가로 볼 때 사무실과 문이 있는 전통적인 사무 공간으로 돌아간 기업은 거의 없다. 그러나 생산성이 15% 줄어들었고 집중하는 데 엄청난 어려움을 겪고 있으며, 개방형 업무 공간에서 몸이 아플 가능성이 두 배로 높다는 등의 연구결과는 개방형 사무실에 대한 반발이 점점 커지는 데 기여해 왔다. 4면이 벽으로 되어 있고 닫을 수 있는 문이 있는 공간을 우리 모두가 좋아하는 한 가지 큰 이유가 있는데 그것은 바로 집중력이다.

사실, 우리는 한꺼번에 여러 일을 처리할 수 없으며, 주의를 산만하게 하는 작은 것들도 최대 20분이나 집중력을 잃게 만들 수 있다. 게다가, 어떤 개방형 사무실들은 우리의 기억력에 악영향을 미칠 수 있다. 우리는 주의를 산만하게 하는 것 없이 한 자리에 앉아 있을 때, 보다 많은 정보를 기억한다. 매일 우리에게 그렇게 분명하게 인지되는 것은 아니지만 개방형 사무실에서는 우리의 기억이 주변으로 사라져 버린다.

(A) The Pros and Cons of the Open Office
 개방형 사무실의 장단점들
(B) The Myth of the Open Office Now Being Challenged
 도전받고 있는 개방형 사무실의 신화 (기존 믿음과는 달리 개방형 사무실은 안 좋다)
(C) The Open Office: the Hub of Collaboration and Bond
 개방형 사무실 : 협력과 유대감의 중심
(D) The Rationale behind the Open Office
 개방형 사무실 이면에 있는 이유 (개방형 사무실이 적합한 이유)

Rudy's Tip MT 구성으로 But 이하가 주제문이다.

독독 3.0 분석독해

But <u>research findings</u> /that we're 15% less productive, we have immense trouble concentrating and we're twice as likely to get sick in open working spaces, /<u>have</u> contributed to a growing backlash against open offices

'주어 동사 - findings have'를 파악하는 것이 요점이다. 동명사 findings 뒤에 동격절 that이 연결되어 주어가 길어진 구조이다.

3
정답 (B)

I found myself in the difficult position of having to choose between not just two but five colleges, all offering fine programs in my field of study. Three of them offered great financial aid, while two of them promised an exciting campus life. I was at a loss. <u>In the end, however, I chose this college because of its convenience.</u> First of all, I could <u>live at home</u> while attending classes, since the campus is located near my neighborhood. Although I did not have a car, <u>taking the bus to my college</u> was not too much trouble. And sometimes, when the weather was nice, I could even <u>ride my bike to the campus</u>.

나는 내 자신이 두 대학이 아닌 다섯 대학 가운데서 선택해야 하는 어려운 처지에 놓여 있음을 발견했다. 그 대학들은 모두 내가 공부하고자 하는 분야에서 훌륭한 프로그램을 제공하고 있었기 때문이었다. 그중 두 곳은 재미있는 대학 생활을 약속한 반면 세 곳에서는 많은 재정 지원을 제안했다. 나는 어찌할 바를 몰랐다. 그러나 마침내 나는 편리함 때문에 이 대학을 선택했다. 무엇보다도, 교정이 우리 동네 근처에 위치해 있었기 때문에 나는 수업에 참석하는 동안 집에서 살 수 있었다. 비록 차는 없었지만, 대학까지 버스를 타는 것은 큰 어려움이 없다. 그리고 때때로 날씨가 화창하면 나는 교정까지 자전거를 탈 수 있다.

Rudy's Tip 삽입문의 'convenience'가 G에 해당하며, 이후 열거구조로 이 편리함을 설명하고 있다.

4
정답 (A)

[C] Race-car drivers are used to going at high speed on the ground. But what do you do if your car totally leaves the ground? That is what happened to Bobby Johns. An unscheduled flight made him lose a big race.

[B] Johns was leading the 1960 Daytona 500-mile race. He was far ahead of his opponents. There were only four miles to go. Everyone thought Johns would easily achieve victory. Johns's car was going more than 130 miles an hour. Suddenly, the car was elevated off the ground. The car spun in the air and landed off the track. Everyone, including Johns, was astounded.

[A] Here is what had happened. The pressure of the air had popped the back window out of Johns's fast-moving car. Wind rushed in through the wide opening. The force of the wind propelled the car through the air. The car sailed more than sixty feet before it came down and stopped. Johns was not injured, but he was scared. He couldn't finish the race.

[C] 자동차 경주 운전자들은 지상에서 빠른 속도로 달리는데 익숙하다. 하지만 자동차가 완전히 지상에서 벗어난다면 어떻게 하겠는가? 이런 일이 Bobby Johns에게 일어났다. 그 계획되어 있지 않았던 비행으로 인해 그는 커다란 경기에서 지고 말았다.

[B] Johns는 1960년 Daytona 500마일 경주에서 앞서가고 있었다. 그는 자신의 경쟁자들보다 훨씬 앞서가고 있었다. 이제 4마일만 가면 끝이었다. 모든 사람들은 Johns가 쉽게 우승할 것이라고 생각했다. Johns의 자동차는 시간당 130마일 이상으로 달리고 있었다. 갑자기 그의 차가 지상으로 들어 올려졌다. 자동차는 공중에서 돌다가 트랙을 벗어난 곳에 내려앉았다. Johns를 포함한 모든 사람들이 깜짝 놀랐다.

[A] 다음이 일어난 일이다. 공기의 압력이 Johns의 빠르게 움직이는 자동차 뒤 유리를 갑자기 빠지게 만들었다. 넓은 구멍으로 바람이 몰려 들어 왔다. 바람의 힘은 자동차를 공중으로 날아가게 했다. 자동차는 내려와 멈출 때 까지 60피트 이상을 떠다녔다. Johns는 다치지는 않았으나 매우 무서웠다. 결국 경주를 끝내지 못하고 말았다.

Rudy's Tip C는 일반적 진술, B는 특정 사람, C는 구체적인 사건에 대한 설명으로 첫 문항으로 C가 제일 적절하다. C에 Bobby가 언급되기에 이것은 B의 첫 문장으로 연결된다.

5-6
정답 (D), (B)

IQ testing has had momentous consequences in our century. In this light, we should investigate Binet's motives, if only to appreciate how the tragedies of misuse might have been avoided if its founder had lived and his concerns been heeded. For American psychologists perverted Binet's intention and invented the hereditarian theory of IQ. They reified Binet's scores, and took them as measures of an entity called intelligence. They assumed that intelligence was largely inherited and developed a series of specious arguments confusing cultural differences with innate properties. They believed that inherited IQ scores marked persons, people and groups for an inevitable station in life. And they assumed that average differences in intelligence were largely the products of heredity, despite manifest and profound variation in quality of life.

지능검사는 금세기에 중요한 영향을 미치고 있다. 이러한 견지에서 볼 때, 만일 그 검사의 창시자가 살아 있고, 그가 관심을 가졌던 부분이 잘 지켜졌더라면 이러한 오용의 비극을 피할 수 있었을 것인가를 알기 위해서 우리는 Binet 검사의 동기들을 조사해 보아야 한다. 왜냐하면, 미국의 심리학자들은 Binet의 의도를 왜곡하고 IQ의 유전이론을 꾸며냈기 때문이다. 그들은 Binet 의 점수를 구체화시켜 이 점수를 지능이라 불리는 실체의 척도로 받아들였다. 그들은 지능은 대체로 물려받는 것이라 가정하고, 문화적 차이를 타고난 능력의 차이와 혼동하여 일련의 그럴듯한 논거를 개발해 놓았다. 그들은 유전된 IQ 지수가 개인들, 사람들과 집단들의 위치를 결정해 준다고 믿었다. 그리고 그들은 명백하고도 커다란 삶의 질의 변화에도 불구하고, 통상적인 지능의 차이를 대체로 유전에 의한 것으로 가정했다.

05 글에 포함되어 있지 않은 진술을 선택하세요.

(A) American psychologists believed that IQ scores were inherited.
미국 심리학자들은 IQ가 유전적이라고 믿었다.

(B) Binet's intention was different from that of American psychologists.
Binet의 의도는 미국 심리학자들의 의도와는 달랐다.

(C) American psychologists used Binet's scores as measures of intelligence.
미국 심리학자들은 Binet 점수를 지능의 척도로서 사용했다.

(D) American psychologists thought that differences in IQ were the products of the environment.
미국 심리학자들은 IQ는 환경의 소산이라고 믿었다.

Rudy's Tip 미국의 심리학자들은 IQ를 유전에서 기인한다고 생각했다. A와 D는 상반되는 문항이다. 이처럼 보기문항에서 의미가 상반되는 문항들이 나란히 등장하면, 둘 중 하나가 정답일 가능성이 매우 높다.

06 글에 따르면, Binet's IQ testing _____.

(A) was only concerned with heredity theory
단지 유전 이론에만 관련되어 있었다.

(B) was wrongly used by American psychologists
미국 심리학자들이 남용했다.

(C) was originated from the station in life of people
사람들의 사회적 지위에서 기인한다.

(D) was indifferent to manifest and profound variation in quality of life
분명하고 커다란 삶의 질과는 무관하다.

Rudy's Tip 미국의 심리학자들이 Binet의 의도를 왜곡했다는 것이 본문의 내용이다.

10분 모의고사 09 해설편

1
정답 (D)

The atomic reactor, people have begun to realize, may be a solution to our energy problem, but it also constitutes a hazard which must be taken into consideration.
원자로는 우리의 에너지 문제에 해결책이 될 수 있다고 사람들이 이해하기 시작했지만, 또한 원자로는 반드시 고려해야만 할 위험을 포함하고 있다.

(A) It dawned on people that the atomic reactor solved the energy problem but that there was a danger in assuming this.
원자로가 에너지 문제를 해결하였지만 여기에는 위험이 있다는 것을 사람들이 깨닫기 시작했었다.

(B) Now, people criticize the atomic reactor for being harmful although it is an ideal means of producing energy.
이제 사람들은 원자로가 에너지 생산에 이상적인 수단임에도 불구하고 해롭다는 이유로 비난하고 있다.

(C) People recognized the dangers of using an atomic reactor but condoned its use anyway.
사람들은 원자로 사용의 위험성을 깨달았지만 어쨌든 원자로의 사용을 용납했다.

(D) People now know that the atomic reactor not only can be beneficial but also can be detrimental.
사람들은 이제 원자로가 유익할 수도 있다는 것뿐만 아니라 해로울 수도 있다는 것을 안다.

Rudy's Tip solution to our energy problem = beneficial
a hazard = detrimental

2

정답 (C)

The science of evolution is taught in all advanced academies. That in another generation evolution will be regarded as uncontradictable as the Copernican system of astronomy, or the Newtonian doctrine of gravitation, can scarcely be doubted. Each of these passed through the same contradiction by theologians. They were charged by the church, as is evolution now, with fostering materialism and atheism.

모든 고등 교육 기관에서 진화론을 가르친다. 다음 세대에는 진화론이 코페르니쿠스의 천문학 이론이나 뉴턴의 중력이론 만큼이나 분명한 것으로 받아들여질 것은 분명하다. 이러한 이론들은 모두 신학자들에게 같은 비판을 겪었다. 지금의 진화론이 유물론과 무신론을 양산해 내면서 비난을 받는 것처럼 예전 이론들도(뉴턴, 코페르니쿠스) 교회의 비난을 받았다.

What does the author predict to be likely to occur?
작가가 일어날 가능성이 높은 것으로 예상하는 것은 무엇인가?

(A) Evolution will never be accepted by the church.
   교회는 진화론을 절대 수용하지 않을 것이다.
(B) The heliocentric theory of Copernicus will contradict the Newtonian doctrine of gravitation.
   코페르니쿠스의 지동설은 뉴턴의 중력이론을 반박할 것이다.
(C) Evolution will universally be accepted as has been the heliocentric theory of Copernicus.
   지동설이 수용된 것처럼 진화론도 보편적으로 수용될 것이다.
(D) The Church will forbid people to accept evolution.
   교회는 사람들이 진화론을 수용하는 것을 금지할 것이다.

Rudy's Tip 본문에 따르면 다음 세대에는 진화론이 보편적으로 수용될 것이라는 문항이 적절하다.

독독 3.0 분석독해

[1] They were charged by the church, **as is evolution now**, with fostering materialism and atheism.
   as is evolution now = as evolution is now charged by the church with fostering materialism and atheism.
   대동사 'is'는 동사와 전명구 모두를 대신한다.

[2] Evolution will universally be accepted **as has been the heliocentric theory of Copernicus**.
   as has been the heliocentric theory of Copernicus = as the heliocentric theory of Copernicus has been accepted

3
정답 (D)

It must be an amazing feeling to go on a concert tour of the world. And it is really so especially if the people who come to see you are enthusiastic about your songs. It takes a special genius to be able to write and sing songs that everyone in the world can listen to and understand. It is not simple to get attention, but once a singer is seen on the air, she has a real chance for success. Some popular singer, like Fergie, now does commercials for Pepsi. So when it's time for a break on TV, everyone who likes her turns up the volume. This is how she becomes more famous as she meets more people. In conclusion, media is important to success for singers.

세계 연주 여행을 가는 것은 놀라운 느낌임이 틀림없다. 그리고 당신을 보러 오는 사람들이 당신 노래에 대해 열광적이라면, 정말로 특히 그러하다. 세상의 모든 사람들이 듣고 이해할 수 있는 노래를 쓰고 부를 수 있는 것은 특별한 재능을 필요로 한다. 주위를 끄는 것은 간단하지 않다. 그러나 일단 가수가 방송에 출연하면 그녀는 성공을 위한 진짜 기회를 갖는다. Fergie 같은 어떤 인기 있는 가수는 Pepsi를 위한 상업광고를 이제 한다. 그래서 TV 중간 광고 시간이 되었을 때, 그녀를 좋아하는 모든 사람은 소리를 높인다. 이것이 그녀가 더 많은 사람을 만나기 때문에 그녀가 더 유명해 지는 방법이다. 결론적으로 방송은 가수들 성공에 중요하다.

Rudy's Tip 삽입문의 TV와 본문의 commercials 연결된다. commercial은 TV광고를 의미하기 때문이다.

4 정답 (C)

[B] How much do we really know about medicine and healing? In hospitals, doctors remove diseased parts, repair injuries, and cure millions of people every year. In those hospitals, research continues daily for better techniques of curing, better medicines, and improved procedures. As a result, the term "modern medicine" is constantly being revised.

[A] One focus of this medical research is on practices of healers in other cultures — they might know something that we don't, something that would be useful in developing our medical culture. The traditions of doctors and healers in one place on this planet can be very dramatically different from the practices of doctors and healers in another part of the world. One report on a doctor's experience below illustrates this point clearly.

[C] The physician, Marlo Morgan, describes her journey in the Australian desert with the people called "the real people." During this hike, one member of the tribe fell and badly broke his leg: the bone had broken into two pieces and one end had broken through the skin. Morgan watched as the real people's healers pulled the foot gently just one and the bone slipped right back into place, and also saw the man get up the next morning and walk the whole day. To Morgan, it was a miracle. To the real people, it is the way they have always practiced medicine, through the wisdom of their culture.

[B] 의학과 치료에 대해 우리가 실제로 얼마나 알고 있을까? 병원에서 의사들이 병든 부분을 제거하고, 상처를 치료해서 매년 수백만의 사람들을 치료한다. 그런 병원에서는 더 나은 치료법, 더 좋은 약, 그리고 향상된 치료 과정을 위해 매일 연구가 계속된다. 그 결과 "현대 의학"이라는 용어는 끊임없이 수정된다.

[A] 이러한 의학 연구의 한 초점이, 다른 문화의 치료사들이 쓰는 방법에 맞추어져 있다. 그들은 우리는 모르지만 우리의 의료 문화를 발전시키는 데 유용한 것을 알고 있을지 모른다. 지구상의 한 지역에 있는 의사나 치료사들의 전통은 다른 지역에 있는 의사나 치료사들의 방법과 아주 극단적으로 다를 수 있다. 아래에 나오는 한 의사의 경험에 대한 보고서는 이런 점을 분명하게 보여 준다.

[C] 내과 의사 Marlo Morgan은 '진짜 사람들'이라 불리는 사람들과의 호주 사막에서의 여행담을 적었다. 이 여행 동안, 그 부족의 한 일원이 넘어져 다리가 심하게 부러졌다. 뼈가 두 조각으로 부러지고 한쪽 끝이 피부를 뚫고 나왔다. Morgan은 그 사람들의 치료사가 발을 단 한 번에 부드럽게 당기고 그 뼈가 미끄러져 제자리로 돌아가는 것을 목격했고, 그 다음 날 아침 그 남자가 일어나 하루 종일 걷는 것도 보았다. Morgan에게 그것은 기적이었다. 그 사람에게는 그것은 그들 문화의 지혜를 통해 그들이 항상 의료를 수행해 온 방법이다.

Rudy's Tip [B] 도입부가 G진술로 첫 문장으로 가장 적절하다. [B]의 마지막 표현이 [A]와 연결. [A]의 마지막 'one report'가 [C] 내과의사의 경험으로 연결된다.

5

정답 (C)

No two cancers are alike; even within an individual patient, tumors may change over time. And doctors are learning that a melanoma growth might have more in common with a lung cancer or a brain cancer than another melanoma. "We are moving away from the concept that all lung cancers are the same and all breast cancers are the same and all colon cancers are the same," says Dr. David Solit, director of the Kravis Center for Molecular Oncology at MSKCC.

유사한 두 개의 암은 없다. 심지어 개별적인 환자 안에서도 종양들은 시간이 지나면서 변한다. 그리고 의사들은 폐암이나 뇌암의 경우에 흑색종 세포 성장이 다른 흑색종 세포에 비해 더 흔하다는 사실을 알아가고 있다. "우리는 모든 폐암들이 동일하고, 모든 유방암들이 동일하고 모든 대장암들이 동일하다는 개념으로부터 벗어나고 있습니다."라고, MSKCC에 있는 Kravis Center for Molecular Oncology의 책임자인 Dr. David는 말한다.

(A) Hospitals should give every cancer patient equal care
　　병원들은 모든 암환자에게 동일한 간호를 해야만 한다.
(B) Tumors come back even after treatment
　　종양은 수술 후에도 재발한다.
(C) No two cancers are alike
　　어떤 두 개의 암들도 동일하지 않다.
(D) All cancers are fundamentally the same
　　모든 암들은 근본적으로 동일하다.

Rudy's Tip GS 구조의 영문으로, 빈칸의 내용은 주제에 해당한다. 언제나 주제가 등장할 경우에는 이어서 논거가 등장한다. 빈칸 바로 뒤에 'change'와 이후에 진술되는 내용을 토대로 정답을 추론할 수 있다.

독독 3.0 분석독해

We are moving away from the concept that ① all lung cancers are the same and ② all breast cancers are the same and ③ all colon cancers are the same.
①+②+③ 모두 the concept을 설명하는 동격절 that에 병렬적으로 연결되어 있는 대등절들이다.

6

정답 (C)

Rooted in romanticism and derived from the idea of natural human rights, European laws have mostly sought to protect creators. America's notion of copyright, on the other hand, sees culture more as a commodity. The constitution of the United States frames copyright as a reward that is granted to authors for a limited time to encourage them to be creative. Yet recently America has followed Europe's lead in extending the term of copyright to 70 years after a creator's death — not so much in belated recognition of authors' rights as in a concession to Hollywood and other important rights-holders, which had lobbied for the changes. In 1998 Disney and other studios even pushed through legislation that extended the copyright on films to 95 years; it became known as the "Mickey Mouse Bill".

낭만주의에 뿌리를 두고 천부인권 사상으로부터 유래했기에 유럽의 법은 대개 저작권자들을 보호하는 것을 추구한다. 반면에 저작권에 대한 미국식 개념은 문화를 상품으로 보는 경향이 강하다. 미국헌법은 저작권을 제한된 시간 동안 예술가들이 창조적이 되도록 독려하기 위한 보상으로 규정한다. 그러나 최근에 미국은 예술가 사후 70년까지 저작권의 보호 기간을 확장하는 유럽의 주장을 따르고 있는데, 저자들의 권리에 대한 뒤늦은 인식 때문이 아니라 저작권보호 연장을 위해 로비를 벌여온 할리우드와 다른 중요한 저작권 소유자들에게 굴복했기 때문이다. 1998년 디즈니와 다른 영화사들은 영화에 대한 저작권을 95년까지 연장하는 입법을 추진하기도 했다. 이것은 미키마우스 법안이라고 알려져 있다.

(A) ① however   ② Consequently
(B) ① similarly   ② Nevertheless
(C) ① on the other hand ② Yet
(D) ① therefore   ② As a result

Rudy's Tip ① 빈칸을 중심으로 앞에는 human rights가, 빈칸에는 commodity가 등장했기에 저작권에 대한 상반된 인식을 알 수 있다. 따라서 역접, 대조의 연결어가 적절하다.
② 빈칸을 중심으로 기존 미국 입장이 유럽의 입장으로 변화한다는 내용이기에 앞 문장과 역접, 대조의 관계이다.

10분 모의고사 10 　해설편

1
정답 (C)

Whether a policy which is "good" in the aggregate sense is also "good" for a particular person is a different matter.
종합적인 의미에서 '좋은' 정책이 특정한 한 사람에게도 '좋을'지는 별개의 문제이다.

(A) In a collective sense, a "good" policy can be generalized to include any kind of individual.
전체적인 의미에서 좋은 '정책'은 어떤 종류의 개인도 포함하도록 일반화될 수 있다.

(B) It does not matter whether a policy which is "good" can be "good" for all individuals.
'좋은' 정책이 모든 개인에게 '좋을'지는 중요하지 않다.

(C) It is wrong to assume that a "good" policy in general will also be "good" for a specific individual.
일반적으로 '좋은' 정책이 특정 개인에게도 '좋을' 것이라 추측하는 것은 옳지 않다.

(D) What is considered "good" for individuals does not necessarily have to be considered when making a policy.
개인들에게 '좋다'고 생각되는 것이 정책을 만들 때 반드시 고려될 필요는 없다.

Rudy's Tip a different matter = wrong to assume
별개의 문제라는 것은 다른 문제라는 의미로, 전체에게 좋은 것이 개인에게도 좋다는 것은 틀렸다는 내용과 동일하다.

2

정답 (D)

We all fear tossing something out only to regret it later on. But if that's your one reason for hanging on to something, it isn't enough. Ask yourself why you're not using it now. The answer can offer clues about whether your possession is worth saving. Take scrapbooking. If you see yourself turning to the hobby in the near future — not 10 years from now when you think you might have more free time, store the supplies. But if you never really enjoyed the activity, or it's been eclipsed by knitting or painting, donate the materials — especially if they're eating up valuable closet space or making you feel guilty. As for the money you spent on them, think of it as a worthy gift to a local Girl Scouts troop, Boys & Girls Club or school art department.

우리 모두는 뭔가를 버렸다가 나중에 가서 버린 것을 후회하게 될까 걱정한다. 그러나 그것이 당신이 뭔가를 계속 보관하는 이유 중의 하나라면 충분하지 않다. 왜 당신이 그것을 지금 사용하지 않고 있는지를 스스로에게 물어보라. 그에 대한 대답은 당신의 소유물이 버리지 않고 남겨 둘 만한 가치가 있는가에 대한 단서를 제공할 수 있다. 스크랩북 만들기를 예로 들어보자. 만약 가까운 미래에 그 취미에 몰입하게 된다면 - 더 많은 자유 시간을 갖게 되는 지금으로부터 10년 안에, 물품들을 보관해라. 그러나 만약 당신이 그 활동을 정말로 즐겨본 적이 없거나, 혹은 뜨개질이나 그림 그리기에 완전히 밀리게 됐다면, 특히 그것들이 귀중한 벽장(수납장) 공간을 차지하고 있다거나 당신에게 죄책감을 느끼게 만들고 있는 경우라면, 스크랩북을 만드는 재료들을 기부하라. 당신이 그 재료들을 마련하는데 쓴 돈에 대해서는, 지역 걸 스카우트 단체나 학생클럽이나 학교 미술부에 값진 선물을 한 것으로 생각하라.

(A) Donation Makes a Difference
    기부는 중요하다.
(B) Tips for Having Good Hobbies
    좋은 취미를 갖기 위한 조언들
(C) Doing Activities Leads to a Healthy Life
    (다양한) 활동들을 하는 것은 건강한 생활을 만든다.
(D) Don't Regret: Throwing Is a Virtue
    후회하지 말라; 버리는 것도 미덕이다. (사용하지도 않는데 짐만 되는 물건들은 정리하라는 의미)

Rudy's Tip GS 구성으로, 사용하지 않는 물건은 버리거나 기부를 하라는 주장이다.

3
정답 (C)

Changes in attitude affect language. As people become more sensitive to the right and needs of individuals, it becomes necessary to change the words we use to describe them. The elderly are now called "senior citizens" and the handicapped are described as "physically challenged." Many of the words we once used had negative feelings attached to them. But new words show an awareness in today's society that differences are good and that everyone deserves respect. Even the names of certain jobs have changed so that workers can be proud of what they do. The trashman, for example, is now called a sanitation worker, a doorman is an attendant, and a janitor is a custodian.

자세의 변화는 언어에 영향을 준다. 개인의 권리와 욕구에 더욱 더 민감하게 되었기 때문에, 우리는 그것들을 설명하는 단어들을 바꿀 필요가 있다. 노인들은 이제 노령자라 불리며, 그리고 장애인은 육체적으로 불편한 사람으로 묘사된다. 우리가 예전에 사용했던 많은 단어는 그것들에 붙어있는 부정적 느낌을 가지고 있었다. 그러나 오늘날의 사회에서 새로운 단어들은 차이점들은 바람직한 것이고, 모든 사람은 존경을 받아야 한다는 인식을 보여준다. 어떤 직업의 이름들은 노동자들이 자신들의 일에 대해 자부심을 갖게 하기 위해서 변경되었다. 예를 들어, 청소원은 이제 공중위생 노동자, 문지기는 안내원이고, 수위는 관리인이라 불리어진다.

Rudy's Tip the words we once used와 negative feelings에 이어서 삽입문의 내용이 연결되어야 논리적이다.

4
정답 (B)

[A] Diana was a clerk in a company. One day she went into Russell's office. She noticed that he looked very tired. In fact, he looked awful. She knew it was not a good time to ask for a raise, but she felt she had to. She tried to think of something casual to say first. It was always best to begin such conversations casually.

[C] "Uh... you're looking a bit tired," she said. "Yes, I have just seen the Financial Controller. It wasn't a very pleasant conversation. I feel burned out today," Russell sighed. Then he mentioned that he had a terrible headache. Diana began to feel sorry for him. She offered to get some aspirins for him from the company store.

[B] "You needn't bother. I can go there myself," he said. "Oh, but I'm going to the store anyway. It's no trouble," she protested. Russell thanked her and gave her some money for the aspirins. She left. It was only after she had closed the door behind her that she remembered the real reason why she had come to see Russell.

[A] Diana는 회사 사무원이었다. 어느 날 그녀는 Russell의 사무실로 들어갔다. 그녀는 그가 매우 피곤해 보인다는 것을 알게 되었다. 사실 그는 몸이 몹시 좋지 않아 보였다. 그녀는 임금을 올려달라는 요구를 하기에 적절한 시기가 아니라는 것을 알았으나, 그 말을 해야만 한다고 생각했다. 그녀는 먼저 부담 없이 할 수 있는 말을 생각해내려고 했다. 언제나 이러한 대화는 부담 없는 말로 시작하는 것이 가장 좋았다.

[C] "음, 약간 피곤해 보이시네요." 그녀가 말했다. "그래요, 방금 재정 담당관을 만나보았어요. 그다지 유쾌한 대화는 아니었어요. 오늘은 몹시 피곤하군요." Russell이 한숨을 쉬며 말했다. 그러고 나서 그는 두통이 아주 심하다는 말을 했다. Diana는 그가 안쓰럽다는 생각이 들기 시작했다. 그녀는 그를 위해 회사 구내매점에 가서 아스피린을 좀 사다 주겠다고 말했다.

[B] "그럴 필요 없어요. 내가 직접 가도 돼요." 그가 말했다. "아, 그렇지 않아도 저는 거기 가려고 했습니다. 힘든 일이 아닙니다." 그녀가 고집하듯이 말했다. Russell은 고맙다고 하며 아스피린 살 돈을 그녀에게 주었다. 그녀는 사무실에서 나왔다. 사무실 문을 닫고 나온 후에야 그녀는 자신이 Russell을 만나러온 진짜 이유가 생각이 났다.

Rudy's Tip C와 B는 둘 다 대명사로 등장하기에 첫 문장으로 적절하지 않다. A의 끝부분이 C의 첫 문장과 연결되고 있다.

5
정답 (B)

Sound waves from an object moving away from you have a lower frequency. So do light waves. The different colors in the spectrum have different frequencies. Violet has light waves of the highest frequency. Red light waves have the lowest frequency. Scientists studied the motion of the stars in distant galaxies. They discovered that the light from these distant galaxies shifted slightly towards the red end of the spectrum and had a lower frequency. Astronomers concluded that these galaxies are moving away from the earth.

당신에게서 멀어져 가는 물체로부터 나오는 음파는 더 낮은 주파수를 갖는다. 광파도 마찬가지이다. 스펙트럼에 있는 다른 색깔들은 다른 주파수를 갖고 있다. 보라색은 가장 높은 주파수의 광파를 갖고 있다. 적색 광파는 가장 낮은 주파수를 갖고 있다. 과학자들은 먼 은하계에 있는 별들의 움직임을 연구했다. 그들은 이 먼 은하계에서 오는 빛이 스펙트럼의 적색 끝 쪽으로 약간 이동한다는 것과 더 낮은 주파수를 갖고 있다는 사실을 알아냈다. 천문학자들은 이 은하계가 지구로부터 멀어지고 있다는 결론을 내렸다.

(A) are getting brighter and brighter
    점점 더 밝아진다.
(B) are moving away from the earth
    지구로부터 멀어지는 중이다.
(C) do not allow even light to escape
    심지어 빛조차 탈출하는 것을 허용하지 않는다.
(D) send light in different directions
    빛을 다른 방향들로 방출한다.

Rudy's Tip 멀어지는 물체는 낮은 주파수의 적색을 띠게 되는데, 멀리 떨어져 있는 은하계의 빛이 적색으로 이동한다는 의미는 은하계가 지구로부터 멀어진다는 의미이다.

6

정답 (D)

What an Indian eats depends on his region, religion, community, and caste. It also depends on his wealth. A vast proportion of the Indian population is made up of the rural poor who subsist on a diet that meets only about 80 percent of their nutritional requirements. Many of the poor, unable to find work all year round, and therefore unable to buy food everyday, have to manage their hunger by fasting on alternate days. In Bengal, the meals of the poor are made up of rice, a little dhal flavored with salt, chillies, and a few spices, some potatoes or green vegetables, tea and paan. Paan, which is an areca nut mixed with spices and rolled up in a betel leaf, is chewed after the meal. **Although it seems a luxury, in fact, the poor use it to stave off hunger.**

인도인이 먹는 것은 그의 종교, 지역, 공동체 그리고 계급에 달려있다. 또한 인도인이 먹는 것은 개인의 부유함에 달려있다. 인도 인구의 대부분은 영양 요구량의 단지 80퍼센트만을 만족시키는 음식으로 연명하는 시골의 가난한 사람들로 구성되어 있다. 가난한 많은 사람들은 일년 내내 일자리를 찾을 수 있는 것은 아니어서 매일 음식을 살 수 없기 때문에 하루걸러 하루씩 굶으면서 자신들의 배고픔을 달랜다. 벵갈에서 가난한 사람들의 식사는 쌀과 소금, 칠리, 그리고 몇몇 향신료를 가미한 약간의 콩 요리, 감자나 채소, 차와 판(paan)으로 이루어졌다. 판은 향신료와 버무려 구장나무 잎으로 말은 빈랑나무 열매로서, 식사 후에 씹어 먹는다. 비록 판은 호화로운 음식처럼 보이지만, 사실 가난한 사람들은 기아를 면하기 위해 판을 먹는다.

(A) Indians' diets vary across their religion and wealth.
　　인도인의 식사는 종교와 재산에 따라 다양하다.
(B) The food the rural poor in India take doesn't meet their nutritional requirements.
　　가난한 인도 시골 사람들이 먹는 음식은 그들의 영양요구량을 충족시키지 못한다.
(C) Many poor Indians go without food every other day.
　　많은 가난한 사람들은 매일 음식 없이 살아간다.
(D) In Bengal, paan is **luxurious food** for the poor.
　　벵갈에서 판은 가난한 사람들에게는 사치스런 음식이다.

Rudy's Tip 본문의 마지막 문장을 통해서 D가 틀린 진술임을 알 수 있다.

10분 모의고사 11 해설편

1
정답 (C)

Chinese is one of the most remarkable pieces of art in language that humankind has ever made. In elementary school, Chinese teachers ask their students to write not only correctly but beautifully. Chinese is different from Western languages such as German, French, or English because it has no alphabet. Instead, it contains 50,000 characters. If a person knows 5,000 of the most commonly used characters, he can read a newspaper. How many characters a person knows indicates how intellectual that person is. Chinese is one of the world's oldest languages and its written form as in most languages, developed from the pictograph.

중국어(한자)는 언어에 있어서 인류가 만든 것 중에서 가장 놀랄만한 예술 작품 중에 하나다. 초등학교에서, 중국어 교사들은 학생들에게 정확할 뿐만 아니라 아름답게 쓰도록 요구하고 있다. 중국어는 독일어, 프랑스어, 또는 영어와 같은 서양 언어와는 다르다. 왜냐면 그것은 알파벳을 가지고 있지 않기 때문이다. 그 대신에 중국어는 50,000개의 문자를 가지고 있다. 만약 한 사람이 가장 널리 사용되는 문자 중 5,000개를 안다면, 그는 신문을 읽을 수 있다. 한 사람이 얼마나 많은 문자를 아느냐 하는 것은 그 사람이 얼마나 지적인가를 가리킨다. 중국어는 세계에서 가장 오래된 언어들 중에 하나이며 대부분의 언어에서처럼 그것의 쓰여진 형태는 그림문자로부터 발전했다.

Rudy's Tip 5만 단어와 how many characters 표현 사이에 위치해야 논리적이다. 중국 전체 한자수가 소개되고 이 중에서 개인이 어느 정도를 아는 것이 적절한지에 관한 내용이 연결되는 것이 적절하기 때문이다.

2
정답 (C)

I hope to organize a political force to protect the pollution-free environment in the city.
나는 무공해 도시 환경을 보호하기 위하여 정치단체를 결성하기를 희망한다.

(A) I am willing to form a government which would stop air pollution.
　　나는 기꺼이 대기오염을 막을 정부를 구성할 것이다.
(B) By organizing the environment to stop pollution, I want to establish the necessary force.
　　오염을 막기 위한 환경을 조직함으로써, 나는 필요한 단체를 설립하기를 원한다.
(C) I want to guard the environment against pollution by establishing a political organization.
　　나는 정치단체를 설립함으로써 오염에 대항하여 환경을 지키기를 원한다.
(D) A political force is to protect the environment from air pollution.
　　정치단체는 대기오염으로부터 환경을 보호해야만 한다.

Rudy's Tip political force = political organization.
protect the pollution-free environment = guard the environment against pollution

3
정답 (A)

I was four, playing outside in the humid Kentucky air. I saw my grandfather's truck and thought, "Granddad shouldn't have to drive such an ugly truck." Then I spied a gallon of paint. Idea! I got a brush and painted white polka dots all over the truck. I was on the roof finishing the job when he walked up, looking as if he were in a trance. "Angela, that's the prettiest truck I've ever seen!" Sometimes I think adults don't stop to see things through a child's eyes. He could have crushed me. Instead, he lifted my little soul.

나는 네 살이었고 습기 찬 켄터키 야외에서 놀고 있었다. 나는 할아버지의 트럭을 보았고 "할아버지가 저런 추한 트럭을 몰아서는 안 돼"라고 생각했다. 그 때, 나는 페인트 한통을 보았고, 좋은 생각이 떠올랐다. 나는 브러시를 집어 들고 트럭 전체를 흰색 물방울무늬로 칠했다. 내가 트럭 지붕에서 칠하는 일을 거의 끝내고 있을 때 할아버지는 정신이 나간 것 같은 표정으로 내게 다가왔다. "Angela, 이 건 내가 본 것 중에서 가장 예쁜 트럭이구나!" 때때로 어른들은 아이들의 눈을 통해서 사물들을 보기 위해서 멈추지 않는다고 생각한다. 할아버지는 나에게 강하게 화를 낼 수도 있었다. 대신 할아버지는 나의 마음을 북돋아 주었다.

(A) Instead, he lifted my little soul 대신에, 내 기분을 북돋아 주었다.
(B) My dreams, however, came true 그러나 내 꿈은 실현되었다.
(C) He thus turned a deaf ear to my wishes 그래서 그는 내 소망을 무시했다.
(D) In the end, I blossomed into a renowned artist 결국, 나는 유명한 예술가가 되었다.

Rudy's Tip 문맥상 'could have pp'는 '~할 수도 있었는데, 하지 않았다'는 의미이다. 따라서 빈칸에는 나를 격려해주는 표현이 적절하다.

4

정답 (B)

In 2005, C. K Prahalad, a University of Michigan Business School professor, wrote a book 'The Fortune at the Bottom of the Pyramid'. He shows how private firms can sometimes find it in their own interest to help solve some of the problems of the poor that are traditionally addressed by aid agencies.

[B] Prahalad gives the example of HLL, a subsidiary of the giant-multinational Unilever. HLL sold a very simple product, soap, which it realized could find a larger market if it was tied to preventing diarrheal diseases of the poor. Hand washing with soap is critical to preventing the spread of the viruses and bacteria that cause diarrhea HLL realized that if it could promote increased awareness among the poor of the benefits of antibacterial soap, it could significantly increase sales.

[A] Getting people to use soap, however, is not as easy as it sounds. Poor people are not well informed about the science of disease transmission. Most poor people wash their hands only if they are visibly dirty, not when their hands are covered with invisible germs after using the latrine or changing a baby's diaper. HLL had to change behavior.

[C] To realize this market potential, HLL had to find ways of gaining the poor's trust in its health-promoting product. Working with the government and aid agencies, it started educational programs, including a program called Lifebuoy Glowing Health, which sent out two-person teams to show schoolchildren how they could avoid infections by washing with Lifebuoy soap. The teams also enlisted the village doctors to speak to the children's parents about how hand washing with soap could prevent diarrhea and other health complications.

2005년·C, K 프라할라드(Prahalad) 미시건 로스 경영대학원 교수는 'The Fortune at the Bottom of the Pyramid'라는 책을 저술했다. 그는 전통적으로 구호단체들이 다뤄왔던 빈곤층 문제들 중 일부를 민간 기업들이 해결하는 데 도움을 주는 것이 어떻게 그들 자신에게도 이익이 되는지를 보여준다.

[B] (책에서) 프라할라드는 거대 다국적기업 유니레버(Unilever)의 자회사인 HLL(힌두스탄 레버 리미티드)을 예로 제시한다. HLL은 매우 단순한 제품인 비누를 팔았는데, HLL은 비누가 빈곤층의 설사병을 예방하는 것과 연관 지어진다면 더 큰 시장을 찾을 수 있을 것이라는 것을 깨달았다. 비누로 손을 씻는 것은 설사를 일으키는 바이러스와 박테리아의 확산을 막는 데 매우 중요하다. HLL은 만일 빈곤층에게 항균비누의 이점에 대한 인식을 높일 수 있다면, 자사의 매출을 상당히 증대시킬 수 있을 것이라는 것을 깨달았다.

[A] 그러나 사람들에게 비누를 사용하도록 하는 것은 생각만큼 쉬운 일이 아니다. 가난한 사람들은 질병 전염의 과학적인 측면을 잘 알지 못한다. 가난한 사람들은 대부분 화장실에 갔다 온 후나 아기 기저귀를 간 후 손에 보이지 않는 세균이 우글거릴 때 손을 씻는 것이 아니라, 눈에 보일 정도로 손이 더러워져야 손을 씻는다. (따라서) HLL은 (가난한 사람들의 행동을 변화시켜야 했다.

[C] 이런 시장 잠재력을 달성하기 위해서, HLL은 자사의 건강증진 제품에 대한 빈곤층의 신뢰를 얻을 방법을 찾아야 했다. HLL은 (인도) 정부와 구호단체들과 협력하여, 2명으로 구성된 팀들을 파견하여 초등학생들이 Lifebuoy 비누로 손을 씻으면 어떻게 감염을 예방할 수 있는지를 알려주는 Lifebuoy Glowing Health라는 프로그램 등 여러 가지 교육 프로그램들을 실시했다. 그 팀들은 또한 마을 의사들에게 요청해 비누로 손을 씻는 것이 설사와 다른 건강상의 합병증을 어떻게 예방할 수 있는지를 아이들의 부모들에게 말해주도록 했다. 그 결과, HLL의 항균비누 매출이 증가했으며, HLL은 수익을 얻는 것과 더불어 마을 주민들에게 질병예방 제품을 사용하도록 설득하는 데도 성공을 거두었다.

Rudy's Tip 도입부에서 민간기업이 빈곤층에서 도움이 될 수 있다는 표현이 B의 예시로 연결된다. B의 주된 내용이 빈곤층의 비누 사용이기에 A의 첫 문장과 호응하고, A의 마지막 문장이 사람들의 태도를 변화시킨 다는 내용으로, C의 첫 문장과 호응한다.

5
정답 (B)

Jim Belushi comes to network television as a loving family man in this show. Happily married with three kids, Jim is an all-American guy's guy, not quick to admit fault, but a softie underneath. He's a contractor in a design firm with his younger, architect brother-in-law, Andy, yet he still finds time to hang out with his six-man garage blues band. Jim's wife, Cheryl, gave up dating corporate guys for a life with a simpler man who makes her laugh. She is champagne and strawberries while Jim is beer, nuts and bratwurst but they're in love. Dana is Cheryl's sister, who works as a VP in an ad agency. She's single and gorgeous, but emotionally short-sighted and self-centered. She gets lots of first dates, not too many second ones. But she adores her two nieces and her baby nephew and she loves verbally sparring with Jim. So that's Jim Belushi, a husband who knows that the key to a good marriage is nodding when your wife talks.

짐 벨루시(Jim Belushi)는 이 프로그램에서 사랑스럽고, 가정에 충실한 남자로 등장한다. 세 아이가 있는 행복한 결혼생활을 하고 있는 짐은 전형적인 미국 남자이다. 잘못을 빨리 인정하지는 않지만 마음은 약하다. 그는 디자인 회사의 도급업자이다. 그곳에서 그보다 어린 처남인 건축가 앤디(Andy)와 함께 일한다. 그는 시간을 내어 6명의 창고에서 연습하는 블루스 밴드와 어울린다. 짐의 아내 셰릴은 그녀를 웃게 만드는 더 소박한 남자와의 삶을 위해 사업가들과 데이트하는 것을 그만뒀다. 그녀가 샴페인과 딸기라면 짐은 맥주와 땅콩, 돼지고기 소시지라고 할 수 있지만, 그들은 서로 사랑한다. 광고회사의 부사장인 다나는 셰릴의 여동생이고, 광고 회사의 부사장이다. 그녀는 미혼이며 매력적이지만 감정적으로 근시안적이고, 자기중심적이다. 그녀는 첫 데이트 경험이 많지만, 두 번 이상 만나는 경우는 그렇게 많지 않다. 그러나 그녀는 자신의 세 조카를 사랑하고 짐과 말다툼하는 것도 좋아한다. 행복한 결혼생활의 열쇠는 아내가 이야기할 때 고개를 끄덕이는 것이라고 알고 있는 남편, 그게 바로 짐 벨루시이다.

(A) Jim is a workaholic.
    짐은 일중독자이다.
(B) Jim's wife met some guys before she married him.
    짐의 아내는 결혼 전 몇 남성들과 교제했다.
(C) Jim and his wife are a perfect match in personality.
    짐과 아내는 성격에 있어서 찰떡궁합이다.
(D) Jim works with his sister-in-law in the same company.
    짐은 같은 회사에서 처제와 함께 일한다.

Rudy's Tip 'gave up dating'을 통해서 B가 맞는 내용임을 알 수 있다.

6

정답 (A)

It is so difficult for human beings to live together; it is difficult for them to associate, however transitorily, and even under the most favorable conditions, without some shadow of mutual offense. Consider the differences of task and of habit, the conflict of prejudices, and the divergence of opinions, which quickly reveal themselves between any two persons and see how much self-control is implicit whenever, for more than an hour or two, they co-exist in seeming harmony. Man is not made for peaceful intercourse with his fellows; he is by nature self-assertive, commonly aggressive, and always critical toward any characteristic which seems strange to him.

인간이 함께 사는 것은 매우 어렵다. 아무리 일시적이라 하더라도 가장 좋은 상황에서조차 어느 정도 서로의 감정을 상하게 하지 않는 것은 어렵다. 두 사람 사이에서 빠르게 드러나는 일과 습관의 차이, 편견으로 인한 갈등, 의견의 차이들을 생각해 보라. 그러면 서로 사이가 좋아 보이는 한 두 시간 이상 동안에도 은연중에 얼마나 큰 자제심을 발휘해야 하는지 알 것이다. 인간은 동료와 평화롭게 지내도록 만들어진 존재가 아니다. 인간은 천성적으로 자신에게 낯선 상대에게는 독단적이고, 공격적이며, 비판적이다.

(A) It is not easy for us to get on peacefully with our fellows.
   인간은 동료들과 평화롭게 지내는 것이 쉽지 않다.
(B) By instinct man is a peace-seeking creature.
   본능적으로 인간은 평화를 추구한다.
(C) Human beings do not offend one another in a favorable situation.
   인간은 우호적인 상황 속에서는 서로를 공격하지 않는다.
(D) The differences of task and of habit often lead to close friendship.
   일과 습관의 차이점들은 친밀한 우정을 낳는다.

Rudy's Tip GS 구성으로 인간은 타인과 공존하기가 어렵다는 것이 주제이다. 첫 문장의 내용과 마지막 문장의 내용이 동일하다.

독독 3.0 분석독해

① **Consider** the differences of task and of habit, the conflict of prejudices, and the divergence of opinions, which quickly reveal themselves between any two persons ① **and see** how much self-control is implicit whenever, for more than an hour or two, they co-exist in seeming harmony.
① '동사 and 동사'의 병렬구조로 '생각하라, 그러면 알게 된다'는 의미로, 명령문 다음에 등장하는 and는 '그러면'이라는 조건의 의미이다.

10분 모의고사 12 해설편

1
정답 (A)

Because of its efficacy in treating many ailments, penicillin has become an important addition to a druggist's stock.
많은 질병을 치료하는 데 있어 효율성 때문에 페니실린은 약사의 저장품에 있어 중요한 추가 물품이 되었다.

(A) Penicillin has become indispensable to druggists because it can treat many different illnesses.
페니실린은 많은 질병을 치료할 수 있기에 약사들에게 없어서는 안 될 물품이 되었다.
(B) Druggists have found penicillin to be the most effective medicine they know.
약사들은 페니실린이 그들이 알고 있는 가장 효과적인 약이라는 것을 알았다.
(C) Druggists were forced to add effective medicines such as penicillin to their drug stores.
약사들은 페니실린처럼 효과적인 약을 그들의 약국에 추가하도록 강요받았다.
(D) Penicillin was necessary to druggists because it could boost their store profits.
페니실린은 약국의 수익을 늘릴 수도 있기에 약사들에게 꼭 필요했다.

Rudy's Tip important addition = indispensable
treating many ailments = treat many different illnesses

2
정답 (B)

The best exercise is one that you enjoy and will do. But otherwise, it's probably running. Running is cheap, easy, as you go out of your house and just do it, and you can't fake it — it's always energetic. Even a jog counts as moderately vigorous exercise. If you are time poor, you need run for only half the time to get the same benefits as other sports. Angelique Brellenthin, of the department of kinesiology at Iowa State University, says it takes 105 minutes of walking to yield the same benefits as a 25-minute run.

가장 좋은 운동은 당신이 즐겨하고 또 하고 싶은 마음이 있는 운동이다. 그렇지 않으면 아마도 달리기가 좋은 운동일 것이다. 달리기는 비용이 저렴하고 쉬우며, 집 밖으로 나가서 그냥 하라는 것처럼, 속임수를 부릴 수 없다. 달리기는 항상 활동적이다. 조깅조차도 적당히 격렬한 운동으로 간주된다. 시간이 없다면 당신은 다른 스포츠와 같은 혜택을 얻기 위해서 시간의 절반만 달려도 된다. 아이오와 주립 대학교의 신체 운동학부 교수인 Angelique Brellenthin은 25분 동안 달리기를 하는 것과 동일한 효과를 얻기 위해서는 105분 동안 걸어야 한다고 말한다.

(A) If you want to speed up your running 달리기 속도를 늘리고 싶다면
(B) If you are time poor 시간이 없다면
(C) With good running shoes 좋은 운동화를 신고
(D) In order to avoid knee pain 무릎 통증을 피하고 싶다면

Rudy's Tip 빈칸 뒤에 '시간'에 대한 표현을 통해서 정답을 추론할 수 있다. IF절과 주절은 연속성 있는 내용이 연결되어야 하기 때문이다.

3 정답 (C)

To pass the civil service examinations in ancient China was no easy matter. Preparation took years, since candidates were required to know thousands of logo-graphs merely to read the classics. Furthermore, they had to memorize whole texts. On the examinations, they wrote essays about particular questions on particular texts. These essays were then evaluated according to the criteria of purity, truthfulness, elegance, and propriety. These criteria were, however, so vague that candidates had little choice but to try to detect the literary preferences of the examiners.

고대 중국에서 관리 등용 시험(공무원 시험)에 합격하는 것은 쉬운 일이 아니었다. 응시자들은 고전을 읽기 위해서 수천 자의 한자를 알도록 요구받았기 때문에 시험 준비는 여러 해 걸렸다. 게다가 그들은 책 전체를 외워야 했다. 시험에서, 그들은 특정한 책의 특정한 지문에 대해 글을 썼다. 이 글은 순수성, 진실성, 우아함, 타당성의 기준에 따라 평가되었다. 그러나 이 기준들은 너무 모호해서 응시자들은 시험관이 학문적으로 선호하는 것을 알아내려고 노력하지 않을 수 없었다.

Rudy's Tip C 앞 essays와 뒤의 these criteria를 통해서 적절한 위치를 파악할 수 있다.

4
정답 (B)

"I'm a company man." This was something many workers were accustomed to saying with pride for most of this century.

[B] It meant that the worker was proud of working for a particular company throughout adulthood. Both blue collar workers and white collar workers often felt loyal to a company and the company returned this loyalty.

[A] But with the loss of thousands of manufacturing jobs in the 1960s and 1970s and of thousands more white collar jobs in 1980s and 1990s, this expression has become a memory.

[C] In the late 1990s, employees felt it was foolish to be loyal to a company that could fire them at any moment.

"나는 회사원입니다."라는 이 말은 근로자들이 금세기 대부분 동안 긍지를 가지고 말하는 데 익숙했던 표현이다.
[B] 그 말은 근로자가 성인이 된 이후로 어떤 특정한 회사를 위해서 일하는 것을 자랑스러워했음을 의미했다. 노동직 근로자와 사무직 근로자 모두 종종 회사에 대해서 충성심을 느꼈고, 회사는 이러한 충성심에 보답을 했다.
[A] 그러나 1960년대와 1970년대에 수많은 제조업 일자리의 상실과 1980년대와 1990년대에 이르러 더 많은 수의 사무직 일자리의 상실로 인해, 이러한 표현은 추억거리가 되었다.
[C] 1990년대 후반에, 고용자들은 언제든지 그들을 해고시킬 수 있는 한 회사에 충성하는 것이 어리석은 일이라고 느꼈다.

Rudy's Tip 도입문의 pride가 B의 'proud of'로 연결된다. A의 But 이후 다른 상황이 제시되고, C가 A와 연결되는 것이 적절하다.

5
정답 (A)

Image processing techniques originally developed by space scientists to analyze pictures taken by spacecraft are being turned to the detection of skin cancer. Researchers at NASA's Jet Propulsion Laboratory, working with dermatologists at Beth Israel Hospital, have adapted the imaging technology to detect the onset of melanoma, a type of cancer that can be treated if detected early enough. The work was initiated by Robert Selzer of JPL's biomedical image processing laboratory in collaboration with Kenneth Arndt, head of the department of dermatology at Beth Israel. Some patients at risk of developing melanoma have so many lesions on their skin that it is difficult for dermatologists to detect and track all changes and thus evaluate treatment. Under the system, photos of patients taken at intervals are sent to the biomedical image processing laboratory where they are scanned into a personal computer and then analyzed by imaging software to indicate changes.

우주선이 찍은 사진들을 분석하기 위해 우주과학자들이 최초로 개발한 화상정보처리기술은 피부암을 감지하는 용도로도 이용되고 있다. NASA의 제트추진연구소의 연구원들은 베스 이스라엘 병원의 피부과 의사들과 협력하여, 초기에 발견하면 치료가 가능한 일종의 암인 흑색종의 징후를 감지하는 데 화상정보처리기술을 적용했다. 이 일은 제트추진연구소의 생물의학 영상정보처리 실험실의 로버트 셀저(Robert Selzer)가 베스 이스라엘 병원의 피부과장인 케네스 안트(Kenneth Arndt)와 협력하여 시작되었다. 흑색종이 발병할 위험이 있는 일부 환자들은 피부에 많은 손상이 있기 때문에 피부과 의사들이 모든 변화를 감지하고 추적해 치료법을 평가해내기가 어렵다. 이 방법 하에서는 일정한 간격을 두고 촬영한 환자의 사진이 생물 의학 영상정보처리 실험실로 보내지며, 이곳에서 이 사진들은 퍼스널 컴퓨터에 실려서 영상 소프트웨어로 분석되어 달라진 부분을 보여준다.

(A) Space Technology on Cancer 암에 대한 우주과학기술 (암 연구에 우주 과학기술을 적용한다는 의미)
(B) The Origin and History of Dermatology (피부학의 기원과 역사)
(C) Image Processing and Home Computer (이미지 처리 기술과 가정용 컴퓨터)
(D) Skin Cancer Causes Death in Deep Space (피부암은 먼 우주에서 죽음을 야기한다)

Rudy's Tip GS 구조의 영문으로 첫 문장이 주제문이다. 우주 사진을 분석하기 위해 만들어진 영상 분석기술을 사람의 피부암 탐지에도 활용한다는 것이 주요 내용이다. 첫 문장 이후에 구체적인 S진술들이 이어지는 구조를 파악하자.

6
정답 (B)

The Wildfoods Festival takes place in the old mining town of Hokitika on the west coast of the South Island. This year, the organizers are preparing for more than 23,000 curious visitors from all over the world, a 10 percent increase in attendance over last year's crowd. Each year, the chefs invent more and more exotic dishes, and you may need to have a strong stomach and be open-minded to try them. This year they are offering new dishes such as insect eggs, scorpions, and venison tongue. Last year's favorites are still available: kangaroo and emu steaks fresh from neighboring Australia, and of course, earthworms and snails. It's a country full of sheep, but don't expect to eat any of them here!

야생음식 축제는 남섬(뉴질랜드의 섬) 서쪽 해안의 오래된 채광 마을인 Hokitika에서 열린다. 이번 해에 주최자들은 호기심 많은 23,000명의 전 세계에서 오는 관광객들을 예상하고 있는데, 이는 작년 보다 10% 증가한 것이다. 해마다 요리사들은 더 이국적인 요리를 개발하기에 당신은 그것들에 도전할 더 강한 비위와 열린 태도가 필요하다. 이번 해에 요리사들은 곤충 알과 전갈, 그리고 사슴 혀와 같은 새로운 요리들을 선보일 것이다. 지난해의 인기 요리도 여전히 맛볼 수 있다. 이웃 호주에서부터 오는 신선한 캥거루와 에뮤(타조) 스테이크, 지렁이와 달팽이 요리도 맛볼 수 있다. 양들이 많은 나라이지만, 그것들을 이 곳에서 맛볼 수 있다는 기대는 하지마라.

(A) The Wildfoods Festival takes place in Australia.
 야생음식 축제는 호주에서 개최된다.
(B) More than 20,000 visitors attended last year's festival.
 작년 축제에는 20,000 이상의 관광객들이 참여했다.
(C) Kangaroo steak is one of this year's new dishes.
 캥거루 스테이크는 올해 새로운 요리 중 하나이다.
(D) Sheep steak is one of last year's favorites.
 양 스테이크는 작년 인기 요리 중 하나이다.

Rudy's Tip 작년보다 10% 증가한 것이 23,000명이기에 작년은 20,000 이상이었다는 것을 유추할 수 있다.

10분 모의고사 13 해설편

1 정답 (A)

Subsequent changes to an original invention do not represent new concepts at all, but rather extensions of the original innovative idea.

최초의 발명에 따른 후속적인 변화들은 전혀 새로운 개념을 나타내지 않으며, 오히려 기존의 혁신적인 아이디어의 확장이다. (최초의 발명 이후에 등장하는 변화들은 발명에 대한 확장, 변형일 뿐이지, 기존 발명과는 다른 새로운 발명은 아니라는 의미)

(A) Nothing that is done to an original invention is completely new.
  최초의 발명에 대해서 이루어진 것은 어떤 것도 완전히 새로운 것이 아니다.
(B) Originality is essentially lost in the innovation of products.
  독창성은 제품의 혁신 가운데 본질적으로 사라진다.
(C) When an original invention changes, so do the perceptions towards it.
  본래의 발명이 변화하게 되면 그 발명에 대한 인식도 변화한다.
(D) New ideas about original inventions are continuously being generated.
  본래의 발명에 대한 새로운 아이디어는 지속적으로 생성된다.

Rudy's Tip not represent new concepts = Nothing new

2

정답 (C)

Although the last days of the Roman Empire may at first appear very different from those of the United States today, there are ominous likenesses. Ancient Rome possessed tremendous military strength, not of the magnitude of our air power, true, but enough to maintain its control over almost all of the known world. Because of the vast expanse of its rule, however, much of its strength was devoted to maintaining order in areas other than within its own borders. Just as in the United States today, Rome was so intensely occupied with establishing and maintaining its political principles in areas other than those within its own borders, its rulers were blind to the full significance of the ominous changes taking place at home. Much of this change consisted of internal conflict induced by the indifference of the affluent Roman to the suffering of the less fortunate. This apathy of the wealthy caused the poor to resort to violence to attract attention to their complaints. This is not unlike our own time when dissenters shoot someone of renown to penetrate the stone wall of indifference.

로마 제국의 말년은 언뜻 보기에는 오늘날 미국의 상황과 매우 다르게 보이지만, 불길한 유사성이 있다. 고대 로마는 굉장한 군사력을 소유하고 있다. 사실, 우리 공군력 정도는 아니지만 당시 알려진 거의 전 세계에 대한 통제력을 충분히 유지할 정도였다. 그러나 엄청난 지배의 확장으로 인해 그들의 힘을 상당 부분 국내보다는 다른 지역에서 질서를 유지하는데 쏟아 부었다. 오늘날의 미국에서처럼, 로마는 자신들의 국내 것보다 다른 지역에서 정치적인 원리를 확립하고 유지하는 데에 너무 집중해서 통치자들은 국내에서 발생하는 불길한 변화들의 중요성을 깨닫지 못했다. 이러한 변화의 많은 부분이 빈곤층의 고통에 대한 부유층의 무관심에서 야기된 내부적 갈등이었다. 부유층의 이러한 무관심은 빈곤층으로 하여금 그들의 불만에 대한 관심을 끌기 위해 폭력에 호소하도록 했다. 이것은 반대자들이 무관심의 벽을 뚫기 위해서 유명인사를 사살하는 우리 시대의 모습과 다르지 않다.

Rudy's Tip 삽입문의 'this apathy' 선행사가 앞 문장의 'indifference'이다. 따라서 선행사 뒤에 위치하는 것이 적절한 자리이다.

3

정답 (B)

Earlier this month, Facebook announced it would be using facial recognition to let users know every time a photo of them had been uploaded to the site. Such a feature would be extremely useful to one man — public-relations professional Jonathan Hirshon, who has managed to stay anonymous online for the past 20 years. He has more than 3,000 friends on Facebook and regularly updates his profile with persona information — where he is going on holiday, what he has cooked for dinner and the state of his health. But what he has never shared on the social network, or anywhere else online, is a picture of himself. It is, he said, his way of "screaming my privacy to the world".

이달 초 페이스북은 사용자들의 사진이 페이스북에 업로드되면 언제든지 사용자들이 알 수 있게 하기 위해 얼굴 인식 기술을 사용할 것이라고 발표했다. 그러한 기능은 홍보 전문가인 Jonathan Hurshon과 같은 사람에게 매우 유용할 것인데 그는 지난 20년 동안 익명으로 온라인에서 활동해 왔다. 그는 페이스북에 3천 명이 넘는 친구가 있으며 휴가 중에 어느 곳을 가고 저녁에 무슨 요리를 했고, 자신의 건강상태가 어떠한지에 대한 신상 정보가 있는 프로필을 정기적으로 업데이트하고 있다. 그러나 그가 소셜 네트워크나 온라인상의 다른 어떤 곳에 한 번도 공유하지 않았던 것은 바로 자신의 사진이다. 그는 그것이 '자신의 사생활을 세상에 공개하는' 자신의 방식이라고 말했다.

(A) share a picture of himself on social media
　　소셜미디어에 자신의 사진을 공유하다(올리다)
(B) stay anonymous online
　　익명으로 남아 있다
(C) keep a secret of himself
　　비밀을 혼자서만 유지하다
(D) leave traces of himself online
　　온라인에서 그의 자신의 흔적을 남기다

Rudy's Tip but 이하의 재진술을 통해서 빈칸의 내용을 추론할 수 있다. 익명성의 핵심은 얼굴을 보이지 않는다는 점이기 때문이다.

4 정답 (A)

The inventor of the first written tablets may have realized the advantage these pieces of clay had over holding memories in the brain: first, the amount of information storable on tablets was endless — one could go on producing tablets again and again in the same way, while the brain's remembering capacity is limited; second, tablets did not require the presence of the memory-holder to retrieve information. Suddenly, something intangible — a number, an item of news, a thought, an order — could be acquired without the physical presence of the message-giver; magically, it could be imagined, noted and passed on across space and beyond time. Since the earliest phases of prehistoric civilization, human society had tried to overcome the obstacles of geography, the finality of death, the erosion of oblivion. With a single act — the incision of a figure on a clay tablet — that first anonymous writer suddenly succeeded in all these seemingly impossible feats.

최초의 문자가 적힌 서판을 발명한 사람은 기억을 두뇌 속에 보유하는 것을 능가하는 이 점토판이 가진 이점을 깨달았을 수도 있다. 첫째, 서판에 저장할 수 있는 정보의 양은 무한하여 서판은 같은 방식으로 반복적으로 계속 만들 수 있지만 두뇌의 기억 용량은 한계가 있다. 둘째, 서판은 정보를 회수하기 위해 기억을 보유한 사람이 그 자리에 있는 것을 필요로 하지 않는다. 갑자기 숫자, 뉴스 항목, 생각, 명령과 같은 무형의 것이 메시지 전달자가 물리적으로 그 자리에 있지 않아도 습득 가능하게 되었고, 마법처럼 그것이 시간과 공간의 경계를 넘어 상상되고 기록되며 전달될 수 있게 되었다. 선사시대 문명의 가장 이른 단계 이래로 인간 사회는 지리적 장애, 죽음이라는 최후, 망각의 침식을 극복하려고 애써 왔다. 점토 서판 위에 형상을 새긴다는 단 하나의 행위로 그 이름을 남기지 않은 최초의 글쓴이는 이 모든 불가능해 보이는 위업을 이루는 데 돌연 성공했다.

(A) remarkable results of storing information on tablets
　　서판에 정보를 저장하는 것의 놀라운 결과
(B) expansion of knowledge in various fields
　　다양한 분야에서의 지식의 확장
(C) different types of memory and storage devices
　　기억과 저장 장치의 다양한 유형
(D) training necessary for improving memory capacity
　　기억 용량을 향상시키기 위해 필요한 훈련

Rudy's Tip GS 구성으로 첫 문장에 이어 first, second 열거 구조가 재진술로 제시되고 있다.

5 정답 (C)

Albert Bruce Sabin was born in Bialystok, Poland. His family settled in New Jersey, USA in 1921. Sabin received his medical degree from New York University in 1931. During World War II, he served in the U.S. Army Medical Corps, where he was involved with the development of a vaccine against dengue fever and the successful vaccination of 65,000 military personnel against the Japanese type of polio. While Jonas Salk developed a vaccine using dead virus, Sabin devised one that used live virus. He later produced a pill vaccine and, in 1955, conducted experiments with prisoners who had volunteered. From 1957 to 1959, the Soviet Union and the other Eastern Bloc nations administered Sabin's pill, with its advantages of oral administration and long-term immunity. It was subsequently accepted in the United States.

Albert Bruce Sabin은 폴란드의 Bialystok에서 태어났다. 그의 가족은 1921년에 미국의 New Jersey에 정착했다. Sabin은 1931년에 뉴욕대학교에서 의학 학위를 받았다. 제2차 세계대전 동안에 그는 미국 육군 의무부대에서 복무했는데, 거기서 그는 뎅기열 백신 개발과 65,000명의 군 인력에 대한 성공적인 일본형 소아마비 백신 접종에 관여했다. 전쟁이 끝난 후에 Sabin은 소아마비에 대한 연구를 계속했다. Jonas Salk가 죽은 바이러스를 이용하여 백신을 개발한 반면에, Sabin은 살아 있는 바이러스를 사용한 백신을 고안했다. 그는 나중에 알약 백신을 만들어 냈으며 1955년에 자원한 재소자들에게 실험을 하였다. 1957년부터 1959년까지 소련과 다른 동구권 국가들은 입을 통해 투여되며 장기간 면역의 장점을 지니고 있는 Sabin의 알약을 투여했다. 그것은 나중에 미국에서 받아들여졌다.

(A) 폴란드에서 출생하여 미국으로 이주했다.
(B) 제2차 세계대전 동안 미군 의무부대에서 복무했다.
(C) 죽은 바이러스를 이용하여 백신을 고안했다.
(D) 자원한 재소자들을 대상으로 실험을 실시하였다.

Rudy's Tip 'Sabin devised one that used live virus' 통해서 틀린 문항을 선별할 수 있다.

6 정답 (C)

Milton Keynes is a dream researcher in Miami, Florida.

[C] He found that people wake up very discouraged after having a bad dream.

[B] He also found that after having a good dream, people feel more optimistic.

[A] Clearly, dreams can have harmful or beneficial effects.

[D] As a result, he believes that we need to learn how to change our bad dreams.

밀튼 케인스는 플로리다주 마이애미에 사는 꿈 연구가이다.

[C] 그는 사람들이 나쁜 꿈을 꾼 후에 매우 낙담하며 깨어나는 것을 발견했다.
[B] 그는 또한 사람들이 좋은 꿈을 꾼 후에는 더 낙관적으로 느낀다는 것을 발견했다.
[A] 확실히, 꿈은 해롭거나 이로운 효과를 가지고 있다.
[D] 결과적으로, 그는 우리의 나쁜 꿈들을 변화시킬 수 있는 방법을 배워야 할 필요가 있다고 믿는다.

Rudy's Tip A는 B, C 결론에 이르는 내용으로 첫 문장으로 적절하지 못하다.

10분 모의고사 14 해설편

1
정답 (B)

Science does not seek to enforce a moral code of behavior in its practitioners, as much as ancient philosophy did.
과학은 과학자들에게 도덕적인 행동규칙을 강요하지 않는다, 고대의 철학이 철학자들에게 그랬던 것만큼.

(A) Like ancient philosophers, practitioners of science should be held accountable for their moral behavior.
고대의 철학자들처럼 과학의 실행자들은 그들의 도덕적 행동에 책임을 져야 한다.

(B) Ancient philosophy placed more pressure on its practitioners to adhere to moral rules regarding behavior than science currently does.
고대의 철학은 현재의 과학이 그러한 것보다 그것의 실행자들에게 행동에 관하여 도덕률을 고수하도록 더 압박을 가했다.

(C) How a moral code of behavior is contested in science differs from how it was done in ancient philosophy.
어떻게 과학에서 행동의 도덕률이 논란되고 있는지는 고대 철학에서 논란되었던 것과 다르다.

(D) Science is more rigorous about regulating its practitioners through a moral code of behavior than in ancient philosophy.
과학은 행동의 도덕률을 통해 그것의 실행자들을 규제하는 것에 관해 고대 철학보다 더 엄격하다.

Rudy's Tip 제시문과 (B)의 대동사를 이해하는 것이 요점이다.
제시문의 'did = sought to enforce a moral code of behavior in its practitioners'
(B) 'does = places more pressure on its practitioners to adhere to moral rules regarding behavior'

2

정답 (B)

It may sound counterintuitive, but excessive freedom of thought leads to "idea anarchy" and a poor level of inventiveness. Most of us have had a firsthand or secondhand experience of a brilliant solution devised by improvising with scant materials at hand. In many cases, a lack of an essential substance or tool requires resourcefulness. If you've ever communicated a big idea concisely on a napkin or managed to score tickets to a soldout concert (without paying a ticket scalper), you can consider yourself resourceful — that is, using existing resources extremely efficiently. Using this same logic, when we place enough constraints around resources, we can prevent ideation anarchy and focus productive thinking into that limited space where the creative solutions are frequently hiding.

직관에 어긋나는 것처럼 들릴지 모르지만, 지나친 생각의 자유는 '아이디어 혼란'과 형편없는 수준의 독창성으로 이어진다. 우리들 대부분은 즉시 쓸 수 있는 부족한 자료를 가지고 임시변통하여 고안해 낸 훌륭한 해결책에 대한 직접 또는 간접 경험을 해 왔다. 많은 경우에, 필수적인 재료나 도구의 부족은 (뛰어난) 문제 해결 능력을 필요로 한다. 대단한 아이디어를 냅킨 위에다가 간결하게 전달해 보았거나 (암표 장수에게 지불하지 않고) 매진된 콘서트의 표를 가까스로 구해본 적이 있다면, 뛰어난 문제 해결 능력을 갖추었다고, 즉 가지고 있는 자료를 아주 효율적으로 사용한다고 여겨도 된다. 이 동일한 논리를 사용하자면, 자료 주변에 충분한 제한을 두게 될 때 관념 작용의 혼란을 막을 수 있고, 창의적인 해결책들이 흔히 숨어 있는 그 제한된 공간 속으로 생산적인 생각을 집중시킬 수 있다.

(A) Enjoy Unrestricted Freedom of Ideas
무제한적인 사상의 자유를 즐겨라.
(B) Lack of Resources Leads to Creativity
부족한 자료들이 창의력을 낳는다.
(C) The More Materials, the More Inspiration
물질이 많을수록, 영감(창의력)이 많아진다.
(D) Small Ideas: The Best Source of Big Ideas
작은 아이디어들 : 획기적인 생각들의 최고의 원천

Rudy's Tip ST 구성으로 과도한 자유가 생각의 혼란을 가져오고, 오히려 제약이 창의력의 근간이 된다는 내용이다.

3

정답 (B)

The ability to detect potential toxins in foods via taste is just one adaptation humans have to protect themselves against food-related illness. Food neophobia is one such proposed adaptation humans share with other animals that may prevent the ingestion of dangerous substances.

[B] Many animals, including humans, have an immediate distrust of new foods. Especially as children, people avoid unfamiliar foods and, when encouraged to try them, do so only in small amounts. Typically, when people taste something that has never been eaten before, the first bite is small and carefully evaluated.

[A] Then, when possible, some amount of time is allowed to pass before a final judgment is made. If the food does not taste bad and the time following its ingestion is not marred by illness, the food may be considered potentially safe and edible.

[C] If, however, the food tastes bad or is associated with sickness, the food may be considered inedible and avoided. This combination of an aversion to new foods and a sensitivity to the association between food and illness provides some protection against potential poisons.

미각을 통해서 음식 안에 들어 있을지도 모르는 독소를 발견하는 능력은 음식 관련 질병으로부터 자신들을 보호하기 위해 인간이 가진 적응의 하나일 뿐이다. 새로운 음식을 싫어하는 것은 위험한 물질의 섭취를 막을 수도 있는, 인간이 다른 동물과 공유하는 그와 같이 의도된 하나의 적응이다.

[B] 인간을 포함한 많은 동물은 새로운 음식에 대해 즉각적인 불신이 있다. 특히 어렸을 때 사람은 낯선 음식을 피하고, 먹어 보라고 권하면 소량으로만 그렇게 한다. 일반적으로 사람이 전에는 먹어 본 적이 없는 무언가를 맛볼 때 최초의 한 입은 크기가 작으며 신중하게 평가가 이루어진다.

[A] 그런 후에 가능하면, 최종 판단이 내려지기 전에 얼마간의 시간이 흐르도록 허용된다. 그 음식의 맛이 나쁘지 않고 그것을 섭취하고 난 이후의 시간이 질병으로 손상되지 않으면 그 음식은 아마도 안전하고 먹어도 되는 것으로 간주될 수 있을 것이다.

[C] 하지만 만일 그 음식의 맛이 나쁘거나 질병과 관련되면 그 음식은 못 먹는 것으로 간주되어 회피될 수도 있을 것이다. 새로운 음식에 대한 혐오감과 음식과 질병 사이의 연관에 대한 예민함의 이러한 결합은 잠재적인 독소로부터 어떤 보호를 제공한다.

Rudy's Tip neophobia가 B의 첫 문장과 연결되고, B 마지막 문장이 A로 연결되고 있다.

4 정답 (B)

What controls the number of times cells divide? The answer may lie with our telomeres, the protective tips on the ends of our chromosomes (a bit like the protective tips on the ends of shoestrings). These tips become shorter each time cells divide. Eventually, when the telomeres have nearly disappeared, the cells stop dividing, causing the cells to age and deteriorate. You might be inclined to think this means that the body has a built-in clock that controls the length of life by limiting cell reproduction.

(A) isolating defective cells 결함이 있는 세포를 격리함
(B) limiting cell reproduction 세포복제를 제한함
(C) allowing for cell expansion 세포 확장을 허용함
(D) preventing the binding of cells 세포의 결합을 막음

무엇이 세포가 분열하는 횟수를 통제하는가? 그 대답은 우리 염색체의 끝에 있는 보호용 말단부인 말단소체에 있을 수도 있다. (신발끈 끝에 있는 보호용 말단부와 약간 비슷한) 이 말단부는 세포가 분열할 때마다 점차 짧아진다. 마침내 말단소체가 거의 사라지면 세포가 분열하는 것을 멈추어, 세포가 노화되고 쇠약해지게 한다. 여러분은 이것이 신체가 세포 복제를 제한함으로써 수명을 통제하는 내장된 시계를 가지고 있다는 것을 의미한다고 생각할 수 있다.

Rudy's Tip 빈칸을 통해서 수명을 제한한다는 의미이기에, 빈칸에는 수명(성장)을 제한할 수 있는 수단에 해당하는 표현이 적절하다. reproduction = cell divide 의미이다.

5

정답 (C)

Coffee beans are seeds that grow inside a coffee plant's fruit, known as a cherry. Normally, two beans are found inside each cherry. However, about 5% of the time there is only one bean. When this happens, it is called a "peaberry." Peaberries are smaller and denser than normal coffee beans. Many people find coffee made from peaberries to be sweeter and more flavorful. But peaberries aren't easy to sort. The problem is that there is no way to tell which cherries contain peaberries just by looking at them. Because of this, they are usually sold mixed in with other coffee beans. Some coffee growers will remove peaberries by hand and sell them separately. However, because of the extra labor required, they are quite expensive.

커피콩은 체리라고 알려진 커피나무의 열매 속에서 자라는 씨앗이다. 보통은 각각의 체리 안에서 두 개의 콩이 발견된다. 그런데 약 5퍼센트의 경우에는 콩이 단 한 개만 있다. 이러한 일이 발생할 때 그것은 'peaberry'라고 불린다. peaberry는 보통의 커피콩보다 더 작고 밀도가 더 높다. 많은 사람들이 peaberry로 만든 커피가 더 달고 더 맛이 좋다고 여긴다. 그러나 peaberry는 분류하기가 쉽지않다. 문제는 눈으로만 봐서는 어느 체리에 peaberry가 들어있는지 구분할 방법이 없다는 것이다. 이 때문에 그것들은 대개 다른 커피콩과 함께 섞여 팔린다. 몇몇 커피 재배업자들은 손으로 peaberry를 따내어 따로 팔기도 한다. 그러나 이에 요구되는 추가적인 노동 때문에 그것들은 상당히 비싸다.

(A) 커피콩 수확량의 약 5퍼센트를 차지한다.
(B) 일반 커피콩보다 크기가 더 작다.
(C) 어느 체리 안에 들어있는지 육안으로 식별이 가능하다.
(D) 보통 다른 커피콩과 섞여서 판매된다.

Rudy's Tip 육안으로는 구별하기 어렵다는 것이 본문의 내용이다.

6
정답 (D)

Each geographical region and each cultural group of persons has its own pottery fashions that rapidly go through short-lived generations. Pottery is easily broken but the resulting fragments are nearly indestructible and leave valuable clues for archaeologists. Fragments enable them to determine the time, place, and size of cultural areas and the changes in these areas. There are hundreds of volumes describing the sequences of pottery styles throughout the world, including both the location and date at which each existed. In the strictest of terms antique pottery is pottery that is at least 100 years old, but today anything that simply looks antique will pass the grade regardless of age. For example, if a farming village was occupied for just a generation or two then its pottery would allow the village site to be dated because it would consist of styles from that period in time.

각각의 지리적인 지역과 각각의 문화적 인구 집단은 단명한 세대를 빠르게 거쳐 가는 자체적인 도기양식을 가지고 있다. 도기는 쉽게 깨지지만, 그 결과로 생긴 파편들은 파괴가 거의 불가능하여 고고학자들에게 귀중한 단서를 남긴다. 파편들 덕택에 고고학자들은 문화권의 시기, 장소 및 규모와 이 권역에서 일어난 변화를 밝힐 수 있다. 전 세계에 걸쳐 도기 양식이 존재했던 위치와 시대를 둘다 포함하여 도기 양식의 순서를 설명하는 수백 권의 책이 있다. 가장 엄밀한 용어로 말하면, 골동품 도기란 적어도 100년이나 된 도기이지만, 오늘날에는 단지 골동품인 것처럼 보이는 것은 무엇이든 연도에 관계없이 등급을 통과하기 마련이다.(골동품으로 인정) 예를 들어, 만약 어느 농촌 마을이 단지 한두 세대 동안만 거주된다 하더라도, 그 도기가 그 마을 터의 연대를 추정할 수 있게 해 주는데, 왜냐하면 그 도기가 시간상으로 그 시기의 양식으로 이루어질 것이기 때문이다.

Rudy's Tip 모두 고고학적 가치(의미)와 관련된 진술이지만, D는 골동품에 관련된 내용으로 고고학적 가치와는 관련성이 없다.

10분 모의고사 15 해설편

1   정답 (C)

Despite its purported neutrality, the study will be compelled to produce results favorable to its sponsors.

연구에 대해 알려진 중립성에도 불구하고, 그 연구는 후원자들에게 유리한 결과를 생산하도록 강요될 것이다.

(A) The results of the study will be unbiased though the people who fund it do not want them to be.

그 연구의 결과들은, 그 연구를 후원한 사람들이 원치 않을지라도 중립적일 것이다.

(B) Some say the research is biased, but really it will only do exactly what people ordered it to do.

어떤 사람들은 그 연구가 편파적이라고 말하지만, 실제로 그 연구는 사람들이 요청한 것만을 정확히 할 뿐이다.

(C) The research claims to be fair, but it will be forced to say good things about the people who paid for it.

그 연구는 공정하다고 주장하지만, 연구에 돈을 지불하는 사람들에 대해 우호적인 것들을 이야기하도록 강요될 것이다.

(D) Even though people say it has to be fair, the report will be supported by financial backers.

사람들은 비록 보고서가 공정해야 한다고 말하지만, 보고서는 재정 후원자들에게 지지를 받을 것이다.

Rudy's Tip purported neutrality = claims to be fair
be compelled to produce results favorable = be forced to say good things

2

정답 (C)

Creative writing may serve many purposes for the writer. Above all, it is a means of self-expression. It is the individual's way of saying, "These are my thoughts and they are uniquely experienced by me." But creative writing can also serve as a safety valve for dormant tensions. This implies that a period of time has evolved in which the child gave an idea some deep thought and that the message on paper is revealing of this deep inner thought. Finally, a worthwhile by-product of creative writing is the stimulus it gives students to be an ardent reader of good literature.

창작은 작가에게 여러 가지로 도움이 될 수 있다. 무엇보다도, 그것은 자기 표현의 수단이 된다. 그것은 "이것들은 나의 생각이며, 저것들은 나에 의해 독특하게 경험된 것이다."를 말하는 한 개인의 표현 방식이다. 그러나 창작은 또한 잠재된 긴장감에 대해서 안전한 배출구 역할을 할 수 있다. 이것은 어린이가 (창작을 하기 위해) 어떤 생각을 일정 기간에 걸쳐 깊이 사고하였으며, 창작은 이런 깊은 내면의 사고를 드러내고 있음을 나타낸다. 마지막으로, 창작의 값진 한가지 부산물은 그것은 학생들에게 훌륭한 문학의 열렬한 독자가 될 수 있는 자극을 제공한다는 것이다.

Creative writing can help release dormant tensions because _____.
창작은 잠재된 긴장을 배출하는데 도움이 될 수 있다. 왜냐하면 _____.

(A) the writer will usually write something autobiographical
작가는 흔히 자서전적인 내용을 집필할 것이다.
(B) creative writing can be attractive to readers.
창작은 독자들에게 매력적일 수 있다.
(C) creative writing can express what the writer has long held within
창작은 작가가 오랫동안 내면에 지니고 있던 것을 표현할 수 있다.
(D) understanding literature means understanding the tensions of the characters
문학을 이해하는 것은 등장인물들의 긴장(갈등)을 이해한다는 것이다.

Rudy's Tip 본문의 revealing의 동의 표현을 찾는 문제이다. reveal = express

3

정답 (B)

We are programmed to be together. Even when we think we are being most individual in the way we present ourselves through the fashions we wear and the way we cut our hair, we are conforming to this truth. Exactitudes is an ongoing photo project started by Dutch photographer Arie Versluis and stylist Elly Yttenbroek in 1995. The two tour the world taking pictures of individuals from social groups wherever they are to be found and get individuals to pose in identical poses. They then display shorts of these individuals in grids of 4×3, so that the similarities are clear. The tattoo section shows that even when we think of the most individualist of fashions — having someone draw on your body — the individuals are clearly doing what other individuals are doing and not being 'different' and unique. Our efforts to be individual are ultimately in vain.

우리는 선천적으로 함께 하는 경향이 있다. 입는 패션과 머리를 자르는 모양을 통해 스스로를 보여주는 방식으로 우리가 가장 개성적이라고 생각할 때조차도, 우리는 이 진실을 따르고 있다. Exactitudes는 네덜란드 사진가인 Arie Versluis와 스타일리스트인 Elly Yttenbroek에 의해 1995년에 시작되어 진행 중인 사진 프로젝트이다. 그 둘은 사회 집단에 속한 사람들이 발견될 수 있는 곳은 어디에서라도 그들의 사진을 찍으며 세계를 돌아다니고, 사람들에게 동일한 자세를 취해보게 한다. 그 다음에 그들은 이 사람들의 사진을 4x3판에 전시하는데, 그래서 그 유사점이 명확해진다. 문신 부문은 우리가 패션에서 가장 개성적인 것, 즉 누군가가 당신 몸에 그리게 하는 것을 생각할 때조차도, 그 사람들은 분명히 다른 사람들이 하고 있는 것을 하고 있으며 '색다르고' 독특한 것이 아니라는 것을 보여준다. 개성적이기 위한 우리의 노력은 결국 헛수고이다.

(A) Fashions are the best way to present ourselves
   패션은 스스로를 보여주는 가장 좋은 방법이다.
(B) Our efforts to be individual are ultimately in vain
   개성적이기 위한 우리의 노력은 결국 헛수고이다.
(C) The common frames that held us together are crashing
   우리를 같이 묶어주었던 공통의 틀이 무너지고 있다.
(D) We are destined to be an 'I-species' rather than a 'we-species'
   우리는 '집단 종족'보다는 '개인 종족'이 될 운명이다.

Rudy's Tip 빈칸은 선행 문장에 대한 재진술이기에, not different를 통해서 빈칸에도 유사한 표현이 적절하다.

4

정답 (B)

Suppose you wish to determine which brand of microwave popcorn leaves the fewest unpopped kernels. You will need a supply of various brands of microwave popcorn to test, and you will need a microwave oven. If you used different brands of microwave ovens with different brands of popcorn, the percentage of unpopped kernels could be caused by the different brands of popcorn or by the different brands of ovens. Under such circumstances, the experimenter would be unable to conclude confidently whether the popcorn or the oven caused the difference. To eliminate this problem, you must use the same microwave oven for every test. In order to reasonably conclude that the change in one variable was caused by the change in another specific variable, there must be no other variables in the experiment. By using the same microwave oven, you control the number of variables in the experiment.

여러분이 어느 상표의 전자레인지용 팝콘이 덜 튀겨진 낱알을 가장 적게 남기는지를 알아내고 싶다고 가정해 보자. 여러분은 조사할 어느 정도 양의 다양한 상표의 전자레인지용 팝콘을 필요로 할 것이고, 전자레인지 한 대도 필요로 할 것이다. 만일 여러분이 여러 다른 상표의 전자레인지를 여러 다른 상표의 팝콘과 함께 사용한다면, 덜 튀겨진 낱알의 비율은 그 여러 상표의 팝콘 또는 그 여러 상표의 전자레인지에 의해 영향을 받을 수 있을 것이다. 그런 상황 하에서는, 실험자가 그 차이에 영향을 미친 것이 팝콘인지 또는 전자레인지인지를 자신 있게 결정할 수 없을 것이다. 이 문제를 제거하려면, 여러분은 모든 조사에 반드시 동일한 전자레인지를 사용해야만 한다. 한 변수에서의 변화가 다른 한 특정 변수에서의 변화에 의해 영향을 받았다고 합리적으로 결론을 내리기 위해서는, 그 실험에 다른 변수들이 있으면 안 된다. 동일한 전자레인지를 사용함으로써, 여러분은 실험에서 변수의 개수를 통제하는 것이다.

(A) importance of safety in experimental work 실험에서 안전의 중요성
(B) need for controlling variables in experiments 실험에서 변수 통제의 필요성
(C) influence of prior knowledge on experiments 실험에 사전 지식이 미치는 영향
(D) benefits of combining experimental methods 실험 과정들을 통합하는 장점들

Rudy's Tip ST 구조로 팝콘과 전자레인지 예시를 통해서 변수 통제의 중요성을 이야기하는 글이다.

5
정답 (C)

What a computer is designed to do is, essentially, arithmetic. Any problem, however complex, can somehow be broken down into a well-defined series of arithmetical operations that can be solved by a computer. The computer is amazing not because of its capability to handle arithmetical operations, but because of the fact that it can perform these operations in one billionth of a second without error. The human brain, on the other hand, is incredibly poor at arithmetic. Unlike computers, it needs and has always needed outside help to solve the simplest problems. We began by counting on our fingers, and have moved on to better things only with the help of pen and paper, Arabic numerals, mechanical calculators and eventually computers.

컴퓨터가 수행하도록 설계되어 있는 일은 본질적으로 계산이다. 어떤 문제든지, 아무리 복잡하더라도, 컴퓨터가 해결할 수 있는 명확한 일련의 계산 작업으로 분해될 수 있다. 컴퓨터가 놀라운 것은 계산 작업을 수행할 수 있는 능력 때문이 아니라, 그러한 작업을 10억분의 1초 만에 실수 없이 수행할 수 있다는 사실 때문이다. 반면에, 인간의 두뇌는 계산에 매우 약하다. 컴퓨터와 달리, 인간의 두뇌는 가장 간단한 문제를 해결하기 위해서도 외부의 도움이 늘 필요했으며 지금도 그러하다. 인간은 손가락으로 계산을 시작하여, 펜과 종이, 아라비아 숫자, 기계식 계산기, 그리고 마침내는 컴퓨터의 도움을 받고서야 더 향상된 방향으로 나아가게 되었다.

Rudy's Tip 'unlike computer, it'에서 it의 선행사가 'human brain'이다.

6

정답 (D)

Whenever anything goes wrong on this globe of ours, it is human tendency for someone, anyone, or all of us to point a long finger of blame at someone or anyone beside ourselves, of course. This finger pointing has certainly been seen with regard to energy shortages and energy-derived pollution problems.

[C] In particular, many critics point the finger of blame for our current and pending shortage of liquid fuels at the environmentalists; however, the U.S. Environmental Protection Agency suggested that a finger of blame pointed at the environmental movement is misdirected.

[A] Although it is true that environmental regulations have caused some increased energy demand and have restricted supply to some extent, it is important to recognize that other factors have been considerably more significant.

[B] These include rapidly escalating demand for energy, energy pricing policies, oil import quotas, lack of incentives to invest in domestic energy facilities, and depletion of domestic oil and gas reserves.

우리의 지구에서 무엇인가 잘못될 때마다 어떤 이, 누군가 또는 우리 모두가 물론 우리 자신 이외의 어떤 이나 누군가를 향해 거센 비난의 손가락질을 하는 것이 인간의 성향이다. 이러한 손가락 겨누기는 에너지 부족과 에너지로부터 비롯된 공해 문제와 관련해서 분명히 목격되어 왔다.

[C] 특히 많은 비판자들은 우리의 현재 그리고 곧 있을 액체 연료의 부족을 환경 운동가들의 탓이라고 손가락질 한다. 그러나 미국 환경보호국은 환경 운동에 겨눠진 비난의 손가락은 겨냥을 잘못한 것이라고 말하였다.
[A] 비록 환경적 규제가 얼마간 증가된 에너지 수요를 야기해 왔고 어느 정도까지는 공급을 제한시켰다는 것은 사실이지만 다른 요인들이 상당히 더 심각했다는 것을 인식하는 것이 중요하다.
[B] 이러한 것(요인)들은 급속도로 증가하는 에너지에 대한 수요, 에너지 가격 정책, 석유 수입 한도, 국내 에너지 시설 투자에 대한 장려책의 부족, 그리고 국내의 석유와 가스 비축량의 고갈을 포함한다.

Rudy's Tip A는 although, B는 These로 시작하기에 첫 문항으로 적절하지 않다.

10분 모의고사 16 해설편

1
정답 (A)

Managers in commerce and industry must increase efficiency to help get us out of the economic slump, and the same applies to public-service managers.

상공업 분야에서 관리자들은 우리들이 경기침체에서 벗어나는 것을 위하여 효율성을 높여야 하고 같은 것이 공공서비스 분야의 관리자들에게도 적용된다.

(A) In order to overcome the economic slump, managers in commerce and industry and public-service managers need to boost efficiency.

경기침체를 극복하기 위해 상공업 분야의 관리자들과 공공서비스 분야의 관리자들은 효율성을 증가시킬 필요가 있다.

(B) To maintain the current economic state, efficiency should be increased by managers in commerce and industry and public-service managers.

현재의 경제상태를 유지하기 위해 효율성은 상공업 분야의 관리자들과 공공서비스 분야의 관리자들에 의해 증가 되어야한다.

(C) Managers in commerce and industry need to negotiate with public-service managers to assist in improving the economy.

상공업분야의 관리자들은 경기회복을 돕기 위해 공공서비스분야의 관리자들과 협상을 할 필요가 있다.

(D) Unlike public-service managers, managers in commerce and industry must do their share for the economy.

공공서비스분야의 관리자들과 달리, 상공업 분야의 관리자들은 경제를 위해 할 수 있는 그들의 역할을 다해야 한다.

Rudy's Tip get us out of the economic slump = overcome the economic slump
the same applies to public-service managers = public-service managers need to boost efficiency

2

정답 (B)

For a long time psychoanalysis was the only psychotherapy practiced in Western society, and it is based on the theories of Sigmund Freud. According to Freud's views, psychological disturbances are due to anxiety about hidden conflicts in the unconscious parts of one's personality. One job of the psychoanalyst, therefore, is to help make the patients aware of the unconscious impulses and desires that are causing the anxiety. However, some symbols in dreams seem to be universal; in other words, they appear to have the same meaning to people everywhere. Psychoanalysts believe that understanding these unconscious motives is very important. If patients can have that kind of understanding, called insight, they have taken the first step toward gaining control over their behavior and freeing themselves of their problems.

정신분석학은 오랫동안 서구사회에서 시행된 유일한 심리치료였으며 Sigmund Freud의 이론에 근거하고 있다. Freud의 견해에 의하면 심리적 장애는 개인 성격의 무의식적인 부분들에 숨어있는 갈등에 대한 불안에서 생겨난다. 그렇기에 정신분석학자가 하는 한 가지 일은 그러한 불안을 야기하는 무의식적인 충동과 욕망을 환자들이 인식할 수 있도록 도와주는 것이다. 그러나 꿈에 등장하는 일부 상징들은 보편적인 것 같다. 다시 말해, 그것들은 모든 사람들에게 동일한 의미를 갖고 있는 것 같다. 정신 분석가들은 이러한 무의식적인 동기들을 이해하는 것이 매우 중요하다고 믿는다. 통찰이라고 불리는 그러한 이해를 할 수 있으면 환자들은 자신들의 행위에 대한 통제와 자신들의 문제를 해결하는 방향으로 첫걸음을 내딛게 된 것이다.

Rudy's Tip B를 제외하고는 모두 정신 분석가들에 대한 진술이다.

3

정답 (D)

The ad hominem fallacy is one of the most common mistakes in reasoning. The fallacy rests on a confusion between the qualities of the person making a claim and the qualities of the claim itself. Let's say my friend, Mike, is an ingenious fellow. It follows that Mike's opinion on some subject, whatever it is, is the opinion of an ingenious person. But it does not follow that Mike's opinion itself is ingenious. To think that, it is would be to confuse the content of Mike's claim with Mike himself. Or let's suppose you are listening to your teacher whom you regard as a bit strange or maybe even weird. Would it follow that the car your teacher drives is strange or weird? Obviously not. Similarly, it would not follow that some specific proposal that the teacher has put forth is strange or weird. A proposal made by an oddball is an oddball's proposal, but it does not follow that it is an oddball proposal.

인신공격의 오류는 추론에 있어서 가장 흔한 실수 중 하나이다. 그 오류는 주장하는 사람의 특징과 그 주장 자체의 특징 사이의 혼란에서 등장한다. 나의 친구인 Mike가 현명한 친구라고 가정해 보자. 어떤 주제에 관한 Mike의 의견은, 그것이 무엇이든 간에, 현명한 사람의 의견이다. 그러나 이것이 Mike의 의견 자체가 현명하다는 결론에 이르는 것은 아니다. 만약 그렇게 생각한다면(Mike 의견도 현명) Mike가 주장하는 내용과 Mike라는 사람 자체를 혼동하게 되는 것이다. 또는 당신이 조금 이상하거나 심지어는 괴상하다고 생각하는 선생님 말씀을 듣고 있다고 생각해 보자. 그렇다면 당신의 선생님이 운전하는 차도 이상하거나 괴상할까? 결코 그렇지 않다. 마찬가지로, 그 선생님이 제시한 일부 세부적인 제안이 이상하거나 괴상하다는 것도 아닐 것이다. 괴짜에 의해 만들어진 제안은 괴짜의 제안이지, 그 제안 자체가 괴짜(이상한) 제안이 되는 것은 아니다.

(A) It is ingenious to suppose that a teacher who owns a strange car also does weird things.
   이상한 차를 소유한 선생님이 괴상한 짓을 할 것이라고 생각하는 것은 창의적이다.
(B) We must accept the reasoning that the qualities of a person determine the qualities of the claim he makes.
   한 사람의 특성이 그 사람이 만드는 그 주장의 특성을 결정짓는다는 추론을 우리는 받아들여야만 한다.
(C) It is odd to claim that common mistakes we make result from confusion between truth and fallacy.
   우리가 하는 흔한 실수는 진실과 오류 사이의 혼동으로부터 기인한다고 주장하는 것은 이상하다.
(D) We must not confuse the qualities of the person making a claim with the qualities of the claim itself.
   우리는 주장을 하는 사람의 특성과 그 주장 자체의 특성을 혼동하지 말아야 한다.

Rudy's Tip GS 구조의 영문으로 서론에 주제가 제시되고, 이어서 예시가 등장하고 있다. 메시지와 메신저는 구분해야 한다는 주장이 요지이다.

4

정답 (B)

Nowadays, most people use passwords and government ID numbers on the Web. They think they are safe, but that may not be true. A new kind of attack is being used by dishonest people to steal IDs and credit card numbers from innocent websurfers.

[C] This new kind of attack is called "fishing." fishing sounds the same as the word "fishing," and it implies a thief is trying to lure people giving away valuable information. How can fishers lure people to do this?

[B] Like real fishermen, they use bait in the form of great online deals or services. For example, phishers might use fake e-mails and false web-sites to cheat people into revealing credit card numbers, and passwords.

[A] In addition, they imitate well-known banks, online sellers, and credit card companies. Successful phishers may convince as many as 5 percent of the people they contact to respond and give away their personal information.

오늘날, 대부분의 사람들은 인터넷에서 암호나 주민등록번호를 사용한다. 그들은 안전하다고 생각하지만 그것은 사실이 아닐 수도 있다. 순진한 인터넷 사용자들로부터 신분 증명 변호와 신용카드 번호를 훔치기 위해 부정직한 사람들에 의해 새로운 종류의 공격이 사용되고 있다.

[C] 이 새로운 종류의 공격은 "피싱(phishing)"이라고 불린다. 피싱은 '낚시(fishing)'와 동일하게 들리며, 그것은 도둑이 사람들을 유인해 귀중한 정보를 앗아가려 한다는 것을 의미한다. 피셔들(phishers)은 이것을 하기 위해 어떻게 사람들을 유혹할까?

[B] 진짜 낚시꾼처럼, 그들은 온라인 거래나 서비스의 형태로 된 미끼를 사용한다. 예를 들어 피셔들은 사람들을 속여 신용카드 번호와 암호를 드러내도록 하기 위해 가짜 이메일과 가짜 암호를 사용할 수도 있다.

[A] 게다가, 그들은 유명한 은행, 온라인 판매자, 그리고 신용카드 회사 등을 모방한다. 성공적인 피셔들은 그들이 접촉하는 사람들의 5퍼센트 정도까지 납득을 시켜 응답을 하여 자신들의 개인 정보를 건네주게 할 수도 있다.

Rudy's Tip B는 대명사 They, A는 in addition으로 첫 문항으로 적절하지 않다.

5

정답 (A)

It is important to understand the impact of wide-scale implementation of digital tools because many of the systems are adopted by many people. This is why organizations must spend some amount of time preparing and researching the process of technology implementation before deciding to add new tools to a system. A good starting point for the implementation of new digital technologies is to anticipate who the users will be and to understand the specific needs of the users. For example, an institution might decide to offer special cell phones to all of its employees, so it must spend some time contemplating who would use the phones, and for what purpose. If the phones are to be used only to stay in touch with the main office, then the phones do not require a built-in camera. The expected use of the technology needs to be the most important criteria before introducing new digital tools.

(A) expected use 예상되는 용도
(B) introduction cost 도입 비용
(C) security system 보안 시스템
(D) overall performance 전반적인 성능

디지털 도구를 대규모로 실제 사용하는 것이 주는 영향을 이해하는 것은 중요한데, 그 이유는 그 시스템 중 많은 것이 많은 사람에 의해 채택되기 때문이다. 이런 이유로 조직은 새로운 도구를 시스템에 추가하기로 결정하기 전에 어느 정도 시간을 들여 기술을 실제로 사용하는 과정을 준비하고 조사해야 한다. 새로운 디지털 기술의 사용을 위한 좋은 출발점은 누가 사용자가 될 것인지 예상하는 것과 그 사용자들의 구체적인 필요를 이해하는 것이다. 예를 들어, 어떤 기관이 특별한 휴대 전화기를 모든 직원들에게 제공하기로 결정할 수 있는데, 그렇다면 그 기관은 어느 정도 시간을 들여 누가, 어떤 목적으로 그 전화기를 사용할 것인지를 생각해야 한다. 그 전화기가 본사와의 연락을 유지하기 위해서만 사용될 것이라면, 그 휴대전화기에는 내장 카메라가 필요 없다. 기술의 예상되는 용도는 새로운 디지털 도구를 도입하기 전에 가장 중요한 기준이 될 필요가 있다.

Rudy's Tip 선행 문장에 '사용자와 사용목적'에 대한 진술이 있기에, 빈칸 또한 사용에 관련된 표현이 가장 적절하다.

6   정답 (D)

People name their children using all sorts of rules and approaches. Sometimes they borrow names from historical or literary heroes, sometimes they follow ancestral naming traditions, and sometimes they just like how a name sounds. In all cases, though, the otherwise meaningless name acquires meaning because it's associated with other concepts that are themselves meaningful. The power of association explains why Adolf, a common boy's name once associated with Swedish and Luxembourger kings, declined in popularity during and after World War II. Most people have a tendency to trust individuals with names that they could easily pronounce. Meanwhile, the name Donald fell from favor when Donald Duck appeared in the 1930s, and parents stopped naming their sons Ebenezer in the 1840s when Charles Dickens's newly published book, A Christmas Carol, featured the miserly Ebenezer Scrooge.

사람들은 모든 종류의 규칙과 접근법을 사용해서 자기 아이들의 이름을 짓는다. 때때로 그들은 역사 혹은 문학에 나오는 영웅의 이름을 빌리고, 때로는 조상의 이름 짓는 전통을 따르고, 그리고 때로는 이름이 들리는 방식을 그냥 좋아한다. 하지만 모든 경우에서 이름이 그 자체로 의미 있는 다른 개념과 연관되기 때문에 그렇지 않으면 의미가 없었을 이름이 의미를 얻는다. 연상의 힘은 한 때 스웨덴과 룩셈부르크 왕들과 연관되었던 남자 아이의 흔한 이름인 Adolf가 왜 제 2차 세계대전 동안과 그 이후에 인기가 떨어졌는지를 설명해준다. (대부분의 사람들은 그들이 쉽게 발음할 수 있는 이름을 가진 사람들을 신뢰하는 경향이 있다.) 한편, Donald라는 이름은 1930년대에 Donald Duck이 나타났을 때 인기가 떨어졌고, Charles Dickens의 새롭게 출간된 책인 'A Christmas Carol'에 구두쇠인 Ebenezer Scrooge가 주인공으로 나온 1840년대에 부모들은 자신들의 아들을 Ebenezer라고 이름 짓는 것을 멈췄다.

Rudy's Tip 이름과 그에 따른 연상 작용에 대한 예시가 본문의 내용이다. 발음하기 편하다는 내용은 본문의 내용과 전혀 관련성이 없다.

 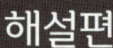

10분 모의고사 17 해설편

1
정답 (C)

Considering all your options means more than taking stock of the pros and cons of any given choice.
모든 방안을 고려한다는 것은 주어진 선택의 찬반을 꼼꼼히 살펴보는 것 이상을 의미한다.

(A) In decision-making, you need to explore all the options available and moreover the pros and cons of a choice.
의사결정과 관련하여 당신은 이용 가능한 모든 방안과 선택의 장점과 단점을 탐구할 필요가 있다

(B) Striking a balance between the pros and cons of a situation is the key to making a wise choice.
상황의 찬반 사이에서 균형을 맞추는 것은 현명한 선택을 하는 열쇠이다.

(C) You have to go beyond just reviewing what the pros and cons are regarding a decision, when you think over what options are available.
이용 가능한 모든 방안을 생각할 때 결정하는 데 있어 장단점을 검토하는 것 이상을 해야 한다.

(D) If the pros outweigh the cons of a decision, then you should reconsider what alternatives are available.
결정하는 데 있어 장점이 단점을 능가한다면, 당신은 이용 가능한 다른 결정을 재고해야 한다.

Rudy's Tip more than taking stock of the pros and cons = go beyond just reviewing what the pros and cons

2
정답 (D)

Poems can be taken apart from time to time, like any well-made objects, but it is important to remember to put them back together properly at the end and check that they still work. Looking at how a poem has built up sound patterns through rhythm, rhyme, alliteration, and other devices, or how word pictures have been built up through images, or meanings made through wordplay, can add a different sort of enjoyment as well as understanding of poems. But poems should not be used just as excuses for feature-spotting, for example hunting down metaphors and similes for the sake of naming the parts. Poems are often left in pieces after this kind of activity as the lesson moves on to another text with the same feature or topic. It should be a rule to read the poem aloud again after any form of analysis, savoring its sounds and images anew.

시(詩)는 그 어떤 잘 만들어진 물건과 마찬가지로 가끔 분해될 수 있지만, 마지막에는 그것을 제대로 다시 합쳐서 여전히 그것이 (시로서) 기능하는지 확인해 보는 것을 명심하는 것이 중요하다. 시가 운율, 각운, 두운, 그리고 다른 장치를 통해서 어떻게 소리 패턴을 만들었는지, 또는 그림을 보는 듯한 생생한 서술이 이미지를 통해서 어떻게 형성되었는지, 또는 (재치 있는) 말장난을 통해서 의미가 어떻게 이루어졌는지를 살펴보는 것은 시에 대한 이해뿐만 아니라 다른 종류의 즐거움도 더할 수 있다. 하지만 시가 특징을 찾아내는 것, 예를 들어 (시의) 부분을 명명하기 위해 은유와 직유를 찾아내는 것을 위한 구실로서만 사용되어서는 안 된다. 이런 종류의 활동 후에 수업이 똑같은 특징 혹은 주제를 가진 또 다른 글로 옮겨 가면서 시는 흔히 조각난 채 남겨진다. 어떤 형태의 분석을 하든지 그 후에는 그 시의 소리와 이미지가 어떻게 서로 들어맞는지를 통찰한 다음에 그 소리와 이미지를 새롭게 음미하면서.

Rudy's Tip GS 구성의 영문으로 첫 문장에 모든 내용이 포괄되어 있다. 또한 첫 문장과 마지막 문장에 동일한 진술에 주목하자.

3

정답 (B)

Scientific experiments should be designed to show that your hypothesis is wrong, and should be conducted completely objectively with no possible subjective influence on the outcome. Unfortunately few, if any, scientists are truly objective. They have often decided long before the experiment is begun what they would like the result to be. This means that very often bias is (unintentionally) introduced into the experiment, the experimental procedure or the interpretation of results. It is all too easy to justify to yourself why an experiment which does not fit with your expectations should be ignored, and why one which provides the results you 'hoped for' is the right one. This can be partly avoided by conducting experiments 'blinded' and by asking others to check your data or repeat experiments.

과학 실험은 여러분의 가설이 틀리다는 것을 보여 주도록 설계되어야 하고, 결과에 대해 있을 법한 그 어떤 주관적 영향도 없이 완벽하게 객관적으로 수행되어야 한다. 불행하게도, 설령 있다 치더라도, 진정으로 객관적인 과학자는 거의 없다. 그들은 흔히 실험이 시작되기 오래 전에 어떤 결과가 나왔으면 좋겠는지를 결정했다. 이것은 빈번히 편견이 실험, 실험 절차 혹은 결과의 해석에 (무심코) 더해진다는 것을 의미한다. 자신의 기대에 어긋나는 실험이 왜 무시되어야 하는지, 그리고 자신이 '기대했던' 결과를 가져다주는 실험이 왜 옳은 것인지를 스스로에게 정당화하는 것은 너무나 쉽다. '앞일을 알지 못한 채' 실험을 하고 다른 사람들에게 여러분의 데이터를 점검하거나 실험을 (똑같이) 다시 해 보라고 요청함으로써 이것을 어느 정도 피할 수 있다.

(A) isolated 고립된
(B) blinded 볼 수 없는(예상할 수 없는)
(C) deceived 속고 있는
(D) informed 알고 있는

Rudy's Tip 실험에서 과학자의 객관성을 강조하는 내용이다. 빈칸은 experiments를 수식하는 분사로 객관성과 관련된 표현이 적절하고, '예상할 수 없는' 실험이란 의미는 실험 결과에 대한 예상을 하지 않고 객관적으로 실험을 수행한다는 의미로 적절하다.

4
정답 (B)

A naturalist named Syevertsoff documented nearly a dozen white-tailed eagles acting as a survey team. Spread across the sky at a considerable distance apart, they were together scanning an estimated twenty-five square miles. For a good half hour, individuals held their respective posts, tracing wide circles in silence, until one finally let out a piercing shriek. Its cry was soon answered by another eagle approaching, followed by a third, a fourth, and so on, till nine or ten eagles came together and soon disappeared. Later that afternoon, Syevertsoff arrived at the place where he had seen the group descend into the gently rolling grasslands hours earlier. There he discovered the birds gathered around the corpse of a horse. Some of the eagles, probably the older ones, who had eaten first, were perched nearby keeping watch while the youngsters dined in safety, surrounded by bands of crows.

Syevertsoff라는 이름의 동식물학자는 거의 12마리에 이르는 흰꼬리수리가 하나의 조사 팀으로 행동하는 것을 기록했다. 상당한 거리를 두고 떨어져서 하늘 곳곳에 퍼져서, 그것들은 어림잡아 25평방 마일을 함께 훑어보고 있었다. 족히 30분 동안, 각각의 수리들은 조용히 큰 원을 따라 돌면서 각자의 자리를 지켰는데, 마침내 한 마리가 찢어지는 듯한 날카로운 소리를 냈다. 그것의 울음소리에 이내 다른 수리가 다가와서 응했고, 세 번째, 네 번째가 뒤따라 마침내 아홉 내지 열 마리의 수리들이 모였고 이내 사라져버렸다. 그날 오후 늦게, Syevertsoff는 수 시간 전에 그 무리가 완만하게 기복이 있는 풀밭으로 내려앉는 것을 보았던 장소에 도착했다. 그곳에서 그는 그 새들이 말 사체 근처에 모여 있는 것을 발견했다. 몇 마리의 수리들은 아마 더 나이가 많은 것들로 먼저 먹었을 텐데, 까마귀 떼들에 둘러싸인 채 새끼들이 안전하게 먹는 동안 근처에서 망을 보면서 앉아 있었다.

Rudy's Tip Its cry의 선행사가 a piercing shriek 이다.

5
정답 (B)

Social stereotypes are often formed initially from some specific experience, or from observations of one or more individuals. These specific impressions become a stereotype when this information is then generalized to apply to all members of a group, regardless of circumstances.

[B] This creates difficulties when circumstances change, but the stereotype does not, or when a stereotype is used as a substitute for gathering accurate information about a person. For example, a friend once reported an experience that his 6-year-old son had at school.

[A] The teacher had asked the children to 'draw a picture of your father relaxing.' When the teacher saw the boy drawing a picture of a man chopping wood, she said, "No, I said draw him relaxing." Bursting into tears, the 6-year-old exclaimed, "But my Daddy does chop wood to relax!"

[C] By contrast, his father's 'work' involved sitting at a desk all day. The teacher's stereotype, not the boy's drawing, was the problem. Stereotypes, as mental schemata, can lead us to prejudge others — and all schemata carry this risk of distorting reality.

사회적 고정관념은 흔히 처음에 어떤 특정한 경험으로부터, 또는 한 사람이나 그 이상의 개인들에 대한 관찰로부터 형성된다. 그리고 나서 이 정보가 일반화되어 상황에 관계없이 한 집단의 '모든' 구성원에게 적용될 때, 이러한 특정한 느낌은 고정관념이 된다.

[B] 상황은 변화하지만, 그 고정관념이 변화하지 않을 때, 또는 고정관념이 한 사람에 대한 정확한 정보를 수집하는 것 대신 사용될 때, 이는 문제를 일으킨다. 예를 들어, 언젠가 한 친구가 자신의 여섯 살 된 아들이 학교에서 경험했던 것을 말했다.

[A] 교사가 아이들에게 '아빠가 편히 쉬고 있는 모습을 그릴 것'을 요청했었다. 교사는 그 사내아이가 나무를 자르고 있는 남자의 그림을 그리고 있는 것을 봤을 때, "아니야, 내가 아빠가 '쉬고 있는' 것을 그리라고 했잖아."라고 말했다. 그 여섯 살 된 사내아이가 눈물을 터뜨리며 "하지만 우리 아빠는 쉬기 위해 '정말로' 나무를 잘라요!"라고 큰 소리로 말했다.

[C] 반대로, 그 아이 아빠의 '일'은 온종일 책상에 앉아 있는 것과 관련이 있었다. 그 사내아이의 그림이 아니라 교사의 고정관념이 문제였던 것이다. 정신적인 도식으로서의 고정관념은 우리가 다른 사람들을 속단할 수 있게 하며, 모든 도식은 현실을 왜곡할 수 있는 이러한 위험을 수반한다.

Rudy's Tip 도입문 마지막 문장과 B의 첫 문장, B의 마지막과 A의 첫 문장이 연결된다.

6
정답 (D)

Tipping is rarely required in Korea. The one exception is in Western-style hotels, restaurants, bars, and nightclubs where a 10% service charge and 10% value added tax will be added automatically to the bill. It is not necessary to tip taxi drivers. From time to time, it might be prudent to offer a small gift to someone who has provided especially good service. In these special circumstances, no doubt that the gift will be received with great appreciation and will help secure future assistance.

팁을 주는 것은 한국에서 좀처럼 요구되지 않는다. 하나의 예외가 있다면 10% 서비스 요금과 10% 부가가치세가 계산서에 자동으로 붙는 서구 스타일의 호텔, 레스토랑, 술집, 그리고 나이트클럽이다. 택시 운전사에게 팁을 주는 것은 불필요하다. 때때로, 특별히 좋은 서비스를 제공한 사람에게 조그만 선물을 주는 것은 세심한 것일 수 있다. 이런 특별한 경우에, 그 선물이 굉장히 감사히 받아들여질 것이고 앞으로의 도움을 보증하는데 도움이 될 것을 확신한다.

(A) The service charge is one form of indirect tipping in Korea.
한국에서 서비스 요금은 간접적인 형태의 팁이다.
(B) Tipping is required in some Korean establishments.
팁은 몇몇 한국의 시설들에서는 요구된다.
(C) Korean taxi drivers do not expect to be tipped.
택시 운전사는 팁을 기대하지 않는다.
(D) Tipping almost always leads to adverse consequences in Korea.
한국에서 팁은 거의 항상 부작용을 가져온다.

Rudy's Tip 마지막 문장을 통해서 틀린 문항을 선별할 수 있다.

10분 모의고사 18 해설편

1
정답 (B)

Any recovery of the natural world will require not only extensive financial funding but conversion deep in the psychic structure of the human.

자연 세계의 회복은 광범위한 재정지원뿐만 아니라 인간의 정신 깊은 곳에서의 변화를 요구한다.

(A) It will be impossible to save the natural world unless humans change their attitudes about investing a vast amount of money in conservation.

인간이 자연보호에 막대한 양의 돈을 투자하는 데 있어서 태도를 바꾸지 않는다면 자연세계를 보존하는 것은 불가능할 것이다.

(B) The natural world can be restored with substantial amounts of money and a change in the minds of humans.

자연 세계는 막대한 양의 돈과 인간정신의 변화와 함께 회복될 수 있다.

(C) Humans recognized that a great amount of funding is necessary to sustain the natural world, which resulted in a shift in mentality.

인간은 자연세계를 유지하기 위해 많은 자금이 필요하다는 것을 인식했는데, 그것이 사고방식의 변화를 가져왔다.

(D) Saving the environment depends more on the consciousness-raising of humans than on the amount of money spent.

환경보호는 사용하는 돈의 양보다 인간의 의식 고양에 더 달려 있다.

Rudy's Tip not only extensive financial funding but conversion deep in the psychic
= substantial amounts of money and a change in the minds

2 정답 (B)

Throughout the centuries, immigrant groups coming to America have attempted to re-create the dishes of their homelands. Often, however, the needed ingredients are unavailable or too expensive. Moreover, in the early-20th century, dietitians and reformers frequently looked upon the food choices and dishes of immigrants with alarm and disdain. Dietitian Bertha M. Wood wrote a cookbook that conveyed many of the then prominent beliefs and stereotypes about immigrants to the United States. Yet she also expressed some sympathy toward the various groups of people who arrived, often penniless, in America. For example, in contrast to the opinion often given by other Americans that immigrants "should learn to eat American food if they are to live here," she countered, "When a person is ill and needs a special diet, it is no time to teach him to eat new foods. It is like hitting a person when he is down. Our milk soups are nutritious, but so are theirs; why not learn what they are and prescribe them? The same is true of other foods."

(A) develop new kinds of dishes
새로운 종류의 요리들을 개발하다.
(B) re-create the dishes of their homelands
고국의 음식들을 재현하다.
(C) accept and learn traditional American dishes
전통적인 미국 음식들을 수용하고 배우다.
(D) change the ingredients of their own traditional dishes
전통 음식의 재료들을 변화시키다.

수 세기에 걸쳐, 미국으로 오는 이민자 집단은 고국의 음식들을 재현하려고 시도해 왔다. 하지만 필요한 재료는 대개 구할 수 없거나 너무 비싸다. 게다가, 20세기 초반에 영양학자들과 개혁가들은 자주 이민자들의 식품 선택과 음식을 불안해하고 경멸스럽게 바라보았다. 영양학자 Bertha M. Wood는 미국으로 오는 이민자들에 대한 그 당시에 두드러진 믿음과 고정관념 중 많은 부분을 전하는 요리책을 썼다. 하지만 그녀는 대개 빈털터리로 미국에 도착한 다양한 집단의 사람들을 향한 어느 정도의 동정도 표현했다. 예를 들어, 다른 미국인들에 의해 흔히 주어지는, 이민자들은 "여기서 살려면 미국 음식을 먹는 것을 배워야 한다."라는 의견과는 대조적으로, "어떤 사람이 아파서 특별한 음식이 필요할 때는 그에게 새로운 음식을 먹도록 가르칠 때가 아니다. 그것은 넘어진 사람을 때리는 것과 같다. 우리의 우유 수프는 영양가가 있지만, 그들의 것도 그러하다. 그것(그들의 음식)이 어떤 것인지를 알고 그것을 처방하는 게 어떤가? 다른 음식들도 마찬가지다."라고 그녀는 반박했다.

Rudy's Tip however 이하에 필요한 재료들과 가격이 비싸다는 내용을 통해서 미국에서 쉽게 구할 수 없는 재료, 음식 관련 내용이 적절하다는 것을 알 수 있다.

3

정답 (A)

Most people feel lonely sometimes, but it usually only lasts between a few minutes and a few hours. For some people, though, loneliness can last for years. Psychologists are studying this complex phenomenon. The most common type of loneliness is temporary. It usually disappears quickly and does not require any special attention. The second kind, situational loneliness, is a natural result of a particular situation — for example, a divorce, the death of a loved one, or moving to a new place. Although this kind of loneliness can cause physical problems, such as headaches and sleeplessness, it usually does not last for more than a year. Situational loneliness is easy to understand and to predict. The third kind of loneliness is the most severe. Unlike the second type, chronic loneliness usually lasts more than two years and has no specific cause. People who experience habitual loneliness have problems socializing and becoming close to others. Many chronically lonely people think there is little or nothing they can do to improve their condition.

대부분의 사람들이 가끔씩 외로움을 느끼지만 대개 이것은 몇 분에서 몇 시간 동안만 지속된다. 하지만 어떤 사람들에게는 외로움이 수년간 지속될 수 있다. 심리학자들은 이 복잡한 현상을 연구하고 있다. 외로움의 가장 흔한 유형은 일시적 외로움이다. 이것은 대개 금방 사라지고 특별한 주의를 요하지 않는다. 두 번째 유형인 상황적인 외로움은 특별한 상황, 예를 들어, 이혼, 사랑하는 이의 죽음, 새로운 장소로의 이동과 같은 상황에 의한 자연스런 결과이다. 이러한 종류의 외로움이 두통, 불면증과 같은 건강상의 문제를 일으킬 수도 있지만, 그것은 대개 일 년 이상 지속되지 않는다. 상황적인 외로움은 이해하고 예측하기 쉽다. 세 번째 유형의 외로움이 가장 심각하다. 두 번째 유형과 달리 만성적 외로움은 2년 이상 지속되는 것이 일반적이며 특별한 원인도 없다. 습관적으로 외로움을 느끼는 사람들은 사회화하거나 다른 이들과 가까워지는 데 문제가 있다. 만성적으로 외로움을 타는 많은 사람들은 그들의 상황을 개선하기 위해 자기가 할 수 있는 일이 거의 없거나 혹은 전혀 없다고 생각한다.

(A) Chronic loneliness is the most severe.
만성적인 외로움은 가장 심각하다.
(B) Situational loneliness usually lasts for two years.
상황적인 외로움은 보통 2년 정도 지속된다.
(C) Habitually lonely people experience sleepless nights.
습관적으로 외로운 사람들은 불면증을 경험한다.
(D) Temporary loneliness does not have a specific cause.
일시적인 외로움은 특별한 원인이 없다.

Rudy's Tip 세가지 외로움 중에서 만성적인 외로움이 가장 위험하다는 내용이 본문과 일치한다.

4

정답 (B)

Elizabeth Gibson was walking down a street on Manhattan's Upper West Side and spied a piece of art squeezed between two garbage bags.

[C] She was tempted to walk away, but then she stopped to reflect about the art. She had a real debate with herself. It had a cheap frame, but she felt it was so overpowering.

[A] So Gibson took it home, where she hung it on her wall. Years later she discovered that the painting was "Three People," which had been painted by the celebrated 20th-century Mexican artist Rufino Tamayo. The painting had been stolen and later thrown away.

[B] Had Gibson come along twenty minutes later, it would have already been picked up by garbage collectors. Instead, the painting was returned to the original owners and auctioned by Sotheby's for over a million dollars.

Elizabeth Gibson은 Manhattan의 Upper West Side의 한 거리를 걷고 있다가 두 개의 쓰레기봉투 사이에 끼어 있는 그림 한 점을 보았다.

[C] 그녀는 그냥 지나칠까 싶은 마음이 있었지만, 그러나 멈춰 서서 그 그림에 대해 깊이 생각했다. 그녀는 정말 곰곰이 생각했다. 그것이 값싼 액자 속에 들어 있었지만 그녀는 그것의 매우 압도적인 힘을 느꼈다.

[A] 그래서 Gibson은 그것을 집으로 가져가 벽에 걸어 두었다. 몇 년 후 그녀는 그 그림이 그 유명한 20세기의 멕시코 화가 Rufino Tamayo가 그린 '세 사람'이라는 것을 알게 되었다. 그 그림은 도난을 당했고, 그 후에 버려졌던 것이다.

[B] Gibson이 20분 후에 도착했더라면 청소부가 그것을 수거했을 것이다. 대신에 그 그림은 원래의 주인에게 반환되어 백만 달러가 넘는 가격으로 소더비즈(Sotheby's)에 의해 경매에 부쳐졌다.

Rudy's Tip A와 B는 대명사 it이 등장하기에 제시문에 이어질 문장으로 적절하지 않다.

5

정답 (B)

People define themselves to the rest of the world by the things they wear, the objects they use, and the things they do. Clothing, jewelry, makeup, and hairstyles help to define the self. In addition, jobs, houses, cars, and recreational and other activities play a role in creating the persona that the world sees. As people go about defining themselves and the world around them, shopping plays a huge role. The things we wear, the goods we use, and the activities in which we engage are all part of our personalities. All of these involve shopping. From this perspective, shopping becomes much more than an activity we carry out in order to acquire goods and services. In fact, it becomes the most central event in people's efforts to define themselves as human beings. Self-definition is one of the most pivotal functions of shopping.

사람은 자신이 입은 의복, 사용하는 물건, 그리고 하는 행동으로 세상의 다른 사람들에게 자신을 규정한다. 의복, 장신구, 화장, 그리고 머리 모양은 자신을 규정하는 데 도움이 된다. 아울러 직업, 주택, 차, 그리고 여가 활동 및 기타 활동은 세상이 보는 개인의 모습을 형성하는 역할을 한다. 사람이 자신과 주변 세상을 규정하기 시작할 때 쇼핑이 큰 역할을 한다. 우리가 입은 의복, 사용하는 제품, 그리고 참여하는 활동은 모두 우리 개성의 일부다. 이 모든 것은 쇼핑을 수반한다. 이런 관점에서 보면, 쇼핑은 재화와 용역을 얻기 위해 우리가 수행하는 활동을 훨씬 넘어서는 활동이 된다. 사실상 쇼핑은 사람이 자신을 인간으로 규정하려는 노력에서 가장 중심적인 일이 된다. 자아 규정은 쇼핑의 가장 중추적인 기능 중 하나이다.

Rudy's Tip ST 구성으로 첫 문장과 마지막 문장이 동일하다.
define themselves = self-definition
the things they wear, the objects they use, and the things they do = functions of shopping

6   정답 (C)

More and more today, English is used by Korean professionals on business in Brazil, by Polish hotel staff welcoming tourists from around the world, or by Indian workers who have taken up jobs in the Gulf States. When the role of a language is to be a tool for communication between non-native speakers, we cannot rationally call it a 'foreign' language. Who is the foreigner, for example, when a speaker from Chile interacts with a colleague from Kazakhstan, using English? In a situation like this, the concept of 'foreigner' and of 'foreign language' is not applicable. Instead, we have a situation where English is acting as a lingua franca. That is to say, it is acting as the common language for speakers whose mother tongues are different.

오늘날 브라질에 있는 한국인 사업 전문가들, 전 세계에서 오는 관광객들을 맞이하는 폴란드인 호텔 직원들이나, 페르시아만 연안 제국에서 직업을 택한 인도인 근로자들에 의해 영어가 점점 더 많이 사용된다. 한 언어의 역할이 비원어민들 간의 의사소통 도구가 되는 것일 때 우리는 그것을 '외국'어라고 부를 수 없는 것이 합리적이다. 예를 들면, 칠레 출신의 한 화자가 카자흐스탄 출신의 동료와 영어를 사용하여 상호대화를 나눌 때 누가 외국인인가? 이와 같은 상황에서는 '외국인'과 '외국어'의 개념이 적용될 수 없다. 그 대신에, 우리는 영어가 lingua franca(국제 공통어)로 역할을 하는 상황에 처한다. 다시 말해, 그것은 모국어가 다른 화자들을 위한 공통어로 역할을 하고 있다.

	(A)	(B)	
(A)	in addition	By contrast	게다가 - 대조적으로
(B)	however	In conclusion	그러나 - 끝으로
(C)	for example	That is to say	예를 들어 - 다시 말해
(D)	by contrast	As a result	대조적으로 - 그 결과

Rudy's Tip (A) 칠레와 카자흐스탄 출신의 사람들이 이야기한다는 구체적인 예시가 등장하고 있다.
(B) lingua franca = common language 재진술 관계이다.

10분 모의고사 19 해설편

1 정답 (C)

There has never been a period of human history altogether free from war, and seldom one of more than a generation which has not witnessed a major conflict.

인류역사상 전적으로 전쟁에서 자유로운(전쟁이 없었던) 시기는 없었고 중요한 갈등을 목격하지 않으며 한 세대 이상을 넘긴 시기는 없었다.

(A) Most periods in human history have been war-free but some generations have experienced war in a significant way.
인류역사상 대부분의 시기는 전쟁이 없었으나 일부 세대는 중요한 의미를 지니는 전쟁을 경험했다.

(B) War has dominated human history, so that every generation has always been in war-like circumstances.
전쟁이 인류 역사를 지배했기 때문에 모든 세대는 항상 전쟁과 같은 상황에 놓여 있었다.

(C) There has rarely been a time in human history when it was carefree from war and when there was no major conflict for generations.
인류역사상 전쟁의 걱정이 없었던 시기는 없었고 수세대에 걸쳐 중요한 갈등이 없었던 시기는 없었다.

(D) Human history is practically based on war and every other generation has seen at least one major battle.
인류 역사는 실제로 전쟁에 기반을 두고 있고 한 세대 걸러서 적어도 중요한 전쟁을 목격해 왔다.

Rudy's Tip 제시문의 never, seldom을 (C)에서는 rarely로 대신하고 있다.

2 정답 (C)

Plug-in hybrids have the potential to make a huge leap over current hybrids. They were first made available to the public in 2010 and were initially quite expensive. It is hoped, though, that models will be available within a few years that will be cost competitive with regular cars. They get 100 miles per gallon or more, but the advantages go way beyond fuel efficiency. It is not an exaggeration to say that plug-in hybrids could help save us from oil dependence, air pollution, and a deteriorating atmosphere. By doing without 80 to 90 percent of the gasoline used by conventional cars, these vehicles could play a key role in our getting unhooked from fossil fuels.

플러그인 하이브리드 자동차는 현재의 하이브리드 자동차를 넘어 거대한 도약을 이룰 수 있는 잠재력을 지니고 있다. 그것은 2010년에 최초로 대중들에게 이용 가능해졌고 처음에는 꽤 비쌌다. 하지만 일반 자동차에 대해 가격 경쟁력이 있는 모델들이 몇 년 내로 이용가능해질 것으로 기대된다. 그것은 갤런당 100마일 이상의 거리를 가지만, 그 이점은 연료 효율을 훨씬 넘어선다. 플러그인 하이브리드 자동차가 석유 의존, 공기 오염, 그리고 악화되고 있는 대기로부터 우리를 구하는 데 도움을 줄 수도 있다고 말해도 과언이 아니다. 기존의 자동차에 의해 사용되는 휘발유의 80~90%가 없어도 됨으로써, 이 자동차는 우리가 화석 연료에서 벗어나는 데 핵심적인 역할을 할 수도 있다.

(A) How Hybrid Cars Work 하이브리드 자동차가 작동하는 방식
(B) The History of Hybrid Cars 하이브리드 자동차의 역사
(C) Plug-in Hybrids: The Next Wave 플러그인 하이브리드 자동차: 차기의 물결
(D) Benefits of Doing Without Your Car 자동차 없이 지내는 것의 이점

Rudy's Tip ST 구성의 영문으로 첫 문장의 잠재력과 이후의 과거에서 미래로 전환되는 시간표시에 주목하자. 과거에서 미래로의 변화를 통해 하이브리드의 밝은 미래를 강조하는 글이다.

3
정답 (B)

The historian of philosophy, whether primarily interested in philosophy or primarily interested in history, cannot help being both a philosopher and a historian. A historian of painting does not have to be a painter; a historian of medicine does not practise medicine. However, a historian of philosophy cannot help doing philosophy in the very writing of history. The link between philosophy and its history is a far closer one. The historical task itself forces historians of philosophy to paraphrase their subjects' opinions, to offer reasons why past thinkers held the opinions they did, to speculate on the premises left tacit in their arguments, and to evaluate the coherence of the inferences they drew. But the supplying of reasons for philosophical conclusions, the detection of hidden premises in philosophical arguments, and the logical evaluation of philosophical inferences are themselves full-blooded philosophical activities. Consequently, any serious history of philosophy must itself be an exercise in philosophy as well as in history.

철학사학자는 철학에 주된 관심이 있든 역사에 관심이 있든 철학자와 사학자 둘 다 될 수밖에 없다. 회화사학자는 화가이어야 할 필요는 없고, 의학사학자는 의료 활동을 하지 않는다. 그러나 철학사학자는 역사를 기술하는 그 자체에서 철학을 연구하지 않을 수 없다. 철학과 그 역사 사이의 관련성은 훨씬 더 밀접한 관련성이다. 역사 과제 자체가 철학사학자로 하여금 연구 대상의 의견을 다른 말로 바꿔 설명하고, 과거의 사상가들이 그들이 가졌던 의견을 가지게 된 이유를 제시하고, 그들의 주장에 암묵적으로 남겨져 있는 전제에 대해 추측하고, 그들이 끌어낸 추론의 일관성을 평가하게 한다. 하지만 철학적 결론에 대한 이유 제시, 철학적 논쟁에 숨겨진 전제의 발견 그리고 철학적 추론에 대한 논리적 평가는 그 자체로 순수한 철학적 활동이다. 결과적으로, 모든 진지한 철학사는 그 자체가 역사뿐만 아니라 철학에 있어서의 활동임에 틀림없다.

Rudy's Tip (A) 전후 문장은 상반된 내용의 마이너스 구조이다.
(B) 전후 문장 모두 철학적 활동에 대한 글로 재진술, 결론 등에 대한 연결어가 적절하다.

4 정답 (D)

Despite the very real problems in the traditional society and the equally real improvements brought about by development, things look different when one examines the important relationships: to the land, to other people, and to oneself. Viewed from this broader perspective, the differences between the old and the new become obvious and disturbing — almost black-and-white. It becomes clear that the traditional nature-based society, with all its flaws and limitations, was more sustainable, both socially and environmentally. It was the result of a dialogue between human beings and their surroundings, a continuing dialogue that meant that, over two thousand years of trial and error, the culture kept changing. The need for wild and undisturbed nature and the need to design nature and the environment are deeply rooted in humans; both must be valued. The traditional Tibetan world view emphasized change, but change within a framework of compassion and a profound understanding of the interconnectedness of all phenomena.

전통 사회의 매우 현실적인 문제와 개발이 가져온 똑같이 현실적인 개선에도 불구하고, 중요한 관계인 땅과의 관계, 다른 사람과의 관계 그리고 자신과의 관계를 검토할 때에는 상황이 다르게 보인다. 이런 더 광범위한 견지에서 보면, 신구의 차이는 거의 흑백과 같이 분명하고 충격적이다. 결점과 한계에도 불구하고 전통적인 자연 기반 사회가 사회적으로 그리고 환경적으로 더욱 지속 가능했다는 것이 분명해진다. 그것은 인간과 이들의 환경 간의 대화, 2,000년이 넘는 시행착오의 기간에 걸쳐, 문화가 계속 변화해 왔다는 것을 의미하는 지속적인 대화의 결과였다. 야생의 누구도 손대지 않은 자연에 대한 욕구와 자연과 환경을 설계하려는 욕구는 인간에 깊이 뿌리박혀 있고, 둘 다 가치 있게 여겨져야 한다. 전통적인 티베트인의 세계관이 변화를 강조했지만, 그 변화는 연민과 모든 현상 간의 상호 연결성에 대한 깊은 이해의 틀 안에서의 변화였다.

Rudy's Tip 전통 사회가 인간과 환경과의 끊임없는 대화의 산물이기 때문에 사회적으로나 환경적으로 더욱 지속 가능한 사회였다는 것이 글의 주된 내용이므로, 야생 자연의 보전과 자연의 개발이 동시에 필요함을 언급한 (D)가 글 전체의 흐름과 무관하다.

5 정답 (D)

Although plankton live near the surface, they don't live on the surface. The ocean surface itself is generally pretty clear. Looking down at the water, one usually sees mostly water, not a plant covering. Thus, the competition for sunlight that often seems to characterize plant life on land seems not to be as important in the oceans. This is due to dissolved nutrients being present only in dilute form, as well as the action of currents, waves, and wind. On land, plants that shoot up the fastest and tallest get more precious sunlight, solar energy that they use for growth. They then cast shade on neighboring, shorter plants, depriving them of energy and tending to impoverish them. That seems to be why trees are tall and why rainforests grow as high as they do.

플랑크톤은 수면 '가까이에' 살지만, 수면 '위에' 살지는 않는다. 바다 수면 그 자체는 일반적으로 매우 투명하다. 물을 내려다 보면, 우리는 대체로 덮고 있는 식물이 아니라 물을 주로 본다. 그래서 자주 육상 식물 생태의 특징이 되는 것으로 보이는 햇빛을 위한 경쟁이 (육상에서만큼) 바다에서는 중요하지 않은 것 같다. 이것은 해류, 파도, 그리고 바람의 작용뿐만 아니라 용해된 영양분이 희석된 형태로만 존재하기 때문이다. 육상에서 가장 빨리 그리고 (키가) 가장 크게 급속히 자라는 식물들은 소중한 햇빛, 즉 그것들이 성장을 위해 이용하는 태양 에너지를 더 많이 얻는다. <u>그러고 나서 그것들은 근처의 더 작은 식물들에 그늘을 드리워서, 그것들로부터 에너지를 빼앗고 그것들을 허약하게 하는 경향이 있다.</u> 그러한 현상이 나무들이 왜 키가 크고, 우림이 왜 그렇게 높이 자라는지의 이유인 것 같다.

Rudy's Tip 주어진 문장은 They가 plants that shoot up the fastest and tallest를 가리키고, then이 문맥상 '가장 빨리 그리고 (키가) 가장 크게 급속히 자라는 식물들은 소중한 햇빛을 더 많이 얻고 나서'의 의미를 나타내므로, 관련 내용을 언급한 문장 다음인 (D)에 들어가는 것이 가장 적절하다.

6   정답 (B)

Any time you use another writer's words or even a close paraphrase of his or her words, you must give that writer credit. If you don't, you've committed the crime of plagiarism. Simply out, plagiarism is using somebody else's words and claiming or pretending that the words are your own. A simple rule of thumb for avoiding plagiarism is: When in doubt, give the original writer credit. If you're applying common information, you do not have to worry about plagiarism. If you say the Earth is round, nobody will accuse you of plagiarism. On the other hand, if you write a research paper stating that 16.5 percent of all merchant marines get seasick, chances are some poor researcher spent months of his or her life to determine that fact. In this case, <u>the researcher deserves the credit</u>.

다른 저자의 말 혹은 심지어 그 저자의 말을 비슷하게 바꾼 표현을 사용할 때마다, 그 저자의 이름을 언급해야 한다. 그러지 않으면, 표절이라는 범죄를 저지른 것이다. 간단히 말해서, '표절'은 누군가 다른 사람의 말을 사용하면서 그 말이 자기 자신의 것이라고 주장하거나 그런 척하는 것이다. 표절을 피하는, 경험에 의거한 간단한 방법은 의심스러울 때는 원저자를 언급하는 것이다. 흔한 정보를 쓸 때는 표절에 대해 걱정할 필요가 없다. 만약 지구가 둥글다고 말한다면 아무도 표절로 비난하지 않을 것이다. 반면, 모든 상선 선원 중 16.5퍼센트가 뱃멀미를 한다고 언급하는 연구 논문을 쓴다면, 아마 어떤 가련한 연구자가 그 사실을 알아내기 위해 자기 인생의 몇 달을 소비하였을 것이다. 이런 경우는 <u>그 연구자가 공로를 인정받을 자격이 있다</u>.

(A) nobody will claim his or her right 아무도 자신의 권리를 주장하지 않을 것이다
(B) the researcher deserves the credit 그 연구자가 공로를 인정받을 자격이 있다
(C) you don't have to worry about plagiarism 표절에 대해 걱정할 필요가 없다
(D) the readers would accuse the original writer 독자는 원저자를 비난할 것이다

Rudy's Tip 빈칸이 있는 문장에 나오는 In this case라는 표현은 바로 앞의 내용인 '전체 상선의 선원 중 16.5퍼센트가 뱃멀미를 한다고 언급하는 연구 논문을 쓰는' 경우이다. 이러한 구체적인 정보를 알아내기 위해 노력한 연구자에 대한 언급이 없으면 표절이 되는 것이므로, 빈칸에는 (B) '그 연구자가 공로를 인정받을 자격이 있다'가 가장 적절하다.

10분 모의고사 20 | 해설편

1
정답 (D)

Jenny said to a waiter, "What's this fly doing in my soup?"
제니는 웨이터에게 "제 수프에서 이 파리가 무얼 하고 있는 것입니까?"라고 말했다.

(A) Jenny asked a waiter what action the fly was taking in her soup.
  제니는 웨이터에게 그 파리가 그녀의 수프에서 어떤 행동을 하고 있는지 물었다.
(B) Jenny asked a waiter what the fly was doing in my soup.
  제니는 웨이터에게 그 파리가 내 수프에서 무얼 하고 있는지 물었다.
(C) Jenny told a waiter that she didn't know what a fly was doing in my soup.
  제니는 웨이터에게 파리가 내 수프에서 무얼 하고 있는지 모르겠다고 말했다.
(D) Jenny complained to a waiter that there was a fly in her soup.
  제니는 웨이터에게 그녀의 수프에 파리가 있다고 항의했다.

Rudy's Tip 제시문의 숨은 의미를 묻는 내용으로, (D)가 적절한 내용이다.

2
정답 (B)

A toy shop selling teddy bears and a range of soft toys wanted to encourage more families with children to visit their shop. They wanted to communicate fun and excitement and to drive the right people to their door.

[B] They came up with the idea of running a hunt-the-bears competition. They took pictures of all their top bears and gave them all a special name. They arranged to put pictures of the bears up in different places in the town centre.
[A] To enter the competition, families had to complete an entry form that requested contact details. The competition involved correctly matching the named bears with a location. All correct entries were entered into a draw to win the bear of their choice.
[C] Competition entry forms had to be delivered to the shop where entrants were given a special gift voucher. This creative marketing idea generated a lot of fun and attracted a crowd of excited kids who all wanted a bear.

봉제 곰 인형과 다양한 봉제완구를 파는 어떤 장난감 가게가 아이들을 동반한 더 많은 가족들이 자신들의 가게를 방문하기를 권유하고 싶어 했다. 그들은 재미와 흥분을 전하고 적절한 사람들을 자신들의 가게로 이끌어 오고 싶어 했다.

[B] 그들은 곰 사냥 대회를 개최하는 아이디어를 생각해 냈다. 그들은 자신들의 최고 인기 있는 곰 인형 모두의 사진을 찍고 곰 인형 모두에 특별한 이름을 붙였다. 그들은 그 곰 사진들을 마을 중심부의 여러 곳에 붙여 두기로 했다.
[A] 대회에 참가하려면 가족들은 상세한 연락처를 요구하는 응모 신청서를 빠짐없이 작성해야 했다. 대회는 이름 붙여진 곰 인형과 위치를 정확히 일치시키는 것을 필요로 했다. 답을 맞힌 모든 응모권은 그들이 선택한 곰을 얻을 수 있는 추첨에 포함되었다.
[C] 대회 응모 신청서는 참가자들에게 특별한 상품권이 주어지는 그 가게로 전달되어야 했다. 이러한 창의적인 마케팅 아이디어는 많은 재미를 만들어 내었고 모두 곰 인형을 원하는 신이 난 수많은 아이를 끌어모았다.

Rudy's Tip 곰 인형 판매를 위한 행사를 개최했다는 내용으로, 동일어구를 찾아가면서 행사가 진행되는 순서를 파악하는 것이 요점이다.

3
정답 (A)

Over the years I have asked thousands of people to do a simple exercise of stating how they intend to influence others every day. I am always both amazed and inspired by the answers people give. A receptionist in a law firm, for example, told me that her intention was that every person who met her all day long got a "shot of friendliness" so that they felt the world was a friendlier place because they encountered her. The list of intentions is inspiring. Some say they want to bring kindness, others goodness, compassion, energy, courage, or hope. Your position does not limit the way you can influence others. This woman was only a receptionist, but she could influence others in a profound way by holding that intention.

지난 수년 동안 나는 수천 명의 사람들에게 매일 자신들이 어떻게 다른 사람에게 영향을 주려고 하는지를 진술하는 간단한 연습을 해 보라고 요청해 왔다. 나는 항상 사람들이 하는 대답에 깜짝 놀라기도 하고 영감을 받기도 한다. 예를 들어, 어느 법률 회사에 근무하는 한 접수계원은 내게 자신의 의도는 하루 동안 그녀를 만났던 모든 사람이 '다정함이라는 주사'를 맞아 그들이 그녀를 우연히 만났기 때문에 세상이 더욱 다정한 곳이라고 느끼게 하는 것이라고 말했다. 의도의 목록은 고무적이다. 친절함을 가져다주고 싶다고 말하는 사람이 있고, 선량함, 온정, 에너지, 용기 또는 희망을 가져다주고 싶다고 말하는 사람도 있다. 여러분의 지위가 다른 사람들에게 영향을 줄 수 있는 방식을 제한하지는 않는다. 이 여성은 단지 접수계원일 뿐이었지만, 그 의도를 가짐으로써 다른 사람들에게 엄청난 영향을 줄 수 있었다.

(A) Your Intention to Influence People Can Make a Difference
사람들에게 영향을 주려는 여러분의 의도가 차이를 만들 수 있다
(B) Don't Impose Your Thoughts on Others
여러분의 생각을 다른 사람에게 강요하지 말라
(C) Facial Expressions Reveal Hidden Intentions
얼굴 표정이 감춰진 의도를 드러낸다
(D) Good Intentions Don't Always Lead to Good Results
좋은 의도가 늘 좋은 결과로 이어지는 것은 아니다

Rudy's Tip GS 구조 영문으로 첫 문장이 주제문이다. 처음과 마지막 문장의 동일어구에 주목해 보자.

4
정답 (C)

Corporate social responsibility means that a corporation should be held accountable for any of its actions that affect people. It implies that negative business impacts on people and society should be corrected if at all possible. It may require a company to give up some profits if its social impacts are seriously harmful to some of the corporation's investors. However, being socially responsible does not mean that a company must abandon its primary economic mission. This also doesn't suggest that socially responsible firms cannot be as profitable as other less socially responsible firms.

기업의 사회적인 책임이란 어떤 기업이 사람들에게 영향을 미치는 그것의 모든 행동에 대해 책임을 져야 한다는 의미이다. 그것은 사람들과 사회에 대한 부정적인 기업의 영향은 가능한 한 바로잡아야 한다는 것을 의미한다. 그것은 어떤 기업의 사회적인 영향이 그 기업의 일부 투자자들에게 심하게 해로운 것이라면 그 기업에게 이익의 일부를 포기하도록 요구할 수도 있다. 하지만 사회적으로 책임이 있다는 것이 한 회사가 그것의 주요한 경제적 임무를 포기해야 한다는 것을 의미하지는 않는다. 또한 이것은 사회적으로 책임이 있는 회사가 다른 사회적인 책임이 덜한 회사만큼 이익을 낼 수 없다는 것을 암시하는 것도 아니다.

Rudy's Tip give up some profits 이후에 'however ~ not abandon ~' 등장해야 마이너스 구조로 적절하다. 또한 also를 통해서도 그 앞에 위치해야 한다는 것을 알 수 있다.

5
정답 (B)

The Internet and communication technologies play an ever-increasing role in the social lives of young people in developed societies. Adolescents have been quick to immerse themselves in technology with most using the Internet to communicate. Young people treat the mobile phone as an essential necessity of life and often prefer to use text messages to communicate with their friends. Young people also increasingly access social networking websites. As technology and the Internet are a familiar resource for young people, it is logical that they would seek assistance from this source. This has been shown by the increase in websites that provide therapeutic information for young people. A number of 'youth friendly' mental health websites have been developed. The information presented often takes the form of Frequently Asked Questions, fact sheets and suggested links. It would seem therefore logical to provide online counselling for young people.

인터넷과 통신 기술은 선진사회에 있는 젊은이들의 사회생활에서 점점 더 큰 역할을 수행한다. 청소년들은 빠르게 과학기술에 몰두해 왔고 대부분이 소통하기 위해 인터넷을 사용하고 있다. 젊은이들은 휴대전화를 생활에 꼭 필요한 필수품으로 다루고 친구들과 소통하기 위해 문자 메시지를 사용하기를 보통 선호한다. 젊은이들은 소셜 네트워킹 웹 사이트에도 점점 더 많이 접속한다. 과학기술과 인터넷이 젊은이들에게 친숙한 수단이기에, 그들이 이 정보원에서 도움을 구할 것이라는 것은 논리적이다. 이것은 젊은이들을 위한 치료법 정보를 제공하는 웹 사이트의 증가에서 증명되었다. 많은 수의 '젊은이 친화적인' 정신 건강 웹사이트들이 개발되어 왔다. 제공되는 정보는 '자주 묻는 질문', 자료표, 추천 링크의 형태를 자주 띤다. 그러므로 젊은이들에게 온라인 상담을 제공해주는 것은 논리적으로 보일 것이다.

(A) might be the victim of identity theft 신분 도용의 희생자가 될
(B) would seek assistance from this source 이 정보원(인터넷)에서 도움을 구할
(C) might enjoy themselves with online games 온라인 게임을 하면서 즐겁게 시간을 보낼
(D) could be satisfied with relationships in real life 현실 생활에서의 관계에 만족할 수 있을

Rudy's Tip 전후 문장을 중심으로 재진술 구조를 띠고 있다. 앞의 resource와 뒤의 information을 통해서 빈칸에는 정보나 도움을 얻을 수 있다는 표현이 적절하다.

6
정답 (C)

An additional trend in consumer behaviour is what is referred to as 'time deepening' in which the individual is involved in more than one activity at the same time. Many people in the home will combine activities such as watching television while ironing, or reading while listening to music; but there are similar trends in travel business contexts as well. An increasing number of people are seeking holidays during which they can focus on an activity such as painting or wine tasting while still enjoying conventional attributes such as climate, scenery and culture. 'Edutainment,' in which entertainment is combined with educational learning, is also apparent in theme parks, heritage centres and contemporary museums and other facilities that are incorporating educational benefits into their service package, such as Chessington World of Adventures and Techniquest.

소비자 행동의 또 하나의 경향은 개인이 동시에 한 가지가 넘는 활동에 참여하는, '시간심화'라고 불리는 것(현상)이다. 많은 사람들이 집에서 다림질을 하며 TV를 시청하거나 음악을 들으며 책을 읽는 것과 같이 활동들을 결합시키는데, 여행 사업 환경에서도 유사한 경향이 있다. 점점 많은 수의 사람들이 그림 그리기 또는 포도주 시음과 같은 활동에 중점을 둘 수 있으면서도 동시에 여전히 기후, 경관, 문화와 같은 기존의 (여행의) 속성을 즐기는 휴가를 추구하고 있다. 오락과 교육적인 학습이 결합되는 '에듀테인먼트'는 Chessington World of Adventures나 Techniquest와 같이, 교육적 혜택을 서비스 패키지에 통합하고 있는 놀이공원, 문화유산 전시 센터, 현대 박물관과 그 밖의 다른 시설에서 또한 뚜렷하게 나타난다.

(A) Edutainment: An Outdated Travel Option 에듀테인먼트 : 구식 여행 방식
(B) A Complete Guide to World Heritage Sites 세계 문화유산에 대한 완벽한 안내
(C) Contemporary Need for Multi-Purpose Travel 다목적 여행에 대한 현대인의 욕구
(D) Why Multitasking May Make You Less Productive 다중 작업이 생산성을 떨어뜨리는 이유

Rudy's Tip ST 구조로 사람들은 다양한 일을 결합시키는데, 최근에 여행사업에서도 여행과 다른 목적을 결합시키는 추세가 등장한다는 것이 요지이다.

10분 모의고사 21 해설편

1 정답 (C)

Based on their school experiences, many students view writing as limited to utilitarian ends : writing to please a teacher or to pass a composition course.
자신들의 학교 경험에 근거하여, 많은 학생들은 글쓰기를 실리적인 목표로만 제한된 것으로 여기고 있다. 즉, 선생님을 만족시키거나 작문 시험에 통과하기 위한 것.

(A) Students learn at school that writing is a short-cut to obtaining good grades in a composition course or showing what they can do to a teacher.
　학생들은 학교에서 작문은 작문 시험에서 좋은 학점을 얻거나 선생님에게 자신들이 무엇을 할 수 있는가를 보여주는 지름길이라는 것을 배운다.

(B) Through schooling, many students learn to consider writing as a means to please the teacher and to obtain a passing grade in a writing course.
　수업을 통해서 많은 학생들은 작문은 선생님을 기쁘게 할 수 있고 작문 시험에 통과할 수 있는 수단이라고 배운다.

(C) Many students attain the perspective from school that writing is to make their teacher happy or obtain a passing grade in a writing course.
　많은 학생들은 학교로부터 작문은 선생님들을 즐겁게 하거나 작문 시험에 통과 학점을 얻는 것이라는 견해를 얻는다.

(D) The school instills in students the notion that they can pass a composition course by pleasing their teacher.
　학교는 학생들에게 선생님들을 기쁘게 해서 작문 시험에 통과할 수 있다는 생각을 주입시킨다.

Rudy's Tip writing to please a teacher or to pass a composition course
= to make their teacher happy or obtain a passing grade in a writing course

2

정답 (D)

Competitive debate is an activity as consuming and, in its own way, as brutal as football. Students spend their days preparing for tournaments in which they will debate a major issue of public policy. These tournaments require them to argue in support of a resolution in one round and then against it in the next. The practical emphasis in debate is on tying logical knots, sounding persuasive, and even speaking so quickly that an opponent cannot respond to all of one's arguments. The point is not to arrive at a fuller understanding of the question at hand or to form genuine convictions. Debaters develop considerable expertise as a result of their preparations, but this is only a means to victory. As for convictions, a premium is placed on not having any; believing in something could interfere with one's ability to win on both sides of the issue. This arrangement may force participants to see both points of view, but it does so in a way that promotes a kind of cynical relativism: no position is better than any other since any position can be successfully defended.

토론 시합은 미식 축구만큼이나 소모적이고 그 나름의 방식으로 격렬한 활동이다. 학생들은 공공 정책의 주요 사안을 논쟁할 토너먼트 방식의 토론 시합을 준비하면서 여러 날을 보낸다. 이런 토너먼트는 한 라운드에서는 그들이 어떤 결의안을 지지하는 주장을 하도록 요구하고 그 다음 라운드에서는 그것에 반대하는 주장을 하도록 요구한다. 토론 시합에서 실제로 강조하는 것은 논리적 매듭을 묶고 설득력 있게 들리게 하며 심지어 상대방이 자기의 모든 주장에 응답을 못하게 할 만큼 말을 빨리 하는 데 있다. 핵심은 다루고 있는 문제에 대한 보다 더 완전한 이해에 도달하거나 진정한 확신을 형성하는 것이 아니다. 토론 시합 참가자들은 자신들의 준비의 결과로 상당한 전문지식을 발달시키지만 이것은 이기기 위한 수단일 뿐이다. 확신에 관해 말하자면, 어떤 확신도 갖지 않는 것이 중요하게 여겨진다. 뭔가를 믿는다는 것은 사안의 (찬반) 양 측면 모두에서 이길 수 있는 자신의 능력에 방해가 될 수 있기 때문이다. 이런 진행 방식은 참가자들이 두 가지 관점을 모두 보도록 만들 수 있겠지만, 어떤 입장이라도 성공적으로 옹호될 수 있기 때문에 그 어떤 입장이 다른 입장보다 더 나은 게 아닌 것이라는 일종의 냉소적 상대주의를 키우는 방식으로 그렇게 한다.

(A) basic rules for resolving a heated debate 뜨거운 논쟁을 해결하기 위한 기본적인 규칙들
(B) various controversial topics for a debate 토론을 위한 다양한 논란이 있는 주제들
(C) attempts to use debate as a learning tool 학습 도구로서 토론을 활용하려는 노력들
(D) potential problems of competitive debates 토론 시합의 잠재적 문제점

Rudy's Tip ST 구성으로 토론 시합의 특징과 부작용을 설명하는 글이다. 난이도 있는 영문으로 첫 문장과 마지막 문장의 부정적인 뉘앙스에 주목하자.

3
정답 (D)

In an attempt to make packaging less harmful to the environment, one company has created a new green packaging material that looks like plastic but turns into compost once it's thrown away. Some grocery stores are already using the material to package their products, and customers are encouraged to return the packaging to the stores later. From there, it is shipped to a recycling facility and processed into organic soil. One current drawback is that this material is much more expensive than traditional plastics, but its cost should come down soon. Plastic substitutes had also been used in products such as mattresses, rugs, and pillows to help the environment. When it does, experts believe green packaging production will become a major industry in the U.S.

환경에 덜 해로운 포장재를 제작하려는 시도로, 한 회사가 플라스틱처럼 보이지만 버려지고 나면 퇴비로 바뀌는 새로운 친환경 포장 재료를 개발했다. 몇몇 식료품점들은 이미 그들의 제품을 포장하기 위해 그 재료를 사용하고 있으며, 고객들은 나중에 그 포장재를 가게에 돌려주도록 권장된다. 그곳에서 그것은 재활용 시설로 보내져 유기 토양으로 가공된다. 현재의 한 가지 단점은 이 재료가 기존의 플라스틱보다 훨씬 더 비싸다는 것이지만, 가격은 곧 내려갈 것이다. 플라스틱 대체물들은 또한 환경을 돕기 위해 매트리스, 깔개, 그리고 베개와 같은 물품들에 사용 되어왔다. 그렇게 되면(가격이 내려가면), 전문가들은 친환경 포장재 생산이 미국에서 주요 산업이 될 것이라고 믿는다.

Rudy's Tip the material = it = this material 흐름을 파악하자.

4   정답 (D)

In a famous experiment, participants were asked to watch a video of six people passing a pair of basketballs to one another. Their instructions were to count how many times the people wearing white shirts passed the ball. Halfway through the video, a man in a gorilla costume walks through the players. Surprisingly, only half of the participants saw him. The others were so focused on the basketballs that they didn't notice. This experiment suggests that our ability to concentrate on multiple tasks at once is limited. The researchers believe this is because there is only a certain amount of information the brain can handle. Once this amount is reached, it stops noticing other things. This is one of the reasons activities like driving while talking on a cell phone are considered dangerous.

한 유명한 실험에서 참가자들에게 6명의 사람들이 2개의 농구공을 서로에게 패스하는 동영상을 보도록 했다. 그들에게 주어진 지시는 흰색 셔츠를 입은 사람들이 몇 번이나 공을 패스하는지를 세는 것이었다. 동영상의 중간에, 고릴라 복장을 한 남자가 선수들 사이로 걸어간다. 놀랍게도 실험 참가자들 중 절반만이 그를 보았다. 나머지는 농구공에 너무 집중한 나머지 보지 못했다. 이 실험은 동시에 여러 가지 과제에 집중하는 우리의 능력에는 한계가 있다는 것을 시사한다. 연구원들은 이것이 뇌가 오직 특정량의 정보만을 처리할 수 있기 때문이라고 여긴다. 이 특정량에 도달하면, 뇌는 다른 것들을 알아차리는 것을 멈춘다. 이는 휴대전화로 통화하면서 운전하는 것과 같은 행위가 위험하다고 여겨지는 이유들 중 하나이다.

(A) we react differently to the same event
    우리는 동일한 사건에 다르게 반응한다.
(B) we have a hard time paying attention for a long time
    우리는 오랫동안 집중하는데, 어려움을 겪는다.
(C) our limited knowledge can cause us to make mistakes
    우리의 제한된 지식은 실수하게 만들 수도 있다.
(D) our ability to concentrate on multiple tasks at once is limited
    동시에 여러 가지 과제에 집중하는 우리의 능력에는 한계가 있다.

Rudy's Tip suggest를 통해 빈칸에는 실험 내용(결과)에 대한 재진술(요약)이 적절하다는 것을 알 수 있다. 패스 숫자를 세면서 동시에 다른 변수에도 주목하는 것이 어렵다는 내용이기에 동시에 집중하는 능력에 한계가 있다는 내용이 적절하다.

5   정답 (B)

When two people have a conversation, the person who is speaking generally makes various gestures coordinated in timing and in meaning with the words being spoken. It is natural to assume that these gestures serve a communicative function by providing visual cues that make the speaker's message easier for the listener to understand. However, that is not the whole story because speakers also make those gestures in different situations. As you may have noticed, speakers often gesture during telephone conversations, even though these gestures are not visible to the listener. Bavelas, Gerwing, Sutton, and Prevost found that speakers make more gestures while talking to someone face-to-face than over the telephone, which suggests that gestures are often used for communication purposes. Why do speakers make any gestures when on the telephone? Perhaps it has become habitual for them to use gestures while speaking, and they maintain this habit even when it is not useful.

두 사람이 대화할 때, 말하고 있는 사람은 대개 말하고 있는 단어와 관련해서 타이밍과 의미에 맞게 조정된 다양한 몸짓을 한다. 화자의 메시지를 청자가 이해하기 더 쉽게 만드는 시각적인 신호를 제공함으로써 이러한 몸짓이 의사 전달의 기능을 한다고 생각하는 것은 당연하다. 하지만 화자들이 또한 다른 상황에서도 그러한 몸짓을 하기 때문에 그것이 전부는 아니다. 여러분이 알아차렸을지도 모르지만, 화자들은 전화 대화 중 자주 몸짓을 하는데, 이러한 몸짓이 청자에게 보이지 않을지라도 그러하다. Bavelas, Gerwing, Sutton, 그리고 Prevost는 화자들이 어떤 사람과 전화상에서보다 대면한 상태에서 대화하는 동안 더 많은 몸짓을 한다는 것을 발견했는데, 이것은 몸짓이 의사소통의 목적으로 자주 사용된다는 것을 보여 준다. 전화 통화를 할 때 화자들은 왜 몸짓을 하는가? 어쩌면 그들이 말을 하면서 몸짓을 사용하는 것이 습관이 되었고, 그들은 이 습관이 쓸모없을 때조차 그것(이 습관)을 유지하는지도 모른다.

Rudy's Tip 삽입문은 however를 기점으로 다른 상황에서도 제스처를 한다는 내용으로, 대면접촉이 아닌 전화를 할 때도 제스처를 취한다는 문장 앞에 위치하는 것이 적절하다.

6

정답 (B)

Ecosystems are generally very efficient in cycling matter, in that most matter is cycled over and over within the ecosystem itself. For example, the carbon atoms in a plant will be incorporated into a deer.

[B] These, in turn, will be incorporated into the tissue of a wolf that eats the deer. When the wolf dies, decomposers will incorporate the same carbon atoms. All of these changes take place within the ecosystem.

[A] Nevertheless, a small amount of matter will be lost from the ecosystem over time. Leaching from rainfall will carry off carbon from decaying organic matter, leaves, and so on. In undisturbed ecosystems, this output loss is roughly balanced by an equal input gain of similar materials.

[C] For instance, carbon enters the ecosystem via weathering of rocks and is carried out of the ecosystem by rainwater. In undisturbed natural ecosystems, both the input and the output are small relative to the amount of matter locked up and recycled within the biomass of the ecosystem itself.

생태계는 일반적으로 물질을 순환시키는데 매우 효율적인데, 대부분의 물질이 생태계 자체 내에서 반복적으로 순환된다는 점에서 그러하다. 예를 들면, 한 식물의 탄소 원자는 사슴에게 합체될 것이다.

[B] 이것은 결과적으로 그 사슴을 잡아먹는 늑대의 조직에 합체될 것이다. 그 늑대가 죽으면, 분해자가 그 동일한 탄소 원자를 합체할 것이다. 이 모든 변화는 그 생태계 내에서 일어난다.

[A] 그럼에도 불구하고, 시간이 흐르면서 소량의 물질이 그 생태계로부터 유실될 것이다. 강우로 인한 용탈은 부패하는 유기 물질, 나뭇잎 등으로부터 탄소를 빼앗아 갈 것이다. 방해받지 않는 생태계에서 이 유출 손실은 비슷한 물질들에 대한 동량의 유입에 의해 대략적으로 균형이 맞추어진다.

[C] 예를 들면, 탄소는 암석의 풍화를 통하여 생태계로 들어오고 빗물에 의해 생태계 밖으로 옮겨진다. 방해받지 않는 자연의 생태계에서 유입과 유출 둘 다 그 생태계 자체의 생물자원 내에서 가두어져서 재순환되는 물질의 양과 비교하여 작다.

Rudy's Tip 도입부의 사슴을 동일어구로 다음 문장을 선별하고 생태계 내에서란 표현과 생태계를 벗어난다는 내용을 nevertheless가 연결하고 있는 구조이다.

10분 모의고사 22

1
정답 (B)

It is no easier for Americans to just listen during a conversation than it is for Korean students to just relax when speaking with foreigners.
미국인들이 대화 중에 단지 듣기만 하는 것은 한국 학생들이 외국인과 대화할 때 긴장을 푸는 것만큼이나 쉽지 않다.

(A) It is not easier for Americans to keep silent during a conversation than it is for Korean students to get excited when speaking with foreigners.
미국인들이 대화 중에 조용히 있는 것은 한국 학생들이 외국인과 대화할 때 흥분하는 것보다 더 어렵다.

(B) It is as difficult for Americans not to speak during a conversation as it is for Korean students not to be nervous when speaking with foreigners.
미국인들이 대화 중에 말을 하지 않는 것은 한국 학생들이 외국인과 대화할 때 긴장하지 않는 것처럼 어렵다.

(C) It is slightly more difficult for Americans to just listen during a conversation than it is for Korean students to get excited when speaking with foreigners.
미국인들이 대화 중에 그냥 듣는 것은 한국 학생들이 외국인과 대화할 때 흥분하는 것보다 약간 더 어렵다.

(D) It is not so difficult for Korean students not to be nervous when speaking with foreigners as it is for Americans not to talk during a conversation.
미국인들이 대화 중에 말을 하지 않는 것만큼 한국 학생들이 외국인과 대화할 때 긴장하지 않는 것은 어렵지 않다.

Rudy's Tip A no more B than C ~ D 'A가 B 아닌 것은 C가 D 아닌 것과 같다'
A와 B의 관계를 C와 D의 관계과 동일하다고 비교하는 구문으로 'as ~ as'로 변환해서 표현하고 있다.

2
정답 (C)

The hallway smelt of boiled cabbage and old rag mats. At one end of it a colored poster, too large for indoor display, had been tacked to the wall. It depicted simply an enormous face, more than a meter wide : the face of a man of about forty-five, with a heavy black moustache and ruggedly handsome features. Winston made for the stairs. It was no use trying the lift. Even at the best of times it was seldom working, and at present the electric current was cut off during daylight hours. It was part of the economy drive in preparation for Hate Week. The flat was seven flights up, and Winston, who was thirty-nine, and had a varicose ulcer above his right ankle, went slowly, resting several times on the way. On each landing, opposite the lift shaft, the poster with the enormous face gazed from the wall. It was one of those pictures which are so contrived that the eyes follow you about when you move.

복도에는 끓인 양배추와 오래된 넝마 같은 매트의 냄새가 가득했다. 복도의 끝자락에는 실내에 장식하기에는 너무 거대한 포스터가 벽에 걸려있었다. 그 포스터에는 1미터가 넘는 거대한 얼굴이 덩그러니 그려져 있었다. 그 얼굴은 45세쯤 되어 보이는 검은색 턱수염이 덥수룩한 억세지만 잘생긴 생김의 얼굴이었다. 윈스턴은 계단을 향했다. 엘리베이터를 타려고 해도 소용없는 일이었다. 가장 상황이 좋은 때조차도 엘리베이터는 거의 작동하지 않았다. 그리고 지금은 낮시간 동안 전류가 차단되어 있기까지 하다. 그것은 Hate Week(캠페인)를 준비하기 위한 절약 운동의 일환이었다. 그의 아파트는 7층에 있어서 오른쪽 발목에 정맥류 궤양이 있는 39세의 윈스턴은 여러 번 쉬면서 매우 느리게 계단을 올랐다. 각 층마다 엘리베이터 통로의 반대편의 엄청난 크기의 사람얼굴이 그려진 포스터가 벽에 서 그를 응시하였다. 그 그림은 당신이 움직일 때 (포스터 인물의) 눈이 당신을 쫓도록 그려진 그림의 일종이었다.

Rudy's Tip 삽입문 'It'의 선행사를 찾는 문제로, it는 전기가 끊긴 것을 의미한다.

3

정답 (A)

When a person watches a television movie or listens to a compact disc, it is reasonably clear that the prime purpose of the communication is entertainment. Television news shows might be watched to gain information, but the television stations are well aware of the importance of presenting news in an entertaining fashion. Are television news and newspaper reporting really just other forms of entertainment? You might argue that listening to the radio in the morning to check traffic conditions is information gathering. Calling a travel agent to make an airline reservation clearly is an example of using the telephone as an information tool. But talking by telephone for hours with a distant friend is an entertaining way to keep in contact and exchange information of what is happening.

한 사람이 텔레비전 영화를 시청하거나 콤팩트디스크를 들을 때, 그 커뮤니케이션의 주된 목적이 오락이라는 것은 상당히 명확하다. 텔레비전 뉴스쇼는 정보를 얻기 위해 시청될 것이지만, 텔레비전 방송국은 즐거움을 주는 방식으로 뉴스를 제공하는 것의 중요성을 익히 알고 있다. 텔레비전 뉴스와 신문 보도는 정말 다른 형태의 오락인가? 여러분은 교통 상황을 점검하기 위해 아침에 라디오를 청취하는 것은 정보 수집이라고 주장할지도 모른다. 항공편 예약을 하기 위해 여행사 직원에게 전화를 하는 것은 명확히 전화를 정보 도구로 사용하는 사례이다. 하지만 몇 시간 동안 멀리 있는 친구와 전화 통화를 하는 것은 연락을 유지하고 일어나고 있는 일에 대한 정보를 교환하는 즐거운 방식이다.

(A) multi-purpose nature of communication 커뮤니케이션의 다목적인 성격
(B) various ways of gaining new information 새로운 정보를 얻는 다양한 방법
(C) telephone as a primary means of communication 커뮤니케이션의 주요 수단으로서의 전화
(D) role of mass media in providing entertainment 오락 제공에서 대중매체의 역할

Rudy's Tip ST 구성으로 커뮤니케이션의 다양한 목적들을 열거와 예시를 통해 제시하고 있다.

4

정답 (D)

We can see the occasional clash between compassion and morality in the lab. Experiments by the psychologist C. Daniel Batson and his colleagues find that being asked to adopt someone else's perspective makes participants more likely to favor that person over others. For example, they are more prone to move a suffering girl ahead of everyone else on a waiting list for a lifesaving procedure. This is compassionate, but it's not moral, since this sort of decision should be based on objective and fair procedures, not on who causes the most intense emotional reaction. Morality is an end in itself, and without humanity, there would be no morality. Part of being a good person, then, involves overriding one's compassion, not cultivating it.

우리는 실험실에서 때때로 동정심과 윤리가 충돌하는 것을 볼 수 있다. 심리학자 C. Daniel Batson과 그의 동료들은 실험에서 다른 어떤 사람의 관점을 취하라고 요구받은 참여자들이 다른 사람보다 그 특정인에게 더 호의를 보이는 경향이 있다는 것을 발견한다. 예를 들어, 실험 참여자들은 구명 절차를 위한 대기명단에서 고통스러워하는 소녀를 다른 누구보다 먼저 옮기는 경향을 보인다. 이러한 종류의 결정은 누가 가장 강렬한 감정반응(동정심)을 불러일으키는가가 아니라 객관적이고 공정한 절차에 근거해야 하는 것이기 때문에 동정적인 것이지만 윤리적인 것은 아니다. 윤리는 그 자체로 목적이며, 인간애가 없으면 윤리도 없을 것이다. 그래서 좋은 사람이 된다는 것은 부분적으로는 자신의 동정심을 키우기보다는 무시하는 것을 포함한다.

Rudy's Tip GS 구조로 본문의 내용은 첫 문장의 재진술이다. 실험을 통해 동정심과 윤리가 상충하는 경우를 제시하고 있기에, 윤리의 특성을 진술한 문장은 본문의 흐름에 어색하다.

5

정답 (D)

Why did Columbus not immediately realize he was not in Asia? Surely the plants and animals and people he discovered were nothing at all like what Marco Polo had reported from his travels eastward from Europe where he had met the Great Khan and absorbed Asian culture.

[B] The answer can be found in the twofold problem of data and theory. What made Columbus confused was poor-quality data coupled with incorrect theory.

[A] Marco Polo's reports of Asia were imperfect at best, allowing huge amounts of wiggle room for interpreting New World data as Old World facts.

[C] Plus, there was no theory of a New World, so in Columbus's mind when he made first contact with the New World on that fateful day in October 1492, where else could he be but in Asia?

콜럼버스는 왜 자신이 아시아에 있는 것이 아니라는 것을 즉시 깨닫지 못했는가? 분명 그가 발견한 식물, 동물, 사람들은 마르코 폴로가 황제를 만나고 아시아 문화를 받아들였던, 유럽에서 동쪽으로 가는 여행에서 보고한 것과 전혀 같지 않았다.

[B] 그 답은 '자료'와 '이론'이라는 이중적인 문제에서 찾을 수 있다. 콜럼버스를 착각하게 한 것은 잘못된 이론과 결부된 질 낮은 자료였다.
[A] 마르코 폴로의 아시아 보고서는 기껏해야 불완전했고, 그것은 신세계 자료를 구세계 사실로 해석할 수 있는 여지를 아주 많이 남기고 있었다.
[C] 게다가 신세계에 대한 어떤 이론도 없었으니 콜럼버스가 1492년 10월 그 운명적인 날 처음 신세계를 접했을 때 그의 생각에는 그가 아시아 '이외에' 다른 어느 곳에 있을 수 있었겠는가?

Rudy's Tip 도입문의 질문에 이어서 답변이 등장하고, 그런 일이 발생한 이유에 대한 진술이 이어지는 것이 논리적이다.

6
정답 (C)

Philosophical questions do not get "solved," as empirical questions do. The empirical question "How many pages are in this book?" has a single, correct answer; all others are wrong. But a philosophical question like "Is abortion wrong?" has more than one plausible answer. Depending on the positions taken on such debatable issues as "life," "personhood," and "rights," we can find even completely opposing arguments that are reasonable and believable. Similarly, we can make a plausible case for saying that we're free to choose anything we want whenever we want to. It is simply a characteristic of philosophical issues that we fall short of absolute certainty.

철학적인 문제들은 경험적인 문제들처럼 '풀리는' 것이 아니다. 경험적인 문제는 "이 책은 몇 페이지로 되어 있는가?"와 같이 단 하나의 정확한 답을 지니는 것이다. 그 외에 다른 모든 답들은 틀린 것이다. 그러나 철학적인 문제는 "낙태는 나쁜가?"와 같이 그럴듯한 답이 하나 이상 있는 것이다. '생명', '개성' 그리고 '권리'와 같은 다소 논쟁의 여지가 있는 주제가 처해 있는 입장에 의거하면서, 우리는 조리 있고 믿을 만한 심지어 완전히 반대되는 주장도 발견할 수 있다. 마찬가지로, 우리는 우리가 원할 때는 언제든지 원하는 어떤 것이라도 선택할 수 있는 자유가 있다는 것을 말할 그럴 듯한 정당성을 만들 수 있다. 이것은 또한 절대적 확신이 부족한 철학적 이슈들의 특징이기도 하다.

(A) Philosophical questions are mostly equivocal.
철학적 문제들은 대체로 애매하다. (복수의 답이 존재)
(B) Various answers can be drawn from philosophical questions.
다양한 문제들이 철학적 문제들에서 도출될 수 있다.
(C) Questions as to what is right or wrong are not philosophical.
무엇이 맞고 틀린지에 대한 문제들은 철학적이지 않다.
(D) Empirical questions are not ambiguous.
경험적 문제들은 애매하지 않다.

Rudy's Tip 'right'에 대한 문제들은 본문에 따르면 철학적인 문제들에 속한다.

10분 모의고사 23 해설편

1
정답 (A)

A world heritage site may be in danger because a country does not have the technical or scientific expertise to salvage an historic building or protect a particular habitat that is home to endangered species.

세계문화유산이 위기에 처한 이유는 국가에서 역사적인 건물을 복구하거나 멸종 위기에 처한 종이 서식하는 특정 서식지를 보호할 수 있는 기술적이거나 과학적인 전문지식을 갖고 있지 못하기 때문이다.

(A) Because a country lacks things that can protect an endangered species or the skills to look after an old building, a world heritage site is at risk of being destroyed.
   국가에서 멸종 위기에 처한 종을 보호하거나 오래된 건물을 지킬 수 있는 기술을 갖지 못하기 때문에 세계문화유산이 파괴될 위험에 처해 있다.

(B) A country that wants to have a world heritage site must improve its knowledge and skills in order to get one.
   세계문화유산을 보유하고픈 국가는 반드시 세계문화유산을 획득하기 위한 지식과 기술을 향상 시켜야 한다.

(C) World heritage sites around the world are in danger because countries do not want to allot resources that take care of their upkeep.
   전 세계의 세계문화유산은 위험에 처해 있으며 그 이유는 국가가 세계문화유산의 유지 관리를 위한 자원의 할당을 원하지 않기 때문이다.

(D) Habitats that support endangered species need to be protected just as much as old buildings are protected as world heritage sites.
   멸종 위기에 처한 종이 살아갈 수 있게 해 주는 서식지는 세계문화유산으로서 오래된 건물이 보호받는 것과 동등한 정도로 보호받아야 한다.

Rudy's Tip 제시문은 2가지 이유로 세계문화 유산이 위험에 처해 있다는 진술이다.
in danger = at risk
not have the technical or scientific expertise to salvage an historic building or protect a particular habitat
= lacks things that can protect an endangered species or the skills to look after an old building

2

정답 (D)

Children of Native American parents are traditionally socialized through an extensive network of relatives. Along with grandparents, uncles and aunts participate with parents in child care, supervision of children, and assurance of love, and cousins are thus considered as close as siblings. Members of this extended family also teach children their tribal values and beliefs along with traditions and rituals. Reflecting a group-oriented culture, the values of cooperation and sharing are emphasized, while competitive behavior is discouraged. As a result, one-third of all Native Americans who marry outside their ethnic group have adopted either white values completely or a mixture of white and traditional values. Children and adolescents are further encouraged to participate in tribal ceremonies and develop an appreciation for their cultural heritage.

아메리카 원주민 부모에게서 태어난 아이들은 전통적으로 넓은 친족망을 통해 사회화된다. 조부모와 함께, 삼촌들과 숙모들이 부모와 함께 보육, 아이 관리, (아이들에게) 확실한 사랑을 보여 주는 활동에 참여하고, 따라서 사촌들은 형제자매들만큼이나 가깝다고 여겨진다. 이 대가족의 구성원들은 또한 아이들에게 전통과 의례와 함께 자기부족의 가치와 신념을 가르친다. 집단 지향적인 문화를 반영한 협동과 공유의 가치가 강조되는 반면, 경쟁적인 행동은 저지된다. 결과적으로, 모든 아메리카 원주민 중에서 자신의 종족 집단 밖에서 결혼하는 3분의 1은 백인의 가치를 전적으로 받아들이거나 백인의 가치와 전통적 가치가 혼합된 것을 채택하였다. 아이들과 청소년들은 더 나아가 부족의 의식에 참여하여 자신들의 문화적 유산에 대한 이해를 기르도록 장려된다.

Rudy's Tip GS 구조로 첫 문장이 주제문으로 본문은 주제문에 대한 재진술이다. 백인의 가치를 수용한다는 내용은 본문의 흐름에 어울리지 않는다.

3

정답 (A)

An edge that happy people have for building physical resources is how well they deal with unexpected, difficult events. How long can you hold your hand in a bucket of ice water? The average duration before the pain gets to be too much is between sixty and ninety seconds. Rick Snyder, a professor at Kansas and one of the fathers of Positive Psychology, used this test on Good Morning America to demonstrate the effects of positive emotion on coping with difficulty. He first gave a test of positive emotion to the regular cast. By quite a margin, Charles Gibson, host of Good Morning America, outscored everybody. Then, before live cameras, each member of the cast put his or her hand in ice water. Everyone, except Gibson, pulled their hands out before ninety seconds had passed. Gibson, though, just sat there grinning, and still had his hand in the bucket when a commercial break was finally called.

신체적 역량을 기르는 데 있어 행복한 사람들이 가진 하나의 장점은 그들이 예기치 않은, 어려운 사건을 참으로 잘 처리한다는 것이다. 여러분은 얼마 동안 얼음물을 담은 양동이 속에 손을 넣고 있을 수 있는가? 고통을 감당할 수 없게 되기 전까지의 평균 지속 시간은 60초에서 90초 사이이다. 캔자스대학의 교수이며 긍정 심리학의 창시자 중 한 사람인 Rick Snyder는 'Good Morning America'라는 방송 프로에서 이 실험을 이용하여 긍정적 감정이 어려움에 대처하는 것에 미치는 영향을 증명해 보였다. 그는 우선 고정 출연진에게 긍정적 감정 실험을 했다. 'Good Morning America'의 진행자인 Charles Gibson이 상당한 차이로 다른 모든 사람보다 더 많은 득점을 올렸다. 그러고 나서 생방송 카메라 앞에서 각 출연자들이 자신의 손을 얼음물에 넣었다. Gibson을 제외한 모든 이가 90초가 지나기 전에 그들의 손을 뺐다. 하지만 Gibson은 싱긋 웃으며 그저 거기에 가만히 앉아 있었고, 마침내 광고 방송이 나올 때까지 여전히 양동이 속에 손을 넣고 있었다.

(A) coping with difficulty 어려움에 대처하는
(B) cooperating with others 타인들과 협력하는
(C) promoting physical fitness 신체 능력을 향상시키는
(D) coming up with new ideas 새로운 생각을 만들어 내는

Rudy's Tip 빈칸은 첫 문장에 대한 예시로 재진술에 해당한다. 행복한 사람들, 즉 긍정적인 태도가 어려움에 미치는 영향이라는 것이 첫 문장으로 빈칸 또한 동일한 내용이 적절하다.

4

정답 (C)

Today in a highly competitive sporting world where one mistake or one slow reaction can ruin a sporting career, good vision is as important to sporting performance as good physical conditioning and consistent mental concentration.

[B] As physical conditioning has already proved its worth, more and more athletes will find value in visual conditioning. Many studies show that athletes have better visual abilities than the normal population.

[C] They are better at focus flexibility, and reveal greater depth perception or better eye-hand coordination, as well as many other excellent visual skills. Their visual system is fine-tuned to aim, anticipate, and respond more quickly to complete a visual task.

[A] It has also been observed that athletes with excellent vision perform better than other athletes. In fact, today at the elite levels, vision is the one thing that makes a difference between a good athlete and an exceptional one.

오늘날 한 번의 실수나 한 차례의 느린 반응이 스포츠 경력을 망쳐 버릴 수 있는 매우 경쟁이 치열한 스포츠계에서, 좋은 시력은 좋은 신체적 컨디션 유지와 지속적인 정신 집중만큼이나 운동수행 능력에 중요하다.

[B] 신체적 컨디션 유지가 이미 그 가치를 입증했듯이, 점점 더 많은 운동선수들이 시각의 컨디션 유지에서 가치를 발견할 것이다. 많은 연구들이 운동선수가 보통 인구보다 더 좋은 시각 능력을 가지고 있다는 것을 보여 준다.

[C] 그들은 여러 많은 탁월한 시각적 기술 이외에도, 초점 유연성이 더 뛰어나고 더 훌륭한 원근 감각과 더 좋은 눈과 손의 협응력을 보인다. 그들의 시각 체계는 시각적 과업을 완성하기 위해 더 빠르게 겨냥하고, 예측하며, 반응하도록 미세 조정되어 있다.

[A] 뛰어난 시력을 가진 운동선수가 다른 운동선수에 비해 더 좋은 경기력을 보여 준다는 사실 또한 관찰되어 왔다. 사실, 오늘날 최상위 수준에서, 시력은 훌륭한 운동선수와 탁월한 운동선수를 가름하는 한 가지이다.

Rudy's Tip 운동에서 시각능력의 중요성을 강조하는 글로, 동일 표현을 따라서 흐름을 파악하자.

5
정답 (A)

Think of your DNA as an ongoing instruction manual for how to build and maintain your body, which remains in use every moment of every day. The cells and enzymes responsible for helping the body to grow, replenish, and repair, continuously refer to those instructions. The manual itself rarely changes, but how it's read does. Nutrients, microbes, and synthetics that enter our bodies — largely but not exclusively through food — can signal which sets of instructions our cells should follow. It's like putting sticky notes on some pages of the manual, while leaving others unread. So you might carry the genetic predisposition for things like cancer, mental illness, ADHD, or obesity, but it's by no means a sure thing that those portions of your DNA will be expressed. Nutrients flag important areas at certain times; thus many "on" and "off" labels come from food.

DNA를 매일 매 순간에 작동하는 우리의 몸을 어떻게 만들고 유지할 것인가에 대한 진행중인 사용설명서라고 생각해보라. 신체가 성장하고, 보충하고, 그리고 치료하는 것을 돕는데 책임을 지고 있는 세포들과 효소들은 지속적으로 그러한 설명을 참조한다. 설명서 자체는 거의 변하지 않지만, '그것이 읽히는 방식'은 변한다. 주로 음식을 통해 우리의 몸으로 들어오지만 전적으로 그렇지는 않은 영양분, 미생물, 그리고 화학 합성물은 우리의 세포가 어떤 일련의 지시를 따라야 하는지 신호를 보낼 수 있다. 이는 설명서의 일부 페이지에 스티커 메모를 붙이고 다른 것들은 읽지 않은 채로 두는 것과 같다. 그래서 여러분은 암, 정신질환, ADHD(주의력결핍 및 과잉행동장애), 또는 비만과 같은 유전적 소인을 지니고 있을지는 모르지만, DNA의 그 부분이 발현되는 것은 결코 확실한 것이 아니다. 영양분은 특정한 시기에 중요한 영역에 표시를 하는데, 그래서 많은 '켜짐'과 '꺼짐' 꼬리표는 음식에서 나온다.

(A) What Is It That Affects How DNA Operates?
　　DNA가 작동하는 방식에 영향을 미치는 것은 무엇인가
　　(DNA는 무엇에 영향을 받아서 작동하는가)
(B) How to Prevent Genetic Diseases in Advance
　　사전에 유전 질환들을 예방하는 방법
(C) Food: An Important Factor for Repairing DNA
　　음식 : DNA를 치유하는데 중요한 요소
(D) Why Are We Forced to Follow a DNA Manual?
　　우리가 DNA 설명서를 준수해야만 하는 이유

Rudy's Tip ST 구성으로 DNA에 영향을 주는 주요소로 음식을 역할을 설명하는 글이다. 처음과 마지막에 'DNA'가 중복되어 등장한 것에 주목하자.

6

정답 (D)

Recent research has begun to shed light on important functions that do not at first glance seem associated with sleep. When people become sleep-deprived, for example, their ability to utilize the food they are consuming falls by about one-third. The ability to make insulin and to extract energy from the brain's favorite dessert, glucose, begins to fail miserably. At the same time, you find a marked need to have more insulin because the body's stress hormone levels begin to rise in an increasingly deregulated fashion. If you keep up the sleep-depriving behavior, you appear to accelerate parts of the aging process. For example, if healthy 30-year-olds are sleep-deprived for six days, parts of their body chemistry soon turn to that of a 60-year-old. And if they are allowed to recover, it will take them almost a week to get back to their 30-year-old systems.

최근의 연구는 언뜻 보기에 잠과 연관되는 것처럼 보이지 않는 중요한 기능들을 밝혀내기 시작했다. 예를 들어, 사람들이 잠이 부족해지면, 그들이 먹고 있는 음식을 활용하는 그들의 능력은 3분의 1가량 떨어진다. 인슐린을 만들어내고 뇌가 가장 좋아하는 디저트인 포도당에서 에너지를 뽑아내는 능력은 형편없이 나빠지기 시작한다. 동시에, 몸의 스트레스 호르몬 수준이 점점 더 통제가 안 되는 방식으로 상승하기 시작하기 때문에, 인슐린을 더 많이 가지려는 뚜렷한 욕구를 가지게 된다. 잠을 부족하게 하는 행동을 계속하게 되면, 노화 과정의 일부를 촉진하는 것처럼 보인다. 예를 들어, 만약 건강한 30세 사람들이 6일 동안 잠이 부족하게 되면, 그들의 신체 화학 작용 중 일부는 이내 60세 사람의 것이 된다. 그리고 회복하도록 허용되면, 자신들의 30살 체계로 돌아가는 데 거의 일주일이 걸릴 것이다.

Rudy's Tip 삽입문의 'aging process'에 대한 재진술로 30-year-old와 60-year-old가 등장하고 있기에 해당 문장 앞에 위치하는 것이 적절하다.

10분 모의고사 24 해설편

1
정답 (C)

The gradations of the moral faculties in the higher animals and man are so imperceptible that to deny to the first a certain sense of consciousness would certainly be an exaggeration of the difference between animals and man.
고등동물과 인간의 도덕적인 능력은 거의 차이가 나지 않기에 전자에(고등동물) 대해서 일정한 의식의 존재를 부정하는 것은 동물과 인간의 차이를 과장하는 것이다.

(A) The differences between higher animals and man are so vast that it is possible to claim that they are truly different.
고등동물과 인간은 차이가 매우 크기에 그들은 완전히 다르다고 주장할 수 있다.

(B) It would be far-fetched to say that higher animals are not inferior to man because they have the same consciousness.
고등동물이 인간과 같은 의식을 지니고 있기 때문에 인간보다 열등하지 않다고 말하는 것은 설득력이 없다.

(C) Higher animals and man have similar moral faculties, so it would wrong be imply that higher animals do not have consciousness.
고등동물과 인간은 유사한 도덕적 능력이 있기에 고등동물이 의식이 없다고 말하는 것은 잘못된 것이다.

(D) To claim that higher animals are not as conscious as man is to refuse to acknowledge many differences between them.
고등동물이 인간만큼 의식이 없다고 주장하는 것은 이들 사이의 많은 차이점을 인정하지 않는 것이다.

Rudy's Tip exaggeration = wrong
similar moral faculties = imperceptible

2

정답 (D)

In 1859, a man released 24 European wild rabbits into a park in Australia. Less than 70 years later, the population had exploded to more than 10 billion rabbits across the nation. Although this number has since decreased to about 300 million, these rabbits are a danger to the ecosystem of Australia. The primary reason is that rabbits eat the same vegetation as Australia's native animals. Rabbits also reproduce more quickly than these native species, and they tend to eat the roots of plants rather than just the leaves, meaning the plants cannot regrow. With less food available, more than 20 species of Australian mammals have gone extinct, as have a number of native plants. What's worse, a lack of plants and grass causes once green areas to turn into lifeless deserts.

1859년에 한 남자가 24마리의 유럽 야생토끼들을 호주의 한 공원에 풀어놓았다. 그로부터 70년도 채 되지 않아 그 나라 전역에 걸쳐 토끼 개체 수가 백억 마리 이상으로 폭발적으로 증가했다. 비록 이 숫자는 그 후에 3억 마리 정도로 줄었지만 이 토끼들은 호주의 생태계에 위험 요소이다. 그 주된 원인은 토끼들이 호주의 토종 동물들이 먹는 것과 같은 식물을 먹기 때문이다. 또한 토끼들은 이 토착종들보다 더 빨리 번식하며, 식물의 잎사귀만 먹기보다는 뿌리를 먹는 경향이 있는데, 이는 식물이 다시 자라날 수 없다는 것을 의미한다. 구할 수 있는 먹이가 줄어들면서, 20종이 넘는 호주의 포유류들이 멸종되었고, 많은 토종 식물들도 마찬가지였다. 엎친 데 덮친 격으로, 식물과 풀의 부족은 한때 녹음이 우거졌던 지역을 생명이 없는 사막들로 바꾸어 놓았다.

(A) the national animal of Australia 호주를 상징하는 동물
(B) an endangered species in Australia 호주의 멸종 위기종
(C) the most popular animal in Australia 호주에서 가장 인기있는 동물
(D) a danger to the ecosystem of Australia 호주 생태계의 위협

Rudy's Tip 빈칸 이후에 토끼들 때문에 몇몇 호주 토종 생물들이 멸종되었고, 녹음이 우거졌던 지역이 사막화되었다는 내용을 통해 빈칸에는 생태계에 대한 위협이 되었다는 것이 적절하다.

3

정답 (B)

The human body shows various responses to stress. When a person experiences stress, the brain releases stress hormones. The hormones signal blood to move to the heart and other organs. People experiencing stress might suddenly feel hot. Their heart may beat faster and their muscles may tense. Their hands and feet might feel cold. Their senses may become sharper. People might feel like they can smell, see, and taste things more clearly. Once the factor causing stress disappears, the stress hormones quiet down. The body gradually goes back to normal.

인간의 몸은 스트레스에 다양한 반응을 나타낸다. 어떤 사람이 스트레스를 겪으면 뇌는 스트레스 호르몬을 분비한다. 이 호르몬들은 혈액에 신호를 보내 심장과 다른 신체기관으로 움직이도록 한다. 스트레스를 겪는 사람들은 갑자기 더워지는 느낌을 받기도 할 것이다. 그들의 심장이 더 빨리 뛰고 그들의 근육이 긴장을 하기도 할 것이다. 그들의 손과 발이 차갑게 느껴지기도 할 것이다. 그들의 감각이 더욱 예리해 지기도 할 것이다. 사람들은 더욱 분명하게 냄새 맡고 보고 맛볼 수 있을 것 같다고 느끼기도 할 것이다. 일단 스트레스를 일으키는 요인이 사라지면, 스트레스 호르몬은 잦아든다. 신체는 점차 정상적인 상태로 돌아가게 된다.

(A) direct effects of stress on memory 스트레스가 기억에 미치는 직접적인 영향들
(B) physical reactions caused by stress 스트레스를 통해 유발되는 신체적 반응들
(C) key factors causing stress hormones 스트레스 호르몬을 야기시키는 핵심 요소들
(D) ways to overcome stressful situations 스트레스를 주는 상황을 극복하는 방식들

Rudy's Tip GS 구조의 영문으로 첫 문장이 주제문이다. 이후에 첫 문장에 대한 다양한 예시가 제시되고 있다.

4   정답 (D)

Many health education campaigns have attempted to motivate people to change their behavior through fear or guilt. Anti-drinking and driving campaigns at Christmas show the devastating effects on families of road accident victims; smoking prevention posters urge parents not to 'teach your children how to smoke.' Increasingly hard-hitting campaigns are used amongst others to raise awareness of the consequences of heavy drinking, smoking and drug use. Whether such campaigns do succeed in shocking people to change their behavior is the subject of ongoing debate. <u>Although fear can encourage a negative attitude and even an intention to change, such feelings tend to disappear over time and when faced with a real decision-making situation.</u> Being very frightened can also lead people to deny and avoid the message. Protection Motivation theory suggests that fear only works if the threat is perceived as serious and likely to occur if the person does not follow the recommended advice.

많은 건강 교육 캠페인은 두려움이나 죄책감을 통해 사람들이 자신의 행동을 바꾸도록 동기를 부여하려고 시도해 왔다. 크리스마스 때의 음주 운전 방지 캠페인은 도로 교통사고 희생자의 가족에게 가해진 끔찍스러운 영향을 보여 주고, 흡연 방지 포스터는 '자녀들에게 담배 피우는 것을 가르치지' 말 것을 부모들에게 촉구한다. 지나친 음주, 흡연, 약물 사용의 결과에 대한 인식을 높이기 위해 무엇보다도 점점 더 강력한 캠페인이 사용되고 있다. 그러한 캠페인이 정말로 사람들에게 충격을 주어 자신들의 행동을 바꾸도록 하는 데 성공하는지는 여전히 진행 중인 논쟁 주제이다. <u>두려움이 부정적인 태도, 심지어는 바꾸고자 하는 의도까지 촉진시킬 수는 있지만 그러한 감정은 시간이 지나면서, 그리고 진짜 의사결정 상황에 직면할 때 사라지는 경향이 있다.</u> 또한 너무 겁먹는 것은 사람들로 하여금 그 메시지를 거부하고 피하도록 유도할 수도 있다. 보호동기이론은 그 위협이 심각한 것으로 인식되고, 또 그 사람이 권고된 조언을 따르지 않을 경우 그 위협이 일어날 것처럼 보이는 경우에만 두려움이 효과가 있다는 것을 시사한다.

Rudy's Tip 삽입문은 양보절이 있기에 주절에 강조점이 있다. 주절은 두려움이라는 감정은 별 실효성이 없다는 내용으로, 뒤에는 이것에 대한 동일한 재진술이 연결되어야 한다. (D) 뒤에 등장하는 내용이 공포가 별 실효성이 없다는 내용이기에 이 문장 앞이 적절한 위치이다.

5　　　　　　　　　　　　　　　　　　　　　　　　　　정답 (B)

Products will no longer be bought and used, but jointly bought, used or rented. Instead of more possessions, people born after the year 1980 (the so-called Generation Y) prefer to have more time for experiences.

[B] Possessing as many items as possible is no longer regarded as an indication of status for them, but is instead seen as a burden. From this perspective, each possession hinders mobility and restricts one's freedom.

[A] Nonetheless, this generation doesn't want to forego pleasure, so those who cannot afford to buy everything tend to swap products instead. In view of the useful lives of objects, the changed mindset initiated by Generation Y seems to make sense.

[C] For example, a power drill is typically used for only 11 minutes a year, and lawn mowers are used only for a few hours every summer in many parts of the world. In a sharing economy, payment is still made using money — or at least digital money — but mutual trust may well turn out to be a kind of new currency.

상품은 더 이상 구입되어 사용되지 않고 공동으로 구입되어 사용되거나 대여될 것이다. 1980년 이후에 출생한 (소위 Y세대라고 불리는) 사람들은 더 많은 소유물 대신에 경험을 위한 더 많은 시간을 갖기를 선호한다.

[B] 가능한 많은 물품들을 소유하는 것은 그들에게 더 이상 지위의 지표로 간주되지 않고 오히려 부담으로 여겨진다. 이런 관점에서 보면 각각의 소유물은 이동성을 방해하고 개인의 자유를 제한한다.
[A] 그렇더라도 이 세대는 욕구를 포기하고 싶지 않아서 모든 것을 살 형편이 되지 않는 사람들은 대신에 상품들을 물물교환하는 경향이 있다. 물건들의 사용 수명의 관점에서 볼 때 Y세대에 의해서 시작된 변화된 사고방식은 타당해 보인다.
[C] 예를 들면 전기 드릴은 보통 1년에 11분 동안만 사용되고 잔디 깎는 기계는 세계 많은 지역에서 매년 여름마다 몇 시간 동안만 사용된다. 공유경제에서는 지불이 여전히 화폐나 최소한 디지털 화폐를 사용해서 이루어지지만 어쩌면 상호 신뢰가 일종의 새로운 화폐로 나타날 것이다.

Rudy's Tip 새로운 세대의 소유 방식에 대한 글로 동일어구와 연결어를 통해서 글의 순서를 파악하자.

6　　　　　　　　　　　　　　　　　　　　　　　　　　　　　정답 (C)

When photography came along in the nineteenth century, painting was put in crisis. The photograph, it seemed, did the work of imitating nature better than the painter ever could. Some painters made practical use of the invention. There were Impressionist painters who used a photograph in place of the model or landscape they were painting. But by and large, the photograph was a challenge to painting and was one cause of painting's moving away from direct representation and reproduction to the abstract painting of the twentieth century. Therefore, the painters of that century put more focus on expressing nature, people, and cities as they were in reality. Since photographs did such a good job of representing things as they existed in the world, painters were freed to look inward and represent things as they were in their imagination, rendering emotion in the color, volume, line, and spatial configurations native to the painter's art.

사진술이 19세기에 등장했을 때 회화는 위기에 처했다. 사진은 자연을 모방하는 일을 여태까지 화가가 할 수 있었던 것보다 더 잘한 것으로 보였다. 몇몇 화가들은 그 발명품을 실제로 활용했다. 자신들이 그리고 있는 모델이나 풍경 대신에 사진을 사용하는 인상파 화가들이 있었다. 하지만 대체로 사진은 회화에 대한 도전이었고 회화가 직접적인 표현과 복제로부터 멀어져 20세기의 추상화로 이동해 가는 한 가지 원인이었다. 그러므로 그 세기의 화가들은 자연, 사람, 도시를 실제 있는 그대로 표현하는 데 더 중점을 두었다. 사진은 사물을 세상에 존재하는 대로 매우 잘 표현했기 때문에, 화가들은 얽매이지 않고 내면을 보며 자신들의 상상 속에서 존재하는 대로 사물을 표현하게 되어 화가의 그림에 고유한 색, 양감, 선, 공간의 배치로 감정을 표현하였다.

Rudy's Tip 사진과의 차별성을 통해서 추상화로 전개되었다는 흐름에서 그림이 사실적인 표현에 집중했다는 내용은 어색하다.

10분 모의고사 25 해설편

1
정답 (D)

No matter which piece of art or architecture you see, there were personal, political, sociological and religious factors behind its creation.
여러분이 어떤 예술 작품이나 건축물을 보든지 간에, 이들 작품이나 건축물이 창조된 이면에는 개인적이고, 정치적이고, 사회학적이고, 종교적인 요소가 존재한다.

(A) If you have personal, political, sociological or religious feelings inside of you, there is also the ability to create art or architecture.
만일 여러분이 자신의 내면에서 개인적이거나, 정치적이거나, 사회학적이거나, 종교적인 느낌이 존재한다면 중요한 예술이나 건축을 창조할 능력이 존재하는 것이다.

(B) The thought that goes into creating art or architecture can be traced back to the origins of personal, political, sociological or religious ideas.
예술이나 건축을 창조하는데 투입되는 생각은 개인적이거나, 정치적이거나, 사회학적이거나, 종교적인 생각의 기원으로 거슬러 올라간다.

(C) Creating something for personal, political, sociological or religious motivations is just what the art and architecture world needs its aficionados to do.
개인적이거나, 정치적이거나 사회학적이거나 종교적인 동기에서 무언가를 창조하는 것은 예술 및 건축 세계에서 그 분야의 애호가들이 하기를 원하는 것이다.

(D) All art and architecture was made because somebody wanted to create something on personal, political, sociological or religious grounds.
모든 예술 및 건축물은 누군가가 개인적이거나 정치적이거나 사회학적이거나 종교적인 이유로 무언가를 창조하길 원했기 때문에 만들어졌다.

Rudy's Tip personal, political, sociological and religious factors behind its creation
= create something on personal, political, sociological or religious grounds

2

정답 (A)

Many cultures of the world see arguing as a pleasurable sign of intimacy. Americans in Greece often get the feeling that they are witnessing an argument when they are overhearing a friendly conversation that is more heated than such a conversation would be if Americans were having it. Linguist Sarah Tannen showed that in the conversations of working class Eastern European Jewish speakers — both male and female — in Philadelphia, a friendly argument was a means of being on good terms with someone. Linguist Jane Frank analyzed the conversation of a Jewish couple who tended to polarize and take argumentative positions in social situations. But they were not fighting. They were staging a kind of public sparring, where both fighters were on the same side.

(A) a pleasurable sign of intimacy 친근함의 즐거운 표시
(B) an effective tool to educate students 학생들을 교육할 수 있는 유용한 도구
(C) a major cause of couples breaking up 커플들이 헤어지는 중요한 이유
(D) an inevitable process in drawing conclusions 결론을 도출하는 필수적인 과정

세상의 많은 문화들은 논쟁을 친근함의 즐거운 표시로 본다. 그리스에 있는 미국인들은 흔히 논쟁을 보고 있다는 느낌을 받는다. 미국인들이 그런 대화를 할 때 보다 격렬한 친근한 대화를 우연히 듣게 될 때. 언어학자 Sarah Tannen은 필라델피아에 사는 동유럽 출신 노동자 계급 유대인 남녀 모두의 대화에서 친근한 논쟁은 누군가와 친한 관계를 유지하는 수단이라는 것을 보여 주었다. 언어학자 Jane Frank는 사회적 상황에서 양편으로 나뉘어 논쟁적인 입장을 취하는 경향이 있는 유대인 부부의 대화를 분석했다. 그러나 그들은 싸우고 있는 게 아니었다. 그들은 두 선수가 같은 편인, 일종의 공개적인 말다툼을 연출하고 있었다.

Rudy's Tip 첫 문장이 주제문인 GS 구조로 본문에 등장하는 예시들을 통해 빈칸을 추론할 수 있다. 그리스 사람들은 대화를 마치 열띤 논쟁을 하는 것처럼 하며, 동유럽 유대인들은 누군가와 친한 관계를 유지하는 수단으로 친근한 논쟁을 하고, 유대인 부부는 공개적인 말다툼을 하듯 대화를 한다는 예시들의 공통점에 해당하는 표현이 빈칸에 적절하다.

3

정답 (D)

One reason why humans take much longer than other species to produce their species-specific "calls" is that at birth the vocal tract of the human infant is disproportionately short compared to the rest of the articulatory system. The oral cavity is broader, the larynx is higher, and the tongue is more forward. This significantly limits the infant's ability to vocalize. It is only at around six months that the vocal tract will become more adult-like and allow the baby to begin babbling language-like sounds. So in humans, the physical capacity to produce language is not present at birth. Nonhuman infant primates take a shorter time to produce adult-like calls, but never progress beyond the use of a fairly limited vocabulary or surpass the single-call level. Human infants, in contrast, show sophisticated sensitivity to language structure prior to production and quickly surpass their primate cousins at every level once production begins.

인간이 다른 종보다 종 특유의 '소리'를 만드는 데 훨씬 더 오래 걸리는 한 가지 이유는 태어날 때 인간 유아의 성도가 나머지 발성 체계에 비해 불균형적으로 짧기 때문이다. 구강은 더 넓고 후두는 더 높으며 혀는 더 앞으로 나와 있다. 이것은 유아가 발성하는 능력을 상당히 제한한다. 약 6개월쯤 되어야만 성도가 더 어른처럼 되어 아기가 언어 비슷한 소리로 옹알이를 시작하게 해 줄 것이다. 따라서 인간에게 있어, 언어를 만드는 '신체적인' 능력이 태어날 때부터 주어지는 것은 아니다. 인간이 아닌 새끼 영장류는 어른과 같은 소리를 내는 데 더 짧은 시간이 걸리지만, 매우 한정된 어휘의 사용 이상으로 진보하거나 한 가지 소리 수준을 절대 넘어서지 못한다. 이와 대조적으로 인간 유아는 발화 이전에 언어 구조에 대한 수준 높은 민감성을 보이며, 일단 발화가 시작되면 자신의 영장류 사촌들을 모든 수준에서 빠르게 능가한다.

Rudy's Tip 삽입문은 인간이 아닌 영장류가 소리를 내는 데 인간보다 더 짧은 시간이 걸리지만 그 이후의 발전에는 한계가 있다는 내용으로 유아는 일단 말을 하기 시작하면 빠르게 발달한다는 내용과 대조되므로 (D)에 들어가는 것이 가장 적절하다.

4

정답 (D)

Efficiency in solving new problems tends to be assumed as a measure of the individual level of intelligence. The more intelligent a person is considered, the quicker he is in his thinking (with other factors held constant). In intelligence testing, a great (and perhaps excessive) emphasis is placed on the time in which test items are accomplished. Most tests demand completion within a certain time-limit; consequently, a slow-thinking subject is bound to solve fewer problems and will therefore rate low on the intelligence scale, though he may be superior to quick thinkers in accuracy. Admittedly, there are numerous practical situations demanding swift solutions (e.g. in combat, in face of technical breakdown), but the ingenuity of the solution is often a more distinct sign of intelligence, though it need not coincide with speed. Intelligence is the antithesis of instinct and habit — the two stereotyped kinds of behavior. The ability to devise new solutions creatively is the principal domain, and hence also the basic criterion of intelligence.

새로운 문제 해결의 효율성은 개인적인 지능 수준의 척도로 여겨지는 경향이 있다. 어떤 사람이 더 똑똑하다고 여겨질수록, 그 사람은 (다른 요인들이 변함 없이 유지될 경우) 생각을 더 빨리한다. 지능 검사에서는 검사 항목이 완수되는 시간에 중점을 많이 (그리고 아마도 과도하게) 둔다. 대부분의 검사는 특정시간 제한 내에서 완료될 것을 요구하고, 결과적으로 생각이 느린 피험자는 더 적은 문제를 해결할 수 밖에 없고, 따라서 그가 정확성에서는 빨리 생각하는 피험자보다 우수할 수 있지만, 지능 등급에서는 낮은 점수를 받을 것이다. 명백하게, 신속한 해결책을 요구하는 실제적인 상황이 무수하게 있으나 (예를 들어, 전투에서, 기술적 고장에 직면하여), 해결책의 독창성은 속도와 일치할 필요는 없지만, 흔히 지능의 더 뚜렷한 표시이다. 지능은 판에 박힌 두 가지 종류의 행동인 본능과 습관의 정반대 이다. 창의적으로 새로운 해결책을 고안하는 능력은 주요 영역이며, 따라서 지능의 기본적인 기준이기도하다.

Rudy's Tip ST 구성의 영문으로 첫 문장과 마지막 문장을 비교해 보면 지능의 기준이 상이하다. 이처럼 글의 처음과 마지막이 다른 경우에는 대부분 글의 후반부에 중심 내용이 등장한다.

5   정답 (C)

Many governments have instituted regulations concerning the humane treatment of animals on fur farms; however, the regulation and methods of enforcement vary widely across the world. For example, European Union legislation includes guidelines for the humane treatment and slaughter of agricultural animals raised for food as well as clothing, including fur. While these guidelines are enforced by routine monitoring carried out by state-authorized agencies, observers find variable results in many countries. <u>Some people say that with so many attractive and sensible alternatives available, animal fur is simply unnecessary, and even purchasing the tiniest bit of fur trim supports a cruel industry.</u> In China, a major supplier of farmed fur, minimal regulatory oversight exists regarding fur farms. Total bans on fur farming are in effect in the United Kingdom and Austria; in the Netherlands, Croatia, and Switzerland, heavy restrictions or partial bans have been established.

많은 정부들이 모피 동물 사육장에서의 동물들에 인도적인 대우에 관한 규정을 제정했지만, 집행의 규정과 방법은 전 세계적으로 매우 다양하다. 예를 들어, 유럽연합의 법률에는 모피를 포함한 의복뿐만 아니라 식용으로 길러진 농장의 동물들의 인도적 대우와 도축지침을 포함한다. 이 지침들은 국가공인기관이 실시하는 정기적인 감시에 의해 집행되고 있지만, 관찰자들은 많은 국가들에게서 다양한 결과를 발견한다. 일부 사람들은 매력적이고 합리적인 아주 많은 대안을 이용할 수 있기 때문에 동물모피는 정말 불필요하며, 가장 작은 모피장식을 구입하는 것조차 잔인한 산업을 지지하는 것이라고 말한다. 사육장에서 생산된 모피의 주요 공급국 인 중국에는 모피동물사육장과 관련된 최소한의 규제감독만이 존재한다. 영국과 오스트리아에서는 모피동물사육에 대한 전면적인 금지법이 시행 중이며, 네덜란드, 크로아티아와 스위스 에서는 엄격한 제한이나 부분적인 금지조치가 확립되었다.

Rudy's Tip GS 구성의 영문으로 첫 문장이 주제문이다. 모피 사육에 대한 규제와 집행이 국가마다 상이하다는 예시들이 등장하기에, 모피제품에 대한 내용은 글의 흐름상 어색하다.

6　　　　　　　　　　　　　　　　　　　　　　　　　정답 (B)

René Descartes is the French philosopher who wrote the famous line "I think, therefore I am." Fortunately for psychology, this was not his only contribution.

[C] In Descartes' time, many people assumed that human behavior was governed entirely by free will or "reason." Descartes disputed this notion and proposed a dualistic model of human nature.

[B] On the one hand, he claimed, we have a body that functions like a machine and produces automatic, involuntary behaviors in response to external stimulation (such as coughing in response to dust). On the other hand, we have a mind that has free will and produces behaviors that we regard as voluntary (such as choosing what to eat for dinner).

[A] Thus, Descartes' notion of mind-body dualism proposes that some human behaviors are automatic reactions that are driven by external stimulation, while other behaviors are freely chosen and controlled by the mind.

르네 데카르트(René Descartes)는 "나는 생각한다. 고로 나는 존재한다."라는 유명한 말을 쓴 프랑스 철학자이다. 다행히도 심리학에는 이것이 그의 유일한 기여는 아니었다.

[C] 데카르트 시대의 많은 사람들은 인간의 행동은 전적으로 자유 의지, 즉 '이성'에 의해 지배된다고 생각했다. 데카르트는 이 개념을 반박하고 인간 본성의 이원론적인 표본을 제안했다.
[B] 한편으로 우리에게는 기계처럼 작동하고 외부의 자극에 대한 반응으로 자동적이고, 비자발적인 행동(먼지에 대한 반응으로 기침하는 것과 같은)을 하는 신체가 있다고 그는 주장했다. 다른 한편으로, 우리에게는 자유 의지를 가지고 자발적이라고 여겨지는 행동(저녁으로 무엇을 먹어야 하는지를 선택하는 것과 같은)을 하는 마음이 있다.
[A] 그러므로 심신 이원론이라는 데카르트의 개념은 인간의 어떤 행동은 외부의 자극에 의해 만들어지는 자동적인 반응인 반면에, 어떤 행동은 마음에 의해서 자유롭게 선택되고 조절되는 것이라고 제안한다.

Rudy's Tip 각 문항의 첫 단어를 통해서 첫 문항을 선별할 수 있다. C는 G진술로 이것을 설명하는 재진술이 이어지는 것이 논리적이다.

10분 모의고사 26 해설편

1

정답 (A)

Like language itself, a technology predisposed us to favor and value certain perspectives and accomplishments and to subordinate others.

언어처럼, 과학기술은 우리가 특정한 견해와 성과들을 더 선호하거나 중시하게 만드는 반면 다른 것들은 하찮은 것으로 생각하게 한다.

(A) Language and technology are similar in that they both highly consider some views and accomplishments but trivialize others.
  언어와 과학기술은 둘 모두가 어떤 입장과 업적은 높이 평가하지만 다른 것들은 사소하게 여긴다는 점에서 비슷하다.
(B) Both technology and language use the same means to rank certain views and assess results on a relative scale.
  과학기술과 언어는 둘 다 특정한 견해를 분류하고 상대적인 기준에 따라 결과들을 평가하는 동일한 방법을 이용한다.
(C) Compared to language, technology is more discriminatory of certain views and results.
  언어와 비교할 때 과학 기술은 특정한 견해와 결과를 더 차별한다. (경시하다)
(D) Technology judges particular views and accomplishments differently than language does.
  과학 기술은 특정한 견해와 업적을 언어와는 다르게 평가한다.

Rudy's Tip to favor and value = highly consider
to subordinate = trivialize

2

정답 (C)

Most people could be forgiven for thinking that human beings are, generation by generation, growing inexorably taller. After all, that certainly seems to be the case with our waistlines. But measurements of human skeletal remains from across the ages made by Richard Steckel, at Ohio State University, tell a different story. Far from gradual evolution from short to tall, Steckel finds that Northern European men living in the Early Middle Ages (9th to 11th centuries AD) were several centimeters taller than their counterparts at the start of the Industrial Revolution around 1750 — and almost as tall as modern humans today. Steckel believes that the height of a population is an indicator of the overall prosperity of the region. He speculates that the differences may be due to a period of warm climate during the Early Middle Ages, which made food plentiful, followed by the Little Ice Age between the 16th and 19th centuries when it would have been scarce.

인간은 세대가 지날수록 멈추지 않고 키가 더 커지고 있다고 대부분의 사람이 생각하는 것도 무리가 아니다. 결국, 그것은 분명 우리의 허리둘레에 대해서는 사실인 것 같다. 하지만 Ohio 주립대학교의 Richard Steckel에 의해 행해진 여러 시대에 걸친 인간의 유골에 대한 측정은 다른 이야기를 한다. 작은 키에서 큰 키로의 점진적인 진화와는 거리가 멀게, Steckel은 중세 초기(서기 9세기에서 11세기)에 살았던 북유럽 남자들이 1750년경 산업혁명이 시작될 때의 북유럽 남자들보다 키가 몇 센티미터 더 컸고, 거의 오늘날의 현대인만큼 키가 컸다는 것을 발견한다. Steckel은 한 인구집단의 키는 그 지역의 전반적인 번영의 지표라고 믿는다. 그는 그 차이가 아마 식량을 풍부하게 했던 중세 초기의 기후가 따뜻했던 일정 기간이 있었고, 그 이후에 식량이 부족했을 16세기에서 19세기까지의 작은 빙하기가 이어진 것 때문이라고 추측한다.

(A) Height Is Affected by Ethnic Origins
키는 인종 기원에 영향을 받는다.
(B) Taller Humans Are Not Good for the Earth
키큰 인류는 지구에 적합하지 않다.
(C) Prosperous Regions May Have Tall Residents
번영한 지역들은 키 큰 인류들을 가질 것이다. (번영한 지역에는 사람들이 키가 크다)
(D) Positive Effects of Humans' Height Increase throughout the history.
인류 키의 긍정적인 효과들은 역사를 거치면서 증가하고 있다.

Rudy's Tip MT 구성으로 시간이 지나면서 키가 커진다는 기존의 견해를 반박하는 것이 글의 주제이다.

3

정답 (C)

Often people who hold higher positions in a given group overestimate their performance, while people in the lowest levels of the group underestimate theirs. While this may not always be true, it does indicate that often the actual position in the group has much to do with the feeling of personal confidence a person may have. Thus, members who hold higher positions in a group or feel that they have an important part to play in the group will probably have more confidence in their own performance.

종종 한 집단에서 낮은 지위에 있는 사람들은 자신의 업무능력을 과소평가하는 반면에, 높은 지위에 있는 사람들은 자신의 업무능력을 과대평가한다. 항상 그런 것은 아니지만, 이러한 사실은 보통 한 집단에서 실제적 지위가 개인이 가지고 있는 자신감과 많은 관계가 있다는 것을 시사한다. 그래서 높은 지위의 사람들이나 자신이 그룹에서 중요한 역할을 한다고 생각하는 구성원들은 자신의 업무능력에 대해 더 많은 자신감을 가지게 될 것이다.

(A) People who hold high positions have more self-confidence than those who don't.
높은 지위에 있는 사람들은 그렇지 않은 사람들보다 자신감이 더 많다.
(B) If we let people know they are an important part of a group, they will probably become more self-confident.
만약 우리가 사람들이 집단에서 중요한 역할을 하고 있다는 것을 알려준다면, 사람들은 더 자신감을 가질 것이다.
(C) People who hold low positions in a group often overestimate their performance.
집단에서 낮은 지위에 있는 사람들은 자주 자신의 능력을 과대평가한다.
(D) People in positions of power in a group may feel they do better work than they really do.
집단에서 권력을 잡은 사람들은 실제보다 자신들이 일을 더 잘한다고 느낄 수 있다.

Rudy's Tip 첫 문장에 모든 내용이 포괄되어 있다. 또한 ③을 제외한 문항들은 모두 지위와 자신감의 플러스 상관관계를 진술하고 있다.

4

정답 (D)

Making judgments will stop the creative process — that is, stop synthesis. People with strong opinions often have difficulty being creative because they are inclined to short-circuit the creative process by making premature judgments. Langer has identified premature judgments as a cause or characteristic of mindlessness. Hobson has suggested that to dream (which is a kind of creative storytelling), people need to set aside their self-reflection systems. Some researchers have suggested that being introspective or self-focused can interfere with making good decisions. We need to learn to suspend judgment long enough for the creative process to run its course.

(A) take risks 위험을 감수하다
(B) activate debate 토론을 활성화하다
(C) control emotions 감정을 조절하다
(D) suspend judgment 판단을 유보하다

판단하는 것은 창의적인 과정, 즉 통합을 중단시킬 것이다. 강한 의견을 가진 사람들은 흔히 창의적이 되는 것에 어려움을 겪는데, 그것은 그들이 섣부른 판단을 함으로써 창의적인 과정을 단절시키는 경향이 있기 때문이다. Langer는 섣부른 판단을 부주의함의 원인이나 특징으로 간주했다. (일종의 창의적인 이야기) 꿈을 꾸기 위해 사람들은 자기반성을 제쳐 둘 필요가 있다고 Hobson은 말했다. 일부 연구자들은 자기 성찰적이 되거나 자신에게 초점을 맞추는 것은 올바른 판단을 내리는 데 방해가 될 수 있다는 것을 보여 주었다. 창의적인 과정이 자연스럽게 전개되도록 우리는 충분히 오랫동안 판단을 유보하는 것을 배울 필요가 있다.

Rudy's Tip GS 구조로 마지막 문장 또한 첫 문장과 동일한 내용에 대한 재진술이다. 따라서 판단을 유보해야 창의적이 된다는 내용이 적절하다.

5

정답 (C)

The power of physics has been due to the fact that it is a very definite science, which has profoundly altered daily life. But this alteration has been proceeded by operating on the environment, not on man himself. Given a science equally definite, and capable of altering man directly, physics would be put in the shade. This is what psychology may become. <u>Until recent times, psychology was unimportant philosophical verbiage — the academic stuff that I learnt in youth was not worth learning</u>. But now there are two ways of approaching psychology which are obviously important: one that of the physiologists, and the other that of psychoanalysis. As the results in these two directions become more definite and more certain, it is clear that psychology will increasingly dominate man's perspective.

물리학의 힘은 그것이 매우 확실한 과학이라는 사실에 기인하는 것이었고, 그것은 일상의 삶을 엄청나게 바꾸어 놓았다. 그러나 이러한 변화는 인간 그 자체가 아니라, 환경에 영향을 미침으로써 진행되어 왔다. 똑같이 확실하고, 인간을 직접적으로 바꿀 수 있는 과학이 주어진다고 하면 물리학은 빛을 잃을 것이다. 이런 과학은 심리학이 될 수 있는 것이다. 최근까지 심리학은 중요하지 않은 철학적 장광설로, 젊었을 적 내가 배운 바로는 배울 가치가 없던 비실용적인 잡동사니였다. 그러나 이제는 심리학에 접근하는 분명히 중요한 두 가지 방법이 있는데, 하나는 생리학자의 방법이고, 나머지 하나는 정신분석의 방법이다. 이 두 가지 방향에서 나타나는 결과가 더욱 확실해지고 더욱 분명해짐에 따라, 심리학은 점점 더 인간의 관점을 지배할 것이 명백하다.

Rudy's Tip 삽입문의 시제에 유의하자. 과거의 사례가 제시되고, 이어서 현재의 변화가 등장하는 대조의 논리구조이다.

6　　　　　　　　　　　　　　　　　　　　　　　　　정답 (A)

Affirmations are a way of turning negative self-talk, which leads to stress, into positive, life-affirming statements. They are always stated in the present tense — 'I am', 'I have' and 'I choose' — and they reflect what you wish to experience, not what you should or could.

[C] Think back to what you say when you might be getting sick or feeling tired: "I don't feel sick," or "I don't have time to be sick." What do both of these statements have in common?

[B] They are negative and focus on what you do not want to happen. More positive and effective statements are, "I feel energetic and healthy," or "I am relaxed and have plenty of time to do what needs to be done." At first it may feel silly to state over and over the exact opposite of what you are feeling.

[A] But with regular practice, you will notice a change. The inner world of your thoughts and feelings will be in line with the outer world of your experience. Your mind and body will work together to produce a positive result.

긍정은 스트레스를 일으키는 부정적인 자기 대화를 긍정적이고 삶을 긍정하는 진술로 바꾸는 한 가지 방법이다. 그것은, '나는 ~이다', '나는 ~을 갖고 있다', '나는 ~을 선택한다' 등과 같이 항상 현재 시제로 진술되며, 여러분이 '해야 하는' 것이나 '할 수도 있는' 것이 아니라, 경험하기를 바라는 것을 반영한다.

[C] 혹시 여러분이 병에 걸리거나 피곤하게 느낄 수 있을 때에 할 수도 있는 "나는 아프지 않아." 혹은 "나는 아플 겨를이 없어." 등과 같은 말을 돌이켜 생각해 보라. 이 진술은 둘 다 어떤 공통점을 지니고 있는가?

[B] 그것들은 부정문이며 일어나지 않기를 바라는 것에 초점을 맞추고 있다. 더 긍정적이고 효과적인 진술은 "나는 활기차고 건강하다고 느껴." 혹은 "나는 편안하며 해야 할 일을 할 시간이 많이 있어." 등이다. 느끼는 것과 정반대의 말을 반복해서 말하는 것이 처음에는 바보스럽게 느껴질 수 있다.

[A] 하지만 꾸준히 연습하면 변화를 발견할 것이다. 생각과 감정의 내면세계가 경험의 외부 세계와 일치하게 될 것이다. 마음과 몸이 협력하여 긍정적인 결과를 만들어 낼 것이다.

Rudy's Tip　A는 'But', B는 'negative'가 등장하기에 첫 문항으로 적절하지 않다.

10분 모의고사 27 해설편

1
정답 (B)

Put differently, an average American can speak the equivalent of two novels per day, although he reads less than three books per year.
달리 말해 평균적인 미국인은 1년에 책을 세 권도 읽지 않지만, 하루에 두 권의 소설에 해당하는 분량을 말할 수 있다.

(A) There are many people in America who do not read what they should and speak too much.
미국에는 읽어야 할 것들은 읽지 않고 말은 너무 많이 하는 사람이 많다.

(B) Americans, though capable of speaking enormous amounts in a day, tend to read only a fraction of that amount each year.
미국인들은 하루에 엄청난 양을 말하지만, 독서량은 1년에 말하는 전체 양으로 보면 일부에 불과하다.

(C) In American society people are relying too much on the spoken word and not enough on the written.
미국 사회에서 사람들은 말에 너무 의존하지만, 글에는 충분히 의지하지 않고 있다.

(D) There is a great void in the level of written versus spoken English in America, and it must change.
미국에서는 글의 수준과 말의 수준 간에 큰 공백이 존재하며 이는 반드시 바뀌어야 한다.

Rudy's Tip 말하는 양에 비해서 독서량이 전혀 균형이 맞지 않는다는 내용이다.
speak the equivalent of two novels per day = speaking enormous amounts in a day
reads less than three books per year = read only a fraction of that amount each year

2

정답 (B)

Until the nineteenth century, when steamships and transcontinental trains made long distance travel possible for large number of people, only a few adventurers, mainly sailors and traders, traveled out of their own countries. "Abroad" was a truly foreign place about which the vast majority of people knew very little indeed. Early map makers therefore had little fear of being accused of mistakes, even though they were often wildly inaccurate. When they compiled maps, imagination was as important as geographic reality. Nowhere is this more evident than in old maps illustrated with mythical creatures and strange humans.

증기선과 대륙횡단 기차가 많은 이들에게 장거리 여행을 가능하게 했던 19세기가 도래할 때까지, 단지 몇몇 모험가들, 주로 선원들과 무역업자들만이 자기 나라를 떠나 여행을 했었다. '해외'는 대다수 사람이 정말 그곳에 대해 거의 알지 못하는 참으로 낯선 곳이었다. 그래서 초기 지도 제작자들은 그들이 종종 크게 틀렸다 할지라도, 실수로 인해 비난받는 것을 거의 두려워하지 않았다. 그들이 지도를 편찬할 때, 상상은 지리적 실제만큼이나 중요했다. 신화적 동물이나 이상한 인간들로 도해된 옛날 지도에서보다 이런 점이 더 분명한 경우는 없다.

(A) Despite their unusual illustrations, maps made before the nineteenth century were remarkably accurate.
이상한 그림들에도 불구하고, 19세기 이전의 지도들은 매우 정확했다.
(B) Old maps often included pictures of imaginary animals.
오래된 지도들은 가상적인 동물들의 모습들을 담고 있었다.
(C) Until the nineteenth century, map makers could draw imaginative animals.
19세기까지, 지도 제작들은 가상적인 동물들을 그릴 수 있었다.
(D) Early map makers were afraid of traveling abroad.
초기 지도제작자들은 해외 여행하는 것을 두려워했다.

Rudy's Tip 마지막 문장에 대한 paraphrase 진술이 (B)이다.

3

정답 (B)

Although we normally think of floods as destructive events, flood plain ecosystems depend on floods. For example, cottonwood tree seeds only develop after a flood, and waterfowl depend on flood plain wetlands. Many species of fish gradually lose out to stronger competitors during normal flows but have adapted better to floods, so their populations increase as a result of flooding. Thus species diversity is maintained by interchanging periods of flooding and normal flow. Deltas are created and expanded by floods. At normal times, when rivers are confined within their banks, the flowing water transports sediment out to sea and deposits it on the ocean floor. But during floods, river water rises above the stream banks and covers the delta land. When the flood waters slow down, they deposit sediment, thus expanding the delta.

우리는 보통 홍수를 파괴적인 사건으로 생각하지만 범람원의 생태계는 홍수에 의존한다. 예를 들어 미루나무의 씨앗은 홍수가 난후에야 발아하며 물새는 범람원의 습지에 의존한다. 많은 종의 물고기는 평상시처럼 (물이) 흐를 동안에는 더 강한 경쟁자들에게 점차적으로 밀리지만 홍수에는 더 잘 적응해 왔기 때문에 그들의 개체 수는 홍수의 결과로 증가한다. 그리하여 범람과 평상시의 (물의) 흐름이 번갈아 일어남으로써 종의 다양성이 유지된다. 삼각주는 홍수에 의해 만들어지고 확장된다. 강물이 강둑 안에 갇혀 있는 평상시에는 흐르는 물이 퇴적물을 바다로 이동시켜 해저에 침전시킨다. 그러나 홍수 때에는 강물이 강둑 위로 넘쳐 삼각주의 땅을 덮는다. 흘러넘친 물이 속도가 느려지면 퇴적물을 침전시켜 삼각주를 확장하게 된다.

(A) importance of preserving water resources
수자원 보존의 중요성
(B) beneficial impacts of floods on ecosystems
홍수가 생태계에 미치는 긍정적인 영향들
(C) how to prevent floods using simple measures
단순한 조치를 이용하면서 홍수를 예방하는 방법
(D) devastating floods that changed world geography
세계 지형을 변화시킨 파괴적인 홍수들

Rudy's Tip GS 구조로 첫 문장이 주제문이다. 이어서 재진술의 예시들이 연결되어 있다. 첫 문장과 마지막 문장의 동일어구에도 주목하자.

4   정답 (C)

Campaign officials want to encourage their supporters to vote. How can they do that? One obvious method is to emphasize the stakes; another is to decrease the cost and burdens, by making it easier for people to get to the polls. But there is another way. It turns out that if you ask people, the day before the election, whether they intend to vote, you can increase the probability of their voting by as much as 25 percent! Or suppose that the goal is to increase new purchases of a certain product, such as cell phones or automobiles. A study of a nationally representative sample of more than forty thousand people asked a simple question: Do you intend to buy a new car in the next six months? The very question increased purchase rates by 35 percent. Or suppose that an official wants to encourage people to take steps to improve their own health. With respect to health-related behavior, significant changes have been produced by measuring people's intentions.

(A) offering a variety of options 다양한 선택을 제공하는
(B) improving the service quality 서비스 질을 향상시키는
(C) measuring people's intentions 사람들의 의향을 측정하는
(D) giving people equal opportunities 사람들에게 동등한 기회를 제공하는

선거 운동원들은 그들의 지지자들이 투표하도록 독려하고 싶어 한다. 어떻게 그들이 그것을 할 수 있을까? 한 가지 명백한 방법은 이해관계를 강조하는 것이다. 또 다른 방법은 사람들이 투표소에 도달하는 것을 더 쉽게 하여 비용과 부담을 줄이는 것이다. 하지만 또 다른 방법이 있다. 여러분이 선거 전날 사람들에게 투표를 할 의향이 있는지를 물으면, 여러분은 그들의 투표 가능성을 25%만큼이나 증가시킬 수 있는 것으로 드러난다! 혹은 목표가 휴대 전화나 자동차와 같은 특정 상품의 새로운 구매를 증가시키는 것이라고 가정해 보자. 전국을 대표하는 4만 명이 넘는 한 샘플에 대한 연구는 하나의 단순한 질문을 던졌다. "향후 6개월 이내에 새 차를 구입할 의향이 있습니까?" 바로 그 질문이 구매율을 35퍼센트 증가시켰다. 혹은 한 관리가 사람들로 하여금 그들 자신의 건강을 향상시키는 조치를 취하도록 장려하고 싶다고 가정해 보자. 건강 관련 행동에 관하여 사람들의 의향을 측정함으로써 아주 큰 변화가 생겨났다.

Rudy's Tip 사람들에게 의향을 묻는 질문만 해도 투표율이 높아지고 구매율이 증가된다는 것이 중심 내용으로 빈칸 또한 의향을 묻는다는 표현이 적절하다.

5

정답 (B)

Technology influenced and even rearranged the traditional divisions between professions and the workforce. The introduction of automation in manufacturing allowed many manufacturing processes to be done by less skilled workers. Also, the new, more complicated technology associated with automated manufacturing required more know-how. Technical know-how became the domain of an increasingly powerful but small group of people. During the 1960s and 1970s, automation also reached the office, with the same results. For example, when the first computers appeared in management, banking, and administration, they were completely puzzling to the average worker, and the few computer "specialists" gained considerable earning power. Meanwhile, some of the tasks secretaries and bookkeepers normally do could now be handled by word-processing and spreadsheet programs that a manager could use himself or herself.

과학기술은 전문 직종과 노동 인력에서의 전통적인 구분에 영향을 끼쳤고 심지어는 이를 재정리하였다. 제조업에서의 자동화 도입은 많은 제조 공정이 덜 숙련된 노동자에 의해 수행되도록 했다. 더불어 자동화된 제조업과 관련된 새롭고 더 복잡한 기술은 더 많은 노하우를 요구하였다. 기술적 노하우는 점점 더 영향력을 발휘하는 소규모 사람들의 영역이 되었다. 1960년대와 1970년대에 자동화가 사무실에까지 이르렀는데 같은 결과를 보였다. 예를 들어 경영과 은행업무, 행정에서 처음 컴퓨터가 등장하였을 때 평범한 직원들에게 컴퓨터는 완전히 난해한 것이어서 소수의 컴퓨터 '전문가들'이 상당한 수익력을 얻었다. 한편, 비서나 회계장부 담당자가 주로 하는 일의 일부는 이제 관리자가 직접 사용할 수 있는 문서 작성과 스프레드시트 프로그램에 의해 다뤄질 수 있게 되었다.

Rudy's Tip 삽입문의 'the same results'의 선행사를 찾는 것이 요점이다. 소수의 사람들이 주도권을 잡는다는 것을 의미하기에 해당 내용의 뒤에 위치하는 것이 적절하다.

6
정답 (B)

A perceptually subjective view gives the audience a closer awareness of what a character is experiencing. Filmmakers may use this technique if they want the audience to feel a stronger sense of connection with a character.

[B] For example, in Joel and Ethan Coen's gangster drama Miller's Crossing, creative editing makes the audience experience the sudden disorientation of being knocked out and then waking up in a confused state.

[A] The entire screen goes black as the lead character, Tom Reagan, is knocked unconscious, so that the audience is effectively 'blacked out' as well. The rest of the scene is not shown until Tom comes around.

[C] The audience therefore has a degree of perceptual subjectivity in this scene because it sees only what Tom sees and not the events that occur while he is unconscious.

지각적 주관은 관객으로 하여금 등장인물이 경험하고 있는 것을 더 면밀히 인식하게 해준다. 관객이 등장인물과 더 강한 유대감을 느끼기를 영화 제작자들이 원할 경우 이 기법을 사용할 수도 있다.

[B] 예를 들면, Joel과 Ethan Coen의 갱스터 극인 'Miller's Crossing'에서, 창의적 편집을 통해 관객은 정신을 잃었다가 혼란스러운 상태로 깨어나는 돌연한 정신적 혼미 상태를 경험하게 된다.
[A] 주인공 Tom Reagan이 의식을 잃은 상태가 되었을 때, 전체 스크린은 암흑상태가 되고, 따라서 관객 또한 사실상 '암흑 상태'가 된다. Tom이 의식을 차리고 나서야 그 나머지 장면이 보인다.
[C] 그러므로 관객은 이 장면에서 어느 정도의 지각적 주관성을 가지게 되는데 (그것은) 관객이 Tom이 보는 것만 보고 Tom이 의식을 잃은 동안 일어나는 사건은 못 보기 때문이다.

주어진 글에서 영화 제작자들이 관객이 등장인물과 더 강한 유대감을 느끼게 하려고 지각적 주관이라는 영화 기법을 사용하기도 한다는 내용이 소개되어 있다. [B]에서 Joel과 Ethan Coen의 갱스터 극인 'Miller's Crossing'에서 사용된 지각적 주관 기법과 효과에 대해 전반적으로 설명한 다음, 그 기법이 해당 영화에서 구체적으로 어떻게 사용되고 있는지에 대해 설명하고 있는 [A]가 온다. [A]에서 언급한 영화기법 사용으로 인해 얻어지는 지각적 주관성과 그 이유를 기술하고 있는 [C]가 마지막에 오게 된다.

Rudy's Tip A와 C는 첫 문장이 도입문의 내용과 연결되지 않고, B와 A는 동일 표현을 통해서 연결되는 것을 파악할 수 있다.

10분 모의고사 28 해설편

1
정답 (D)

Business investment in Britain is weak by the standards of other rich countries — one reason why its recovery has been so sluggish.
영국의 기업 투자는 다른 부유한 국가의 기준에서 봤을 때 약한데 이는 영국의 회복이 지금까지 부진한 이유이다.

(A) As other rich countries received business investment from far and wide, Britain's slow recovery scared all potential investors off.
다른 부유한 국가들은 사방에서 기업 투자를 얻을 수 있었지만 영국의 느린 회복은 잠재적인 모든 투자자들을 겁줘서 쫓아내고 말았다.

(B) On seeing the lack of business investment in Britain, other rich countries were deterred from helping the recovery.
영국의 기업 투자가 부족하다는 사실을 알게 되자 다른 부유한 국가들은 회복을 돕기를 그만두게 되었다.

(C) Business investment in Britain remains low as a direct result of its slow recovery as other rich countries see furtive investment.
다른 부유한 국가들은 은밀히 이루어지는 투자를 목격하는 와중에 영국의 기업 투자는 느린 경제 성장의 직접적인 결과로 인해 낮다.

(D) As a result of the lack of business investment in Britain compared to other rich countries, its recovery has been lethargic.
다른 부유한 국가와 비교해 영국의 기업 투자가 부족한 결과 영국 경제의 회복은 활발하지 못하다.

Rudy's Tip Business investment in Britain is weak = the lack of business investment
its recovery has been so sluggish = its recovery has been lethargic

2

유전자 연구의 목적이 아닌 것은?

정답 (C)

Genes are part of the center of every living cell. In the form of DNA, this biological genetic material determines the characteristics of every living thing. Medical geneticists are scientists that study DNA and genes for many purposes. First, they study to learn how living things such as viruses and bacteria cause illness. Second, they try to find the gene that cause certain diseases to pass from parents to their children. Third, they try to prevent or repair birth defects. Fourth, they expect to change gene structure to improve health and increase longevity. Fifth, they want to change the biological characteristics of humans in ways that are beneficial to society.

(A) to lengthen human life-span 수명을 연장하는 것
(B) to discover the relationship between virus and diseases 질병과 바이러스의 관계를 발견하는 것
(C) to lower the birthrate of human babies 출산율을 낮추는 것
(D) to cure genetically transmitted diseases 유전 질환들을 치료하는 것

유전자는 모든 살아있는 세포의 핵심적인 부분이다. 이 생물학적 유전 물질은 DNA의 형태로 모든 생물체의 특징을 결정짓는다. 의학 유전학자란 DNA와 유전자를 여러 가지 목적으로 연구하는 과학자이다. 첫째로, 그들은 바이러스와 박테리아 같은 생물체가 어떻게 질병을 일으키는지를 연구한다. 둘째로, 부모에서 자식에게로 전해지는 특정 질병의 원인 유전자를 찾아내려고 한다. 셋째로, 선천성 기형을 치료하고 예방하려고 노력한다. 넷째로, 유전자의 구조를 변형시켜 건강을 증진하고 수명을 늘릴 수 있길 기대한다. 다섯째로, 사회에 유익한 방향으로 인간의 생물학적 특징을 변형시키고 싶어 한다.

Rudy's Tip 유전연구의 목적을 열거식으로 제시하고 있는 구조이다.

3

정답 (C)

For many years, behavioral scientists believed a sharp distinction existed between such instinctive behaviors and acquired behaviors, which they classified as learning. To many, a behavior had to be either instinctive or learned. Ethologists, viewing behavior from an evolutionary perspective, emphasized the importance of instinctive behaviors to survival in nature. Behavioral psychologists, interested in mechanisms of learning under controlled conditions, believed that all complex behaviors are acquired by a nervous system that starts off at birth as a clean slate. To some, instinct seemed nearly irrelevant.

This philosophical conflict between the importance of genes (or "nature") and the significance of environmental factors and learning during development (or "nurture") raged fiercely for many years. We now know that both nature and nurture are important in shaping many complex behaviors. Genetic instructions guide the growth of the neurons and synapses that make behavior possible; however, individual experience can change both the structure and the function of cells and synapses. The behaviors that mature animals display, like many other visible characteristics, depend on both genes and environment. To understand this still-controversial area, we must look closely at both instinctive behaviors and learned responses.

(A) Evolutionary Aspects of Human Behaviors
  인간 행동들의 진화론적 측면들
(B) The Significance of Environmental Factors for Humans
  인간에 대한 환경적 요소들의 중요성
(C) The Making-up of Behaviors: Instinct vs. Learning
  행동의 구성 요소 : 본능(선천) : 학습(후천)
(D) Various Ways of Survival in Nature
  자연에서 생존의 다양한 방식들

오랫동안 행동주의 과학자들은 그러한 본능적인 행동과 그들이 학습으로 분류하고 있는 후천적인 행동 사이에 상당한 차이가 있다고 믿어 왔다. 여러 사람들에게 있어 행동은 본능적이거나 학습된 것, 둘 중의 하나여야만 했다. 진화론적 관점에서 행동을 바라보는 생태학자들은 자연 속에서 생존하는 데 있어 본능적인 행동이 중요하다고 강조했다. 통제된 조건 아래에서의 학습 메커니즘에 관심이 있는 행동심리학자들은 모든 복잡한 행동들은 태어날 때 백지 상태로 시작되는 신경체계에 의해 얻어진다고 믿었다. 몇몇 사람들에게는, 본능은 거의 무관한 것처럼 보였다.

유전자(또는 '본성')의 중요성과 환경적 요인 및 성장하는 동안의 학습(또는 '양육') 사이의 이러한 철학적 대립은 오랜 세월 동안 맹렬하게 고조되었다. 우리는 지금 수많은 복잡한 행동을 형성하는 데 있어서 본성과 교육이 모두 중요하다는 것을 알고 있다. 유전적인 명령은 행동을 가능하게 하는 신경세포와 시냅스의 성장을 지배한다. 그러나, 개개인의 경험은 세포와 시냅스의 구조와 기능을 모두 바꿀 수 있다. 많은 다른 눈에 띄는 특징들과 같이, 성숙한 동물들이 보여주는 행동들은 유전자와 환경 모두에 좌우된다. 여전히 논쟁의 여지가 있는 이와 같은 영역들을 이해하기 위해서, 우리는 본능적인 행동들과 학습된 반응들 모두를 면밀하게 고찰해야 한다.

Rudy's Tip 선천과 후천을 강조하는 대조 구조이다. 첫 문장과 마지막 문장에 동일한 표현이 등장한 것에 주목하자.

4

정답 (A)

Let's move on to the concept of how we create our own reality. A good example is exam tension. This is a very common stress that has a clear cause: mild tension or anxiety is normal during an exam.

[C] It helps students improve their focus and pace. But when this stress is severe, students may experience negative thoughts or beliefs such as 'I will fail' or 'I can't remember anything.'

[B] These thoughts can often create physical symptom such as fear, sleep loss, lack of appetite, nausea, restlessness, frequent urination, headaches, aggression, irritability and dizziness.

[A] This can in turn have a severe impact on performance. For some, the fear will become real and they will indeed fail the exam and thus confirm their negative beliefs. In other words, fear can create precisely what we don't want.

어떻게 우리가 자신의 현실을 만드는가에 대한 개념으로 옮겨가 보자. 좋은 예는 시험과 관련된 긴장감이다. 이것은 명확한 원인을 가진 매우 흔한 스트레스인데, 약간의 긴장감이나 불안감은 시험 중에 나타나는 정상적인 반응이다.

[C] 그것은 학생들이 자신들의 집중력과 속도를 향상하는 데 도움을 준다. 하지만 이 스트레스가 심해지면, 학생들은 '나는 실패할 거야.' 또는 '나는 어떤 것도 기억할 수가 없어.'와 같은 부정적인 사고나 믿음을 겪게 될 수도 있다.

[B] 이러한 사고는 흔히 두려움, 수면 손실, 식욕 부진, 메스꺼움, 안절부절못함, 빈뇨, 두통, 공격성, 신경과민, 어지러움과 같은 신체적 증상을 유발할 수 있다.

[A] 이것은 결과적으로 실행(현실)에 심각한 영향을 끼칠 수 있다. 어떤 사람들에게, 그 두려움은 현실적인 것이 될 것이고 그들은 실제로 시험에 실패하여 자신의 부정적인 믿음을 확인하게 될 것이다. 다시 말하면, 두려움이 바로 우리가 원하지 않는 것을 만들어 낼 수 있는 것이다.

Rudy's Tip 선행사와 대명사, 동일어구를 찾아보자.

5   정답 (C)

The United States was founded on a spirit of dominion over nature. "My family, I believe, have cut down more trees in America than any other name!" boasted John Adams. Benjamin Lincoln, a Revolutionary War general, spoke for most Americans of his day when he observed in 1792, "Civilization directs us to remove as fast as possible that natural growth from the lands." The Adams-Lincoln mode of thought did make possible America's rapid expansion to the Pacific, the Chicago school of architecture, and Henry Ford's assembly line. Our growing environmental awareness casts a colder light on these accomplishments, however. Since 1950 more than 25 percent of the remaining forests on the planet have been cut down. Recognizing that trees are the lungs of the planet, few people still think that this represents progress.

미국은 자연에 대한 지배라는 정신을 바탕으로 세워졌다. "미국에서 내 가족이 다른 어떤 가문보다 더 많은 나무를 잘랐다고 나는 믿는다!"라고 John Adams는 자랑했다. 독립 전쟁 당시 장군이었던 Benjamin Lincoln이 1792년에 "문명은 우리에게 대지에서 저 성장물(나무)을 가능한 한 빠르게 제거할 것을 명한다."라고 말했을 때 그는 당시의 대부분의 미국인을 대변한 것이었다. Adams와 Lincoln의 사고방식은 태평양을 향한 미국의 급속한 팽창, 시카고 건축학파 그리고 Henry Ford의 (대량 생산을 위한) 조립 라인을 정말로 가능하게 했다. 하지만 환경에 대한 우리의 증대되는 인식이 이러한 성과물에 대해 더 냉정한 시선을 던지고 있다. 1950년 이래로 지구에 남아있는 숲의 25퍼센트가 넘는 부분이 잘려나갔다. 나무가 지구의 허파라는 사실을 인식하고 있기에, 이것이 발전을 의미한다고 여전히 생각하는 사람은 거의 없다.

Rudy's Tip 'these accomplishments'의 선행사를 찾는 문제로 치환할 수 있다. 미국의 빠른 발전과 대량 생산등을 의미하기에 이 문장 뒤에 위치하는 것이 적절하다.

6

정답 (B)

Mark Twain observed, "We are all ignorant, but about different things." One mistake technical professionals make when writing for non-technical readers is assuming their readers are as knowledgeable as they are about the subject. This is a fatal assumption that will only result in confusion and frustration for your reader. Also, a great deal of your time will be spent generating additional messages to the reader trying to explain what should have been clear the first time. Just because it's clear to you does not make it clear to your reader. If you are an engineer or accountant writing to others in your field, then perhaps there will be less need to explain all aspects of your message. If you're writing to the senior vice president of marketing, who is not familiar with software applications, then you will need to "walk" that reader through your message. Remember that when it comes to technical knowledge, writers and readers are hardly equal.

(A) good readers can be good writers 좋은 독자가 좋은 작가가 될 수 있다
(B) writers and readers are hardly equal 작가와 독자는 거의(전혀) 동등하지 않다
(C) readers don't necessarily trust writers 독자들이 반드시 작가들을 신뢰하는 것은 아니다
(D) writers and readers have the same purpose 작가와 독자는 같은 목적을 가지고 있다

"우리는 모두 무지하다. 다만 서로 다른 것들에 대해서."라고 Mark Twain은 말했다. 비전문적인 독자에게 글을 쓸 때 전문가가 저지르는 한 가지 실수는 그들의 독자들이 그 주제에 대해 그들 만큼이나 지식이 있다고 추정하는 것이다. 이것은 여러분의 독자에게 혼란과 좌절을 가져다 줄 뿐인 아주 잘못된 추정이다. 또한, 처음에 분명했어야 할 것을 설명하려 애쓰면서 추가적인 메시지를 독자에게 만들어내는 데 여러분의 많은 시간이 소모될 것이다. 단지 그것이 여러분에게 분명하다는 것이 여러분의 독자에게 그것이 분명하게 되는 것이 아니기 때문이다. 여러분이 자신의 분야에 있는 다른 사람에게 글을 쓰는 엔지니어나 회계사라면, 그때는 아마도 여러분의 메시지의 모든 측면을 설명할 필요는 덜 할 것이다. 여러분이 마케팅 부서의 상무에게 글을 쓰는데 그 사람이 소프트웨어 응용 프로그램에 익숙하지 않다면, 여러분은 그 독자에게 여러분의 메시지를 '차근차근 보여줄' 필요가 있을 것이다. 전문적인 지식에 관한 한, 필자와 독자는 거의 동등하지 않다는 것을 기억하라.

Rudy's Tip 전문적인 지식에 관한 글을 쓸 때, 독자가 비전문가인 경우 전문가인 필자만큼의 지식이 없다는 사실을 명심하고 쉽고 자세하게 설명하라는 내용으로 빈칸은 본문의 내용을 요약하는 진술이 적절하다.

10분 모의고사 29 해설편

1
정답 (D)

Commonly found in architecture and design, the art nouveau style can be seen in many of the world's cities and perhaps most famously in the Parisian Metro stations.
건축물과 디자인에서 흔히 발견되는 아르누보 양식은 전 세계의 수많은 도시에서 볼 수 있으며 가장 유명한 곳은 파리 지하철역일 것이다.

(A) The architecture and design of many of the world's cities is a direct imitation of the art nouveau style intended to be unique to Paris' Metro stations.
전 세계의 수많은 도시의 건축물 및 디자인은 파리의 지하철역에만 독특하게 사용되고 있는 아르누보 양식을 직접적으로 모방한 것이다.

(B) The Metro stations in Paris were created in the art nouveau style that had already become popular in the architecture and design of cities around the world.
파리의 지하철역은 전 세계 도시 건축물 및 디자인에서 이미 널리 쓰인 아르누보 양식으로 만들어졌다.

(C) As the world's cities begin to understand the effect the art nouveau style can have on architecture and design, the Parisian Metro stations become more popular.
전 세계의 도시 건축물과 디자인에 아르누보 양식이 미치는 영향력을 이해하기 시작하면서 파리의 지하철역이 더욱 유명해졌다.

(D) All over the world's cities, especially the Metro stations in Paris, the art nouveau style can be seen in architecture and design.
전 세계의 도시에서, 특히 파리의 지하철역에서 아르누보 양식을 건축물과 디자인에서 찾을 수 있다.

Rudy's Tip most famously in the Parisian Metro = especially the Metro stations in Paris

2

정답 (B)

Cialdini is an expert in the field of influence. The book is a comprehensive study on the psychology of influence. It is an indispensible tool for professionals involved in sales and marketing and negotiations, but it has practical applications for everyday social interactions as well. Cialdini explains techniques, a.k.a. weapons of influence, that can be used to gain compliance from others. These techniques are drawn from real-life situations. While he constantly cites academic sources and laboratory experiments, the book remains accessible to the casual, non-academic reader. Illustrations, cartoons, and "reader's reports" are sprinkled throughout, which helps the book stay firmly grounded in practicality. The study questions at the end of the chapter help to pull each chapter's ideas together. To critics of the book many of the ideas presented are seen as common sense, but I really think that everyone can benefit from reading this book.

(A) Cialdini is the author of the new book.
   치알디니는 새 책의 저자이다.
(B) Cialdini regard the book as too academic.
   치알디니는 그 책을 너무 학문(학술)적 이라고 생각한다.
(C) Some practical techniques are introduced in the book.
   몇몇 실용적인 기술들이 책에 소개되어 있다.
(D) The book is written for readers of general backgrounds.
   그 책은 일반적인 지식을 가지고 있는 독자들을 위해서 집필되었다.

치알디니(Cialdini)는 설득 분야의 전문가이다. 그 책은 설득의 심리학에 대한 포괄적인 연구서이다. 그것은 영업, 마케팅, 협상 관련 전문가들에게는 필수불가결한 서적이다. 그러나 그것은 또한 일상적인 사회적 상호작용에 있어서 실제로 응용이 되기도 한다. 치알디니는 설득의 무기라고도 알려진 기술들을 설명하는데 이것은 다른 사람들로부터 동의를 얻기 위해 사용된다. 이러한 기술들은 실제 상황들로부터 나온다. 그는 계속 학문적인 자료들과 실험실에서의 연구들을 언급하지만, 그 책은 학식이 별로 없거나 비전문적인 독자들도 쉽게 접근할 수 있다. 실례, 만화 그리고 '독자 보고서'들이 전체에 산재해 있다. 이것들은 이 책이 확실히 실용성에 근거한 것이 되게끔 한다. 각 장의 마지막에는 공부해야 할 질문들이 있는데 이것은 각 장의 개념들을 총괄적으로 이해하는 데 도움이 된다. 비평가들에게 있어 이 책에 제시된 많은 개념들은 상식으로 여겨지겠지만, 나는 정말로 모든 사람들이 이 책을 읽음으로써 도움을 받을 수 있다고 생각한다.

Rudy's Tip 설득 분야의 실용서적이기 때문에 학문적이라는 표현은 적절하지 않다.

3

정답 (A)

Sugar's effects are ironic; that is, they have the opposite effect from the one you intended. You wanted to feel less hungry and nasty, and you ended up feeling more hungry and nasty. TV has a similar effect, but on happiness instead of hungriness. You watch TV because you want to be entertained, relaxed, involved — you want to feel happy. Unfortunately, although TV can be relaxing, it is only occasionally entertaining and very rarely involving. So, you end up bored, which makes you think you should watch more TV, and you can guess the consequences. Everyone needs a little time to watch TV or just do nothing, just like everyone needs a little sugar now and then. A problem arises when you assume that <u>if a little is good, then more must be better</u>. I guarantee that prolonged periods of sitting in front of the TV and eating sugary snacks will not make you happy in the long run.

(A) if a little is good, then more must be better
조금이 좋다면, 더 많은 양은 틀림없이 더 좋을 것이다.
(B) happiness can be achieved in a few easy ways
행복은 몇 가지 쉬운 방식들을 통해 얻을 수 있다.
(C) when sugar is consumed, your body energy increases
설탕을 소비할 때, 신체 에너지가 증가한다.
(D) there is an interaction between happiness and health
행복과 건강 사이에는 연관성이 존재한다.

설탕의 효과는 모순적이다. 즉, 여러분이 의도했던 것과 반대의 효과를 가진다. 여러분은 배고픔을 덜고 불쾌한 기분을 달래고 싶었지만, 결국 더 배고프고 더 불쾌하게 되고 말았다. TV도 유사한 효과가 있지만, 배고픔에 대해서가 아닌 행복에 대해서다. 여러분은 재미를 느끼고, 편안함을 느끼며, 열중하고 싶어서, 즉 행복감을 느끼고 싶어서 TV를 본다. 유감스럽게도, TV가 편안함을 줄 수 있긴 하지만 가끔만 재미를 주고 거의 몰두하게 하지 못한다. 그래서 여러분은 결국 따분해지는데, 이것은 TV를 더 많이 봐야겠다는 생각이 들게 하고, 그 결과는 여러분이 추측할 수 있다. 누구나 때때로 약간의 설탕이 필요한 것과 같이, 누구나 TV를 보거나 그저 아무 일도 하지 않는 약간의 시간이 필요하긴 하다. 문제는 여러분이 <u>조금이 좋다면 그보다 많은 양은 틀림없이 더 좋을 것이라고</u> 생각할 때 발생한다. 단언하건대 장시간 동안 TV 앞에 앉아 있는 것과 설탕이 많이 들어간 간식을 먹는 것은 결국에는 여러분을 행복하게 하지 않을 것이다.

Rudy's Tip 약간의 설탕과 TV 시청이 행복감과 즐거움을 준다고 해서 그것을 즐기는 시간을 증가시켰을 때 더 많은 행복감과 즐거움이 있는 것은 아니라는 것이 이 글의 중심 내용이다. 빈칸 뒤 문장은 빈칸에 대한 재진술이기에 양과 만족감은 비례하지 않는다는 내용이 적절하다.

4   정답 (A)

Most modern nations contain a lot of cultural diversity within their boundaries. This is especially true for nations with a history of colonialism. For example, the internationally recognized national borders of most African and South Asian countries are a product of their history as colonies, not of their indigenous cultural or ethnic identities. That is, more often than not, colonizing nations created boundaries between "their" colonies to further their own interests rather than to reflect cultural distinctions and ethnic divisions. Thus, modern India has dozens of languages and cultural identities, as do most sub-Saharan African nations like Kenya and Tanzania. The government of the People's Republic of China recognizes 56 minority peoples, some of whom theoretically have traditional homelands labeled autonomous regions on maps.

대부분의 현대 국가들은 국경 안에 많은 문화적 다양성을 포함한다. 이것은 식민주의의 역사를 가진 국가들에게 특히 해당된다. 예를 들어, 대부분의 아프리카와 남아시아 국가들의 국제적으로 인정된 국경은 토착의 문화적 또는 민족적 정체성이 아니라 식민지로서의 그들의 역사의 산물이다. 즉, 대개 식민지를 만드는 나라들은 문화적 차이와 민족적인 분할을 반영하기보다는 자신들의 이익을 증진시키기 위해 '그들 소유의' 식민지들 사이에 경계를 만들었다. 이렇게 하여, 현대 인도는 케냐와 탄자니아 같은 사하라 이남의 대부분의 아프리카 국가들이 그런 것처럼 수십 개의 언어와 문화적 정체성을 갖고 있다. 중화 인민 공화국 정부는 56개의 소수 민족을 인정하고 있는데, 그들 중 일부는 이론적으로는 지도에 자치구라고 이름 붙여진 전통적인 모국을 갖고 있다.

Rudy's Tip
(A) 앞에서 식민주의의 역사를 가진 나라 안에 많은 문화적 다양성이 있다고 말하고 뒤에서 이러한 나라들의 예를 들고 있으므로, For example이 들어가야 한다.
(B) 앞에서 식민지를 만드는 나라들이 문화나 민족을 반하여 경계를 만들지 않았다는 말이 나오고, 뒤에서 그것에 대한 결과로 한 나라 안에 많은 언어나 문화적 정체성이 존재하게 되었다고 했으므로, Thus가 들어가야 한다.

5   정답 (B)

To produce the distinctive sounds of laughter, we make use of a number of muscles that control our breathing and vocal apparatus. The normal human breathing cycle consists of inspiration, inspiration pause, expiration, and expiration pause.

[B] Regardless of where the person happens to be in this cycle, laughter typically begins with an initial forced exhalation, which brings the lung volume down to around functional residual capacity (i.e., the volume that remains after a normal expiration).

[A] This is followed by a sustained sequence of repeated, rapid, and shallow expirations, which, when accompanied by phonation, produce the "ha-ha-ha" of laughter. By the end of this expiratory laugh bout, the lungs reach the air volume remaining in the lungs after maximal expiration.

[C] Thus, laughter typically occurs at a low lung volume, forcing out more air from the lungs than occurs during normal breathing. Following a laughter bout, a quick inhalation occurs, filling the lungs once again to normal capacity. Another laughter bout may then follow.

웃음이라는 독특한 소리를 생산하기 위해 우리는 우리의 호흡 기관과 발성 기관을 통제하는 많은 근육을 이용한다. 인간의 정상적인 호흡 주기는 들숨(흡기), 들숨 후 휴지, 날숨(호기), 그리고 날숨 후 휴지로 구성된다.

[B] 사람이 이 주기의 어떤 부분에 있게 되는지와 관계없이 웃음은 전형적으로 최초의 강제적인 날숨으로 시작되는데 그것은 폐용량이 기능적 잔량(즉, 정상적인 날숨 후에 남아 있는 부피) 근처까지 작아지게 한다.

[A] 이것에 지속적인 일련의 반복적이고 신속하며 얕은 날숨이 이어지는데, 그것은 발성이 수반되었을 때, '하, 하, 하'하는 웃음소리를 생산한다. 이 날숨의 웃음 한바탕이 끝날 무렵 폐는 최대 날숨 후에 폐에 남아 있는 공기량에 이른다.

[C] 따라서 웃음은 전형적으로 낮은 폐용량에서 발생하며, 정상적인 호흡 동안에 발생하는 것보다 더 많은 공기를 폐로부터 강제로 배출시킨다. 웃음 한바탕 다음에는 신속한 흡입이 발생하여 다시 폐를 정상적인 용량으로 채운다. 또 다른 웃음 한바탕이 그 다음에 따를 수 있다.

Rudy's Tip 웃음에 따른 호흡의 과정을 설명하는 글이다. 대명사와 동일어구를 파악하자.

6

정답 (A)

Has your creativity ground to a stop? Instead of letting frustration get the better of you, try to sit back and take a few deep breaths. Did you know that drawing a deep breath gives your creativity a boost by increasing the negative ions in oxygen? The negatively charged oxygen circulates throughout the brain, refreshing the neurons and, because these negative ions promote alpha waves of longer amplitude in the brain, which are associated with creative thinking, suddenly your creativity receives a boost. So, next time your creative spirit feels burdened, spend two minutes taking deep breaths, breathing in and out every five seconds, and repeat the cycle at least 12 times.

(A) Breathe Deep for Inspiration 영감을 위한 심호흡
(B) Frustration Makes Hope 절망이 희망을 만든다
(C) Can Memory Be Boosted? 기억력은 향상 될 수 있을까?
(D) Don't Fear Ridiculous Ideas 우스운 생각들을 두려워하지 마라

여러분의 창의력이 서서히 멈추었는가? 좌절감에 사로잡히지 말고, 의자에 깊숙이 앉아 몇 번 심호흡하라. 심호흡이 산소내의 음이온을 증가시켜 여러분의 창의력에 활력을 불어넣는다는 것을 알고 있었는가? 음전하를 띤 산소는 뇌의 곳곳을 순환하면서 신경 세포에 생기를 주고, 이 음이온이 창의적 사고와 연관된 더 큰 진폭의 알파파를 뇌 속에 촉진하기 때문에 돌연 여러분의 창의력은 활력을 얻게 된다. 그러므로, 다음에 여러분의 창의적 기운이 눌린 듯한 기분이 들 때에는, 5초마다 숨을 들이쉬고 내쉬면서 2분 동안 심호흡을 하고, 적어도 12번 그 과정을 반복하라.

Rudy's Tip GS 구조로 심호흡이 창의력을 향상시킨다는 서론에 주제가 제시되어 있다.

10분 모의고사 30 해설편

1
정답 (A)

After thousands of years of studying and treating every aspect of it, there are still many facets of the brain that remain mysterious.
수천 년 동안 뇌를 연구하고 뇌의 모든 측면을 취급한 이후에도 뇌에는 여전히 불가사의함이 남아있는 수많은 측면이 존재한다.

(A) Despite having spent many years trying to work out what goes on in the brain, much of it still remains a mystery.
　　뇌에서 무슨 일이 진행되고 있는지 해결하기 위해 많은 시간을 보냈지만 뇌의 상당 부분은 여전히 수수께끼로 남았다.

(B) Understanding the brain has been at the forefront of medical advances for years and years, and finally we are close to understanding its true origins.
　　뇌를 이해하는 것이 오랫동안 의학 발달에 선두에 있어왔다. 그리고 마침내 우리는 뇌의 진정한 기원을 이해하려고 한다.

(C) Although it has taken many years to get to this point, it seems the inner workings of the brain have at last been untangled.
　　여기까지 이르기까지 오랜 시간이 걸렸지만, 뇌의 내부 작동원리가 마침내 해결된 듯 보인다.

(D) Even though we have spent so long studying the brain, to this day we are no closer to understanding it than before.
　　비록 우리가 뇌를 연구하기 위해 오랜 시간을 보냈지만 오늘까지도 예전처럼 뇌를 이해하지 못하고 있다.

Rudy's Tip many facets of the brain that remain mysterious
= much of it still remains a mystery

2   정답 (B)

Of all the mystic places, the most enigmatic — and the source of many of the rest, in the view of some people — is the lost island of Atlantis. The subject of more than 2,000 books and countless articles and poems, Atlantis has been traced to a long list of sites and regions in the world. Thousands of years after it supposedly sank into the cold and gloomy depths of the Atlantic Ocean, the island continent of Atlantis lives on as one of history's most tantalizing puzzles. If indeed such a place existed, it was a civilization unequaled before or since. Yet its chroniclers say that it vanished in little more than a single day, leaving not a trace behind. Plato described Atlantis as an idyllic land with beautiful gardens and a balmy climate — a place where people lived lives of cultivated leisure in magnificent mansions.

(A) Atlantis is believed to have declined gradually.
   아틀란티스는 서서히 침몰했다고 전해진다.
(B) Atlantis was the place where savages used to live.
   아틀란티스는 원시인들이 거주했던 장소였다.
(C) The existence of Atlantis has been unconfirmed.
   아틀란티스의 존재는 확인되지 않았다.
(D) The idea of paradise has nothing to do with Atlantis.
   천국에 대한 생각과 아틀란티스는 아무 관련성이 없다.

모든 신비한 장소 중에서도 가장 수수께끼 같은 곳은, 그래서 사람들의 생각에 많은 다른 신비한 곳들의 원천으로 여겨지는 곳은 바로 아틀란티스의 잃어버린 섬이다. 2000여 권의 책과 셀 수 없이 많은 기사와 시의 주제인 아틀란티스는 세계의 여러 유적지와 장소의 긴 목록에서 그 소재(所在)가 추적되고 있다. 그 섬이 아마도 차갑고 어두운 대서양의 깊은 곳으로 빠져들어 간 지 몇 천 년 후, 아틀란티스 섬 대륙은 역사적으로 가장 궁금증을 불러일으키는 풀리지 않는 문제점 중의 하나로 남아있다. 그러한 곳이 실제로 존재했다면 그것은 전에도 후에도 그 유례를 찾아볼 수 없는 문명이었다. 하지만 그곳에 대한 연대기 작가가 말하기를 그것은 하루아침에 사라진 것이나 마찬가지이고 흔적을 남기지 않았다고 한다. 플라톤은 아틀란티스를 아름다운 정원과 온화한 기후를 가진 멋진 땅, 즉 사람들이 훌륭한 저택에서 우아한 여가를 즐기며 살던 곳으로 묘사했다.

Rudy's Tip 본문과 일치하는 내용은 존재가 확인되지 않는다는 문항 뿐이다.

3

정답 (D)

I would like to introduce what I've come to call the lasagna principle — the notion that our capacity to enjoy different activities is limited and unique. Lasagna is my favorite food, and every time I visit my parents, my mother prepares a tray of it. This does not, however, mean that I want to eat lasagna all day and every day. The same principle applies to my favorite activities, such as writing and watching movies, as well as to my favorite people. The mere fact that my family is the most meaningful thing in my life does not mean that spending eight hours a day with them is what would make me happiest; and not wanting to spend all my waking hours with them does not imply that I love them any less. I derive a great deal of pleasure and meaning from being with other people, but I also need my daily quota of solitude. Identifying the right activity, and then the right quantity for each activity leads to the highest quality of life.

(A) Striving and struggling for a worthwhile goal
　　가치있는 목표를 위해 노력하고 투쟁하라.
(B) Protecting myself from external forces that I can't control
　　자신이 통제할 수 없는 외부적 압력들로부터 자신을 보호하라.
(C) Staying positive and constructive, and focusing on favorite activities
　　긍정적, 발전적 태도를 취하고 좋아하는 활동들에 집중하라.
(D) Identifying the right activity, and then the right quantity for each activity
　　적절한 활동과 각 활동에 대한 적절한 양을 확인해라.

나는 '라자냐 원리'로 부르게 된 것을 소개하고 싶은데, 그것은 서로 다른 활동을 즐기는 우리의 능력은 제한적이고 고유하다는 개념이다. 라자냐는 내가 가장 좋아하는 음식이고, 내가 부모님을 방문할 때마다 어머니는 그것을 한 접시 준비하신다. 그러나 이것이 내가 온종일 그리고 매일 라자냐를 먹기 원한다는 것을 의미하지는 않는다. 같은 원리가 내가 가장 좋아하는 사람뿐만 아니라 글쓰기와 영화 감상과 같이 내가 가장 좋아하는 활동에도 적용된다. 내 가족이 내 인생에서 가장 의미가 있다는 단순한 사실이 그들과 하루에 여덟 시간을 함께 보내는 것이 나를 가장 행복하게 만들 것이라는 것을 의미하지는 않으며, 내가 깨어 있는 모든 시간을 그들과 함께 보내고 싶지 않다는 것이 내가 그들을 조금이라도 덜 사랑함을 암시하는 것은 아니다. 나는 다른 사람들과 함께 있는 것으로부터 많은 기쁨과 의미를 얻지만, 내게는 또한 고독의 일일 할당량이 필요하다. 적절한 활동을 확인한 다음, 각각의 활동에 대한 적절한 양을 확인하는 것이 최고의 삶의 질로 이끈다.

Rudy's Tip 최고의 삶의 질을 위해 자신이 좋아하는 일을 할 때 자신이 원하는 활동의 적절한 양을 하는 것이 중요하다는 내용이다. 빈칸은 앞 문장에 대한 재진술이기에 활동과 양을 규정한다는 내용이 적절하다.

4   정답 (D)

Small children have smaller stomachs. They need concentrated foods, high in calories but low in volume. This is one of the main causes of infant malnutrition. In many countries, children are poorly fed but adults are not. It would be a mistake to believe that adults eat everything and leave nothing for the children. Parents (and especially mothers) watch out for their children. They would happily give up their own food in order to feed their children. The problem is that many times the only food available to families consists of vegetables and roots high in fibre but low in calories. Adults can eat all they need, as their stomachs are big enough. And in enough quantity, any food will fatten a person. Small children, as hard as they try, cannot eat the amount of vegetables needed, because they don't have enough room in their stomach.

(A) types of foods that are good for small eaters
    소식가에게 좋은 음식 종류
(B) simple ways to lose weight in the healthy way
    건강하게 체중을 줄이는 간단한 방법
(C) development of eating habits among children
    아이들의 식습관 발달
(D) reasons that small children may not get enough calories
    어린아이들이 충분한 열량을 섭취하지 못하는 이유

어린아이들은 위가 더 작다. 그들에게는 열량은 높지만 양이 적은 농축 식품이 필요하다. 이것이 유아 영양실조의 주요 원인 중 하나이다. 많은 나라에서, 아이들은 잘 먹지 못하지만 어른들은 그렇지 않다. 어른들이 모든 것을 먹고 아이들을 위해 아무것도 남기지 않는다고 믿는 것은 오해일 것이다. 부모들(특히 엄마들)은 자신들의 아이들에게 주의를 기울인다. 그들은 자기 아이들에게 먹이기 위해 자신의 음식을 기꺼이 포기할 것이다. 문제는 많은 경우 가족이 먹을 수 있는 유일한 음식이 섬유질은 풍부하지만 열량이 낮은 채소와 뿌리로 이루어진다는 것이다. 어른은 위가 충분히 크기 때문에 그들이 필요로 하는 모든 것을 먹을 수 있다. 그리고 충분한 양이라면 어떤 음식도 사람을 살찌울 수 있다. 어린아이들은 그들의 위에 공간이 충분하지 않기 때문에, 아무리 애를 써 봐도 필요로 하는 양만큼의 채소를 먹을 수 없다.

Rudy's Tip GS 구성으로 서론과 마지막 문장이 동일하다. 따라서 아이들이 충분한 영양을 얻지 못하는 이유가 주제로 적절하다.

5 정답 (D)

Barry Mazur, one of the world's leading mathematicians, has always been a prodigy. He left the Bronx High School of science after his junior year in order to go directly to MIT. He left MIT after his sophomore year to go to Princeton for graduate studies. Barry told me that he also left Princeton after one year to go study in England. To make a long story short, the only degree that Mazur ever got was the PhD from Princeton. <u>This fact evidently caused the reason of headaches as Barry's career unfolded.</u> When he would submit his NSF grant proposals, they would invariably be returned with a request for information about his high school diploma and college degree. The Administrative Assistant, Mary McQuillen, would write back and say, "This is not an omission; PhD is Professor Mazur's only degree."

세계적인 일류 수학자 중 한 명인 Barry Mazur는 항상 영재였다. 그는 곧바로 MIT에 진학하기 위해 3학년을 마치고 Bronx 과학 고등학교를 떠났다. 그는 대학원 공부를 하려고 Princeton에 가기 위해 2학년을 마친 후 MIT를 떠났다. Barry는 자신이 영국으로 공부를 하러 가기 위해 1년 후에 또 Princeton을 떠났다고 내게 말했다. 요약하자면, Mazur가 취득한 유일한 학위라고는 Princeton에서 얻은 박사 학위뿐이었다. <u>Barry가 사회생활을 해 나가면서 이 사실은 두통의 이유가 되었다.</u> 그가 NSF(전미과학재단) 보조금 제안서를 제출하면, 그것들은 예외 없이 그의 고등학교 졸업 증서와 대학 학위에 관한 정보의 요구와 더불어 되돌아오곤 했다. 행정 조교인 Mary McQuillen은 "이것은 누락이 아닙니다. 박사 학위가 Mazur 교수님이 가진 유일한 학위입니다."라는 내용의 회신을 쓰곤 했다.

Rudy's Tip This fact가 Mazur가 고등학교와 대학교를 계속 조기 수료하면서 유일하게 취득한 학위가 Princeton의 박사 학위뿐이라는 것을 의미하고, headaches가 그의 보조금 제안서가 계속 되돌아오는 것을 의미하므로, (D)에 들어가는 것이 가장 적절하다.

6

정답 (C)

In the 19th century, the UK government nearly surrendered to a powerful foe — the smell of human excrement. By that summer, the River Thames had become such a large repository of human waste that the stench drove all of London to its knees.

[C] The problem had been decades in the making. Since experts at the time believed the spread of contagious disease was solely airborne, little thought was given to the dangers of disposing of London's sewage in the Thames. Media outlets like the Times had editorialized for years about the need to clean up the river, but nothing changed.

[A] Then came the great heat wave of 1858. That summer was a scorcher in England. It boiled the waste in the Thames, which released noxious odors of increasing pungency. The situation grew so desperate that everyone agreed that something had to be done. Figuring out the solution was the next challenge, and after debates and arguments, Disraeli finally passed a bill in July 1858 authorizing the construction of a system of embankments and tunnels that would lead the sewage out of the city.

[D] As work got underway, Joseph Bazalgette, the chief engineer who led the project, spoke publicly about its problems. "It was tremendously hard work," Bazalgette said. Despite the difficulties, the embankment project gradually became part of the crafting of a more modern city. A new underground-railway system was also built as part of the effort. The embankment wasn't completed until 1874, but by 1861 residents were raving about the transformation.

[B] For all the suffering it caused, the Great Stink of 1858 eventually became a blessing for London. Not only was the Thames cleansed over the next decade but the whole city was infrastructurally and visibly improved by Thames embankments, which carried the sewage while at the same time easing road traffic from the congested thoroughfare, embracing the new underground railway system and enhancing the look of London above ground.

19세기, 영국정부는 인간 배설물의 냄새라는 강력한 적에 거의 항복할 뻔했다. 여름이 되면 이미, 템스(Thames)강은 인간이 배설한 똥오줌의 거대한 매장지가 되어, 그 악취에 런던시 전체가 무릎을 꿇고 말았다.

[C] 이 악취문제는 수십 년 동안 쌓여왔다. 당시 전문가들은 전염병이 오직 공기로만 전염된다고 믿었기 때문에 템스 강에 오물을 버리는 것의 위험성에 대해서는 거의 생각해 보지 않았다. 영국의 타임스(The Times)지 같은 언론들은 수년 간 템스 강을 정화할 필요성에 대해 사설을 통해 입장을 밝혀왔지만 달라진 것은 아무 것도 없었다.

[A] 그러다가 1858년 엄청난 폭염이 찾아왔다. 영국의 그해 여름은 모든 걸 태워 버릴 듯이 더웠다. 엄청난 폭염은 템스 강의 똥오줌을 부글부글 끓게 만들었고, 이것은 점점 더 자극적인 유독한 냄새를 뿜어냈다. 상황은 너무나 절망적으로 변해갔기 때문에 무언가를 해야 한다는 데 모두가 동의했다. 해결책을 생각해 내는 것이 그 다음의 도전 과제였으며, 수많은 논쟁과 토론을 거친 후 (당시 영국 총리였던) 디즈 레일리(Disraeli)는 마침내 1958년 7월, 오물을 도시 밖으로 보내는 제방과 터널의 건설을 승인하는 법안을 통과시켰다.

[D] 건설공사가 진행됨에 따라 그 공사 프로젝트를 진두지휘했던 최고 기술자인 조셉 배절제트(Joseph Bazalgette)는 그 공사의 문제점에 대해 공개적으로 밝혔다. "이 공사는 엄청나게 어려운 작업이었어요." 라고 배절제트가 말했다. 많은 어려움에도 불구하고, 제방축조 프로젝트는 점점 현대 도시의 모습을 만드는 데 한 부분이 되었다. 새로운 지하철 시스템도 또한 그 노력의 일환으로 만들어졌다. 제방은 1874년 이 돼서야 완공되었지만, 1861년에 이미 주인들은 그 변화에 대해 극찬을 아끼지 않고 있었다.

[B] 1858년의 대악취(the Great Stink)는 그로 인한 모든 고통에도 불구하고, 결국 런던에게 축복이 되었다. 템스 강이 그 후 10년 동안 정화되었을 뿐 아니라 런던 시 전체가 템스 강둑 덕택에 기간시설 면으로나 시각적으로나 개선이 되었는데, 이 템스 강둑은 오물을 흘려 보내면서도 동시에 교통이 혼잡한 거리에서 교통체증을 완화시키고 새로운 지하철 시스템을 채택하고, 런던의 지상 외관도 더 나아지게 했다.

Rudy's Tip 템스강 공사에 대한 글로 각 문항의 첫 문장에 대명사, 연결어, 공통어구를 중심으로 순서를 파악해 보자.